American Youth Gangs at the Millennium

American Youth Gangs at the Millennium

Finn-Aage Esbensen
University of Missouri at St. Louis

Stephen G. Tibbetts
California State University, San Bernardino

Larry Gaines
California State University, San Bernardino

WAVELAND
PRESS, INC.
Long Grove, Illinois

For information about this book, contact:
Waveland Press, Inc.
4180 IL Route 83, Suite 101
Long Grove, IL 60047-9580
(847) 634-0081
info@waveland.com
www.waveland.com

Contents

SECTION II
VARIETIES OF GANGS   109

SECTION III
GANG ACTIVITIES   215

Section IV
Responding to Youth Gangs   297

*Prepared specifically for *American Youth Gangs at the Millennium.*

Introduction

During the last fifteen years of the twentieth century, there was a virtual explosion of attention to youth gangs and youth violence that prompted the proliferation of numerous myths and misperceptions about American youth gangs. The articles assembled in this book seek to address the status of youth gangs in America at the turn of the twenty-first century. Some of these articles are reprinted works that were written by leading gang researchers, while other articles were solicited specifically for this book in order to provide the most current information about youth gangs.

The book is divided into four main sections that explore the following topical areas: (1) the current trend in youth gang violence, (2) examination of the characteristics of youth gangs, (3) assessment of the diversity of gangs and gang activity, and (4) potential responses to gangs and violence. However, before exploring these specific issues, we provide an introductory section that seeks to highlight some underlying themes that are interwoven throughout the selected readings: definitional issues; risk factors associated with gang membership; the nature of gang violence; the role of girls in gangs; and the importance of theory and research as the basis for gang policies.

Youth gangs and violence are interwoven terms that evoke concern, if not fear, throughout the population. The early 1990s can be characterized as a period of gang hysteria in the United States; "Bloods" and "Crips" became terms familiar to rural residents who had never ventured into "gang-infested" urban centers. Media hype about the new generation of "superpredators" and the short-lived crack "epidemic" contributed to widespread concern about youth violence (e.g., Blumstein, 1995; DiIulio, 1995). Given the fact that the annual number of street-gang-motivated homicides in Chicago increased fivefold between 1987 and 1994 (from 51

1

to 240), while gang-related homicides more than doubled in Los Angeles County from 1987 to 1992 (387 to 803) (Howell, 1999:209), it is small wonder that there was heightened concern about gang violence.

Youth collective violence, however, is not a new phenomenon. Whether we visit the historical writings of Shakespeare about the Montagues and Capulets or the 1990s media images of *Boyz in the Hood*, youth gangs and group violence have been a characteristic of adolescent life for centuries. The prominence of gangs and associated violence, however, tends to fluctuate across time. In fact, after a relatively prominent gang problem in the 1950s and 1960s in the United States, by the early 1980s some writers (Bookin-Weiner and Horowitz, 1983) asked whether the gang problem had disappeared. As if in response to this query, the 1980s and 1990s witnessed a re-emergence of gang activity, including violent offending. Are these fluctuations an artifact of media, researcher, and law-enforcement interest or do they reflect real changes in behavior?

WHAT IS A GANG?

What is a gang, and what constitutes a gang-related crime? While these questions may seem esoteric, definitions of these terms are of the utmost importance. Unfortunately, considerable disagreement exists on this topic (Ball and Curry, 1995; Decker and Kempf-Leonard, 1991; Howell, 2003; Klein, 1969; W. B. Miller, 1975, 1980; Needle and Stapleton, 1983).

Failure to employ a standard definition of youth gangs and gang membership has at least two implications for gang research and for gang-related public policy. First, the need to accurately estimate the size of the gang problem is necessary so that adequate resources can be allocated to the problem. Second, we need to accurately describe the characteristics and location of the "gang" problem.

Let us provide you with two examples of the consequences of not having a standard definition. First, Esbensen and colleagues (see article 2 in this volume) report that depending upon the specific definition used, the prevalence of youth gang membership in their study ranged from 2.3 percent to 16.8 percent. Clearly, to say that 2.3 percent (i.e., 1 out of 45) of youths are gang involved leads to quite a different social and justice system response than to say that one out of every six youths in a neighborhood is gang involved! The magnitude of the problem increases sevenfold when a single item is used to measure gang membership compared to when gang membership is restricted to youths who identify themselves as "core" members of a delinquent peer group with some level of organization (i.e., leaders, specific roles, meetings, initiation rites, or colors). A second example taps the characteristics of gang-identified youths. In the Esbensen et al. study, the official law-enforcement stance in one of the study sites was that there were no girls in gangs in that jurisdiction. However, survey results from a school sample indicated that almost half of the gang members in that city were female and, importantly, those gang girls reported involvement in a variety of violent crimes. The law-enforcement official and survey researcher not only have a different picture of the extent and nature of the gang problem, they would also have different suggestions for a community response.

Varying definitions produce different pictures of gangs and gang members. In general, law-enforcement data from National Youth Gang Surveys (Egley, Howell, and Major in this volume) paint a picture of inner city, minority males (generally from single-parent households). Ethnographic studies of older and more homogenous samples of gang members tend to confirm this picture. Surveys involving younger samples, however, call into question the extent to which these stereotypes accurately depict youth gang members.

At this point we will forgo engaging in an insightful but tedious discussion of gang definitions and simply state that the bulk of gang research tends to include the following: a social **group** that uses **symbols**, engages in verbal and nonverbal communications to declare their "**gang-ness**," that has a sense of **permanence** and gang-identified **territory** or **turf**, and lastly, is involved in **criminal activity.** (Definitional issues are discussed in considerable detail in article 2 of this volume.)

WHAT ARE THE RISK FACTORS
ASSOCIATED WITH JOINING A GANG?

During the past twenty or so years, a considerable body of research identifying risk factors associated with various forms of adolescent problem behavior has emerged. This body of research has identified a number of risk factors in various domains (e.g., family, school, community, individual, and peer) while focusing primarily on the relationships between these risk factors and violent offending. A few researchers have also examined risk factors and gang membership specifically. The bulk of this research (whether focused on general or specific forms of delinquency) can be classified as being atheoretical—relying primarily on establishing co-occurrence or correlation of key constructs.

Clearly exceptions to the nontheoretical approach exist (see, for example, article 1 by Howell, article 3 by Huff, and article 8 by Hill et al.). Perhaps the most widely cited research utilizing the risk-factors approach is the work of David Hawkins and Richard Catalano (1993). They developed the Social Development Model that has informed U.S. juvenile justice policy and program development throughout much of the 1990s (Howell, 2003). That model identifies the following risk factors: *community* risk factors—availability of drugs and firearms, media portrayals of violence, community norms favorable to drug use and crime, transition and mobility, economic deprivation, and low neighborhood attachment and community disorganization; *family* risk factors—family history of problem behavior, family management problems, family conflict, favorable parental attitudes and involvement in problem behavior; *school* risk factors—early and persistent antisocial behavior, academic failure, lack of commitment to school; and *individual/peer* risk factors—rebelliousness, delinquent peers, early initiation in problem behavior, favorable attitudes to norm violation, and constitutional factors.

The majority of the risk-factor literature has been applied to delinquency and violent offending and less so to gang activity. Given the close association between violent offending and gang membership, however, much of the general risk-factor literature is also applicable to gangs.

At this point it is worth noting the changing nature of youth gangs in American society, and in society in general. Based on multiple sources, we know that youth gangs of one sort or another exist in virtually every state in the United States. In recent National Youth Gang Surveys (see article 4 by Egley, Howell, and Major), more than 15 percent of rural communities indicated that they had youth gangs. Likewise, there is growing evidence that youth gangs are emerging in Europe (Klein et al., 2001), Australia, and elsewhere (although we have not yet heard of gangs in Antarctica!). These gangs do not necessarily fit the youth gang stereotypes of the 1950s. Maxson and Klein (1995) proposed a typology for studying gangs. Two of these types appear to be more common and account for a large number of new gangs and gang members; the neo-traditional (relatively short history, territorial, with crime versatility and more than 50 members) and the compressed (small—less than 50, brief history, narrow age range of members, may or may not be territorial, and versatile crime patterns) gangs.

Research has also identified protective factors that appear to insulate at-risk youth from gang membership. While some criminologists suggest that protective and risk factors are simply polar opposites of each other, this interpretation does not fully explicate the complex nature of these various influences. Risk factors include such factors as exposure to delinquent peers, low level of parental supervision, and low levels of perceived guilt associated with norm violation. Protective factors, as identified in a frequently cited review by Brewer, Hawkins, Catalano, and Neckerman (1995), include the following three domains: *individual*—for example, gender, intelligence, or resilient temperament; *social bonding*—such as warm, supportive, affective relationships or attachments with family or others; and *healthy beliefs and clear standards*—including family and community norms opposed to crime and violence and supportive of educational success and healthy development.

To help frame the discussion of risk and protective factors that appears in the readings included in this text, we turn to Michael Rutter (1987), who suggested that protective factors may serve the following purposes: (1) to reduce riskiness itself—i.e., involvement in the risk, (2) to reduce the likelihood of negative chain reactions, (3) to promote self-esteem and self-efficacy, and (4) to open up opportunities of a positive kind. Thus, protective factors prevent or reduce the probability of certain negative outcomes. At the same time, we must realize that some events or factors may have differential consequences for different people in similar situations. Similarly, the same events and/or factors may have different effects on the same person at different stages of the life cycle. For instance, having a child at age 30 may be a protective factor whereas having a child at 16 may be a risk factor. Along the same vein, what may be protective for one youth may be a risk factor for another. For example, based on the gang literature, having a child at age 16 has a different effect for females than for males; becoming a mother has been found to increase the likelihood of leaving the gang (i.e., a protective factor) whereas becoming a father has no consequence. Likewise, it may be that going to school may reduce exposure to violence in the home for some but increase exposure to delinquent peers for others.

The complex nature of risk and protective factors has direct relevance for prevention and intervention strategies. It has been established that the presence of delinquent peers is the most influential cause of not only delinquency but also gang affiliation. In addition, it appears that association with conventional peers counteracts the effect of delinquent peers. It has also been learned from recent research that parenting skills and practices can increase resiliency. This focus on risk and protective factors has guided much of the prevention and intervention programming of the past decade (see article 16 by Huff and article 18 by Esbensen et al.). An array of school-based prevention programs (e.g., Botvin's Life Skills program, G.R.E.A.T., Peer Mediation, the Perry Preschool Project, etc.) target life skills, conflict resolution, and communication skills. Other programs such as the Boys & Girls Clubs of America's (B&GCA) Targeted Outreach Program enhance commitment to school through monitoring youths' activities. Big Brothers Big Sisters of America and other similar mentoring programs also seek to enhance protective factors. These programs not only address risk factors but also may serve as protective factors. Research has suggested that the more protective factors an individual has, the more resilient they are (Smith et al., 1995). Based on findings from the Rochester Youth Development Study, protective factors (conceived of as being more distal factors associated with the family and early development) had more impact in early adolescence than they did later. One reasonable interpretation of this finding is that protective factors are modified across the life course. So parenting and family programs may be important for early teen years but not subsequent years. That is, it is necessary to realize that while parental monitoring and supervision may be effective in reducing initial gang joining (ages 12–14), these factors may prove ineffective as the child enters mid-adolescence. At this point, positive peer networks may be more important.

WHAT IS THE NATURE OF GANG VIOLENCE?

Gangs and gang members are engaged in a number of activities other than violent crimes. In fact, throughout most of the day, gang members are like other adolescents—going to school, working, hanging out, eating with family or friends (e.g., Esbensen, Huizinga, and Weiher, 1993; Fleisher, 1998; Klein, 1995). Criminal activity and violence in particular are relatively rare occurrences in the context of other gang activities. Having said that, it is still a widely documented finding that gang members are responsible for a disproportionate amount of crime. Not all of this criminal activity involves violence. For example, between 1987 and 1990, there were 17,085 criminal offenses classified as street-gang related in Chicago. Of these, 288 were homicides, over half (8,828) were classified as nonlethal violent offenses (i.e., assaults and batteries), drug offenses (both sale and possession) accounted for approximately one-third of the offenses (5,888), and the remaining 2,081 offenses included all other offense types (Block and Block, 2001).

It should also be noted that there is considerable variation in the activities of different gangs. Some gangs are best classified as drug gangs, others as violent gangs, and yet others as lacking specialization. "Levels of gang violence differ from one city to another . . . from one community to another . . . from one gang to another . . . and even among cliques within the same gang . . ." (Howell, 1998:9; article 1 of this volume). The one constant is that most gangs and gang members engage in violent crime at a rate higher than nongang youths in the same environment.

Gang membership enhances involvement in delinquent activity of all kinds (e.g., Battin-Pearson, Thornberry, Hawkins, and Krohn, 1998; Esbensen and Huizinga, 1993; Huizinga, 1997; Thornberry and Burch, 1997). Comparisons of gang and nongang youths consistently and historically have produced significant differences in both the prevalence and frequency of offending between these two groups. According to self-report surveys, gang youths account for approximately 70 percent of all self-reported violent offending in adolescent samples (Huizinga, Weiher, Espiritu, and Esbensen, 2003; Thornberry, Krohn, Lizotte, Smith, and Tobin, 2003). In research involving 15-year-old youths, the researchers report that gang members committed twice as many violent acts as did youths who were not gang members but had delinquent friends. And, when compared with youths who did not have delinquent friends, the gang youths reported committing seven times as many violent acts during the past year (Battin, Hill, Abbott, Catalano, and Hawkins, 1998).

Based on three years of field research of active gang members in St. Louis, Decker (1996) concluded that violence was a normative aspect of gang life. Violence, or the threat of violence, helps to account for the formation and spread of gangs through a process of contagion. That is, an initial act of violence is seen as requiring some form of retaliation, perhaps as retribution or, more likely, to uphold the honor or reputation of the offended individual or group. If retaliation is not enacted, the threat of further victimization persists. Intergroup violence serves to unite the group and to accentuate group cohesiveness. Involvement in violence creates a fear of the gang among neighborhood residents that further isolates gang members from social institutions from which they already have experienced alienation.

Gang violence, especially homicide, became highly visible in the late 1980s and early 1990s. In 1994, for example, Los Angeles experienced 370 gang homicides—an average of one gang homicide each and every day—accounting for 44 percent of all homicides in that city that year (Maxson and Klein, 2001; see also article 14 of this volume). Despite a decrease in gang violence at the end of the century, gang homicides still accounted for 1,061 deaths nationwide in 1998 (Curry, Maxson, and Howell, 2001).

One notable difference between the youth gangs of yesteryear and those of the 1990s is the prominence of guns. Today's gang members are heavily armed (e.g., Decker and Van Winkle, 1996; Sheley and Wright, 1995; Thornberry et al., 2003). No longer are bats, chains, and switchblades the weapons of choice. These have been replaced by handguns and semi-automatic weapons. Part of this change has been linked to participation in drug trafficking. For example, researchers in New York (Lizotte, Krohn, Howell, Tobin, and Howard, 2000:830) report:

> Gang members carry guns to protect themselves and their turf from rival gangs, who, in turn, must arm. Drug dealers carry guns to ply their trade. This necessitates gun carrying by their best customers, which, in turn, ensures and reinforces the dealer's carrying. These boys see many of their peers armed with guns, and they feel a need to arm in response.

How Involved are Girls in Gangs and Gang Violence?

As with violent youth crime, gang membership has traditionally been viewed as a male phenomenon and girls have been systematically excluded from gang research (e.g., Campbell, 1991; Chesney-Lind, 1993; and Esbensen and Winfree, 1998). This exclusion of females from gang research has contributed to a paucity of studies examining sex differences in violent offending and the role of gang membership in violent behavior. This lack of research has resulted in several misconceptions about female gang involvement and violent crime. Recent research, however, has begun to address this gap in the literature (e.g., Deschenes and Esbensen, 1998, 1999; Maxson and Whitlock, 2002; J. Miller, 1998, 2001; Miller and Brunson, 2000; Miller and Decker, 2001; Moore and Hagedorn, 2001; Peterson, Miller, and Esbensen, 2001).

Current estimates of the magnitude of gang involvement by females have a wide range. Whereas official records indicate that fewer than 10 percent of gang members are female (Curry, Ball, and Fox, 1994; Howell, 1994), self-report studies consistently find rates between 20 and 46 percent (Bjerregaard and Smith, 1993; Campbell, 1991; Esbensen, Huizinga, and Weiher, 1993; Esbensen and Winfree, 1998; Fagan, 1990; Moore, 1991). While homicide does appear to be the domain of male gang members (e.g., Decker and Van Winkle, 1996; Miller and Decker, 2001), it appears that these female gang members are active in other forms of violent offending. Gang girls commit a wide variety of offenses similar to the pattern exhibited by gang boys, only at a slightly lower frequency. However, male gang members are more involved in more serious violent behavior (being involved in gang fights, carrying weapons, using weapons) than are female gang members. Victimization experiences tend to be the strongest predictors of violent behavior, suggesting that some violence may be reciprocal or retaliatory fighting amongst youths.

An important finding from research is that engaging more frequently in violence was correlated with one's attitudes towards violence and lack of guilt, regardless of sex (Deschenes and Esbensen, 1999). In examination of differences between gang girls and nongang girls, significant differences were found for both behavior and attitudes. Attitudes about violence were markedly different between gang and nongang girls. The gang girls were much more likely than the nongang girls to view hitting and use of physical violence as appropriate responses in various situations (Deschenes and Esbensen, 1998).

RESPONSES TO GANG VIOLENCE

The past 60 years have seen a variety of gang prevention and intervention strategies. These include efforts focused on environmental factors and provision of improved opportunities [e.g., the Chicago Area Project (CAP) developed by Shaw and McKay, 1942; the Midcity Project evaluated by Miller, 1962; and the Mobilization for Youth Program, Bibb, 1967]; programs with a distinct social-work orientation [e.g., most notably the detached worker approach reported by Klein, 1971; and Spergel, 1966]; and a strategy of gang suppression by law enforcement. The majority of these programs have experienced short life spans due to the absence of any immediately noticeable effect or due to a change in administrative priorities.

Many current efforts to establish gang policy are rooted in theory and/ or are based on evaluation results. Prevention strategies such as the Office of Juvenile Justice and Delinquency Prevention's (OJJDP) Comprehensive Strategy (see Howell, 2003) are based on the assessment of risk and protective factors (see articles 3, 8, and 16). Intervention and suppression strategies such as those depicted in articles 17 and 19 find their theoretical base in deterrence theory.

CONCLUSION

Gangs are locally grown problems and adapt to their particular environments, but certain underlying characteristics and group structures appear to provide common underlying elements (group identity, permanence across some period of time, involvement in illegal activity as a prominent aspect of the group, and a tendency to congregate in public domains). Due to the customized and local nature of youth gangs, there exist a number of different impressions and many misperceptions about gangs. At times the descriptions of youth gangs are similar to the diverse descriptions provided by the proverbial blind individuals exposed to only one part of an elephant (i.e., the tusks, trunk, tail, etc.). Their descriptions, while accurate, are nonetheless incomplete and do not provide sufficient knowledge with which to respond to the entire elephant. Our knowledge of gangs at the beginning of the twenty-first century is in a similar state; we have a lot of information, we just don't have the complete picture. Researchers, practitioners, and policy makers all have their own opinions about the validity of their gang picture and are certain that the "tusk" is an accurate reflection of the gang problem. It is our hope that this collection of readings will allow readers to have a slightly better understanding of the issues associated with American youth gangs at the millennium.

References

Ball, R. A., & Curry, G. D. (1995) The Logic of Definition in Criminology: Purposes and Methods for Defining Gangs. *Criminology* 33:225–245.

Battin, S. R., Hill, K. G., Abbott, R. D., Catalano, R. F., & Hawkins, J. D. (1998) The Contribution of Gang Membership to Delinquency Beyond Delinquent Friends. *Criminology* 36(1):93–115.

Battin-Pearson, S. R., Thornberry, T. P., Hawkins, J. D., & Krohn, M. D. (1998) Gang Membership, Delinquent Peers, and Delinquent Behavior. *Juvenile Justice Bulletin*. Washington, DC: U.S. Department of Justice.

Bibb, M. (1967) Gang Related Services of Mobilization for Youth. In M. W. Klein (Ed.), *Juvenile Gangs in Context: Theory, Research, and Action*. Englewood Cliffs, NJ: Prentice-Hall.

Bjerregaard, B., & Smith, C. (1993) Gender Differences in Gang Participation, Delinquency, and Substance Use. *Journal of Quantitative Criminology* 4(3): 329–355.

Block, C. R., & Block, R. (2001) Street Gang Crime in Chicago. In J. Miller, C. L. Maxson, & M. W. Klein (Eds.), *The Modern Gang Reader, 2nd Ed*. Los Angeles: Roxbury Press.

Blumstein, A. (1995) Violence by Young People: Why the Deadly Nexus? *National Institute of Justice Journal* August: 2–9.

Bookin-Weiner, H., & Horowitz, R. (1983) The End of the Youth Gang: Fad or Fact? *Criminology* 21:585–602.

Brewer, D. D., Hawkins, J. D., Catalano, R. F., & Neckerman, H. J. (1995) Preventing Serious, Violent, and Chronic Offending: A Review of Evaluations of Selected Strategies in Childhood, Adolescence, and the Community. In J. C. Howell, B. Krisberg, J. D. Hawkins, & J. J. Wilson (Eds.), *A Sourcebook: Serious, Violent, and Chronic Juvenile Offenders*. Thousand Oaks, CA: Sage Publications.

Campbell, A. (1991) *The Girls in the Gang, 2nd Ed*. Cambridge, MA: Basil Blackwell.

Chesney-Lind, M. (1993) Girls, Gangs and Violence: Anatomy of a Backlash. *Humanity and Society* 17:321–344.

Curry, G. D., Ball, R. A., & Fox, R. J. (1994) *Gang Crime and Law Enforcement Record Keeping. Research in Brief*. Washington, DC: U.S. Department of Justice, Office of Justice Program, National Institute of Justice.

Curry, G. D., Maxson, C. L., & Howell, J. C. (2001) *Youth Gang Homicides in the 1990's. OJJDP Fact Sheet*. Washington, DC: U.S. Department of Justice, Office of Juvenile Justice and Delinquency Prevention.

Decker, S. H. (1996) Collective and Normative Features of Gang Violence. *Justice Quarterly* 13:243–264.

Decker, S. H., & Kempf-Leonard, K. (1991) Constructing Gangs: Social Definitions and Youth Activities. *Criminal Justice Policy Review* 4:271–291.

Decker, S. H., & Van Winkle, B. (1996) *Life in the Gang: Family, Friends, and Violence*. New York: Cambridge University Press.

Deschenes, E. P., & Esbensen, F.-A. (1998) Violence among Girls: Does Gang Membership Make a Difference? In M. Chesney-Lind & J. M. Hagedorn (Eds.), *Female Gangs in America*. Chicago: Lake View Press.

Deschenes, E. P., & Esbensen, F.-A. (1999) Violence and Gangs: Gender Differences in Perceptions and Behavior. *Journal of Quantitative Criminology* 15:63–96.

DiIulio, J. (1995) The Coming of the Superpredators. *Weekly Standard* November 27:23.

Esbensen, F.-A., & Huizinga D. (1993) Gangs, Drugs, and Delinquency in a Survey of Urban Youth. *Criminology* 31:565–589.

Esbensen, F.-A., & Winfree, L. T., Jr. (1998) Race and Gender Differences Between Gang and Non-Gang Youth: Results from a Multi-Site Survey. *Justice Quarterly* 15(4): 505–526.

Esbensen, F.-A., & Deschenes, E. P. (1998) A Multi-site Examination of Youth Gang Membership: Does Gender Matter? *Criminology* 36:799–828.

Esbensen, F.-A., Huizinga, D., & Weiher, A. W. (1993) Gang and Nongang Youth: Differences in Explanatory Factors. *Journal of Contemporary Criminal Justice* 9:94–116.

Esbensen, F.-A., Winfree, L. T., Jr., He, N., & Taylor, T. J. (2001) Youth Gangs and Definitional Issues: When is a Gang a Gang, and Why Does it Matter? *Crime and Delinquency* 47(1):105–130.

Fagan, J. (1990) Social Processes of Delinquency and Drug Use among Urban Gangs. In C. R. Huff (Ed.), *Gangs in America*. Newbury Park, CA: Sage.

Fleisher, M. (1998) *Dead End Kids*. Madison: University of Wisconsin Press.

Hawkins, J. D., & Catalano, R. F. (1993) *Risk-focused Prevention Using the Social Development Strategy*. Seattle: Developmental Research and Programs, Inc.

Hawkins, J. D., Catalano, R. F., & Associates. (1992) *Communities That Care*. San Francisco: Jossey-Bass.

Hill, K. G., Howell, J. C., Hawkins, J. D., & Battin-Pearson, S. R. (1999) Childhood Risk Factors for Adolescent Gang Membership: Results from the Seattle Social Development Project. *Journal of Research in Crime and Delinquency* 36(3):300–322.

Howell, J. C. (1994) Recent Gang Research: Program and Policy Implications. *Crime and Delinquency* 40:495–515.

Howell, J. C. (1998) Youth Gangs: An Overview. *Juvenile Justice Bulletin*. Washington, DC: U.S. Department of Justice.

Howell, J. C. (1999) Youth Gang Homicides: A Literature Review. *Crime & Delinquency* 45:208–241.

Howell, J. C. (2003) *Preventing and Reducing Juvenile Delinquency: A Comprehensive Framework*. Thousand Oaks, CA: Sage Publications.

Huff, C. R. (1998) *Comparing the Criminal Behavior of Youth Gangs and At-Risk Youths. Research in Brief*. Washington, DC: U.S. Department of Justice.

Huizinga, D. (1997) Gangs and the Volume of Crime. Paper presented at the Annual Meeting of the Western Society of Criminology, Honolulu, HI.

Huizinga, D., Weiher, A. W., Espiritu, R., & Esbensen, F.-A. (2003) Delinquency and Crime: Some Highlights from the Denver Youth Survey. In T. P. Thornberry & M. D. Krohn (Eds.), *Taking Stock: An Overview of Findings From Longitudinal Studies*. New York: Plenum Press.

Klein, M. W. (1969) On Group Context of Delinquency. *Sociology and Social Research* 54:63–71.

Klein, M. W. (1971) *Street Gangs and Street Workers*. Englewood Cliffs, NJ: Prentice-Hall.

Klein, M. W. (1995) *The American Street Gang*. New York: Oxford University Press.

Klein, M. W., Kerner, H.-J., Maxson, C. L., & Weitekamp, E. G. M. (2001) *The Eurogang Paradox: Street Gang and Youth Groups in the U.S. and Europe*. Amsterdam: Kluwer Academic Publishers.

Lizotte, A. J., Krohn, M. D., Howell, J. C., Tobin, K., & Howard, G. J. (2000) Factors Influencing Gun Carrying Among Young Urban Males Over the Adolescent-Young Adult Life Course. *Criminology* 38:811–834.

Maxson, C. L. (1999) Gang Homicide: A Review and extension of the Literature. In D. Smith & M. A. Zahn (Eds.), *Homicide: A Sourcebook of Social Research*. Thousand Oaks, CA: Sage Publications.

Maxson, C. L., & Klein, M. W. (1995) Investigating Gang Structures. *Journal of Gang Research* 3:33–40.

Maxson, C. L., & Klein, M. W. (2001) Defining Gang Homicide: An Updated Look at the Member and Motive Approaches. In J. Miller, C. L. Maxson, & M. W. Klein (Eds.), *The Modern Gang Reader, 2nd Ed*. Los Angeles: Roxbury Press.

Maxson, C. L., & Whitlock, M. L. (2002) Joining the Gang: Gender Differences in Risk Factors for Gang Membership. In C. R. Huff (Ed.), *Gangs in America, 3rd Ed*. Thousand Oaks, CA: Sage Publications.

Miller, J. (1998) Gender and Victimization Risk among Young Women in Gangs. *Journal of Research in Crime and Delinquency* 35:429–453.

Miller, J. (2001) *One of the Guys: Girls, Gangs, and Gender*. New York: Oxford University Press.

Miller, J., & Brunson, R. K. (2000) Gender Dynamics in Youth Gangs: A Comparison of Male and Female Accounts. *Justice Quarterly* 17: 419–448.

Miller, J., & Decker, S. H. (2001) Young Women and Gang Violence: Gender, Street Offending, and Violent Victimization in Gangs. *Justice Quarterly* 18:115–140.

Miller, W. B. (1962) The Impact of a 'Total Community' Delinquency Control Project. *Social Problems* 10:168–191.

Miller, W. B. (1975) *Violence by Youth Gangs and Youth Groups as Crime Problem in Major American Cities*. Washington, DC: U.S. Government Printing Office.

Miller, W. B. (1980) Gangs, Groups, and Serious Youth Crime. In D. Schichor & D. H. Kelly (Eds.), *Critical Issues in Juvenile Delinquency*. Lexington, MA: D. C. Heath and Co.

Moore, J. (1991) *Going Down to the Barrio: Homeboys and Homegirls in Change*. Philadelphia, PA: Temple University Press.

Moore, J., & Hagedorn, J. M. (2001) *Female Gangs: A Focus on Research*. Washington, DC: U.S. Department of Justice, Office of Justice Programs, Office of Juvenile Justice and Delinquency Prevention.

Needle, J., & Stapleton, W. V. (1983) *Report to the National Juvenile Justice Assessment Centers, Policy Handling of Youth Gangs*. Washington, DC: Office of Juvenile Justice and Delinquency Prevention, U.S. Department of Justice.

Peterson, D., Miller, J., & Esbensen, F.-A. (2001) The Impact of Sex Composition on Gangs and Gang Member Delinquency. *Criminology* 39:411–440.

Rutter, M. (1987) Psychosocial Resilience and Protective Mechanisms. *American Journal of Orthopsychiatry* 57:316–331.

Shaw, C. R., & McKay, H. D. (1942) *Juvenile Delinquency and Urban Areas*. Chicago: University of Chicago Press.

Sheley, J. F., & Wright, J. D. (1995) *In the Line of Fire: Youth, Guns, and Violence in Urban America*. Hawthorne, NY: Aldine De Gruyter.

Smith, C. A., Lizotte, A. J., Thornberry, T. P., & Krohn, M. D. (1995) Resilient Youth: Identifying Factors that Prevent High-risk Youth from Engaging in Delinquency and Drug Use. In J. Hagan (Ed.), *Delinquency in the Life Course*. Greenwich, CT: JAI.

Spergel, I. A. (1966) *Street Gang Work: Theory and Practice*. Reading, MA: Addison-Wesley.

Thornberry, T. P., & Burch, J. H., II. (1997) Gang Members and Delinquent Behavior. *Juvenile Justice Bulletin*. Washington, DC: U.S. Department of Justice.

Thornberry, T. P., Krohn, M. D., Lizotte, A. J., Smith, C. A., & Tobin, K. (2003) *Gangs and Delinquency in Developmental Perspective*. New York: Cambridge University Press.

SECTION I

Definitions and Current Trends

Until the 1990s, little was known about the prevalence of youth gangs in society. There had been no national surveys and there was no national clearinghouse to gather and distribute information about gangs. In an attempt to remedy this situation, Walter Miller conducted a survey of law-enforcement agencies in twelve cities in 1975. He found that six of these agencies had gang problems and based on this survey, he estimated that there were between 28,500 and 81,500 gang members in 760 to 2,700 gangs in the United States. This early effort by Miller laid the foundation for subsequent national surveys, including the 1988 study in which 68 of 94 cities reported experiencing gang crime problems (Spergel and Curry, 1990). These surveys of law-enforcement agencies, while including a larger sample of cities, failed to include towns and rural areas. As such, little was known about gang issues outside of the larger U.S. cities.

By the 1990s, it appeared that gangs had spread beyond the large urban areas and researchers widened their sampling frames to include these previously ignored areas. Curry, Ball, and Fox (1994), for instance, expanded their 1992 sample of law-enforcement agencies to include 11 counties, 43 smaller cities, and 79 of the largest U.S. cities. Of these 133 jurisdictions, 121 (91%) reported gang crime problems. In 1994, Curry, Ball, and Decker (1996) surveyed 428 jurisdictions. This sample included all cities with populations exceeding 150,000 ($n = 115$), a sample of cities with populations between 25,000 and 150,000, and the 11 counties included in the 1992 survey. Based upon this survey, 57 percent of all jurisdictions reported gang problems with estimates of total gang membership at 378,807 within 8,625 gangs. The 2000 National Youth Gang Center (NYGC) survey estimates that there were 772,500 gang members in 24,500 gangs (Egley and Arjunan, 2002). Since 1996, when there were an estimated 846,428 gang members in 30,818 gangs, the NYGC has reported a steady decline in the prevalence of youth gangs (Egley, 2002). In this volume, article 4 by Arlen Egley, James Howell, and Aline Major provides an excellent overview of the results from the NYGC from 1996 through 2002.

With this apparent proliferation of gangs to small towns and rural counties, one concern was that the Chicago and Los Angeles gangs were establishing satellite gangs throughout the United States. An important finding from a survey of law-enforcement officers refuted this common belief (Maxson, 1998). Gangs were not establishing satellite affiliates across the country; rather, the proliferation of gangs was attributable to social and familial movement. Gangs developed in response to local conditions—not due to a national conspiracy to establish drug distribution networks.

Commensurate with the growing awareness of the dispersion of gangs was an emphasis on achieving consensus on a definition of gang affiliation and gang-related crime. James Howell (article 1) provides a thorough and informative overview of a number of the issues surrounding the increasing attention paid to youth gangs during the 1990s. Complementing the emergence of law-enforcement data on youth gangs, survey researchers studying general adolescent samples also began to explore youth gangs. For instance, Esbensen and Huizinga (1993), using a very restrictive definition of gang membership, found that eight percent of their sample of Denver youths reported gang affiliation at some point during a four-year study period. Thornberry and Burch (1997), utilizing a more inclusive definition of gang member status, reported that 30 percent of a school-based sample in Rochester indicated that they were gang members at some point prior to the end of high school. In an 11-city study of eighth-grade students attending public schools, Esbensen and Deschenes (1998) reported that gang membership ranged from a low of five percent in Will County, Illinois to a high of almost 16 percent of students in Milwaukee.

The issues associated with the importance of clearly defining the terms "youth gang" and "gang member" are discussed in article 2 by Finn Esbensen, Thomas Winfree, Ni He, and Terrance Taylor. They examined the impact of varying the definition of gang membership among a sample of school-aged adolescents. Depending on which definition was used, anywhere from two percent to 17 percent of their sample would be considered gang involved. In addition to investigating the effect of varying definitions on the magnitude of the youth gang problem, these researchers also examined the extent to which the definition impacted the demographic, attitudinal, and behavioral characteristics of gang members. They found that self-identification, a technique that has become increasingly more common in gang research, is a robust measure of gang status.

In article 3, Ron Huff provides an overview of the criminal behavior of youths involved with gangs and those at risk of joining a gang. His four-city study of "emergent" gang cities (i.e., those in which gangs are relatively recent occurrences) produced findings consistent with other studies conducted during the 1990s. Among these findings are the following: (1) While gang members are more involved in drug sales than other at-risk youths, drug trafficking is not controlled by the gang; (2) There was actually little pressure to join gangs—those youths who declined joining suffered milder reprisals than did the youths who actually joined the gang; (3) Most youths did not become gang involved until age 14; and (4) Gang youths were more likely than the at-risk youths to possess weapons. These findings are then used to frame possible policy responses, with an emphasis on prevention efforts.

References

Curry, G. D., Ball R. A., & Fox, R. J. (1994) Gang Crime and Law Enforcement Record Keeping. *Research in Brief.* Washington, DC: U.S. Department of Justice, Office of Justice Program, National Institute of Justice.

Curry, G. D., Ball, R. A., & Decker, S. H. (1996) Estimating the National Scope of Gang Crime from Law Enforcement Data. *Research in Brief.* Washington, DC: U.S. Department of Justice, Office of Justice Program, National Institute of Justice.

Egley, A., Jr. (2002) *National Youth Gang Survey Trends From 1996 to 2000.* Washington, DC: U.S. Department of Justice.

Egley, A., Jr., & Arjunan, M. (2002) *Highlights of the 2000 National Youth Gang Survey.* Washington, DC: U.S. Department of Justice.

Esbensen, F.-A., & Deschenes, E. P. (1998) A Multi-site Examination of Youth Gang Membership: Does Gender Matter? *Criminology* 36:799–828.

Esbensen, F.-A., & Huizinga, D. (1993) Gangs, Drugs, and Delinquency in a Survey of Urban Youth. *Criminology* 31:565–589.

Maxson, C. L. (1998) Gang Members on the Move. *Bulletin.* Washington, DC: U.S. Department of Justice, Office of Justice Program, Office of Juvenile Justice and Delinquency Prevention.

Miller, W. B. (1975) *Violence by Youth Gangs and Youth Groups as Crime Problem in Major American Cities.* Washington, DC: U.S. Government Printing Office.

Spergel, I. A., & Curry, G. D. (1990) Strategies and Perceived Agency Effectiveness in Dealing with the Youth Gang Problem. In C. R. Huff (Ed.), *Gangs in America.* Newbury Park, CA: Sage Publications.

Thornberry, T. P., & Burch, J. H., II. (1997) Gang Members and Delinquent Behavior. *Juvenile Justice Bulletin.* Washington, DC: U.S. Department of Justice.

Youth Gangs
An Overview

James C. Howell

INTRODUCTION

The United States has seen rapid proliferation of youth gangs[1] since 1980. During this period, the number of cities with gang problems increased from an estimated 286 jurisdictions with more than 2,000 gangs and nearly 100,000 gang members in 1980 (Miller, 1992) to about 4,800 jurisdictions with more than 31,000 gangs and approximately 846,000 gang members in 1996 (Moore and Terrett, in press).[2] An 11-city survey of eighth graders found that 9 percent were currently gang members, and 17 percent said they had belonged to a gang at some point in their lives (Esbensen and Osgood, 1997).

Other studies reported comparable percentages and also showed that gang members were responsible for a large proportion of violent offenses. In the Rochester site of the OJJDP-funded Program of Research on the Causes and Correlates of Delinquency, gang members (30 percent of the sample) self-reported committing 68 percent of all violent offenses (Thornberry, 1998). In the Denver site, adolescent gang members (14 percent of the sample) self-reported committing 89 percent of all serious violent offenses (Huizinga, 1997). In another study, supported by OJJDP and several other agencies and organizations, adolescent gang members in Seattle (15 percent of the sample) self-reported involvement in 85 percent of robberies committed by the entire sample (Battin et al., 1998).

Howell, James C. 1998, August. "Youth Gangs: An Overview," *Juvenile Justice Bulletin*. Washington, DC: Office of Juvenile Justice and Delinquency Prevention.

This article reviews data and research to consolidate available knowledge on youth gangs that are involved in criminal activity. Following a historical perspective, demographic information is presented. The scope of the problem is assessed, including gang problems in juvenile detention and correctional facilities. Several issues are then addressed by reviewing gang studies to provide a clearer understanding of youth gang problems. An extensive list of references is provided for further review.

HISTORY OF YOUTH GANGS

Youth gangs may have first appeared in Europe (Klein, 1996) or Mexico (Redfield, 1941; Rubel, 1965). No one is sure when or why they emerged in the United States. The earliest record of their appearance in the United States may have been as early as 1783, as the American Revolution ended (Sante, 1991; Sheldon, 1898). They may have emerged spontaneously from adolescent play groups or as a collective response to urban conditions in this country (Thrasher, 1927). Some suggest they first emerged following the Mexican migration to the Southwest after the Mexican Revolution in 1813 (Redfield, 1941; Rubel, 1965). They may have grown out of difficulties Mexican youth encountered with social and cultural adjustment to the American way of life under extremely poor conditions in the Southwest (Moore, 1978; Vigil, 1988). Gangs appear to have spread in New England in the early 1800s as the Industrial Revolution gained momentum in the first large cities in the United States: New York, Boston, and Philadelphia (Finestone, 1976; Sante, 1991; Spergel, 1995).

Gangs began to flourish in Chicago and other large cities during the industrial era, when immigration and population shifts reached peak levels (Finestone, 1976). Early in American history, gangs seem to have been most visible and most violent during periods of rapid population shifts. Their evolution has been characterized by an ebb and flow pattern that "at any given time more closely resembles that of, say, influenza rather than blindness," as Miller (1992:51) has observed. The United States has seen four distinct periods of gang growth and peak activity: the late 1800s, the 1920s, the 1960s, and the 1990s (Curry and Decker, 1998). Gang proliferation, in other words, is not a constant.

In the modern era, youth gangs have been influenced by several trends. In the 1970s and 1980s, because of increased mobility and access to more lethal weapons, many gangs became more dangerous (Klein, 1995; Klein and Maxson, 1989; Miller, 1974, 1992; Spergel, 1995). Gang fights previously involving fists or brass knuckles increasingly involved guns. The growing availability of automobiles, coupled with the use of more lethal weapons, fueled the growth of drive-by shootings, a tactic that previously took the form of on-foot hit-and-run forays (Miller, 1966). Gangs of the 1980s and 1990s seem to have both more younger and more older members than before (Miller, 1992; Spergel, 1995), more members with prison records or ties to prison inmates (Hagedorn, 1988; Miller, 1992; Moore, 1990; Vigil, 1988), and more weapons of greater lethality (Block and Block, 1993; Miller, 1992; National Drug Intelligence Center, 1995). They are less concerned with territorial affiliations (Fagan, 1990; Klein, 1995), use alcohol and drugs more extensively (Decker and Van Winkle, 1996; Fagan, 1990; Thornberry, 1998), and are more involved in drug trafficking (Battin et al., 1998; Fagan, 1990; Miller, 1992; Taylor, 1989; Thornberry, 1998).

Some youth gangs appear to have been transformed into entrepreneurial organizations by the crack cocaine epidemic that began in the mid-1980s (Sanchez-Jankowski, 1991; Skolnick et al., 1988; Taylor, 1989). However, the extent to which they have become drug-trafficking organizations is unclear (Howell and Decker, in press). Some youth groups, many of which are not considered bona fide gangs, are not seriously involved in illegal activities and provide mainly social opportunities for their membership (Fagan, 1989; Vigil, 1988). Some gangs seldom use drugs and alcohol, and some have close community ties (Fagan, 1989; Sanchez-Jankowski, 1991; Vigil, 1988).

DEMOGRAPHIC CHARACTERISTICS

The average age of youth gang members is about 17 to 18 years (Curry and Decker, 1998), but tends to be older in cities in which gangs have been in existence longer, like Chicago and Los Angeles (Bobrowski, 1988; California Attorney General's Gang Unit, 1996; Klein, 1995; Spergel, 1995). The typical age range is 12 to 24. Although younger members are becoming more common, it is the older membership that has increased the most (Hagedorn, 1988; Moore, 1990; Spergel, 1995). Male gang members outnumber females by a wide margin (Miller, 1992; Moore, 1978), and this span is greater in late adolescence than in early adolescence (Bjerregaard and Smith, 1993; Esbensen and Huizinga, 1993; Moore and Hagedorn, 1996). Gangs vary in size by type of gang. Traditional (large, enduring, territorial) gangs average about 180 members, whereas specialty (e.g., drug trafficking) gangs average only about 25 members (Klein and Maxson, 1996). In large cities, some gangs number in the thousands and even tens of thousands (Block and Block, 1993; Spergel, 1995).

In the early 19th century, youth gangs in the United States were primarily Irish, Jewish, and Italian (Haskins, 1974; Sante, 1991). According to a recent national law enforcement survey, the ethnicity of gang members is 48 percent African-American, 43 percent Hispanic,[3] 5 percent white, and 4 percent Asian (Curry, 1996). However, student surveys show a much larger representation of white adolescents among gang members.

In a survey of nearly 6,000 eighth graders in 11 sites (Esbensen and Osgood, 1997), 31 percent of the students who said they were gang members were African-American, 25 percent were Hispanic, 25 percent were white, 5 percent were Asian, and 15 percent were of other racial and ethnic groups.[4] Bursik and Grasmick (1993) point out that, despite the disproportionate representation of minority group members in studies as compared with white youth, "blacks and Hispanics have no special predisposition to gang membership. Rather, they simply are overrepresented in those areas most likely to lead to gang activity."

Miller (1974:220) notes that "observers of any given period tend to relate the characteristics of gangs to those of the particular ethnic groups prominent in the urban lower class during that period . . . , roughly, the more prevalent the lower-class populations, the more gangs." Spergel (1995:60) agrees, but with an important caveat: "Contemporary youth gangs are located primarily in lower-class, slum, ghetto, barrio, or working-class changing communities, but it is not clear that either class, poverty, culture, race or ethnicity, or social change per se primarily accounts [sic] for gang problems." Spergel's observation appears to be correct, because gangs have recently become much more prevalent in rural counties, small cities, and towns (Moore and Terrett, in press), for reasons that are not well understood.

Gang Specialization

Certain offenses are related to different racial/ethnic youth gangs. African-American gangs are relatively more involved in drug offenses; Hispanic gangs, in "turf-related" violence; Asian and white gangs, in property crimes (Block et al., 1996; Spergel, 1990). Numerous ethnographic studies have provided excellent descriptions of Hispanic gangs in Los Angeles. They tend to be structured around age-based cohorts, based in a specific territory (barrio), and characterized by fighting (Moore, Vigil, and Garcia, 1983). The gang provides family-like relationships for adolescents who feel isolated, drifting between their native and adopted cultures and feeling alienated from both (Vigil, 1990a, 1990b; Vigil and Long, 1990). Hispanic gangs have strong links to the neighborhood, or barrio, which tie them to the larger culture (Moore, 1978); much of their violence is related to defense of neighborhood turf. In contrast, African-American gangs in large cities tend to replace traditional social networks that linked youth with legitimate work opportunities (Anderson, 1990). Thus, these gangs tend to be involved in entrepreneurial activities more than other ethnic/racial gangs and may evolve from "scavenger" groups to turf gangs and drug-trafficking gangs (Taylor, 1989).

Use of violence to protect the neighborhood, or gang turf, from rival gangs is also a predominant goal in Chicago (Block and Block, 1993), San Diego (Pennell et al., 1994), and St. Louis (Decker and Van Winkle, 1996). Violence is rarely planned and generally occurs spontaneously among gangs (Decker and Van Winkle, 1996; Sanchez-Jankowski, 1991; Pennell et al., 1994) in response to a wide variety of situations (Horowitz and Schwartz, 1974; Sanders, 1994).

Numerous ways of classifying gangs other than by ethnicity have been devised (Spergel, 1995), although the gangs' complexity, variations, and changing structure practically defy static categories. One way of viewing gangs is along a continuum of degree of organization (Gordon, 1994), from youth groups who hang out together in shopping malls and other places; to criminal groups, small clusters of friends who band together to commit crimes such as fencing operations; to street gangs composed of groups of adolescents and young adults who form a semistructured operation and engage in delinquent and criminal behavior; to adult criminal organizations that engage in criminal activity primarily for economic reasons. The latter, also called criminal gangs, are not considered youth gangs. Distinguishing among these various forms of gangs is often not easy; in some areas, groups may evolve from less formal to more formal organizations along this continuum.

Female Gang Delinquency

Data on the number of female youth gang members have not yet been gathered nationwide; however, several estimates are available. Miller (1992) estimated that approximately 10 percent of gang members were females. Among law enforcement agencies that reported male and female membership data in a 1992 survey, gang membership was estimated to be nearly 6 percent female (Curry, 1995b). In their 11-city survey of eighth graders, Esbensen and Osgood (1997) report that 38 percent of the students who said they were gang members were females. Recent studies of large adolescent samples in urban areas, funded through OJJDP's Program of Research on the Causes and Correlates of Delinquency, report that female membership is higher in early adolescence (Bjerregaard and Smith, 1993; Esbensen and Huizinga, 1993). Among all adolescents, female involvement may be increasing proportionally with male gang involvement (Klein, 1995). Surveys have been incapable of measuring these changes nationwide because data and information systems at the local level are inadequate. Nevertheless, these and other studies of urban samples (Fagan, 1990; Winfree et al., 1992) suggest growing involvement of females in gangs concomitant with gang proliferation.

Are independent female gangs increasing? The initial survey of cities with gang problems indicates that by far the most common female gangs are auxiliary gangs affiliated with male gangs (Miller, 1975). Subsequent surveys suggest an increase in independent female gangs (Curry, Ball, and Decker, 1996; Curry, 1995a, 1995b; National Drug Intelligence Center, 1995). However, Moore (1991:41) suggests that "the general notion that gang girls have moved away from . . . 'traditional [auxiliary] roles' must be taken with a grain of salt." Based on her review of gang research,

Chesney-Lind (1993) contends that there is little evidence to support the notion of a new breed of violent female gangsters breaking into this historically male-dominated phenomenon.

Are female gang members becoming involved in more serious and violent offending? This question cannot be answered definitively because national trend data are not available. Chicago data on gang-related offenses during the 30-year period from 1965 to 1994 show that females represented only 5 percent of victims and 1 percent of offenders (Block et al., 1996). Female gang violence was more likely to involve simple battery or assault rather than homicide, and female nonviolent crimes consisted mainly of liquor law violations.

In the OJJDP-funded Causes and Correlates study site of Denver, Esbensen and Huizinga (1993) found that delinquent behavior was much more prevalent among female gang members than nongang females. However, incidence rates were not significantly higher. In Rochester, another Causes and Correlates study site, Bjerregaard and Smith (1993) also found that female gang members were significantly more likely to engage in serious delinquency than nongang females. However, in contrast to Denver, the incidence rates in Rochester in every offense category were significantly higher among female gang members than among nongang females. Fagan (1990) also found high levels of involvement in serious delinquency among female gang members in Chicago, Los Angeles, and San Diego. Prevalence rates in all behavior categories, including violent offenses, were higher among female gang members than among nongang males.

SCOPE OF THE PROBLEM

Assessing the scope of the youth gang problem in the United States is difficult. No consensus exists on what constitutes a youth gang. Many jurisdictions deny the existence of gangs. Others incorrectly, many experts believe, characterize less serious forms of adolescent law-violating groups as gangs (Miller, 1992). Some call gangs by other names, such as "crews" or "posses," although some of these are not bona fide gangs; rather, they are specialized groups engaged in predatory crimes or drug trafficking (Miller, 1992). It appears that communities are likely to label troublesome adolescent groups as gangs if the public perceives them to be a problem (Miller, 1992). Although youth gang definitions vary, most include the following elements: a self-formed group, united by mutual interests, that controls a particular territory, facility, or enterprise; uses symbols in communications; and is collectively involved in crime (Curry and Decker, 1998; Miller, 1992).

Youth Gang Proliferation

Few systematic data are collected routinely on youth gangs at the city or county level, with the exception of a few gang information systems. In the past, intermittent surveys were relied on for assessing the national scope of the gang problem (Curry et al., 1992; Curry, Ball, and Decker, 1996; Klein, 1995; Knox et al., 1996; Miller, 1975, 1992; Needle and Stapleton, 1983). In 1996, the National Youth Gang Center surveyed more than 3,000 law enforcement agencies, 87 percent of which responded, to obtain a more complete count of jurisdictions with gang problems (Moore and Terrett, in press).

Almost three-fourths of cities surveyed with populations of 25,000 or more reported youth gangs in 1996 (Moore and Terrett, in press). Respondents in large cities reported the highest level of gang activity (74 percent), followed by suburban counties (57 percent), small cities (34 percent), and rural counties (25 percent). Most respondents reported that their gang problem began quite recently, with 1994 the most frequently cited year. The average year of onset varied with the type of locality: 1989 for large cities, 1990 for suburban counties, 1992 for small cities, and 1993 for rural counties. Thus, the youth gang problem in this country is substantial and affects communities of all sizes.

Youth gangs are especially widespread in certain cities with chronic gang problems such as Chicago (Block et al., 1996) and Los Angeles (Klein, 1995). Chicago is said to have about 132 gangs (Block et al., 1996), with an estimated membership of 30,000 to 50,000 hardcore gang members (Chicago Crime Commission, 1995). Members of Chicago's four largest and most criminally active gangs, the Black Gangster Disciples Nation, the Latin Disciples, the Latin Kings, and the Vice Lords, number about 19,000 and account for two-thirds of all gang-motivated crimes and for more than half of the city's gang-motivated homicides (Block and Block, 1993). Police in Los Angeles estimate that the city has more than 58,000 gang members (National Youth Gang Center, 1997), making it the U.S. city with the most gang members.

Gang Problems in Juvenile Detention and Correctional Facilities

Three surveys have assessed youth gang problems in juvenile detention and correctional facilities. The OJJDP-funded Conditions of Confinement: Juvenile Detention and Corrections Facilities study (Parent et al., 1994) included a survey of all detention and correctional facility administrators. Administrators in detention centers and training schools were asked to estimate the proportion of confined juveniles who had problems in particular areas, including gang involvement. In both the detention center and training school populations, facility administrators estimated that about 40 percent of the confined youth were involved in gangs (Leiter, 1993, cited in Snyder and Sickmund, 1995).

A 1990 Juvenile Correctional Institutions Survey (Knox, 1991) found that 160 respondents, more than three-fourths (78 percent) of responding institutions, reported a gang problem for some period of time. Fifty-two percent of the responding institutions reported that more than 10 percent of confined youth were involved in gangs. More than one-third (40 percent) reported gang involvement of female inmates. The survey inquired about problems gangs presented in the institutions. Assaults on correctional officers were reported by 14 percent of respondents; among these, 28 percent reported more than one incident. Of the 150 reported assaults on correctional officers, 11 resulted in hospitalization. Approximately one-third of all responding institutions reported one or more incidents in which violence involving gang members resulted in serious injury.

In a sample of inner-city high schools and juvenile correctional facilities in 4 states, Sheley and Wright (1993, 1995) surveyed more than 800 male serious offenders in 6 juvenile correctional facilities located near urban areas experiencing youth gang problems. Two-thirds (68 percent) of the inmates self-reported affiliation with a gang or a "quasi-gang." Gang members were much more likely than nongang members to have possessed guns: 81 percent of gang and quasi-gang members owned a revolver, and about three-fourths owned an automatic or semiautomatic handgun. Eighty-four percent of the inmates said they carried a gun at least "now and then" in the year or two before being incarcerated, and 55 percent said "all" or "most of the time."

Gangs clearly present significant problems in juvenile detention and correctional facilities. There is evidence that, in addition to contributing to institutional violence, gangs form in these facilities and recruit members there (Moore, Vigil, and Garcia, 1983). The formation of gangs probably is related to inmates' need for protection from other inmates. The Chicago Vice Lords originated in the Illinois State Training School for Boys when several residents decided to form a new gang by pooling their affiliations with other gangs, hoping to form the toughest gang in Chicago (Dawley, 1992; Keiser, 1969). Confinement in a juvenile correctional facility is one of the strongest predictors of adult prison gang membership (Ralph et al., 1996).

Programs are needed to break the cycle of street-level youth gang involvement, further involvement in juvenile detention and correctional facilities and prisons, and continued gang involvement in the communities to which former inmates return.

Community and Economy

A major source of variation in youth gang violence is found in relationships between the gang and the community. J. F. Short, Jr., contends that the concept of gangs used in gang research is too narrow, in that it does not take into account the relevance of gangs and gang membership in other social settings (personal communication to the author, April 24, 1996). First, the gang's relevance goes beyond its relationship to individual gang members. For example, gangs serve as carriers of community traditions and culture (Miller, 1958; Moore, 1978). Second, a youth's identification with a gang affects how others react to him or her. To illustrate, Esbensen and Huizinga (1993) found that negative labeling of gang members is linked to elevated offenses.

Much remains to be learned about the relationship between gangs and their neighborhoods or communities. Sanchez-Jankowski (1991) identified four factors that motivate gangs to make concerted efforts to establish ties with the community. First, the gang needs a "safe haven." Second, it needs a recruitment pool from which to draw its membership. Third, the community provides the gang with important information (e.g., on gangs in other parts of the city). Fourth, the gang needs the community ties for psychological reasons: "A bonding occurs between the gang and the community that builds a social adhesive that often takes a significant amount of time to completely dissolve" (Sanchez-Jankowski, 1991:201). These are important features of youth gangs. Sanchez-Jankowski (1991) has argued that community ambivalence toward gangs exists because many of the gang members are children of residents, the gangs often provide protection for residents, residents identify with gangs because of their own or relatives' prior involvement, and the gangs in some instances have become community institutions; personal interests (fear of too much policing, fear of too much gang activity) also figure in community perceptions of gangs.

Another reason for ambivalence toward, or acceptance of, gangs could be the changing economy. Recent gang theory has focused on the effects of the changing urban economy on gang-neighborhood dynamics (Bursik and Grasmick, 1993). The transition during the 1970s from a manufacturing to a service-based economy in the United States drastically changed economic conditions, reducing the demand for low-skilled workers in an increasingly service-oriented, high-tech society, restricting their access to the labor market, and blocking their upward mobility, creating what Glasgow (1980) first called the underclass (see also Wilson, 1987, 1996). Fagan (1996) describes the underclass's plight as being permanently excluded from participating in mainstream labor market occupations. As a result, members of the underclass must rely on other economic alternatives: low-paying temporary jobs, part-time jobs in the secondary labor market, some form of welfare or dependence on friends and relatives, or involvement in drug trafficking and other profitable street crimes (Moore, 1988). Several gang researchers (Bursik and Grasmick, 1993; Decker, 1996; Hagedorn, 1988; Moore, 1978, 1985; Sullivan 1989; Vigil, 1988) have argued that crime, delinquency, gangs, and youth violence have increased in the 1980s and 1990s as a result of these postindustrial society conditions.

WHY DO YOUTH JOIN GANGS?

Decker and Van Winkle (1996) view joining youth gangs as consisting of both pulls and pushes. Pulls pertain to the attractiveness of the gang. Gang membership can enhance prestige or status among friends (Baccaglini,

1993), especially girls (for boys) (Decker and Van Winkle, 1996), and provide opportunities to be with them (Slayton, Stephens, and MacKenna, 1993). Gangs provide other attractive opportunities such as the chance for excitement (Pennell et al., 1994) by selling drugs and making money (Decker and Van Winkle, 1996). Thus, many youth see themselves as making a rational choice in deciding to join a gang: They see personal advantages to gang membership (Sanchez-Jankowski, 1991).

Social, economic, and cultural forces push many adolescents in the direction of gangs. Protection from other gangs and perceived general well-being are key factors (Baccaglini, 1993; Decker and Van Winkle, 1996). As noted above, some researchers contend that the "underclass" (Wilson, 1987) status of minority youth serves to push them into gangs (Hagedorn, 1988; Moore, 1978; Taylor, 1989; Vigil, 1988). Feeling marginal, adolescents join gangs for social relationships that give them a sense of identity (Vigil and Long, 1990). For some youth, gangs provide a way of solving social adjustment problems, particularly the trials and tribulations of adolescence (Short and Strodtbeck, 1965). In some communities, youth are intensively recruited or coerced into gangs (Johnstone, 1983). They seemingly have no choice. A few are virtually born into gangs as a result of neighborhood traditions and their parents' earlier (and perhaps continuing) gang participation or involvement in criminal activity (Moore, 1978).

Risk Factors for Gang Membership

Table 1 summarizes risk factors for youth gang membership that have been identified in studies using many types of research methods, including cross-sectional, longitudinal, and ethnographic (observational) studies. Examination of this table suggests that the present state of knowledge of risk factors for gang membership is not refined. Because so many risk factors have been identified, it is difficult to determine priorities for gang prevention and intervention programs without an in-depth assessment of the crime problem that identifies the most prevalent risk factors.

Long-term studies of large samples of urban adolescents in Rochester, NY (Thornberry, 1998), and Seattle (Hill et al., in press) have identified causal risk factors for gang membership. Both studies, the former funded by OJJDP and the latter supported by OJJDP and other agencies and organizations, measure risk factors in the community, family, school, peer group, and individual attribute domains. Because both studies are collecting data on their respective samples over a long period of time, risk factors measured in early adolescence can be used to predict gang membership at points later in adolescence. The identification of early risk factors indicates priorities for prevention and intervention programs.

In the Rochester study, Thornberry (1998) found predictors of gang membership among males in all five of the domains listed above. The most important community risk factor is growing up in neighborhoods in which the level of social integration (attachment) is low. Neither high levels of

Table 1   Risk Factors for Youth Gang Membership

Domain	Risk Factors	Sources
Community	Social disorganization, including poverty and residential mobility	Curry and Spergel, 1988
	Organized lower-class communities	Miller, 1958; Moore, 1991
	Underclass communities	Bursik and Grasmick, 1993; Hagedorn, 1988; Moore, 1978, 1985, 1988, 1991; Moore, Vigil, and Garcia, 1983; Sullivan, 1989
	Presence of gangs in the neighborhood	Curry and Spergel, 1992
	Availability of drugs in the neighborhood	Curry and Spergel, 1992; Hagedorn, 1988, 1994a, 1994b; Hill et al., in press; Kosterman et al., 1996; Moore, 1978, 1991; Sanchez-Jankowski, 1991; Taylor, 1989
	Availability of firearms	Lizotte et al., 1994; Miller, 1992; Newton and Zimring, 1969
	Barriers to and lack of social and economic opportunities	Cloward and Ohlin, 1960; Cohen, 1960; Fagan, 1990; Hagedorn, 1988, 1994b; Klein, 1995; Moore, 1990; Short and Strodtbeck, 1965; Vigil, 1988
	Lack of social capital	Short, 1996; Sullivan, 1989; Vigil, 1988
	Cultural norms supporting gang behavior	Miller, 1958; Short and Strodtbeck, 1965
	Feeling unsafe in neighborhood; high crime	Kosterman et al., 1996; Vigil, 1988
	Conflict with social control institutions	Vigil, 1988
Family	Family disorganization, including broken homes and parental drug/alcohol abuse	Bjerregaard and Smith, 1993; Esbensen, Huizinga, and Weiher, 1993; Hill et al., in press; Vigil, 1988
	Troubled families, including incest, family violence, and drug addiction	Moore, 1978, 1991; Vigil, 1988
	Family members in a gang	Curry and Spergel, 1992; Moore, 1991; Moore, Vigil, and Garcia, 1983
	Lack of adult male role models	Miller, 1958; Vigil, 1988
	Lack of parental role models	Wang, 1995
	Low socioeconomic status	Almost all studies
	Extreme economic deprivation, family management problems, parents with violent attitudes, sibling antisocial behavior	Hill et al., in press; Kosterman et al., 1996
School	Academic failure	Bjerregaard and Smith, 1993; Curry and Spergel, 1992; Kosterman et al., 1996
	Low educational aspirations, especially among females	Bjerregaard and Smith, 1993; Hill et al., in press; Kosterman et al., 1996
	Negative labeling by teachers	Esbensen and Huizinga, 1993; Esbensen, Huizinga, and Weiher, 1993
	Trouble at school	Kosterman et al., 1996
	Few teacher role models	Wang, 1995
	Educational frustration	Curry and Spergel, 1992
	Low commitment to school, low school attachment, high levels of antisocial behavior in school, low achievement test scores, and identification as being learning disabled	Hill et al., in press

Table 1 *continued*

Domain	Risk Factors	Sources
Peer Group	High commitment to delinquent peers	Bjerregaard and Smith, 1993; Esbensen and Huizinga, 1993; Vigil and Yun, 1990
	Low commitment to positive peers	Esbensen, Huizinga, and Weiher, 1993
	Street socialization	Vigil, 1988
	Gang members in class	Curry and Spergel, 1992
	Friends who use drugs or who are gang members	Curry and Spergel, 1992
	Friends who are drug distributors	Curry and Spergel, 1992
	Interaction with delinquent peers	Hill et al., in press; Kosterman et al., 1996
Individual	Prior delinquency	Bjerregaard and Smith, 1993; Curry and Spergel, 1992; Esbensen and Huizinga, 1993; Kosterman et al., 1996
	Deviant attitudes	Esbensen, Huizinga, and Weiher, 1993; Fagan, 1990; Hill et al., in press; Kosterman et al., 1996
	Street smartness; toughness	Miller, 1958
	Defiant and individualistic character	Miller, 1958; Sanchez-Jankowski, 1991
	Fatalistic view of the world	Miller, 1958
	Aggression	Campbell, 1984a, 1984b; Cohen, 1960; Horowitz, 1983; Miller, Geertz, and Cutter, 1962; Sanchez-Jankowski, 1991
	Proclivity for excitement and trouble	Miller, 1958; Pennell et al., 1994
	Locura (acting in a daring, courageous, and especially crazy fashion in the face of adversity)	Moore, 1991; Vigil, 1988
	Higher levels of normlessness in the context of family, peer group, and school	Esbensen, Huizinga, and Weiher, 1993
	Social disabilities	Short and Strodtbeck, 1965; Vigil, 1988
	Illegal gun ownership	Bjerregaard and Lizotte, 1995; Lizotte et al., 1994; Vigil and Long, 1990
	Early or precocious sexual activity, especially among females	Kosterman et al., 1996; Bjerregaard and Smith, 1993
	Alcohol and drug use	Bjerregaard and Smith, 1993; Curry and Spergel, 1992; Esbensen, Huizinga, and Weiher, 1993; Hill et al., in press; Thornberry et al., 1993; Vigil and Long, 1990
	Drug trafficking	Fagan, 1990; Thornberry et al., 1993
	Desire for group rewards such as status, identity, self-esteem, companionship, and protection	Curry and Spergel, 1992; Fagan, 1990; Horowitz, 1983; Horowitz and Schwartz, 1974; Moore, 1978, 1991; Short and Strodtbeck, 1965
	Problem behaviors, hyperactivity, externalizing behaviors, drinking, lack of refusal skills, and early sexual activity	Hill et al., in press; Kosterman et al., 1996
	Victimization	Fagan, 1990

neighborhood disorganization nor high levels of violence predict gang membership. Among family variables, poverty, absence of biological parents, low parental attachment to the child, and low parental supervision all increase the probability of gang membership. Three school variables are very significant risk factors: low expectations for success in school (both by parents and students), low student commitment to school, and low attachment to teachers. Along with school factors, peers have a very strong impact on gang membership. Associating with delinquent friends and unsupervised "hanging around" with these delinquent friends are a potent combination. Important individual risk factors identified in the Rochester study are low self-esteem, numerous negative life events, depressive symptoms, and easy access to drugs or favorable views toward drug use. Finally, youth who use drugs and are involved in delinquency— particularly violent delinquency—are more likely to become gang members than are youth who are less involved in delinquency and drug use. In sum, "youth who grow up in more disorganized neighborhoods; who come from impoverished, distressed families; who do poorly in school and have low attachment to school and teachers; who associate with delinquent peers; and engage in various forms of problem behaviors are at increased risk for becoming gang members" (Thornberry, 1998:157).

Seattle researchers discovered somewhat similar risk factors compared with Thornberry's analysis for both male and female gang membership (Hill et al., in press; Kosterman et al., 1996). The most important community factor identified in the Seattle study is growing up in neighborhoods where drugs are readily available. Several family variables are important: family instability, extreme economic deprivation, family management problems, parents with violent attitudes, and sibling antisocial behavior. Numerous school factors have been identified, including low educational aspiration, low commitment to school, low school attachment, high levels of antisocial behavior in school, low achievement test scores, the identity of being learning disabled, and low grades. The most important peer group factor is associating with law-violating peers. Individual risk factors are the early use of alcohol and marijuana, prior delinquency, hyperactivity, externalizing behaviors (hostility, aggression, and rule breaking), poor skills in refusing offers to engage in antisocial behavior, and early sexual activity. Being a male, feeling unsafe in the neighborhood, and residing in a poor family put youth at high risk for gang involvement, regardless of other community, family, school, or peer risk factors (Kosterman et al., 1996). However, the greater the number of risk factors to which youth are exposed, the greater their risk of joining a gang in adolescence. Children who experience 7 or more risk factors at ages 10 to 12 are 13 times more likely to join a gang in adolescence than children who experience only 1 risk factor or none at those early ages (Hill et al., in press).

YOUTH GANGS AND VIOLENCE

Youth gang violence from the 1950s to the 1980s has a curious history. Miller (1992:2) contended that the national perspective of gangs during this period was dominated by a New York City media view: "a flowering in the 1950s, death in the 1960s, revival in the early 1970s, and dormancy in the later 1970s." His survey of gang problems in major American cities (Miller, 1975, 1992) proved the latter part of this media theory to be wrong. Miller's study showed that gang violence was very prevalent in the 1960s and 1970s. He argued that nothing had changed from the 1950s; rather, media and public attention were diverted from gangs to the Vietnam War, the civil rights movement, and ensuing riots.

Miller's (1992) study indicated that gangs had become more dangerous than ever in the 1970s. He attributed this to four major motives: honor, defense of local turf, control [of facilities], and gain [of money and goods]. In the 1970s, "gang crime was more lethal than at any time in history; more people were shot, stabbed, and beaten to death in gang-related incidents than during any previous decade . . . and the prevalence and sophistication of firearms used was unprecedented" (Miller, 1992:142).

Except for gangs that specialize in violence, such as small Chicago Latino gangs (Block et al., 1996), violence is a rare occurrence in proportion to all gang activities (Maxson, 1995; Miller, 1966; Strodtbeck and Short, 1964). It should be noted that violent behavior is not the only behavior in which gang members partake. For the most part, gang members "hang out" and are involved in other normal adolescent social activities, but drinking, drug use, and drug trafficking are also common (Battin et al., 1998; Decker and Van Winkle, 1996; Esbensen, Huizinga, and Weiher, 1993). Although a direct comparison cannot be made, it is apparent that the relative proportion of violence in gang behaviors has increased since the 1950s.

The introduction to this article notes that youth gang members commit a disproportionate share of offenses, including nonviolent ones. In the Seattle study supported by OJJDP, gang members (15 percent of the sample) self-reported committing 58 percent of general delinquent acts in the entire sample, 51 percent of minor assaults, 54 percent of felony thefts, 53 percent of minor thefts, 62 percent of drug-trafficking offenses, and more than 59 percent of property offenses (Battin et al., 1998). In the OJJDP-funded Causes and Correlates study, Denver gang members (14 percent of the sample) self-reported committing 43 percent of drug sales and 55 percent of all street offenses (Esbensen and Huizinga, 1993). In the same study, Rochester gang members (30 percent of the sample) self-reported committing 70 percent of drug sales, 68 percent of all property offenses, and 86 percent of all serious delinquencies (Thornberry, 1998). Curry, Ball, and Decker (1996) estimated that gang members accounted for nearly 600,000 crimes in 1993.

Gang members also commit serious and violent offenses at a rate several times higher than nongang adolescents. In Denver, gang members committed approximately three times as many serious and violent offenses as nongang youth (Esbensen and Huizinga, 1993). Even greater differences were observed in Rochester (Bjerregaard and Smith, 1993), where gang members committed about seven times as many serious and violent delinquent acts as nongang adolescents. Seattle gang youth (ages 12–18) self-reported more than five times as many violent offenses (hitting someone, fighting, and robbery) as nongang youth (Hill et al., in press). In Rochester, two-thirds of chronic violent offenders were gang members for a time (Thornberry, Huizinga, and Loeber, 1995). As Moore (1991:132) has observed, "gangs are no longer just at the rowdy end of the continuum of local adolescent groups—they are now really outside the continuum."

How strong are the effects of gang membership on the behavior of individual members? Studies in the three cities showed that the influence of the gang on levels of youth violence is greater than the influence of other highly delinquent peers (Battin et al., 1998; Huizinga, 1997; Thornberry, 1998). Youth commit many more serious and violent acts while they are gang members than they do after they leave the gang (Esbensen and Huizinga, 1993; Hill et al., 1996; Thornberry et al., 1993). However, the influence of a gang is long lasting. In all three sites, although gang members' offense rates dropped after they left the gang, they still remained fairly high (Esbensen and Huizinga, 1993; Hill et al., 1996; Thornberry et al., 1993). Drug use and trafficking rates, the most notable exceptions to offense rate drops, remained nearly as high after members left the gang as when they were active in it (Hill et al., 1996). This study also showed that in comparison with single-year gang members, multiple-year members had much higher robbery and drug-trafficking rates while in the gang.

Gangs are highly criminogenic in certain cities and communities. Studies have not yet determined what accounts for the high levels of individual serious and violent offense rates in gangs or the lasting effects of gang involvement. Are the individual characteristics of gang members a key factor? These characteristics could be important (Yablonsky, 1962), but Esbensen, Huizinga, and Weiher (1993) found no differences in the extent to which Denver gang members, nongang street offenders, and nonoffenders were involved in eight different conventional activities: holding schoolyear jobs, holding summer jobs, attending school, and participating in school athletics, other school activities, community athletics, community activities, and religious activities. Nor have long-term studies succeeded in identifying characteristics that distinguish gang members from other serious, violent, and chronic offenders. The main difference between the two groups is gang members' higher propensity for violence (Esbensen, Huizinga, and Weiher, 1993; Horowitz, 1983; Sanchez-Jankowski, 1991; Vigil, 1988); however, this could be because more violent adolescents may be recruited into gangs.

Gang norms also constitute an important factor in the elevated level of violence in gang peer groups: "Violence that is internal to the gang, especially during group functions such as an initiation, serves to intensify the bonds among members" (Decker and Van Winkle, 1996: 270). Most gangs are governed by norms supporting the expressive use of violence to settle disputes (Short and Strodtbeck, 1965) and to achieve group goals associated with member recruitment, defense of one's identity as a gang member, turf protection and expansion, and defense of the gang's honor (Block and Block, 1993). Gang sanctioning of violence is also dictated by a code of honor that stresses the inviolability of one's manhood and defines breaches of etiquette (Horowitz, 1983; Sanchez-Jankowksi, 1991). Violence is also a means of demonstrating toughness and fighting ability and of establishing status in the gang (Short and Strodtbeck, 1965).

These norms—coupled with the fact that violence is contagious (Loftin, 1986) and clustered in space, escalates over time (Block and Block, 1991), and likely spreads more quickly among youth who are violence prone—may explain why the level of violence in gangs is higher than in other delinquent peer groups. Willingness to use violence is a key characteristic distinguishing gangs from other adolescent peer groups (Horowitz, 1983; Sanchez-Jankowski, 1991; Sanders, 1994). Violence also serves to maintain organization within the gang and to control gang members (Decker and Van Winkle, 1996; Horowitz, 1983; Sanchez-Jankowski, 1991; Yablonsky, 1962).

Levels of gang violence differ from one city to another (Miller, 1974), from one community to another (Block and Block, 1993), from one gang to another (Fagan, 1989), and even among cliques within the same gang (Moore, 1988). Violence in a particular clique changes as the group evolves: "Violence is a variable. Violence is not something inevitable and fixed with gangs" (Moore, 1988:225). Decker (1996) delineates a seven-step process that accounts for the peaks and valleys in levels of gang violence. The process begins with a loosely organized gang:

- Gang members feel loose bonds to the gang.
- Gang members collectively perceive a threat from a rival gang (which increases gang cohesion).
- A mobilizing event occurs—possibly, but not necessarily, violent.
- There is an escalation of activity.
- One of the gangs lashes out in violence.
- Violence and activity rapidly de-escalate.
- The other gang retaliates.

Although our society has substantial basis for fearing the violence of certain gangs, most gang violence is directed at other gangs. Of nearly 1,000 gang-related homicides in Chicago from 1987 to 1994, 75 percent were intergang, 11 percent were intragang, and 14 percent involved nongang victims murdered by gang members (Block et al., 1996). Most of the intergang conflicts are concentrated in specific areas of cities with gang problems. These disputes over turf are generally played out in fights along the borders of disputed territory. Also, as Block and colleagues point out (1996:11), "Spatial analysis suggests a 'marauder' pattern, in which members of rival gangs travel to the hub of their enemy's territory in search of potential victims." Violent episodes generally occur within a mile of the attacker's residence. Rivalries with other gangs, not vengeance against society, provide the motivation for gang growth and expansion.

Guns

Adolescent propensity for violence and gun ownership and use are closely linked. Juvenile males who own guns for protection rather than for sport are six times more likely to carry guns, eight times more likely to commit a crime with a gun, four times more likely to sell drugs, almost five times more likely to be in a gang, and three times more likely to commit serious and violent crimes than youth who do not own guns for protection (Lizotte et al., 1994). Gangs are more likely to recruit adolescents who own firearms, and gang members are more than twice as likely as nongang members to own a gun for protection, more likely to have peers who own guns for protection, and more likely to carry their guns outside the home (Bjerregaard and Lizotte, 1995).

Gangs have always been armed with weapons of some sort (Newton and Zimring, 1969; Strodtbeck and Short, 1964). Recent studies have found that most violent gang members illegally own or possess a firearm (Sheley and Wright, 1993, 1995), and the lethality of assaults appears to have increased steadily (Block and Block, 1993) because of the availability and use of deadlier weapons. Gang members arm themselves because they believe their rivals have guns. According to Decker and Van Winkle (1996:23), "The proliferation of guns and shootings by gang members escalates violence by creating a demand for armaments among rival gangs." They feel they need more guns, and more sophisticated ones, so they will not be caught at a disadvantage (Horowitz, 1983).

Homicides

Although current national data on youth gang homicides is sparse, they may be following the national homicide pattern, which is in a downturn (Federal Bureau of Investigation, 1997). The growing use of more lethal weapons in gang assaults has been driving gang homicides. For example, from 1987 to 1990, virtually all of the increase in Chicago gang-motivated homicides appears to be attributable to an increase in the use of high-caliber, automatic, or semiautomatic weapons (Block and Block, 1993). The Blocks found that during a period in which there was no increase in street gang assaults, gang homicides increased, indicating that the lethality of weapons (deaths per incident) accounted for the greater number of homicides (see also Zimring, 1996). In Los Angeles, the proportion of gang-related homicides involving firearms increased from 71 percent in 1979 to 95 percent in 1994, mainly because of the increased use of handguns, particularly semiautomatics (Hutson et al., 1995). Surprisingly, assault weapons are rarely used in gang-related drive-by shootings and other homicides (Hutson, Anglin, and Pratts, 1994; Hutson et al., 1995; National Drug Intelligence Center, 1995).

National trend data on gang homicides are scant. Miller (1982) provided the first national tabulation of gang homicides, reporting a total of 633 gang-related killings in major gang cities in 1980. Since that time, gang homicides have increased dramatically, reaching epidemic proportions in certain cities like Chicago and Los Angeles.[5] The annual number of youth and adult gang-motivated homicides in Chicago increased almost fivefold between 1987 and 1994, then dropped slightly in 1995 (Block et al., 1996; Maxson, in press[a]). Youth and adult gang-related homicides in Los Angeles County more than doubled from 1987 to 1992, from 387 to 803 (Klein, 1995), dropped slightly in 1993, climbed back to the 800 level by 1995, then dropped by 20 percent in 1996 (Maxson, in press[a]). Los Angeles County Sheriff's Department data reported by the California Department of Justice (1998) also indicate this drop in gang-related homicides.

Chicago and Los Angeles alone accounted for more than 1,000 youth and adult gang homicides in 1995 (Maxson, in press[a]). Data on youth gangs in particular reveal that a member's risk of being killed is 60 times greater than that of the general population (Morales, 1992), and even higher in certain cities. For example, Decker and Van Winkle (1996) found that in St. Louis, the gang member homicide rate is 1,000 times higher than the U.S. homicide rate. National data on gang homicides were gathered in the 1995 National Youth Gang Survey (National Youth Gang Center, 1997) and again in 1996.[6]

Gang homicides have characteristics that distinguish them from nongang homicides (Maxson, Gordon, and Klein, 1985). Homicides by gang members are more likely to take place in public settings (particularly on the street), involve strangers and multiple participants, and involve automobiles (drive-by shootings). Gang homicides are three times more likely than nongang homicides to involve fear of retaliation. Unlike other homicides, gang homicides fluctuate from one racial/ethnic group to another at a given point in time and in different community areas within the same city (Block and Christakos, 1995). Gang homicide trends are also characterized by periodic spurts (Block, 1993), peaking, retreating to higher plateaus than before, then surging upward again. Spurts in gang homicides are explained largely by turf disputes between gangs (Block et al., 1996; Block and Block, 1993; Block and Christakos, 1995). The spurts are not citywide, but occur in specific neighborhoods and involve particular gangs. Each homicide peak tends to correspond to a series of escalating confrontations, usually over control of territory—either traditional street gang turf or an entrepreneurial drug market (Block and Christakos, 1995).[7]

Drive-by shootings

Gang-related drive-by shootings have increased in certain cities. Interestingly, killing is a secondary intent; promoting fear and intimidation among rival gangs is the primary motive (Hutson, Anglin, and Eckstein, 1996).

From 1989 through 1993, 33 percent of Los Angeles gang-related homicides were drive-bys (Hutson, Anglin, and Eckstein, 1996), resulting in 590 homicides. In Chicago, from 1965 through 1994, only 120 gang homicides resulted from drive-by shootings (about 6 percent of the total), most of which (59 percent) occurred after 1984 (Block et al., 1996).

Drug Trafficking

Although youth gangs appear to be increasing their involvement in drug trafficking, empirical research has not documented extensive networks of drug trafficking as an organized activity managed by youth gangs. The consensus among the most experienced gang researchers is that the organizational structure of the typical gang is not particularly suited to the drug-trafficking business (Klein, 1995; Moore, 1990; Spergel, 1995; Waldorf, 1993).

Some gang members become involved in drug trafficking by acting on their own, and some by involvement in gang cliques. Several researchers have identified drug-trafficking gangs and cliques within gangs established for drug distribution purposes (Decker and Van Winkle, 1996; Fagan, 1989; Sanchez-Jankowski, 1991; Skolnick et al., 1988; Taylor, 1989; Waldorf, 1993). In Chicago (Block et al., 1996), Detroit (Taylor, 1989), Milwaukee (Hagedorn, 1988, 1994a, 1994b), and San Francisco (Waldorf, 1993), a few gangs have developed lucrative drug-trafficking enterprises, and in some cases most of their violence is associated with drug trafficking. Chicago's Vice Lords and the Black Gangster Disciples are notable examples (Block and Block, 1993; Block et al., 1996).

Much has been made of the supposed relation between adolescent drug trafficking and violence (Blumstein, 1995a, 1995b; Fox, 1996). However, several gang studies have found the relation between these two behaviors to be weak or nonexistent. Despite a high prevalence of drug trafficking among Seattle gang members, accelerated adolescent involvement in drug trafficking after joining a gang, and a strong correlation between drug trafficking in mid-adolescence and selling drugs in late adolescence, a recent analysis of longitudinal data showed that gang involvement in drug trafficking is not a strong predictor of violence (Howell et al., in press). Several other gang studies have produced similar findings (Decker and Van Winkle, 1996; Esbensen and Huizinga; 1993; Fagan, 1989; Klein, Maxson, and Cunningham, 1991; Maxson, 1995).

Drug use, drug trafficking, and violence overlap considerably in gangs (Howell and Decker, in press). Moreover, gang involvement appears to increase individual involvement in drug use, drug trafficking, gun carrying, and violence and, perhaps, to prolong involvement in drug sales.

Although drug use is strongly associated with drug trafficking, which is strongly associated with gun carrying and other serious and violent crimes, drug trafficking is not necessarily a direct cause of more frequent violent offending except in established youth and adult drug-trafficking gangs. More research is needed to resolve this issue.

Gang migration

There is some discrepancy between research results and law enforcement investigatory agency reports on youth and adult gang migration and drug trafficking (see Maxson, Woods, and Klein, 1996). This discrepancy has many determinants, including different research methods used in the various studies, different definitions, and different information sources. Most of this gap may be accounted for by variations in definitions of gangs—and also the lack of a clear distinction between youth gangs and adult criminal organizations in reports of gang migration and drug trafficking. Some of the apparent affiliation of small local youth gangs with large gangs in major cities, indicated by similar gang names, may involve imitation or symbolism (Decker and Van Winkle, 1996). Fortunately, the gap is being narrowed, as seen through recent studies reported below.

Some possible expansion. A California study (Skolnick, 1989; Skolnick et al., 1988) suggested that the two major Los Angeles gangs, the Crips and the Bloods, were expanding their drug-trafficking operations to other cities. The National Drug Intelligence Center (NDIC) (1994) reported "a noticeable spread of Bloods/Crips gangs across the United States in the late 1980s and early 1990s." Gangs claiming affiliation with the Bloods or Crips were reported in 180 jurisdictions in 42 States. In a 1996 survey of 301 local law enforcement agencies (National Drug Intelligence Center, 1996), Chicago-based gangs were reported in 110 jurisdictions in 35 States.

Common reasons to migrate. A 1992 nationwide gang migration study of youth and adult gangs surveying 1,100 U.S. cities shows that the most common reasons to migrate (movement of members from one city to another) are social considerations, including family moves to improve the quality of life and to be near relatives and friends (Maxson, in press[b]; Maxson, Woods, and Klein, 1996). Drug franchising is not the principal driving force. Migrants usually arrive individually rather than with gang companions, and existence of local gangs precedes migrating gang members in almost every instance. Only one-fifth of cities reporting gang migration attributed their gang problem to this factor. However, cities reporting gang migration said local crime rates or patterns generally were affected by migrants, primarily through increases in theft, robbery, and other violent crimes: "Gang migrants were generally not perceived as having a substantial impact on the local drug market, probably because of their relatively low numbers" (Maxson, Woods, and Klein, 1996:27). In reference to youth gangs, most gang problems are "homegrown" (Klein,

1995). Several local studies of drug-trafficking youth gangs also have not found migration to be an important factor (Decker and Van Winkle, 1996; Hagedorn, 1988; Huff, 1989; Rosenbaum and Grant, 1983; Waldorf, 1993; Zevitz and Takata, 1992; see also Maxson, in press[b]).

Drug trafficking is a small factor. The availability of more intelligence has enabled investigatory agencies to track the movement of youth and adult gangs more precisely. The *NDIC Street Gang Symposium* (NDIC, 1995) concluded that, as the exception rather than the rule, some well-organized street gangs are engaged in interstate drug trafficking. As youth and adult gang members relocate throughout the country for various reasons, the gang's drug-trafficking connections are indirectly expanded. This new information is fairly consistent with the findings of the Maxson migration study.

It is clear that some youth gangs have extended their drug-trafficking operations to other states and cities. Their impact on local markets could be significant. Some of the migrant connections may be initiated by distant gangs for the purpose of obtaining drugs or guns (Decker and Van Winkle, 1996). However, gang migration for drug-trafficking purposes is mainly limited to within-the-region movement. Further research is needed on the impact of migrating gangs on local drug trafficking.

Homicide and the drug trade
Because the growth in youth gang violence coincided with the crack cocaine epidemic (Inciardi, 1986; Inciardi and Pottieger, 1991; Klein, 1995), the two developments appeared to be interrelated (Klein, Maxson, and Cunningham, 1991; Moore, 1990). Nonempirical assessments conducted by local governmental agencies (California Council on Criminal Justice, 1989; Skolnick et al., 1988), the U.S. Congress (Clark, 1991; General Accounting Office, 1989), and by the executive branch of the Federal Government (Bryant, 1989; Drug Enforcement Administration, 1988; Hayeslip, 1989; McKinney, 1988) concluded that gangs were instrumental in the increase in crack cocaine sales and that their involvement in drug trafficking resulted in a growth in youth violence, including homicide.

The presumed strong correlation between youth and adult gang-related homicides and drug trafficking has been questioned in several studies. Studies in Boston (Kennedy, Piehl, and Braga, 1996; Miller, 1994), Chicago (Block and Block, 1993; Block et al., 1996), Miami (Inciardi, 1990; Sampson, 1985, 1988), Los Angeles (Hutson et al., 1995; Klein, Maxson, and Cunningham, 1991; Maxson, 1995; Meehan and O'Carroll, 1992), and St. Louis (Decker and Van Winkle, 1996) consistently show a low correlation between gang-related homicides and drug trafficking (see Howell, 1997). Two caveats explain important exceptions.

First, some youth and adult gang homicides are related to the drug business, from a low of 2 percent in Chicago for the period from 1965 to 1994 (Block et al., 1996) up to 34 percent in Los Angeles for the years

1988 and 1989 (Maxson and Klein, 1996). Although most gang drug wars appear to involve adult criminal organizations, some do involve youth gangs. These can produce a large number of drug-related homicides, particularly in the case of prolonged gang wars.

Second, drug trafficking contributes indirectly to youth and adult gang homicides. Although studies indicate that drug trafficking is an infrequent cause of youth and adult gang homicide, the existence of gang drug markets provides a context in which gang homicides are more likely to occur (Hagedorn, in press). Most youth and adult gang homicides involve intergang conflicts and drug markets bring rival gang members into proximity with one another (Block et al., 1996).

There is no question that in particular communities in certain cities, youth gangs are very active in drug trafficking. However, the common stereotypes of the relationships between gangs, drug trafficking, and violence are sensationalized (Moore, 1990). Where drug-related violence occurs, it mainly stems from drug use and dealing by individual gang members and from gang member involvement in adult criminal drug distribution networks more than from drug-trafficking activities of the youth gang as an organized entity (see Howell and Decker, in press).

Youth gang homicides result more from intergang conflict than from the drug trade (Block et al., 1996; Block and Block, 1993). Most are due to impulsive and emotional defense of one's identity as a gang member, defense of the gang and gang members, defense and glorification of the reputation of the gang, gang member recruitment, and territorial disputes. Most drug distribution network groups involving youth grew out of criminal organizations formed solely for crack distribution and bear little resemblance to traditional youth gangs (Fagan, 1996; Inciardi, 1990; Moore, 1990). These findings suggest that interventions should be designed to target youth and adult gang homicides and drug trafficking as separate phenomena, except in cases in which street gang drug markets overlap with violence "hot spots" (areas with high gang crime rates) (Block et al., 1996).

CHANGING COMPOSITION OF YOUTH GANGS

The popular image of youth gangs is that they are becoming more formally organized and more threatening to society, and therefore should be feared. Supergangs with thousands or tens of thousands of members, including adults, have existed at least since the 1960s (Spergel, 1995). Like other gangs, they grow in times of conflict or crisis and decrease in size at other times (Spergel, 1990). Some gangs with a high proportion of adult members have very sophisticated organizational networks, much like large corporations (see McCormick, 1996). The Black Gangster Disciples Nation (BGDN) exemplifies such an evolution from a relatively disorganized criminal street gang to a formal criminal organization (Spergel, 1995). Its corporate hierarchy (see McCormick, 1996) comprises a chairman of the board, two boards of directors (one for prisons, another for the streets), governors (who control drug trafficking within geographical areas), regents (who supply the drugs and oversee several drug-selling locations within the governors' realms), area coordinators (who collect revenues from drug-selling spots), enforcers (who beat or kill members who cheat the gang or disobey other rules), and "shorties" (youth who staff drug-selling spots and execute drug deals). From 1987 to 1994, BGDN was responsible for more than 200 homicides (Block et al., 1996). One-half of their arrests were for drug offenses and only one-third were for nonlethal violence.

Klein (1995:36) observed that "the old, traditional gang structure of past decades seems to be declining." In an earlier era, youth gangs might have comprised several hundred members and were generally age graded, consisting of several discrete subgroups based on age (Klein and Crawford, 1967; Moore, 1991; Miller, 1974). Both youth and adult gangs had these characteristics. Recently, however, age-graded and geographically based youth and adult gangs have become less common (see Klein and Maxson, 1996). These have given way "to relatively autonomous, smaller, independent groups, poorly organized and less territorial than used to be the case" (Klein, 1995:36). Leadership "is complex, fluid and responsive, more diffuse than concentrated, and depends in large part on the particular activity being conducted" (Miller, 1974:217). Even large youth gangs composed of allied "sets" may not be well organized and may be in a constant state of flux because of the various subgroups, changing leadership, and limited number of hardcore members (Sanders, 1994).

Although they are very much in the minority, youth and adult drug gangs are more predominant now than in the 1970s and 1980s. Klein (1995) identifies a number of common differences between youth gangs and drug gangs, recognizing that there is some overlap in these dimensions (see table 2).

The racial/ethnic composition of gangs also appears to be changing. African-American and Hispanic gangs still predominate, but law enforcement agencies in a number of cities are now reporting Asian and South Pacific groups, more white gangs, and more racial/ethnic mixing than in the past (Klein, 1995).

The growth of adult prison gangs is also a fairly recent development (Ralph et al., 1996). These gangs began to be a significant factor in State prisons in the late 1960s and early 1970s, and some states are now reporting an increase in gang-related inmate violence. Moreover, there is evidence that prison gangs in Texas, for example, are exporting their operations to large urban areas in the state (Ralph et al., 1996). These developments are of concern because when adult gang member inmates return to their home communities, they give vitality to local youth gangs (Moore, 1988).

Table 2 Common Differences Between Street Gangs and Drug Gangs

Street Gangs	Drug Gangs
Versatile ("cafeteria-style") crime	Crime focused on drug business
Larger structures	Smaller structures
Less cohesive	More cohesive
Looser leadership	More centralized leadership
Ill-defined roles	Market-defined roles
Code of loyalty	Requirement of loyalty
Residential territories	Sales market territories
Members may sell drugs	Members do sell drugs
Intergang rivalries	Competition controlled
Younger on average, but wider age range	Older on average, but narrower age range

Source: Klein, 1995:132.

SOLUTIONS

Space limitations here preclude extensive discussion of program options.[8] Although no program has been demonstrated through rigorous evaluation (of which there has been little) to be effective in preventing or reducing serious and violent youth gang delinquency, a number of promising strategies are available.

Preventing children and adolescents from joining gangs appears be the most cost-effective long-term strategy. The Bureau of Alcohol, Tobacco and Firearms has implemented a school-based gang prevention curriculum, Gang Resistance Education and Training (G.R.E.A.T.). Evaluation has shown positive preliminary results (Esbensen and Osgood, 1997). Students who completed the G.R.E.A.T. program reported lower levels of gang affiliation and self-reported delinquency, including drug use, minor offending, property crimes, and crimes against persons. Further evaluation will determine the effectiveness of this program.

The Comprehensive Community-Wide Approach to Gang Prevention, Intervention, and Suppression Program, developed by Spergel and his colleagues (Spergel et al., 1994; see also Thornberry and Burch, 1997), contains 12 program components for the design and mobilization of community efforts by police, prosecutors, judges, probation and parole officers, corrections officers, school officials, employers, community-based agency staff such as street outreach workers, and a range of grassroots organization staff. Variations of this model are currently being implemented and tested in five sites under OJJDP support.

An early pilot of this model, the Gang Violence Reduction Program, has been implemented in Chicago. Preliminary evaluation results (after 3 years of program operations) are positive (Spergel and Grossman, 1997; see also Thornberry and Burch, 1997). Positive results include a lower level of serious gang violence among the targeted gangs than among comparable gangs in the area. There also is noted improvement in residents' perceptions of gang crime and police effectiveness in dealing with that crime. In addition, there are fewer arrests for serious gang crimes (especially aggravated batteries and aggravated assaults) by members of targeted gangs as compared with control youth from the same gangs and members of other gangs in Chicago. The project also was able to hasten the departure of youth from the gang while reducing their involvement in violence and other crimes (Spergel, Grossman, and Wa, 1998). These results are attributed to the project's coordinated approach combining community mobilization, suppression, and social intervention, which appears to be more effective than the traditional, mainly suppression-oriented, approach.

Studies reviewed in this article show that many serious, violent, and chronic offenders are gang members, at least at some point during adolescence. Thus, it is important for the juvenile and criminal justice systems to target gang offenders. Targeting gang members for graduated sanctions (including priority arrest, adjudication, vertical prosecution,[9] intensive probation supervision, incarceration, and transfer to the criminal justice system) can also be accomplished by implementing OJJDP's Comprehensive Strategy for Serious, Violent, and Chronic Juvenile Offenders (Howell, 1995; Wilson and Howell, 1993).

One successful intervention that can be implemented in such a comprehensive strategy is the Tri-Agency Resource Gang Enforcement Team (TARGET), which supports gang interdiction, apprehension, and prosecution. This California program integrates and coordinates the work of the Westminster Police Department, the Orange County District Attorney, and the County Probation Department (Capizzi, Cook, and Schumacher, 1995). The Gang Incident Tracking System (GITS) identifies and tracks gang members, providing the information base for the TARGET program. TARGET uses intelligence gathering and information sharing to identify and select appropriate gang members and gangs for intervention.

Police should not be expected to assume sole responsibility for gang problems, yet gang suppression remains the predominant strategy that jurisdictions use to deal with gangs. Suppression tactics have recently been expanded in three ways:

- State laws increasing criminal sanctions for gang crime and gang involvement and local ordinances and enforcement of specific criminal codes that restrict gang activities.
- Multiagency and multijurisdictional strategies bringing together several law enforcement agencies in a collective approach.
- Collaborative approaches tying together all sectors of the community.

A gang suppression model, the Boston Gun Project (Clark, 1997; Kennedy, Piehl, and Braga, 1996), is employing a coerced use-reduction strategy targeting gun violence involving gang members. To carry out its deterrence strategy, the Boston Police Department's Youth Violence Strike Force, through Operation Nite Lite, uses probation and police officers who patrol the streets in teams to identify gang members, enforce conditions of probation, and increase sanctions for probation and parole violations. Evaluation results are not yet available, although gun homicide victimization among 14- to 24-year-olds in the city is reported to have fallen by two-thirds after the project began (Kennedy, 1997), including a 27-month period in which no juvenile homicide occurred (Harden, 1997). Because homicides were dropping nationwide among this age group when the project began, the evaluation will compare Boston's homicide trends to a sample of other cities.

Communities should organize a collaborative approach to gang problems from the outset rather than beginning with a predominantly suppression strategy.

The program model that proves to be most effective is likely to contain multiple components, incorporating prevention, social intervention, rehabilitation, suppression, and community mobilization approaches, supported by a management information system and rigorous program evaluation.

Community responses must begin with a thorough assessment of the specific characteristics of the gangs themselves, crimes they commit, other problems they present, and the localities they affect. Other articles in this series (Howell, in press) provide guidance to communities in assessing their potential gang problems and in crafting solutions. Principles for effective gang strategies are provided, along with promising and effective program models.

CONCLUSION

Youth gang problems are proliferating across the United States, even in small cities and towns. At the same time, the composition of youth gangs is changing. Smaller, less structured gangs are emerging, and although drug trafficking is generally not an organized activity managed by gangs, drug gangs are more predominant now than in previous decades. The racial/ethnic composition of gangs also is changing, and gangs are becoming more organized.

Gang violence—particularly homicide—has increased, owing mainly to availability and use of more dangerous weapons, especially automatic and semiautomatic handguns. This violence also has been linked to gangs' proclivity to be associated with drug trafficking. New research, however, questions the extent to which gang-related drug sales are a major cause of violence. It appears that most gang violence is related to conflicts with other gangs.

Most gang problems are homegrown. Gang migration appears to contribute little to local gang problems, including drug trafficking, except within geographic regions. There is some discrepancy between research results and investigatory agency reports on youth and adult gang migration and drug trafficking; however, much of this can be explained by the studies' use of different research methods, definitions, and information sources.

Although significant progress is being made in identifying the major risk factors for youth gang involvement, much more information is needed to specify the developmental sequence by which these risk factors operate. This knowledge will be very useful in the development of prevention and intervention programs. Progress also is being made in developing comprehensive programs that combine prevention, social intervention and rehabilitation, and suppression of gang violence. Because of a dearth of program evaluations, however, little is known about the effectiveness of these interventions. The current evaluation of OJJDP's five-site program may shed more light on the effectiveness of comprehensive programs.

A key issue in combating youth gangs is providing a uniform definition for them—distinguishing them from troublesome youth groups and adult criminal organizations. Youth gangs and adult criminal organizations have different origins, and they serve unique purposes for participants. Efforts to develop effective long-term interventions must take these differences into account.

Notes

[1] This overview relies on definitions of the term "youth gang" offered by the leading gang theorists and researchers. For the purposes of this review, a group must be involved in a pattern of criminal acts to be considered a youth gang. These groups are typically composed only of juveniles, but may include young adults in their membership. Prison gangs, ideological gangs, hate groups, and motorcycle gangs are not included. Likewise, gangs whose membership is restricted to adults and that do not have the characteristics of youth gangs are excluded (see Curry and Decker, 1998). Unless otherwise noted, the term "gangs" refers to youth gangs.

[2] Sheriff's departments were asked to report data only on unincorporated areas in an effort to reduce redundancies. Respondents were allowed to use their own definition of a gang, with the guidance that "youth gang" was defined as "a group of youths in the [respondent's] jurisdiction that the [respondent or other] responsible persons in the [respondent's] agency or community are willing to identify or classify as a 'gang.'" Motorcycle gangs, hate or ideology groups, prison gangs, and adult gangs were excluded. See Moore (1997) and National Youth Gang Center (1997) for results of the 1995 National Youth Gang Survey.

[3] Hispanic (Spanish-speaking) ethnic groups include Mexicans, Mexican-Americans, Latinos, and Puerto Ricans.

[4] Percentages total to 101 due to rounding.

[5] Law enforcement agencies define gang homicides differently (see Maxson and Klein, 1990). In the broader definition (used in Los Angeles), "gang-related" homicide, the basic element is evidence of gang membership on the side of either the suspect or the victim. In the narrower definition (used in Chicago), a "gang-motivated" homicide is considered to be a gang crime only if the preponderance of evidence indicates that the incident grew out of a street gang function. Using the latter, more restrictive definition in counting gang homicides will produce totals about half as large as when the former, broader definition is used.

[6] OJJDP's recently published Program Summary *1995 National Youth Gang Survey*, which was prepared by the National Youth Gang Center, does not include the data collected in the survey on homicide. These data are currently being analyzed by the National Youth Gang Center, and a report is forthcoming.

[7] The relation between homicide and drug trafficking will be discussed later in this article.

[8] See Howell (1998) for a detailed historical review of program evaluations.

[9] The prosecutor who files a case remains responsible for it throughout the prosecution process.

References

Anderson, E. 1990. *Streetwise: Race, Class, and Change in an Urban Community.* Chicago, IL: University of Chicago Press.

Baccaglini, W. F. 1993. *Project Youth Gang-Drug Prevention: A Statewide Research Study.* Rensselaer, NY: New York State Division for Youth.

Battin, S. R., Hill, K. G., Abbott, R. D., Catalano, R. F., and Hawkins, J. D. 1998. The contribution of gang membership to delinquency beyond delinquent friends. *Criminology* 36:93–115.

Bjerregaard, B., and Lizotte, A. J. 1995. Gun ownership and gang membership. *The Journal of Criminal Law and Criminology* 86:37–58.

Bjerregaard, B., and Smith, C. 1993. Gender differences in gang participation, delinquency, and substance use. *Journal of Quantitative Criminology* 9:329–355.

Block, C. R. 1993. Lethal violence in the Chicago Latino community. In *Homicide: The Victim/Offender Connection*, edited by A. V. Wilson. Cincinnati: Anderson, pp. 267–342.

Block, C. R., and Block, R. 1991. Beginning with Wolfgang: An agenda for homicide research. *Journal of Crime and Justice* 14:31–70.

Block, C. R., and Christakos, A. 1995. *Major Trends in Chicago Homicide: 1965–1994.* Research Bulletin. Chicago: Illinois Criminal Justice Information Authority.

Block, C. R., Christakos, A., Jacob, A., and Przybylski, R. 1996. *Street Gangs and Crime: Patterns and Trends in Chicago.* Research Bulletin. Chicago: Illinois Criminal Justice Information Authority.

Block, R., and Block, C. R. 1993. *Street Gang Crime in Chicago.* Research in Brief. Washington, DC: U.S. Department of Justice, Office of Justice Programs, National Institute of Justice. NCJ 144782.

Blumstein, A. 1995a. Violence by young people: Why the deadly nexus? *National Institute of Justice Journal* (August): 1–9.

Blumstein, A. 1995b. Youth violence, guns, and the illicit-drug industry. *Journal of Criminal Law and Criminology* 86:10–36.

Bobrowski, L. J. 1988. Collecting, organizing and reporting street gang crime. Unpublished report. Chicago: Chicago Police Department, Special Functions Group.

Bryant, D. 1989 (September). *Communitywide Responses Crucial for Dealing with Youth Gangs.* Program Bulletin. Washington, DC: U.S. Department of Justice, Office of Justice Programs, Office of Juvenile Justice and Delinquency Prevention. NCJ 119465.

Bursik, R. J., Jr., and Grasmick, H. G. 1993. *Neighborhoods and Crime: The Dimension of Effective Community Control.* New York: Lexington Books.

California Attorney General's Gang Unit. 1996. Number of gang members by age. Unpublished report. Los Angeles: California Department of Justice, Division of Law Enforcement.

California Council on Criminal Justice. 1989. *Task Force Report on Gangs and Drugs.* Sacramento: California Council on Criminal Justice.

California Department of Justice. 1998 (February). Gang-related homicides. *Intelligence Operations Bulletin* 119.

Campbell, A. 1984a. Girls' talk: The social representation of aggression by female gang members. *Criminal Justice and Behavior* 11:139–156.

Campbell, A. 1984b. Self-definition by rejection: The case of gang girls. *Social Problems* 34:451–466.

Capizzi, M., Cook, J. I., and Schumacher, M. 1995. The TARGET model: A new approach to the prosecution of gang cases. *The Prosecutor* (Fall): 18–21.

Chesney-Lind, M. 1993. Girls, gangs and violence: Anatomy of a backlash. *Humanity and Society* 17:321–344.

Chicago Crime Commission. 1995. Gangs. Public enemy number one, 75 years of fighting crime in Chicagoland. Unpublished. Chicago: Report of the Chicago Crime Commission.

Clark, C. S. 1991. Youth gangs. *Congressional Quarterly Research* 22:755–771.

Clark, J. R. 1997. LEN salutes its 1997 People of the Year, the Boston Gun Project Working Group. *Law Enforcement News* 23(1):4–5.

Cloward, R. A., and Ohlin, L. E. 1960. *Delinquency and Opportunity: A Theory of Delinquent Gangs.* New York: The Free Press.

Cohen, A. K. 1960. *Delinquent Boys: The Culture of the Gang.* Glencoe, IL: The Free Press.

Curry, G. D. 1995a. Gang community, gang involvement, gang crime. Paper presented at the American Sociological Association Annual Meeting, Washington, DC.

Curry, G. D. 1995b (November). Responding to female gang involvement. Paper presented at the annual meeting of the American Society of Criminology, Boston, MA.

Curry, G. D. 1996. National youth gang surveys: A review of methods and findings. Unpublished. Tallahassee, FL: Report prepared for the National Youth Gang Center.

Curry, G. D., Ball, R. A., and Decker, S. H. 1996. *Estimating the National Scope of Gang Crime From Law Enforcement Data.* Research in Brief. Washington, DC: U.S. Department of Justice, Office of Justice Programs, National Institute of Justice. NCJ 161477.

Curry, G. D., Ball, R. A., Fox, R. J., and Stone, D. 1992. *National Assessment of Law Enforcement Anti-Gang Information Resources.* Final Report. Washington, DC: U.S. Department of Justice, Office of Justice Programs, National Institute of Justice. NCJ 147399.

Curry, G. D., and Decker, S. H. 1998. *Confronting Gangs: Crime and Community.* Los Angeles: Roxbury.

Curry, G. D., and Spergel, I. A. 1988. Gang homicide, delinquency, and community. *Criminology* 26:381–405.

Curry, G. D., and Spergel, I. A. 1992. Gang involvement and delinquency among Hispanic and African-American adolescent males. *Journal of Research in Crime and Delinquency* 29:273–291.

Dawley, D. 1992. *A Nation of Lords: The Autobiography of the Vice Lords,* 2d ed. Prospect Heights, IL: Waveland.

Decker, S. H. 1996. Collective and normative features of gang violence. *Justice Quarterly* 13:243–264.

Decker, S. H., and Van Winkle, B. 1996. *Life in the Gang: Family, Friends, and Violence.* New York: Cambridge University Press.

Drug Enforcement Administration. 1988. Crack cocaine availability and trafficking in the United States. Unpublished report. Washington, DC: U.S. Department of Justice, Drug Enforcement Administration.

Elliott, D. S. 1994. Serious violent offenders: Onset, developmental course, and termination. The American Society of Criminology 1993 Presidential Address. *Criminology* 32:1–21.

Esbensen, F., and Huizinga, D. 1993. Gangs, drugs, and delinquency in a survey of urban youth. *Criminology* 31:565–589.

Esbensen, F., Huizinga, D., and Weiher A. W. 1993. Gang and non-gang youth: Differences in explanatory variables. *Journal of Contemporary Criminal Justice* 9:94–116.

Esbensen, F., and Osgood, D. W. 1997. *National Evaluation of G.R.E.A.T.* Research in Brief. Washington, DC: U.S. Department of Justice, Office of Justice Programs, National Institute of Justice. NCJ 167264.

Fagan, J. E. 1989. The social organization of drug use and drug dealing among urban gangs. *Criminology* 27:633–669.

Fagan, J. E. 1990. Social process of delinquency and drug use among urban gangs. In *Gangs in America*, edited by C. R. Huff. Newbury Park, CA: Sage Publications, pp. 183–219.

Fagan, J. E. 1996. Gangs, drugs, and neighborhood change. In *Gangs in America*, 2d ed., edited by C. R. Huff. Thousand Oaks, CA: Sage Publications, pp. 39–74.

Federal Bureau of Investigation. 1997. *Uniform Crime Reports 1996*. Washington, DC: U.S. Department of Justice, Federal Bureau of Investigation.

Finestone, H. 1976. *Victims of Change*. Westport, CT: Greenwood.

Fox, J. A. 1996. *Trends in Juvenile Violence: A Report to the United States Attorney General on Current and Future Rates of Juvenile Offending*. Boston, MA: Northeastern University.

General Accounting Office. 1989. *Nontraditional Organized Crime*. Washington, DC: U.S. Government Printing Office.

Glasgow, D. G. 1980. *The Black Underclass: Poverty, Unemployment and Entrapment of Ghetto Youth*. San Francisco: Jossey-Bass.

Gordon, R. M. 1994. Incarcerating gang members in British Columbia: A preliminary study. Unpublished study. Victoria, BC: Ministry of the Attorney General.

Hagedorn, J. M. 1988. *People and Folks: Gangs, Crime and the Underclass in a Rustbelt City*. Chicago: Lakeview Press.

Hagedorn, J. M. 1994a. Homeboys, dope fiends, legits, and new jacks. *Criminology* 32:197–217.

Hagedorn, J. M. 1994b. Neighborhoods, markets, and gang drug organization. *Journal of Research in Crime and Delinquency* 31:264–294.

Hagedorn, J. M. In press. Gang violence in the post-industrial era. In *Juvenile Violence*, Crime and Justice Series, edited by M. Tonry and M. Moore. Chicago: University of Chicago.

Harden, B. 1997. Boston's approach to juvenile crime encircles youth, reduces slayings. *The Washington Post* (October 23):A3.

Haskins, J. 1974. *Street Gangs: Yesterday and Today*. Wayne, PA: Hastings Books.

Hayeslip, D. W., Jr. 1989. *Local-Level Drug Enforcement: New Strategies*. Research in Action, No. 213. Washington, DC: U.S. Department of Justice, Office of Justice Programs, National Institute of Justice. NCJ 116751.

Hill, K. G., Hawkins, J. D., Catalano, R. F., Kosterman, R., Abbott, R., and Edwards, T. 1996 (November). The longitudinal dynamics of gang membership and problem behavior: A replication and extension of the Denver and Rochester gang studies in Seattle. Paper presented at the annual meeting of the American Society of Criminology, Chicago, IL.

Hill, K. G., Howell, J. C., Hawkins, J. D., and Battin, S. R. In press. Childhood risk factors for adolescent gang membership: Results from the Seattle Social Development Project. University of Washington.

Horowitz, R. 1983. *Honor and the American Dream: Culture and Identity in a Chicano Community.* New Brunswick, NJ: Rutgers University Press.

Horowitz, R., and Schwartz, G. 1974. Honor, normative ambiguity and gang violence. *American Sociological Review* 39:238–251.

Howell, J. C., ed. 1995. *Guide for Implementing the Comprehensive Strategy for Serious, Violent, and Chronic Juvenile Offenders.* Washington, DC: U.S. Department of Justice, Office of Justice Programs, Office of Juvenile Justice and Delinquency Prevention. NCJ 153571.

Howell, J. C. 1997. *Juvenile Justice and Youth Violence.* Thousand Oaks, CA: Sage Publications.

Howell, J. C. 1998. Promising programs for youth gang violence prevention and intervention. In *Serious and Violent Juvenile Offenders: Risk Factors and Successful Interventions,* edited by R. Loeber and D. P. Farrington. Thousand Oaks, CA: Sage Publications, pp. 284–312.

Howell, J. C. In press. *Youth Gang Programs and Strategies.* Bulletin. Washington, DC: U.S. Department of Justice, Office of Justice Programs, Office of Juvenile Justice and Delinquency Prevention.

Howell, J. C., and Decker, S. H. In press. *The Gangs, Drugs, and Violence Connection.* Bulletin. Washington, DC: U.S. Department of Justice, Office of Justice Programs, Office of Juvenile Justice and Delinquency Prevention.

Howell, J. C., Hill, K. G., Battin, S. R., and Hawkins, J. D. In press. *Youth Gang Involvement in Drug Trafficking and Violent Crime in Seattle.* Seattle, WA: University of Washington.

Huff, C. R. 1989. Youth gangs and public policy. *Crime and Delinquency* 35:524–537.

Huizinga, D. 1997. The volume of crime by gang and nongang members. Paper presented at the annual meeting of the American Society of Criminology, San Diego, CA.

Hutson, H. R., Anglin, D., and Eckstein, M. 1996. Drive-by shootings by violent street gangs in Los Angeles: A five-year review from 1989 to 1993. *Academic Emergency Medicine* 3:300–303.

Hutson, H. R., Anglin, D., Kyriacou, D. N., Hart, J., and Spears, K. 1995. The epidemic of gang-related homicides in Los Angeles County from 1979 through 1994. *The Journal of the American Medical Association* 274:1031–1036.

Hutson, H. R., Anglin D., and Pratts, M. J. 1994. Adolescents and children injured or killed in drive-by shootings in Los Angeles. *New England Journal of Medicine* 330:324–327.

Inciardi, J. A. 1986. *The War on Drugs: Heroin, Cocaine, Crime, and Public Policy.* Palo Alto, CA: Mayfield.

Inciardi, J. A. 1990. The crack-violence connection within a population of hardcore adolescent offenders. In *Drugs and Violence: Causes, Correlates, and Consequences,* edited by M. E. De La Rosa, Y. Lambert, and B. Gropper. NIDA Research Monograph 103. Rockville, MD: U.S. Department of Health and Human Services, National Institutes of Health, National Institute on Drug Abuse, pp. 92–111.

Inciardi, J. A., and Pottieger, A. E. 1991. Kids, crack, and crime. *Journal of Drug Issues* 21:257–270.

Johnstone, J. W. 1983. Recruitment to a youth gang. *Youth and Society* 14:281–300.

Keiser, R. L. 1969. *The Vice Lords: Warriors of the Street.* New York: Holt, Rinehart and Winston.

Kennedy, D. M. 1997. Pulling levers: Chronic offenders, high-crime settings, and a theory of prevention. *Valparaiso University Law Review* 31:449–484.

Kennedy, D. M., Piehl, A. M., and Braga, A. A. 1996. Youth violence in Boston: Gun markets, serious youth offenders, and a use-reduction strategy. *Law and Contemporary Problems* 59:147–196. Special Issue.

Klein, M. W. 1995. *The American Street Gang.* New York: Oxford University Press.

Klein, M. W. 1996. Gangs in the United States and Europe. *European Journal on Criminal Policy and Research* 63–80. Special Issue.

Klein, M. W., and Crawford, L. Y. 1967. Groups, gangs and cohesiveness. *Journal of Research in Crime and Delinquency* 4:63–75.

Klein, M. W., and Maxson, C. L. 1989. Street gang violence. In *Violent Crime, Violent Criminals*, edited by M. E. Wolfgang and N. A. Weiner. Newbury Park, CA: Sage Publications, pp. 198–234.

Klein, M. W., and Maxson, C. L. 1996. Gang structures, crime patterns, and police responses. Unpublished report. Los Angeles, CA: Social Science Research Institute, University of Southern California.

Klein, M. W., Maxson, C. L., and Cunningham, L. C. 1991. Crack, street gangs, and violence. *Criminology* 29:623–650.

Knox, G. W. 1991. *An Introduction to Gangs.* Barren Springs, MI: Vande Vere Publishing.

Knox, G. W., McCurrie, T. F., Laskey, J. A., and Tromanhauser, E. D. 1996. The 1996 National Law Enforcement Gang Analysis Survey: A research report from the National Gang Crime Research Center. *Journal of Gang Research* 3:41–55.

Kosterman, R., Hawkins, J. D., Hill, K. G., Abbott, R. D., Catalano, R. F., and Guo, J. 1996 (November). The developmental dynamics of gang initiation: When and why young people join gangs. Paper presented at the annual meeting of the American Society of Criminology, Chicago, IL.

Leiter, V. 1993. *Special Analysis of Data from the OJJDP Conditions of Confinement Study.* Cambridge, MA: Abt Associates.

Lizotte, A. J., Tesoriero, J. M., Thornberry, T. P., and Krohn, M. D. 1994. Patterns of adolescent firearms ownership and use. *Justice Quarterly* 11:51–73.

Loftin, C. 1986. Assaultive violence as a contagious social process. *Bulletin of the New York Academy of Medicine* 62:550–555.

Maxson, C. L. 1995 (September). *Street Gangs and Drug Sales in Two Suburban Cities.* Research in Brief. Washington, DC: U.S. Department of Justice, Office of Justice Programs, National Institute of Justice. NCJ 155185.

Maxson, C. L. In press[a]. Gang homicide. In *Homicide Studies: A Sourcebook of Social Research*, edited by D. Smith and M. Zahn. Thousand Oaks, CA: Sage Publications.

Maxson, C. L. In press[b]. *Gang Members on the Move.* Bulletin. Washington, DC: U.S. Department of Justice, Office of Justice Programs, Office of Juvenile Justice and Delinquency Prevention.

Maxson, C. L., Gordon, M. A., and Klein, M. W. 1985. Differences between gang and nongang homicides. *Criminology* 23:209–222.

Maxson, C. L., and Klein, M. W. 1990. Street gang violence: Twice as great, or half as great? In *Gangs in America*, edited by C. R. Huff. Newbury Park, CA: Sage Publications, pp. 71–100.

Maxson, C. L., and Klein, M. W. 1996. Defining gang homicide: An updated look at member and motive approaches. In *Gangs in America*, 2d ed., edited by C. R. Huff. Thousand Oaks, CA: Sage Publications, pp. 3–20.

Maxson, C. L., Woods, K., and Klein, M. W. 1996 (February). Street gang migration: How big a threat? *National Institute of Justice Journal* 230:26–31.

McCormick, J. 1996. The "Disciples" of drugs—and death. *Newsweek* (February 5):56–57.

McKinney, K. C. 1988 (September). *Juvenile Gangs: Crime and Drug Trafficking.* Bulletin. Washington, DC: U.S. Department of Justice, Office of Justice Programs, Office of Juvenile Justice and Delinquency Prevention. NCJ 113767.

Meehan, P. J., and O'Carroll, P. W. 1992. Gangs, drugs, and homicide in Los Angeles. *American Journal of the Disabled Child* 146:683–687.

Miller, W. B. 1958. Lower class culture as a generating milieu of gang delinquency. *Journal of Social Issues* 14:5–19.

Miller, W. B. 1966. Violent crimes in city gangs. *Annals of the American Academy of Political and Social Science* 364:96–112.

Miller, W. B. 1974. American youth gangs: Past and present. In *Current Perspectives on Criminal Behavior*, edited by A. Blumberg. New York: Knopf, pp. 410–420.

Miller, W. B. 1975. *Violence by Youth Gangs and Youth Groups as a Crime Problem in Major American Cities.* Washington, DC: U.S. Department of Justice, Office of Justice Programs, Office of Juvenile Justice and Delinquency Prevention. NCJ 137446.

Miller, W. B. 1992. (Revised from 1982.) *Crime by Youth Gangs and Groups in the United States.* Washington, DC: U.S. Department of Justice, Office of Justice Programs, Office of Juvenile Justice and Delinquency Prevention. NCJ 156221.

Miller, W. B. 1994. Boston assaultive crime. Memorandum sent to J. C. Howell.

Miller, W. B., Geertz, H., and Cutter, H. S. G. 1962. Aggression in a boys' streetcorner group. *Psychiatry* 24:283–298.

Moore, J. P. 1997. *Highlights of the 1995 National Youth Gang Survey.* Fact Sheet #63. Washington, DC: U.S. Department of Justice, Office of Justice Programs, Office of Juvenile Justice and Delinquency Prevention. FS009763.

Moore, J. P., and Terrett, C. P. In press. *Highlights of the 1996 National Youth Gang Survey. Fact Sheet.* Washington, DC: U.S. Department of Justice, Office of Justice Programs, Office of Juvenile Justice and Delinquency Prevention.

Moore, J. W. 1978. *Homeboys: Gangs, Drugs and Prison in the Barrios of Los Angeles.* Philadelphia: Temple University Press.

Moore, J. W. 1985. Isolation and stigmatization in the development of an underclass: The case of Chicano gangs in East Los Angeles. *Social Problems* 33:1–13.

Moore, J. W. 1988. Introduction: Gangs and the underclass: A comparative perspective. In *People and Folks*, by J. Hagedorn. Chicago: Lake View, pp. 3–17.

Moore, J. W. 1990. Gangs, drugs, and violence. In *Drugs and Violence: Causes, Correlates, and Consequences*, edited by M. De La Rosa, E. Y. Lambert, and B. Gropper. Research Monograph No. 103. Rockville, MD: National Institute on Drug Abuse, pp. 160–176.

Moore, J. W. 1991. *Going Down to the Barrio: Homeboys and Homegirls in Change.* Philadelphia: Temple University Press.

Moore, J. W., and Hagedorn, J. M. 1996. What happens to girls in the gang? In *Gangs in America*, 2d ed., edited by C. R. Huff. Thousand Oaks, CA: Sage Publications, pp. 205–218.

Moore, J. W., Vigil D., and Garcia, R. 1983. Residence and territoriality in Chicano gangs. *Social Problems* 31:182–194.

Morales, A. 1992. A clinical model for the prevention of gang violence and homicide. In *Substance Abuse and Gang Violence*, edited by R. C. Cervantes. Newbury Park, CA: Sage Publications, pp. 105–118.

National Drug Intelligence Center. 1994. *Bloods and Crips Gang Survey Report.* Johnstown, PA: U.S. Department of Justice, National Drug Intelligence Center.

National Drug Intelligence Center. 1995. *NDIC Street Gang Symposium.* No. 94M0119-002A. Johnstown, PA, November 2–3, 1994. Johnstown, PA: U.S. Department of Justice, National Drug Intelligence Center.

National Drug Intelligence Center. 1996. *National Street Gang Survey Report.* Johnstown, PA: U.S. Department of Justice, National Drug Intelligence Center.

National Youth Gang Center. 1997. *1995 National Youth Gang Survey.* Washington, DC: U.S. Department of Justice, Office of Justice Programs, Office of Juvenile Justice and Delinquency Prevention. NCJ 164728.

Needle, J., and Stapleton, W. V. 1983. *Police Handling of Youth Gangs.* Washington, DC: U.S. Department of Justice, Office of Justice Programs, Office of Juvenile Justice and Delinquency Prevention. NCJ 088927.

Newton, G. D., and Zimring, F. E. 1969. *Firearms and Violence in American Life: A Staff Report to the National Commission on the Causes and Prevention of Violence.* Washington, DC: U.S. Government Printing Office.

Parent, D., Leiter, V., Livens, L., Wentworth, D., and Stephen, K. 1994. *Conditions of Confinement: Juvenile Detention and Corrections Facilities.* Washington, DC: U.S. Department of Justice, Office of Justice Programs, Office of Juvenile Justice and Delinquency Prevention. NCJ 145793.

Pennell, S., Evans, E., Melton, R., and Hinson, S. 1994. *Down for the Set: Describing and Defining Gangs in San Diego.* San Diego, CA: Criminal Justice Research Division, Association of Governments.

Ralph, P., Hunter, R. J., Marquart, J. W., Cuvelier, S. J., and Merianos, D. 1996. Exploring the differences between gang and non-gang prisoners. In *Gangs in America*, 2d ed., edited by C. R. Huff. Thousand Oaks, CA: Sage Publications, pp. 241–256.

Redfield, R. 1941. *Folk Culture of Yucatan.* Chicago: University of Chicago Press.

Rosenbaum, D. P., and Grant, J. A. 1983. *Gangs and Youth Problems in Evanston: Research Findings and Policy Options.* Evanston, IL: Center for Urban Affairs and Policy Research, Northwestern University.

Rubel, A. J. 1965. The Mexican American palomilla. *Anthropological Linguistics* 4:29–97.

Sampson, E. H. 1985 (May 14). *Dade youth gangs.* Final report of the Grand Jury, Circuit Court of the Eleventh Judicial Circuit of Florida in and for the County of Dade. Miami, FL: Dade County District Attorney.

Sampson, E. H. 1988 (May 11). *Dade County gangs—1988.* Final report of the Grand Jury, Circuit Court of the Eleventh Judicial Circuit of Florida in and for the County of Dade. Miami, FL: Dade County District Attorney.

Sanchez-Jankowski, M. S. 1991. *Islands in the Street: Gangs and American Urban Society.* Berkeley: University of California Press.

Sanders, W. 1994. *Gangbangs and DriveBys: Grounded Culture and Juvenile Gang Violence.* New York: Aldine de Gruyter.

Sante, L. 1991. *Low Life: Lures and Snares of Old New York.* New York: Vintage Books.

Sheldon, H. D. 1898. The institutional activities of American children. *The American Journal of Psychology* 9:424–448.

Sheley, J. F., and Wright, J. D. 1993. *Gun Acquisition and Possession in Selected Juvenile Samples*. Research in Brief. Washington, DC: U.S. Department of Justice, Office of Justice Programs, National Institute of Justice and Office of Juvenile Justice and Delinquency Prevention. NCJ 145326.

Sheley, J. F., and Wright, J. D. 1995. *In the Line of Fire: Youth, Guns and Violence in Urban America*. Hawthorne, NY: Aldine De Gruyter.

Short, J. F., Jr. 1996. *Gangs and adolescent violence*. Boulder, CO: Center for the Study and Prevention of Violence.

Short, J. F., Jr., and Strodtbeck, F. L. 1965. *Group Process and Gang Delinquency*. Chicago: University of Chicago.

Skolnick, J. H. 1989. Gang organization and migration—drugs, gangs, and law enforcement. Unpublished manuscript. Berkeley: University of California, Berkeley.

Skolnick, J. H., Correl, T., Navarro, E., and Rabb, R. 1988. The social structure of street drug dealing. Unpublished Report to the Office of the Attorney General of the State of California. Berkeley: University of California, Berkeley.

Slayton, C., Stephens, J. W., and MacKenna, D. W. 1993. *Kids Speak Out: Opinions, Attitudes, and Characteristics of Fort Worth Gang and Non-Gang Members*. Fort Worth, TX: Fort Worth Gang Research Project.

Snyder, H., and Sickmund, M. 1995. *Juvenile Offenders and Victims: A National Report*. Washington, DC: U.S. Department of Justice, Office of Justice Programs, Office of Juvenile Justice and Delinquency Prevention. NCJ 153569.

Spergel, I. A. 1990. Youth gangs: Continuity and change. In *Crime and Justice: A Review of Research*, vol. 12, edited by M. Tonry and N. Morris. Chicago: University of Chicago, pp. 171–275.

Spergel, I. A. 1995. *The Youth Gang Problem*. New York, NY: Oxford University Press.

Spergel, I. A., Chance, R., Ehrensaft, K., Regulus, T., Kane, C., Laseter, R., Alexander, A., and Oh, S. 1994. *Gang Suppression and Intervention: Community Models*. Washington, DC: U.S. Department of Justice, Office of Justice Programs, Office of Juvenile Justice and Delinquency Prevention. NCJ 148202.

Spergel, I. A., and Grossman, S. F. 1997. The Little Village Project: A community approach to the gang problem. *Social Work* 42:456–470.

Spergel, I. A., Grossman, S. F., and Wa, K. M. 1998. *The Little Village Project: A Three Year Evaluation*. Chicago: University of Chicago.

Strodtbeck, F. L., and Short, J. F., Jr. 1964. Aleatory risks versus short-run hedonism in explanation of gang action. *Social Problems* 12:127–140.

Sullivan, M. L. 1989. *Getting Paid: Youth Crime and Work in the Inner City*. Ithaca, NY: Cornell University Press.

Takata, S. R., and Zevitz, R. G. 1990. Divergent perceptions of group delinquency in a midwestern community: Racine's gang problem. *Youth and Society* 21:282–305.

Taylor, C. S. 1989. *Dangerous Society*. East Lansing: Michigan State University Press.

Thornberry, T. P. 1998. Membership in youth gangs and involvement in serious and violent offending. In *Serious and Violent Offenders: Risk Factors and Successful Interventions*, edited by R. Loeber and D. P. Farrington. Thousand Oaks, CA: Sage Publications, pp. 147–166.

Thornberry, T. P., and Burch, J. H. 1997. *Gang Members and Delinquent Behavior*. Bulletin. Washington, DC: U.S. Department of Justice, Office of Justice Programs, Office of Juvenile Justice and Delinquency Prevention. NCJ 165154.

Thornberry T. P., Huizinga, D., and Loeber, R. 1995. The prevention of serious delinquency and violence: Implications from the program of research on the causes and correlates of delinquency. In *A Sourcebook: Serious, Violent, and Chronic Juvenile Offenders*, edited by J. C. Howell, B. Krisberg, J. D. Hawkins, and J. J. Wilson. Thousand Oaks, CA: Sage Publications, pp. 213–237.

Thornberry, T. P., Krohn, M. D., Lizotte, A. J., and Chard-Wierschem, D. 1993. The role of juvenile gangs in facilitating delinquent behavior. *Journal of Research in Crime and Delinquency* 30:55–87.

Thrasher, F. M. 1927. *The Gang*. Chicago: University of Chicago Press.

Vigil, J. D. 1988. *Barrio Gangs: Street Life and Identity in Southern California*. Austin: University of Texas Press.

Vigil, J. D. 1990a. Cholos and gangs: Culture change and street youth in Los Angeles. In *Gangs in America*, edited by C. R. Huff. Newbury Park, CA: Sage Publications, pp. 116–28.

Vigil, J. D. 1990b. Street socialization, locura behavior and violence among Chicano gang members. In *Research Conference on Violence and Homicide in Hispanic Communities*, edited by J. F. Kraus, S. B. Sorenson, and P. D. Juarez. Los Angeles: UCLA Publication Series.

Vigil, J. D., and Long, J. M. 1990. Emic and etic perspectives on gang culture. In *Gangs in America*, edited by C. R. Huff. Newbury Park, CA: Sage Publications, pp. 55–70.

Vigil, J. D., and Yun, S. C. 1990. Vietnamese youth gangs in Southern California. In *Gangs in America*, edited by C. R. Huff. Newbury Park, CA: Sage Publications, pp. 146–162.

Waldorf, D. 1993. Don't be your own best customer—Drug use of San Francisco gang drug sellers. *Crime, Law and Social Change* 19:1–15.

Wang, Z. 1995. Gang affiliation among Asian-American high school students: A path analysis of a social developmental model. *Journal of Gang Research* 2:1–13.

Wilson, J. J., and Howell, J. C. 1993. *Comprehensive Strategy for Serious, Violent, and Chronic Juvenile Offenders*. Washington, DC: U.S. Department of Justice, Office of Justice Programs, Office of Juvenile Justice and Delinquency Prevention. NCJ 143453.

Wilson, W. J. 1987. *The Truly Disadvantaged: The Inner City, the Underclass, and Public Policy*. Chicago: University of Chicago.

Wilson, W. J. 1996. *When Work Disappears*. New York: Alfred A. Knopf.

Winfree, T. L., Fuller, K., Vigil, T., and Mays, G. L. 1992. The definition and measurement of gang status: Policy implications for juvenile justice. *Juvenile and Family Court Journal* 43:29–37.

Yablonsky, L. 1962. *The Violent Gang*. New York: Macmillan.

Zevitz, R. G., and Takata, S. R. 1992. Metropolitan gang influence and the emergence of group delinquency in a regional community. *Journal of Criminal Justice* 20:93–106.

Zimring, F. E. 1996. Kids, guns, and homicide: Policy notes on an age-specific epidemic. *Law and Contemporary Problems* 59:25–38. Special Issue.

2

Youth Gangs and Definitional Issues

When Is a Gang a Gang, and Why Does It Matter?

Finn-Aage Esbensen, L. Thomas Winfree, Jr.,
Ni He, & Terrance J. Taylor

Social science research is predicated on the practice of employing definitions that allow for replication and independent assessment of any set of research findings. As a general observation, gang research in the United States suffers from definitional shortcomings and calls into question its ability to inform policy makers and expand criminological knowledge. There is little, if any, consensus as to what constitutes a gang and who is a gang member, let alone what gangs do, either inside or outside the law (Ball & Curry, 1995; Decker & Kempf-Leonard, 1991; Gardner, 1993; Klein, 1969; Miller, 1975, 1980; Needle & Stapleton, 1983). When describing their conceptual and operational definitions, many contemporary gang researchers note the absence of definitional consensus. They subsequently identify two widely used benchmarks for assessing whether a given social group is a gang: (1) youth status, defined as an age classification ranging between 10 and the early 20s or even older, and (2) the

Esbensen, Finn-Aage, Winfree, L. Thomas, Jr., He, Ni, and Taylor, Terrance J. "Youth Gangs and Definitional Issues: When Is a Gang a Gang, and Why Does It Matter?" *Crime & Delinquency*, Vol. 47, pp. 105–130, copyright © 2001 by Sage Publications, Inc. Reprinted by permission of Sage Publications, Inc.

engagement by group members in law-violating behavior or, at a minimum, "imprudent" behavior. What follows this declaration often takes the following rather vague form: "The definition of gangs used here relies on the work of the leading experts in the field" (see, for example, Howell, 1998, p. 1). The irony, of course, is that even the "experts" cannot agree on what constitutes a gang or gang behavior, and many experts find fault with nearly every definition.

Failure to employ universal definitions of youth gangs and gang membership has numerous implications for gang research and gang-related public policy. For example, research on the extent and nature of the gang problem faces three possible outcomes: (1) accurately stating the gang problem with the best definition for the research question, (2) underestimating it with a far too narrow definition, or (3) overestimating it if the definition is too broad, capturing individuals, groups, and behavior that are of little interest to the intended audience. Of importance, then, is the question guiding the research reported in this article: When is a gang a gang and why does it matter?

The possibility of under- or overestimating gang membership is far from a trivial matter. Resource allocation and public concern (i.e., fear of gang crime) are largely shaped by reports of the magnitude of the problem. Estimates of gang members in the United States in the mid-1990s ranged from about 660,000 to perhaps as many as 1.5 million (Office of Juvenile Justice and Delinquency Prevention, 1997; Curry, Ball, & Decker, 1996; Knox, 1996), numbers that at least one gang expert characterized as "probably conservative because many jurisdictions deny, often for political and image reasons, that there is a problem, especially in the early stages of youth gang development in a community" (Huff, 1998, p. 1). Public policies, particularly law enforcement practices, respond in very direct ways to these numbers, whether the estimates are for the nation or a single community. Hence, how gang is defined impacts the numerator in any per capita rate, let alone the gross number of gangs or gang members.

In addition to the issue of accurately estimating the size of the gang problem is the concern of accurately assessing the epidemiology of gang members. Quite disparate estimates exist with regard to the demographic composition of youth gangs (Esbensen & Winfree, 1998). Law enforcement data paint a picture of inner-city, minority males (generally from single-parent households) (National Youth Gang Center, 1999). Ethnographic studies of older and more homogeneous samples tend to confirm this picture. Surveys, however, call into question the extent to which these stereotypes accurately depict youth gang members.

In this article, we attempt to disentangle some of the definitional questions that arise. Do gang definitions used in community or school-based surveys, for example, produce overestimates of gang youths? That is, do surveys include youths who would not be considered gang members by law enforcement? Or, alternatively, are law enforcement estimates too narrow in scope, excluding individuals who should be included as gang members? Will more restrictive definitions in survey research produce lower prevalence estimates? Will these more restrictive definitions change the demographic depiction of gang members? More specifically, does the application of a more restrictive definition of gang membership in survey data produce estimates of gang membership and depictions of gang members that are more similar to those derived from law enforcement data?

Clearly, the definitions of gang and gang membership used by researchers and policy makers have important implications for both research results and the ways in which policy makers employ those findings. The present study, then, provides multiple answers to a single compound research question: When is a gang a gang, and why does it matter? We propose that by shifting from a less restrictive definition through increasingly more restrictive ones, the analysis should yield valuable insights into the overall gang phenomenon.

DEFINING THE GANG

Nearly from the onset of twentieth-century gang research, a popular strategy for defining gangs was to let the youths do it themselves (i.e., those who claimed membership). Thrasher (1927/1963), recognizing the scientific need "to discover what is typical rather than what is unique," centered his definition of a gang on its natural history, those characteristics that made it unique and distinct from other "types of collectives" (p. 37). His list of definitional characteristics included (a) a spontaneous and unplanned origin, (b) intimate face-to-face relations, (c) a sense of organization, solidarity, and morale that is superior to that exhibited by the mob, (d) a tendency to move through space and meet a hostile element, which can precipitate cooperative, planned conflict, a morale-boosting activity in itself, (e) the creation of a shared esprit de corps and a common tradition or "heritage of memories," and (f) a propensity for some geographic area or territory, which it will defend through force if necessary (Thrasher, 1927/1963, pp. 36–46). Nowhere in his definition, however, does Thrasher mention delinquent or law-violating behavior as a criterion for a gang. Certainly, he acknowledged that the criminal gang was one type, but he also stressed that among his 1,313 gangs were some that were good and some that were bad (Thrasher, 1927/1963, pp. 47–62; see also Bursik & Grasmick, 1993).

Almost 50 years after Thrasher, Klein (1971) argued persuasively for the self-definition of gang members: a gang is "any denotable adolescent group of youngsters who (a) are generally perceived as a distinct aggregation by others in their neighborhood, (b) recognize themselves as a denotable group (almost invariably with a group name), and (c) have been involved in a sufficient number of delinquent incidents to call forth a consistent negative response from neighborhood residents and/or law enforcement agencies" (p. 428). As Bursik and Grasmick (1993) have further noted, the first two criteria are easily met by a number of social groups, including Greek fraternities and, we might add, Greek sororities, the Boy and Girl Scouts, and Police Athletic League members, among others. Even if the fraternities identified by Bursik and Grasmick exhibited the third quality and enjoyed a "dangerous" reputation on campus, they would not, in all likelihood, come to the attention of the law enforcement community's groups that target gangs. The qualitative differences between how fraternities compared to street gangs fulfill the first two criteria tend to neutralize much of the behavioral element and lead to it being reclassified as "college pranks," unless, as has happened, someone is seriously injured or dies.

Ball and Curry (1995) have provided perhaps the most cogent and erudite treatment of definitional alternatives and issues surrounding the term *gang*. After engaging in a lengthy linguistic analysis of various ways to define *gang*, they proposed that "gang definitions would do better to focus on the abstract, formal characteristics of the phenomenon rather than connotative, normative content" (Ball & Curry, 1995, p. 240). In this regard, they mirrored the much earlier concerns of Short (1968), who stated, "It is clear . . . that in most cases gangs and subcultures are not coterminous and that among gang boys most delinquencies do not involve the total group . . . and the behavior of gang members is a function not only of participation in the subculture of the gang, but of other subcultures as well, e.g., social class and ethnicity associates with neighborhood residence" (p. 11).

This caveat—its early and recent versions—has generally fallen on deaf ears. Largely conceptual treatments of gangs, such as those offered by Curry and Decker (1998), include a merger of Thrasher's (1927/1963) and Klein's (1971) elements, including being a social group, using symbols, engaging in verbal and nonverbal communications to declare their "gangness," a sense of permanence, gang identified territory or turf, and, lastly, crime (pp. 2–6). Maxson (1998) emphasizes that not only are adjectives often necessary to make sense of gangs, as in drug gangs and street gangs, but gangs also exhibit a remarkably fluid social structure (p. 2).[1] Moreover, "the terms 'wannabe,' 'core,' 'fringe,' 'associate,' 'hardcore,' and 'O.G.' (original gangster) reflect the changing levels of involvement and the fact that the boundaries of gang membership are penetrable" (Maxson, 1998, p. 2).

Quantitative data-based gang researchers continue to employ crime, and thereby Ball and Curry's (1995) connotative behavioral content, as a defining criterion. For example, Battin, Hill, Abbott, Catalano, and Hawkins (1998) disposed of the gang question with the following: "Gang membership at ages 14 and 15 was measured by the question, 'Do you belong to a gang?' To validate gang membership, follow-up questions about the gang's name and characteristics were asked" (p. 97) (see Battin-Pearson, Thornberry, Hawkins, & Krohn, 1998).

Winfree, Fuller, Bäckström, and Mays (1992) explored the empirical utility of both parts of this procedure for defining gang membership. That is, they employed two definitions of gang membership in answering the following two-part question: What is the effect of changing the definition of gang membership on (a) the level of gang involvement and (b) the prediction of self-reported group-context offending? They reported that the self-designation method alone yielded nearly equal numbers of wannabes (i.e., youths indicating that they had been interested in joining a gang), former gang members (i.e., youths indicating that they had been involved with gangs in the past but not now), and currently active gang members (i.e., youths indicating a continuing involvement in gangs); however, a restrictive definition, such as that employed by Battin and associates (1998), revealed that most of the sample, more than 70%, were wannabes, with active gang members outnumbering former gang members two to one (Winfree et al., 1992, p. 33). They also found that the same set of predictors revealed more about self-nomination gang membership than the restrictive definition (Winfree et al., 1992, p. 35). Winfree and associates (1992) suggested three reasons for this anomaly: first, youths in "near-gangs" may feel considerable motivation to demonstrate their "gang-worthiness" by participating in group-context offending; second, the sample of "true" gang members may not include the most criminally active ones as they may not be in school; and third, those criminally active youths still in school may have absented themselves from the survey (pp. 35–36) (see Winfree, Bäckström, & Mays, 1994). In essence, changing the definition of what constitutes a gang and membership in that gang can alter the findings even within the same sample.

DELINQUENCY THEORY, GANGS, AND CRITERION-RELATED VALIDATION

The current research question comports well with a criterion-related validity check. We elected to include in the analyses variables drawn from the key constructs associated with Akers's (1985, 1994) variant of social learning theory and Gottfredson and Hirschi's (1990) self-control theory. As Kerlinger (1973) has noted, "in criterion-related validation, which is often practical and applied research, the basic interest is usually more in the criterion, some practical outcome, than in the predictors. . . . A test high in criterion-related validity is one that helps investigators make successful decisions in assigning people to treatments, conceiving treatments broadly" (pp. 459–460). In this case, we are interested in what happens to the relationships between the theoretical variables and gang membership when we change the definition of what constitutes a *gang*. The goal, then, would be to look at the utility of such variable labels as gang for theorists and practitioners.

Social learning theory has logical links to gang behavior, especially given the social nature of much gang-related offending (Bjerregard & Smith, 1993; Hill, Howell, Hawkins, & Battin-Pearson, 1999; Maxson, Whitlock, & Klein, 1998; Winfree et al., 1994). In particular, many social learning variables have demonstrated predictive efficacy for gang membership and gang-related delinquency, including differential associations, or the extent to which one's peers are involved in delinquent versus prosocial activities; positive and negative social reinforcers, here measured as commitment to negative peers and positive peers; and differential definitions, defined as neutralizations and perceived level of guilt for misbehavior (Esbensen & Deschenes, 1998; Winfree, Bernat, & Esbensen, in press). Similarly, gang membership and gang-related misbehavior fit closely with Gottfredson and Hirschi's (1990) concept of analogous behaviors, ones commonly observed in low self-control individuals (Decker & Van Winkle, 1996; Deschenes & Esbensen, 1999; Fleisher, 1998; Lynskey, Winfree, Esbensen, & Clason, 2000). Key among the self-control variables, and ones included in this analysis, are the level of parental monitoring, or the extent to which parents are aware of their children's location, activities, and friends; impulsivity, or a propensity to engage in actions without thinking through all of the consequences; and risk-seeking, a tendency to engage in actions that entail more than a modicum of danger to the participants (Arneklev, Grasmick, Tittle, & Bursik, 1993; Gibbs & Giever, 1995; Gibbs, Giever, & Martin, 1998; Gottfredson & Hirschi, 1990).

We are not, strictly speaking, testing either of these theories or even the specific variables included in this analysis. Rather, based on our research question, we posit tests of five different definitions of self-declared gang membership and their links to theoretical constructs. That is, we are predicting gang membership, variably defined as an either/or condition, from social learning and self-control variables. Our objectives in this research are twofold: (a) to what extent are the prevalence and characteristics of gang members altered by varying the operational definition of youth gang membership? and (b) to what extent are theoretical concepts derived from social learning theory and self-control theory capable of distinguishing gang from nongang youth under five increasingly restrictive definitions of gang membership?

THEORETICAL AND POLICY IMPLICATIONS

The two questions posed above are of significance for both theoretical and policy relevant reasons. First, what we know about delinquency in urban areas is largely based on youth gang research; many advances in delinquency research and theory have taken gangs as their focal point (Esbensen & Winfree, 1998). Consequently, it is not surprising that theory-based gang studies often employ gang membership and other group-context criminality as dependent variables. For example, Cloward and Ohlin's (1960) *Delinquency and Opportunity*, a work that introduced differential opportunity theory as an expansion of both anomie and differential association theories, was subtitled *A Theory of Delinquent Gangs*.[2] Citing Thrasher's work on urban gangs, Cloward and Ohlin noted that collective alternative solutions to the commonly felt problems of urban youth do not create a gang until a group of youth "becomes a conflict group." As a general rule, then, theory-based youth gang studies have begun with the assumption that for a given social group to be a gang, it must engage in some negativistic, law-violating behavior, among other things. The delinquent gang is subsequently viewed as a likely venue in which to test or develop a delinquency theory. To what extent has this definitional decision by researchers and theorists impacted the variance found in the dependent variable and, in some cases, its ties to explanatory variables?

For policy makers, the perceived need to control gangs and gang behavior has led to the passage of antigang laws and codes. Although many of these legal actions have been challenged, most have withstood the legal scrutiny of the appellate courts. For example, persons convicted of violating the federal Criminal Street Gangs Statute (1999) can receive an additional sentence enhancement of up to 10 years. Some states, like California, have adopted sentence enhancements for persons found to have committed a felony "for the benefit of, at the direction of, or in association with any criminal street gang, with the specific intent to promote, further, or assist in any criminal conduct by gang members" (California Penal Code, 1999, section 186.22 [b][1]). In fact, "actively participating in any criminal street gang" can, by itself, result in a jail or prison sentence in California (California Penal Code, 1999, section 186.22[al]. As a further example of legislation intended to control gang members, Illinois statutorily denies probation to persons convicted of forcible felonies if the offenses were related to the activities of organized gangs.[3] Given the lack of consensus about what constitutes gang membership, is it viable to implement policies that subject individuals to criminal justice processing due to their alleged gang status?

RESEARCH DESIGN

Site Selection and Sample

During Spring 1995, eighth-grade students in 11 cities—Las Cruces (NM), Omaha (NE), Phoenix (AZ), Philadelphia (PA), Kansas City (MO), Milwaukee (WI), Orlando (FL), Will County (IL), Providence (RI), Pocatello (ID), and Torrance (CA)—completed self-administered questionnaires as part of the National Evaluation of the Gang Resistance Education and Training (GREAT) program (Esbensen & Osgood, 1999). The final sample consisted of 5,935 eighth-grade public-school students, representing 42 schools and 315 classrooms. Passive parental consent, in which excluded students were those whose parents did not want their children participating, was used at all sites except one. Torrance relied on active consent, in which parents had to return signed permission forms for their children. Participation rates, or the percentage of children providing answers to the questionnaires, varied between 98% and 100% at the passive consent sites. At the four active consent schools, the participation rates varied from a low of 53% to a high of 75% (Esbensen et al., 1997). Comparison of school district data indicates that the study sample is representative of eighth-grade students enrolled in public schools in these 11 communities.

This public school-based sample has the standard limitations associated with school-based surveys, such as exclusion of private school students, exclusion of truants, sick, and/or tardy students, and the potential underrepresentation of high-risk youth. With this caveat in mind, the current sample is composed of nearly all eighth-grade students in attendance on the days questionnaires were administered in these 11 jurisdictions. The sample includes primarily 13- to 15-year-old students attending public schools in a broad cross-section of communities across the continental United States. This is not a random sample and strong generalizations cannot be made to the adolescent population as a whole. However, students from these 11 jurisdictions do represent the following types of communities: large urban areas with a majority of students belonging to a racial or ethnic minority (Philadelphia, Phoenix, Milwaukee, and Kansas City), medium-sized cities (population ranges between 100,000 and 500,000) with considerable racial and/or ethnic heterogeneity (Providence and Orlando), medium-sized cities with a majority of White students but a substantial minority enrollment (Omaha and Torrance), a small city (fewer than 100,000 inhabitants) with an ethnically diverse student population (Las Cruces), a small, racially homogeneous (i.e., White) city (Pocatello), and a rural community in which more than 80% of the student population is White (Will County). Such a sample is appropriate to the prototypical prevention approach exemplified by GREAT, which addresses a social problem through a simple intervention delivered to the broadest possible population, rather than concentrating a more intensive program on a smaller high-risk population. Furthermore, Maxson and Klein (1994) and Curry et al. (1996) document that gangs are not exclusively an urban phenomenon, as is often suggested. They report that gangs also exist in communities with populations of less than 25,000. According to the 1995 National Youth Gang Survey, law enforcement agencies in nine of the sites represented in this study reported active youth gangs in their jurisdictions during 1995 (National Youth Gang Center, 1997).

Measures

Gang Definition

Our primary purpose in this article is to examine the criterion-related validity of the self-nomination technique of gang membership. We explore this issue by assessing the effect of five different definitions on attitudes and behaviors. Self-report studies rely on respondent self-identification of gang membership, similar to police reliance on gang members "claiming" affiliation. Just as the police often require additional criteria to be met (i.e., using gang signs, wearing colors, and associating with known gang members), self-report surveys often include follow-up questions that provide confirmation of gang affiliation. In the current study, respondents were asked two filter questions: "Have you ever been a gang member?" and "Are you now in a gang?" These two questions provide our first two levels of gang membership. Three increasingly more restrictive definitions of gang membership were then created. Although there is some disagreement concerning inclusion of illegal activity as a requisite for gang membership (Ball & Curry, 1995; Bursik & Grasmick, 1993; Short, 1968), it is our position that participation in criminal activity is a key element that distinguishes youth gangs from other youth groups. As such, aside from self-nomination, our first criterion for designation as a delinquent gang member was for the respondent to indicate that their gang was involved in at least one of the following illegal activities: getting in fights with other gangs, stealing things, robbing other people, stealing cars, selling marijuana, selling other illegal drugs, or damaging property.

The next criterion required gang members to indicate that their gang had some level of organization. Specifically, the survey respondents were asked if the following described their gang: "there are initiation rites, the gang has established leaders, the gang has symbols or colors." An affirmative response to all three of these descriptors led to designation as an "organized gang" member.

The last criterion used to determine gang membership was an indicator of whether individuals considered themselves a core member or a peripheral member. This classification was determined by their response to the following instructions. A five-ringed concentric circle (i.e., a target) was drawn on the chalkboard and students were asked to think of the circle as their gang and to indicate "how far from the center of the gang are you?" Those students indicating they were in the inner two circles were classified as "core," whereas those indicating they were in circles 3 through 5 were classified as "peripheral" members (see Appendix A for a listing of the five definitions).

Demographic, Attitudinal, and Behavioral Measures

Demographic, attitudinal, and behavioral measures were obtained from students completing the self-administered questionnaires. Responses to five questions describe the demographic composition of our sample and allow for comparisons of gang and nongang youth. Students provided the following background information:

- their sex;
- family structure (i.e., do they live with both their mother and father [including step-parents], with only their mother, with only their father, or some other situation);
- their race (White, African American, Hispanic, Asian, or other);
- their age; and
- the highest level of schooling completed by their mother and father.

Attitudinal measures used in these analyses are representative of social learning theory and self-control theory. Due to the cross-sectional nature of this sample, we do not attempt to conduct theory testing, but we do use theoretical concepts to explore the relationship between gang membership and indicators of these two theoretical perspectives. Indicators of self-control theory include the following: parental monitoring, impulsivity, and risk-seeking. Social learning theory is represented by the following measures: delinquent peers, pro-social peers, commitment to negative peers, commitment to positive peers, neutralization (tolerance of fighting under specified situations), and perceived guilt. Unless otherwise indicated, the scales (which are described in more detail in Appendix B) were adapted from the National Youth Survey (Elliott, Ageton, & Huizinga, 1985) or the Denver Youth Survey (Huizinga, Esbensen, & Weiher, 1991).

We also obtained measures of self-reported delinquency and drug use. Students were provided a list of 17 behaviors and 5 different drugs and then asked to indicate if they had ever committed the act or used the drug. If the students answered yes, they were asked to indicate how many times they had engaged in the behavior during the past 12 months. In addition to a general delinquency measure, we created five subscales of behavior: status offenses, minor offenses, property offenses, crimes against person, and drug sales (items included in these subscales are listed in Appendix B).

RESULTS

Bivariate Analyses

The demographic composition of gangs using the five different definitions of gang affiliation is reported in table 1. A total of 4,773 (82.6%) respondents indicated that they had never been in a gang, whereas 994 (16.8% of the sample) answered yes to the question of ever having been a gang member. In columns 3 and 4 (identified as Gang 1 and Gang 2), we distinguish between those youth who reported ever being in a gang from those who reported current gang membership (522 or 8.8% of the sample). Likewise, under the remaining three columns, we include those

Table 1 Demographic Characteristics of Gang Members

			Gang 1	Gang 2	Gang 3		Gang 4		Gang 5	
	Total Sample n = 5935	Never in Gang n = 4773	Ever in Gang n = 483	Now in Gang n = 522	Non-Gang n = 502	Delinquent Gang n = 467	Non-Gang n = 692	Organized Delinquent n = 275	Non-Gang n = 827	Core Gang n = 137
Age (M)	13.8	13.8	14	14.1	14	14.1	14	14.1	14.1	14
Gender (%)*										
Male	48	45	59	63	59	63	61	60	62	54
Female	52	55	41	37	41	37	39	40	38	46
Race (%)*										
White	41	44	26	24	25	24	24	27	24	30
Black	27	25	30	31	30	31	32	28	32	23
Hispanic	19	17	30	25	30	25	29	25	28	22
Other	14	14	15	19	15	20	16	20	16	25
Family Structure (%)*										
Single	31	30	35	41	35	41	36	41	37	40
Intact	62	64	56	47	55	46	53	46	52	46
Other	7	6	10	13	10	13	11	13	11	15
Parents' education (%)*										
< high school	10	9	13	16	13	17	14	15	14	18
High school	24	24	27	27	28	27	28	26	28	24
> high school	66	68	60	57	60	57	58	59	58	57

$p < .01$. All chi-square tests comparing gang youth with those never in a gang are statistically significant.

youth who no longer fit the increasingly restrictive criteria as nongang members. Of primary importance is to highlight the degree to which prevalence estimates of gang membership are an artifact of measurement. In this sample, the prevalence of gang membership could be said to be any one of the following: 17% based on the "ever" gang member question; 9% according to the "current" gang member question; 8% are "delinquent" gang members; slightly less than 5% are "organized" gang members; and only 2% are "core" gang members.

The second column in table 1 reveals that 45% of those youth who had never been in a gang were male, 44% were White, 30% lived in single-parent homes, and 68% reported that at least one of their parents had more than a high school education (i.e., attended some college or more). Compared to the "never in gang" youth, all five definitions of gang member status indicate that gang members are more likely to be male (ranging from 54% male in the most restrictive definition to 63% male under the less restrictive gang definitions). Gang members are also more likely to be a racial or ethnic minority, to live in single-parent homes, and to have parents who have not graduated from high school. Contrary to what we had expected, the most restrictive definition did not produce a picture of gang members that was more consistent with law enforcement data than was the least restrictive definition. That is, the core gang members, relative to the "ever" gang members, were not more likely to be male or members of racial and ethnic minorities, a finding inconsistent with law enforcement-based surveys.

In table 2, we report the mean scores for both gang and nongang youths on the self-control and social learning measures. Here we see that the gang members reported increasingly lower levels of parental monitoring with each new restriction to gang membership. And, in each instance, the gang members' perceptions of parental monitoring were statistically significantly different from the nongang members. The same pattern holds for each theoretical construct. As the definition of gang membership becomes increasingly more restrictive, the expressed attitudes of the gang members become increasingly more antisocial. That is, gang members are more impulsive, engage in more risk-seeking behavior, have more delinquent friends, have fewer pro-social peers, report less perceived guilt, have a greater tendency to view fighting as appropriate behavior, are more committed to delinquent peers, and are less committed to positive peers. In short, as the definition of gang membership takes on more characteristics of the media image of an organized, delinquent street gang, the members express more antisocial attitudes.

The same pattern evidenced with respect to attitudes is reflected in behavioral self-reports. With each increasingly restrictive definition, the gang members reported greater participation in illegal activity. For example, whereas the mean number of crimes committed against persons for the youth who were never in a gang was 0.60, those youth who were cur-

Table 2 *t* Tests of Attitudinal Variables by Gang Memberships

	Total Sample	Never in Gang	Gang 1 Ever in Gang	Gang 2 Now in Gang	Gang 3 Non-Gang	Gang 3 Delinquent Gang	Gang 4 Non-Gang	Gang 4 Organized Delinquent	Gang 5 Non-Gang	Gang 5 Core Gang
Self-control theory										
Parental monitoring	3.72	3.82	3.49	3.16	3.49	3.12	3.39	3.13	3.36	3.01
Impulsivity	2.85	2.78	3.05	3.25	3.05	3.25	3.1	3.3	3.12	3.39
Risk-seeking	3.06	2.95	3.41	3.7	3.4	3.74	3.47	3.79	3.5	3.92
Social learning theory										
Guilt	2.31	2.42	2.03	1.66	2.03	1.63	1.93	1.6	1.89	1.54
Commitment to negative peers	2.4	2.23	2.71	3.5	2.71	3.54	2.94	3.52	3.01	3.7
Commitment to positive peers	3.8	3.93	3.54	3.04	3.53	2.99	3.38	3.01	3.34	2.95
Neutralization, fight	3.98	3.85	4.36	4.66	4.36	4.7	4.46	4.72	4.49	4.75
Pro-social peers	2.97	3.08	2.68	2.36	2.68	2.34	2.6	2.3	2.57	2.23
Delinquent peers	2	1.82	2.43	3.1	2.43	3.19	2.59	3.27	2.68	3.4

Note: All *t* tests of the attitudinal variables by gang membership are statistically significant at the .01 level: never in gang/nongang in each gang definition, never in gang/gang in each gang definition, nongang/gang in each gang definition.

rently core members of a delinquent youth gang reported committing an average of 3.69 (six times as many) crimes against person. For each of these self-report subscales, the ratio of offending for core gang members and never gang members ranged from 4:1 for status offenses to 22:1 for drug sales (see table 3).

Multivariate Analyses

To examine the extent to which demographic characteristics and attitudes can predict gang membership, we conducted a series of logistic regression analyses. Step-wise forward inclusion procedures were used to identify the relative predictive power of demographic variables and the indicators of social learning and self-control theories. For parsimony, we report only the final models for each gang definition in table 4. One notable observation is that the effect of demographic variables becomes less important with each increasingly restrictive definition. Whereas all but the family structure variable were significant in the ever gang member definition, none of the demographic characteristics was statistically significant in the full model predicting core gang membership.

These summary models highlight the importance of peers (both having delinquent peers and expressing a commitment to negative peers) and of attitudes about right and wrong (perceptions of guilt and tolerance of fighting). Importantly, it is exposure to delinquent peers that is vital, not association with pro-social peers. In each model, the delinquent activity of the peer group was predictive of gang membership. Battin et al. (1998), in an examination of the simultaneous effects of gang membership and delinquent peers on both self-reported and court-reported delinquency, noted that gang membership "contributed directly to delinquency and substance use above and beyond association with delinquent peers" (p. 106). Thus, it is not simply a case that the variable representations for delinquent peers and gangs are measuring the same thing. Having delinquent peers and belonging to a gang are two different states; however, the former would appear to be predictive of the latter. As noted by Esbensen and Huizinga (1993), among others (Cairns & Cairns, 1991; Hill et al., 1999; Thornberry, Krohn, Lizotte, & Chard-Wierschem, 1993), aggressive and delinquent youth and youth who have shown a propensity to enjoy the company of like-minded youth are more likely to become gang youth.

In addition to peer variables, the variables that are most predictive of gang membership are the respondents' perceptions of guilt and the degree to which they indicate that fighting is an appropriate response in specific situations. To measure guilt, respondents were asked to indicate how guilty they would feel if they engaged in one of 16 different delinquent acts (corresponding to those included in the self-report inventory). Acceptance of physical violence as a suitable response to conflict was measured by three questions tapping the appropriateness of getting in a physical fight if, for example, someone was threatening to hurt friends or family. As

Table 3   t Tests of Behavioral Variables by Gang Memberships

	Total Sample M	Never in Gang M	Gang 1 Ever in Gang M	Gang 2 Now in Gang M	Gang 3		Gang 4		Gang 5	
					Non-Gang M	Delinquent Gang M	Non-Gang M	Organized Delinquent M	Non-Gang M	Core Gang M
Status offenses	1.92	1.47	3.21	5.14	3.22	5.42	3.75	5.56	3.95	5.94
Minor offenses	1.31	0.92	2.25	4.08	2.22	4.32	2.8	4.2	3.01	4.37
Property offenses	0.83	0.57	1.29	2.93	1.27	3.09	1.72	3.14	1.9	3.37
Crimes against person	0.82	0.6	1.21	2.65	1.2	2.85	1.52	3.13	1.67	3.69
Drug sales	0.5	0.21	0.86	3.16	0.83	3.52	1.36	3.89	1.6	4.79
Drug use	1.29	0.92	2.23	4.07	2.23	4.24	2.69	4.41	2.86	5.06
Delinquency, total	0.99	0.67	1.67	3.52	1.66	3.76	2.14	3.92	2.32	4.41

Note: All three-way t tests of the behavioral variables by gang membership are statistically significant at the .01 level: never in gang/nongang in each gang definition, never in gang/gang in each gang definition, nongang/gang in each gang definition.

Table 4 Predicting Gang Membership: Logistic Regression Analysis

	Ever in Gang			Now in Gang			Delinquent Gang			Organized Delinquent			Core Gang		
	B	SE	Exp(B)	B	SE	Exp(B)	B	SE	Exp(B)	B	SE	Exp(B)	B	SE	Exp(B)
Demographics															
Age	0.26*	0.06	1.3	0.26*	0.08	1.29	0.26*	0.09	1.31	.01	0.09	1.1	-0.08	0.1	0.92
Female	-0.29*	0.09	0.75	-0.24	0.12	0.78	-0.17	0.13	0.84	0.07	0.15	1.08	0.34	0.2	1.4
Race															
Black	0.68*	0.12	1.98	0.64*	0.16	1.9	0.65*	0.17	1.91	0.16	0.21	1.18	-0.03	0.28	0.98
Hispanic	0.93*	0.12	2.54	0.65*	0.16	1.92	0.64*	0.17	1.89	0.35	0.2	1.41	0.13	0.26	1.13
Other	0.88*	0.13	2.42	0.93*	0.18	2.53	0.86*	0.19	2.35	0.60*	0.22	1.82	0.63	0.27	1.88
Family															
Single parent	0.09	0.1	1.1	0.33*	0.13	1.4	0.33*	0.13	1.4	0.39	0.16	1.47	0.32	0.21	1.37
Other	0.34	0.16	1.41	0.46	0.2	1.58	0.48	0.21	1.62	0.52	0.25	1.68	0.65	0.31	1.92
Social learning															
Neutral fight	0.42*	0.06	1.52	0.60*	0.1	1.35	0.61*	0.11	1.85	0.61*	0.14	1.84	0.65*	0.2	1.91
Delinquent peers	0.58*	0.06	1.79	0.71*	0.08	2.03	0.80*	0.08	2.24	0.80*	0.1	2.22	0.79*	0.13	2.21
Pro-social peers	-0.04	0.07	0.94	-0.03	0.09	0.97	0.01	0.1	1.01	0.01	0.12	1.01	0.01	0.15	1.01
Commitment to negative peers	0.15*	0.04	1.16	0.33*	0.06	1.39	0.33*	0.06	1.38	0.18*	0.07	1.19	0.16	0.1	1.18
Commitment to positive peers	-0.02	0.04	0.98	-0.05	0.05	0.95	-0.06	0.06	0.94	0.01	0.07	1.01	0.02	0.09	1.02
Guilt	-0.77*	0.1	0.46	-0.91*	0.14	0.4	-0.93*	0.15	0.39	-1.03*	0.19	0.36	-1.03*	0.27	0.36
Self-control															
Impulsivity	0.06	0.07	1.06	0.09	0.09	1.1	0.03	0.09	1.03	0.14	0.11	1.15	0.14	0.14	1.15
Parental monitoring	-0.04	0.06	0.96	-0.04	0.07	0.96	-0.08	0.08	0.92	-0.03	0.09	0.97	-0.02	0.12	0.98
Risk-seeking	0.04	0.06	1.05	-0.09	0.08	0.92	-0.06	0.09	0.95	-0.04	0.1	0.96	0.06	0.14	1.06
Model χ^2	1227.08*			1057.42*			1040.29*			617.71*			350.11*		
Degree of freedom	16			16			16			16			16		
Nagelkerke R^2	0.344			0.397			0.414			0.341			0.306		

*p < .01

seen in the bivariate analyses (table 2), the core gang members had a mean of 1.54 on the 3-point guilt scale (with 1 indicating *not at all guilty* and 3 representing *very guilty*) compared to a mean of 2.42 for those never in a gang. For the neutralization to fighting measure, the core gang members averaged a score of 4.75 on a 5-point scale (5 indicates *strongly agree*), whereas those youth who reported never being in a gang averaged 3.85. These latter two findings comport well with the general discussion of normative saliency for social deviance (Krohn, Akers, Radosevich, & Lanza-Kaduce, 1982; Sellers, Winfree, & Griffiths, 1993), and that concept's link to social learning theory's differential definitions (Akers, 1985). As we report, gang members, youth who have been shown by other researchers to be more violent and delinquency-engaged than other comparable youth, even delinquents (Howell, 1998, pp. 8–11; Huff, 1998; Thornberry & Burch, 1997), exhibit lower perceptions of guilt and greater tolerance for physical violence.

DISCUSSION

So what have we learned? When is a gang a gang, and why does it matter? These questions result in somewhat different answers for researchers, theorists, and policy makers. For researchers, it is important to refine measurement: to assess the validity and reliability of the measures being used. For theorists, it is important to better understand factors associated with gang membership and associated behaviors, whether testing or constructing theory. For policy makers, it is important to know the extent and nature of the gang problem to allow for development of appropriate policies and programs. Clearly, the primary domains of interest for theorists, researchers, and policy makers are not mutually exclusive and, in fact, are closely intertwined.

Considerable debate has centered around the attributes that constitute a gang and the criteria necessary to classify someone a gang member. Miller (1980), Klein (1995), Short (1996), Spergel (1995), and others have been engaged in this debate for three decades with little success in resolving their differences. Of particular concern in this debate have been the following questions: Is involvement in delinquent activity a prerequisite for classifying a youth group a gang? Must a youth group possess some level of organizational structure to be classified as a gang? Are self-nomination techniques valid measures of gang membership? and Are core members more antisocial than peripheral gang members? We are not presumptuous enough to suggest that we can accomplish what has eluded others. However, with the data at hand, we have been able to undertake analyses of a large, although limited, sample of young adolescents that contribute new insights to this debate. We turn first to a discussion of the gang member issues prior to consideration of the gang definition concerns.

In one way or another, gang research, as well as law enforcement classification of gang activity, has relied on self-nomination (i.e., "claiming") of gang members. That is, if a person has claimed to be a gang member, that has been adequate grounds for inclusion in a study of gangs or for special prosecution by the justice system. To what extent is such a crude measure a valid predictor of gang membership? Our findings lend credence to the continued reliance on this technique that is often summarized by the following colloquialism: "If it walks like a duck and talks like a duck, it is a duck." The largest observed differences in attitudes and behaviors are those found in comparing youths who reported never having been gang members and those who reported prior gang involvement. Whatever it is that this one question captures, the respondents clearly reacted to the stimulus and the gang members reported substantially more antisocial attitudes and behaviors than the nongang youths. As additional restrictions were placed on the criteria necessary for classification as a gang member, the attitudes and behaviors of the gang members became increasingly more antisocial, with the relatively small sample of core gang members manifesting the most extreme responses.

So, if a person claims gang affiliation, what does this mean? What is a gang? Our methodological approach does not allow a direct response to this question. However, we can address this question indirectly by filtering respondents out of the gang based on the conceptual criteria identified by researchers and theorists as requisites for gang status. As discussed above, the simple question "Have you ever been a gang member?" was understood by the respondents in such a manner that one can surmise that there exists a shared understanding of what this term means, not only by former and current gang members, but also by nongang youth. Does the imposition of conceptually determined criteria alter the size, composition, or characteristics of the gang? Exclusion of current gang youth who did indicate their gang was involved in delinquent activity resulted in elimination of 55 (11%) of the 522 current gang members and only minimal change in the reported attitudes and behaviors. Further reduction in the size of the gang sample and expression of more negative attitudes and behaviors were produced with the additional criterion that the gang possess organizational components. Clearly, conceptually based definitions of gang membership have significant ramifications for estimates about the size of the gang problem and for descriptions of the attitudes and behaviors of gang members. However, personal characteristics (i.e., sex, age, race) remain relatively stable, regardless of definition.

From a research perspective, we can conclude that the self-nomination technique is a particularly robust measure of gang membership capable of distinguishing gang from nongang youth. The magnitude of the gang problem, as measured by prevalence rates of gang membership, varies substantially (from a high of 16.8% when using the ever gang member question to 2.3% for delinquent, organized core gang members), but the demographic characteristics of the gang members remain relatively stable across definitions. Likewise, whereas the filtering (i.e., exclusion of respondents not meeting the restricted definition) process results in an increasingly more antisocial gang member, as reflected in reported attitudes and behaviors, the largest difference is between the never gang and the ever gang youth.

From a theoretical perspective, what is the relevance of our findings? With a broad definition of gangs and gang membership, we are left with the impression that demographic characteristics are significant predictors (older, male, and minority youth) of gang membership. However, as we invoke conceptual restrictions on those youth claiming gang status, the theoretical predictors from social learning theory (especially association with delinquent peers, perceptions of guilt, and neutralizations for fighting) supersede the importance of demographic characteristics.

The varying prevalence estimates of gang membership and the changes in attitudes and behavior have distinct policy relevance. Obviously, the definition used greatly affects the perceived magnitude of the gang problem. By restricting gang membership status to gangs that are involved in delinquent activity and have some level of organization, we reduce the size of the gang problem substantially. A similar finding was recently discovered in the law-enforcement estimates provided to the National Youth Gang Center (NYGC). In its 1998 survey, the NYGC included a restricted definition for the survey respondents to use. Analyses incorporating this restricted definition indicate that earlier NYGC estimates may have overestimated the number of youth gangs in the United States by 35% and the number of youth gang members by 43% (Klein, personal correspondence). In terms of resource allocation, not to mention public hysteria, such definitional issues assume considerable importance.

From a policy perspective, the validity of the self-nomination method lends credence to the police practice of targeting youth who claim gang affiliation. However, caution needs to be exercised. Although it is the case that the largest distinction in this study is that between those youths who claim to never have been a gang member and those who claim gang affiliation at some time, it is vital to note that those gang members who no longer claim gang status are substantially more pro-social in both attitudes and behavior than are those persisting in their membership, a finding consistent with longitudinal results from the Denver and Rochester studies (e.g., Esbensen & Huizinga, 1993; Thornberry et al., 1993). Law enforcement, therefore, should be encouraged to remove former members from their gang lists.

Additional policy issues surround responses to youth gangs. Civil injunctions, antiloitering statutes, and sentence enhancements aimed at gang members may be too encompassing of their targeted audience. Whereas some of these approaches have received legal support (e.g., sentencing enhancements), others have failed to receive judicial backing (e.g., Chicago's Gang Congregation Ordinance). Given the permeability of gang membership, policies linking legal action to an individual's perceived status may erroneously criminalize that individual. As such, we suggest that legislation targeting gang status should be discouraged in favor of legislation focused on actual behavior.

APPENDIX A:
Gang Definitions

GANG 1: Have you ever been a gang member?
GANG 2: Are you now a gang member?
GANG 3: Are you now a gang member? And
Does your gang do any of the following things? (Yes to at least one)

- get in fights with other gangs?
- steal things?
- rob other people?
- steal cars?
- sell marijuana?
- sell other illegal drugs?
- damage or destroy property?

GANG 4: Current gang member and gang is delinquent
Do the following describe your gang? (Yes to all three)

- there are initiation rites
- the gang has established leader
- the gang has symbols and colors

GANG 5: Current gang member, gang is delinquent, and has organizational aspects
Self-identification as a "core" member.

APPENDIX B:
Attitudinal Measures and Summary Scale Characteristics

Unless otherwise indicated, these measures were adopted from the National Youth Survey (Elliott et al., 1985) or the Denver Youth Survey (Huizinga et al., 1991).

Parental Monitoring: Four items measuring communication with parents about activities, e.g., "My parents know who I am with if I am not at home."

Scale Mean = 3.72   Scale Standard Deviation = .81   Alpha = .74

Risk Seeking (Grasmick, Tittle, Bursik, & Arneklev, 1993): Four items about risk-taking behavior, e.g., "Sometimes I will take a risk just for the fun of it:"

Scale Mean = 3.06   Scale Standard Deviation = .94   Alpha = .82

Impulsivity (Grasmick et al., 1993): Four items measuring impulsive behavior, e.g., "I often act on the spur of the moment without stopping to think."

Scale Mean = 2.85   Scale Standard Deviation = .74   Alpha = .63

Commitment to Negative Peers: Three questions such as "if your friends were getting you in trouble at home, how likely is it that you would still hang out with them?

Scale Mean = 2.40   Scale Standard Deviation = 1.14   Alpha = .84

Commitment to Positive Peers: Two questions such as "If your friends told you not to do something because it was against the law, how likely is it that you would listen to them?

Scale Mean = 3.80   Scale Standard Deviation = 1.12   Alpha = 37

Neutralization: Three items tapping the respondent's belief that it is okay to get in physical fights if extenuating factors are present. For instance, "It's okay to get in a physical fight with someone if they hit you first."

Scale Mean = 3.98   Scale Standard Deviation = .97   Alpha = .83

Guilt: 16 questions asking how guilty the youth would feel if they did such things as "hit someone with the idea of hurting them" or "using alcohol."

Scale Mean = 2.31   Scale Standard Deviation = .56   Alpha = .94

Positive Peer Behavior: Eight items about the kinds of pro-social things in which friends are involved.

Scale Mean = 2.97   Scale Standard Deviation = .80   Alpha = .84

Negative Peer Behavior: 16 items about illegal activities in which the friends are involved.

Scale Mean = 1.99   Scale Standard Deviation = .86   Alpha = .94

Status Offenses: Skipped classes without an excuse. Lied about your age to get into someplace or to buy something.

Minor Offenses: Avoided paying for things such as movies, bus, or subway rides. Purposely damaged or destroyed property that did not belong to you.

Property Offenses: Stole or tried to steal something worth less than $50. Stole or tried to steal something worth more than $50. Went into or tried to go into a building to steal something. Stole or tried to steal a motor vehicle.

Crimes Against Person: Hit someone with the idea of hurting them. Attacked someone with a weapon. Used a weapon or force to get money or things from people. Shot at someone because you were told to by someone else.

Drug Sales: Sold marijuana. Sold other illegal drugs such as heroin, cocaine, crack, or LSD.

Drug Use: Used tobacco products. Used alcohol. Used marijuana. Used paint, glue, or other things you inhale to get high. Other illegal drugs.

Total Delinquency: A summary index consisting of all the items included in the scales for status offenses, minor offenses, property offenses, crimes against a person, and drug sales plus three additional items: (1) carried a hidden weapon, (2) illegally spray painted a wall or a building, and (3) was involved in gang fights.

Notes

[1] Also, as previously observed, Howell (1998), in his overview of the American gang scene, notes that most researchers use the terms *youth gangs* and *gangs* interchangeably, although the latter term has many other uses in which youth are only tangentially involved.

[2] Cohen's (1955) *Delinquent Boys: The Culture of the Gang* introduced his reaction formation theory, another gang-based exploration of general juvenile delinquency from a more social psychological perspective. It is interesting that Cohen defines the behavior of gangs—delinquent subcultures—as nonutilitarian, malicious, and negativistic (pp. 27–29). In so doing, Cohen also relies on Thrasher's earlier work and the research of Shaw and McKay (1942), the latter work playing an important role in explaining gang delinquency's versatility, or gang members' willingness to get involved in a wide variety of antisocial and illegal activities. Unlike Cloward and Ohlin's (1960) *Delinquency and Opportunity, Delinquent Boys* is long on theory and short on empirical proof.

[3] Before July 1, 1994, an organized gang was defined as "an association of 5 or more persons, with an established hierarchy, that encourages members of the association to perpetrate crimes or provides support to the members of the association who do commit crimes" (Illinois Compiled Statutes Annotated, 1999, Chapter 730, Section 5-5-3[c][2][J]). After July 1, 1994, "'Streetgang' or 'gang' or 'organized gang' or 'criminal street gang' means any combination, confederation, alliance, network, conspiracy, understanding, or other similar conjoining, in law or in fact, of 3 or more persons with an established hierarchy that, through its membership or through the agency of any member engages in a course or pattern of criminal activity" (Illinois Compiled Statutes Annotated, 1999, Chapter 730, Section 5-5-3[c][2][J]).

References

Akers, R. L. (1985). *Deviant behavior: A social learning approach* (3rd ed.). Belmont, CA: Wadsworth.

Akers, R. L. (1994). *Criminological theory: Introduction and evaluation.* Los Angeles: Roxbury.

Arneklev, B. J., Grasmick, H. G., Tittle, C. R., & Bursik, R. J. (1993). Low self-control and imprudent behavior. *Journal of Quantitative Criminology, 9,* 225–247.

Ball, R. A., & Curry, G. D. (1995). The logic of definition in criminology: Purposes and methods for defining gangs. *Criminology, 33,* 225–245.

Battin, S. R., Hill, K. G., Abbott, R. D., Catalano, R., & Hawkins, J. D. (1998). The contributions of gang membership to delinquency beyond delinquent friends. *Criminology, 36,* 67–92.

Battin-Pearson, S. R., Thornberry, T. P., Hawkins, J. D., & Krohn, M. D. (1998). *Gang membership, delinquent peers, and delinquent behavior.* OJJDP Juvenile Justice Bulletin. Washington, DC: Department of Justice.

Bjerregard, B., & Smith, C. (1993). Gender differences in gang participation, delinquency, and substance use. *Journal of Quantitative Criminology, 4,* 329–355.

Bursik, R. J., Jr., & Grasmick, H. G. (1993). Neighborhoods and crime: The dimensions of effective community control. New York: Lexington Books.

Cairns, R. B., & Cairns, B. D. (1991). Social cognition and social networks: A developmental perspective. In D. J. Pepler & K. H. Rubin (Eds.), *The development and treatment of childhood aggression*. Hillsdale, NJ: Erlbaum.

California Penal Code. Part 1, Title 7, Chapter 11, 186.22 (1999).

City of Chicago v. Morales, et al., 524 U.S. 975. (Ill. 1998).

Cloward, R. A., & Ohlin, L. E. (1960). *Delinquency and opportunity: A theory of delinquent gangs*. New York: Free Press.

Cohen, A. K. (1955). *Delinquent boys: The culture of the gang*. New York: Free Press.

Criminal Street Gangs Statute, 18 U.S.C.A. §521 (1999).

Curry, G. D., Ball, R. A., & Decker, S. H. (1996). *Estimating the national scope of gang crime from law enforcement data*. Research in Brief. Washington, DC: U.S. Department of Justice, Office of Justice Programs, National Institute of Justice.

Curry, G. D., & Decker, S. H. (1998). *Confronting gangs: Crime and community*. Los Angeles, CA: Roxbury.

Decker, S., & Van Winkle, B. (1996). *Life in the gang: Family, friends, and violence*. New York: Cambridge University Press.

Decker, S. H., & Kempf-Leonard, K. (1991). Constructing gangs: Social definition and youth activities. *Criminal Justice Policy Review*, 5, 271–291.

Deschenes, E. P., & Esbensen, F.-A. (1999). Violence and gangs: Gender differences in perceptions and behaviors. *Journal of Quantitative Criminology*, 15, 53–96.

Elliott, D. S., Ageton, S. S., & Huizinga, D. (1985). *Explaining delinquency and substance use*. Beverly Hills, CA: Sage.

Esbensen, F.-A., & Deschenes, E. P. (1998). A multisite examination of youth gang membership: Does gender matter? *Criminology*, 36, 799–827.

Esbensen, F.-A., Deschenes, E. P., Vogel, R. E., West, J., Arboit, K., & Harris, L. (1997). Active parental consent in school-based research: An examination of ethical and methodological issues. *Evaluation Review*, 20, 737–753.

Esbensen, F.-A., & Huizinga, D. (1993). Gangs, drugs and delinquency in a survey of urban youth. *Criminology*, 31, 565–589.

Esbensen, F.-A., & Osgood, D. W. (1999). Gang Resistance Education and Training (G.R.E.A.T.): Results from the national evaluation. *Journal of Research in Crime and Delinquency*, 36, 194–225.

Esbensen, F.-A., & Winfree, L. T., Jr. (1998). Race and gender differences between gang and nongang youths: Results from a multisite survey. *Justice Quarterly*, 15, 505–526.

Fleisher, M. (1998). *Dead end kids*. Madison: University of Wisconsin Press.

Gardner, S. (1993). *Street gangs*. New York: Franklin Watts.

Gibbs, J. J., & Giever, D. M. (1995). Self-control and its manifestations among university students: An empirical test of Gottfredson and Hirschi's general theory. *Justice Quarterly*, 12, 231–255.

Gibbs, J. J., Giever, D. M., & Martin, J. S. (1998). Parental management and self-control: An empirical test of Gottfredson and Hirschi's general theory. *Journal of Research in Crime and Delinquency*, 35, 40–70.

Gottfredson, M. R., & Hirschi, T. (1990). *A general theory of crime*. Stanford, CA: Stanford University Press.

Grasmick, H. G., Tittle, C. R., Bursik, R. J., Jr., & Arneklev, B. J. (1993). Testing the core assumptions of Gottfredson and Hirschi's general theory of crime. *Journal of Research in Crime and Delinquency*, 30, 5–29.

Hill, K. G., Howell, J. C., Hawkins, J. D., & Battin-Pearson, S. R. (1999). Child-hood risk factors for adolescent gang membership: Results from the Seattle Social Development Project. *Journal of Research in Crime and Delinquency*, 36, 300–322.

Howell, J. C. (1998). *Youth gangs: An overview.* Juvenile Justice Bulletin. Washington, DC: Office of Juvenile Justice and Delinquency Prevention.

Huff, C. R. (1998). *Comparing the criminal behavior of youth gangs and at-risk youths.* Research in brief. Washington, DC: National Institute of Justice.

Huizinga, D., Esbensen, F.-A., & Weiher, A. W. (1991). Are there multiple paths to delinquency? *Journal of Criminal Law and Criminology*, 82, 83–118.

Illinois Compiled Statutes Annotated. 730. Chapter V. Article 5 (1999).

Kerlinger, F. N. (1973). *Foundations of behavioral research* (2nd ed.). New York: Holt, Rinehart and Winston.

Klein, M. W. (1969). Violence in American juvenile gangs. In D. J. Mulvihill, M. M. Tumin, & L. A. Curtis (Eds.), *Crime of violence, volume 13, a staff report to the National Commission on the Causes and Prevention of Violence.* Washington, DC: Government Printing Office.

Klein, M. W. (1971). *Street gangs and street workers.* Englewood Cliffs, NJ: Prentice Hall.

Klein, M. W. (1995). *The American street gang: Its nature, prevalence, and control.* New York: Oxford University Press.

Knox, G. W. (1996). The 1996 national law enforcement gang analysis survey. *Journal of Gang Research*, 3, 41–55.

Krohn, M. D., Akers, R. L., Radosevich, M. J., & Lanza-Kaduce, L. (1982). Norm qualities and adolescent drinking and drug behavior. *Journal of Drug Issues*, 12, 343–359.

Lynskey, D. P., Winfree, L. T., Jr., Esbensen, F.-A., & Clason, D. L. (2000). Linking gender, minority group status, and family matters to self-control theory: A multivariate analysis of key self-control concepts in a youth-gang context. *Juvenile and Family Court Journal*, 1 (3), 1–20.

Maxson, C. L. (1998). *Gang members on the move.* OJJDP Juvenile Justice Bulletin. Washington, DC: Department of Justice.

Maxson, C. L., & Klein, M. W. (1994). *Gang structures and crime patterns in U.S. cities.* Paper presented at the annual meeting of the American Society of Criminology, November, Miami, FL.

Maxson, C. L., Whitlock, M. L., & Klein, M. W. (1998). Vulnerability to street gang membership: Implications for practice. *Social Service Review*, 72, 70–91.

Miller, W. B. (1975). *Violence by youth gangs and youth groups as a crime problem in major American cities.* Washington, DC: National Institute for Juvenile Justice and Delinquency Prevention.

Miller, W. B. (1980). Gangs, groups and serious youth crime. In D. Shichor & D. H. Kelly (Eds.), *Critical issues in juvenile delinquency.* Lexington, MA: D.C. Heath and Co.

National Youth Gang Center. (1997). *1995 national youth gang survey.* Washington, DC: U.S. Department of Justice, Office of Justice Programs, Office of Juvenile Justice and Delinquency Prevention.

National Youth Gang Center. (1999). *1996 national youth gang survey.* Washington, DC: U.S. Department of Justice, Office of Justice Programs, Office of Juvenile Justice and Delinquency Prevention.

Needle, J. A., & Stapleton, W. V. (1983). *Reports of the national juvenile justice assessment centers: Police handling of youth gangs.* Washington, DC: Office of Juvenile Justice and Delinquency Prevention.

Office of Juvenile Justice and Delinquency Prevention. (1997). *Highlights of the 1995 national youth gang survey.* OJJDP Fact Sheet. Washington, DC: Department of Justice.

Sellers, C. S., Winfree, L. T., Jr., & Griffiths, C. T. (1993). Legal attitudes, permissive norm qualities, and substance abuse: A comparison of American Indians and non-Indian youths. *Journal of Drug Issues, 23,* 493–513.

Shaw, C. R., & McKay, H. D. (1942). *Juvenile delinquency and urban areas.* Chicago: University of Chicago Press.

Short, J. F. (1968). Introduction: On gang delinquency and the nature of subcultures. In J. F. Short (Ed.), *Gang delinquency and delinquent subcultures.* New York: Harper and Row.

Short, J. F. (1996). Foreword: Diversity and change in U.S. gangs. In C. R. Huff (Ed.), *Gangs in America* (2nd ed.). Thousand Oaks, CA: Sage Publications.

Spergel, I. A. (1995). *The youth gang problem: A community approach.* New York: Oxford University Press.

Thornberry, T. P., & Butch, J. H., III (1997). *Gang members and delinquent behavior.* OJJDP Juvenile Justice Bulletin. Washington, DC: Department of Justice.

Thornberry, T. P., Krohn, M. D., Lizotte, A. J., & Chard-Wierschem, D. (1993). The role of juvenile gangs in facilitating delinquent behavior. *Journal of Research in Crime and Delinquency, 30,* 55–87.

Thrasher, F. M. (1963). *The gang: A study of one thousand three hundred thirteen gangs in Chicago.* Chicago: University of Chicago Press. Abridged with a new introduction by James F Short, Jr. (Original work published 1927).

Winfree, L. T., Jr., Bäckström, T. V., & Mays, G. L. (1994). Social learning theory, self-reported delinquency, and youth gangs: A new twist on a general theory of crime and delinquency. *Youth & Society, 26,* 147–177.

Winfree, L. T., Jr., Bernat, F. P., & Esbensen, F.-A. (in press). Hispanic and Anglo gang membership in two southwestern cities. *The Social Science Journal.*

Winfree, L. T., Jr., Fuller, K., Bäckström, T. V., & Mays, G. L. (1992). The definition and measurement of "gang status": Policy implications for juvenile justice. *Juvenile and Family Court Journal, 43,* 20–37.

Comparing the Criminal Behavior of Youth Gangs and At-Risk Youths

C. Ronald Huff

For years, observers have noted that youth-gang-related crime has been growing, but a picture of the extent and precise nature of crimes committed by gang members is only now beginning to emerge. Are gangs really responsible for increases in crime or are youths who grow up in very difficult circumstances but do not join gangs committing just as many crimes?

This study explored the differences between the criminal behavior of youth gang members and nongang, but similarly at-risk, youths. The research revealed that criminal behavior committed by gang members is extensive and significantly exceeds that committed by comparably at-risk but nongang youth.[1] Furthermore, the research suggests important implications for preventing involvement in and intervening in youth gang activity.

A gang is described as a well-defined group of youths between 10 and 22 years old. Most research on youth gangs in the United States has concluded that the most typical age range of gang members has been approximately 14–24, though researchers are aware of gang members as young as 10 and that in some areas (e.g., southern California where some Latino gangs originated more than 100 years ago), one can find several generations in the same family who are gang members with active gang members in their thirties.

Huff, C. Ronald. 1998, October. "Comparing the Criminal Behavior of Youth Gangs and At-Risk Youths," *Research in Brief*. Washington, DC: National Institute of Justice.

By all accounts, the number of youth gangs and their members continues to grow. For example, one recent nationwide study found 58 percent of the jurisdictions surveyed reported that they have active youth gangs.

There are an estimated 23,388 youth gangs with 664,906 members in all 50 States.[2] These numbers are probably conservative estimates[3] because many jurisdictions deny, often for political and image reasons, that there is a problem, especially in the early stages of youth gang development in a community.[4]

Responding to the growing magnitude of the problem, the National Institute of Justice (NIJ) sponsored a research project that focused on the nature and extent of youth gang behavior in Denver and Aurora (a large suburb of Denver), Colorado, and Broward County in south Florida. In addition, a companion study, underwritten by a research grant from Ohio's Office of Criminal Justice Services (with funds provided by the Office of Juvenile Justice and Delinquency Prevention),[5] explored the criminal behavior of gang versus nongang youths in Cleveland, Ohio, and the nature and extent of criminal behavior committed over time by a sample of leaders and hardcore members of youth gangs in Columbus, Ohio, dating to 1986.

Denver, Aurora, and Broward County were selected for this study because: (1) they provided emergent, rather than chronic, gang environments and opportunities to study gang formation at an early stage of development; (2) they comprised a combination of central cities and suburbs, providing an opportunity to assess differences within and across metropolitan areas; and (3) they are demographically diverse, as are the racial and ethnic compositions of the youth gangs in these areas.

YOUTH INVOLVEMENT IN CRIME

Exhibit 1, compiled from interviews with gang members in Denver, Aurora, Broward County, and Cleveland, shows how deeply they are involved in specific types of criminal behavior. While results vary from one region to another, the overall picture that emerges is that gangs engage in a wide array of criminal behaviors, including those involving weapons and violence. These data include only what gang members said about their own criminal behavior. The same general patterns emerged, but at much higher levels, when gang members were asked about other members' behavior.

Self-reported criminal behavior varies across sites and across regions for many reasons. With respect to this study, there are some age variations in the samples across sites and some differences across specific gangs with respect to the types of crimes they commit. Previous research on gangs has consistently found that there are topologies of gangs and that the criminal behaviors committed by the members of different gangs vary. With respect to such behaviors as drug sales and drug use, the national data produced

Exhibit 1 Type of Criminal Behavior in Which Gang Members Report Being Involved

	Aurora N=49	Broward Co. N=50	Cleveland N=47	Denver N=41
Guns in School	53.1%	46.0%	40.4%	46.3%
Knives in School	50.0	58.3	38.3	37.5
Concealed Weapons	87.8	84.0	78.7	88.1
Drug Use	49.0	76.0	27.7	51.2
Drug Sales (School)	26.5	34.0	19.1	38.1
Drug Sales (Other)	75.0	58.0	61.7	64.3
Drug Theft	31.9	44.9	21.3	23.1
Drive-by Shooting	51.0	68.0	40.4	50.0
Homicide	12.2	20.0	15.2	19.5
Auto Theft	44.9	67.3	44.7	61.9
Theft-Other	59.2	80.0	51.1	52.4
Assault Rivals	81.6	94.0	72.3	71.4
Assault Own Members	31.3	40.0	30.4	26.2
Assault Police	28.6	22.0	10.6	31.0
Assault Teachers	26.5	16.3	14.9	26.8
Assault Students	58.3	66.0	51.1	53.7
Mug People	26.5	52.0	10.6	33.3
Assault in Streets	42.9	56.0	29.8	52.4
Intimidate/Assault Vict/Wit	39.6	46.0	34.0	47.6
Intimidate/Assault Shoppers	31.3	42.0	23.4	40.5
Shoplifting	57.1	62.0	30.4	45.0
Check Forgery	4.1	18.0	2.1	4.8
Credit Card Theft	12.2	46.0	6.4	9.5
Sell Stolen Goods	44.9	70.0	29.8	52.4
Bribe Police	12.2	10.0	10.6	11.9
Burglary (Unoccupied)	26.5	64.0	8.5	42.9
Burglary (Occupied)	8.3	34.0	2.1	14.6
Arson	12.2	12.0	8.5	14.3
Kidnapping	6.1	4.0	4.3	9.5
Sexual Assault/Molestation	4.1	4.0	2.1	0.0
Rape	2.0	4.0	2.1	0.0
Robbery	14.3	30.0	17.0	26.2

by DUF (Drug Use Forecasting) studies reveal significant variation across sites and regions also.

Do gang members commit more crimes than their at-risk peers, or are the various forces that affect youths living in similar circumstances so compelling that criminal behavior is unrelated to the existence of gangs in these areas? Consider the following data from Cleveland, where the gang and at-risk samples were scientifically comparable by age, gender, race/ethnicity, education completed, work during the past year, and whether they grew up in a two-parent family.

As exhibit 2 shows, gang members are far more likely to commit certain crimes, such as auto theft; theft; assaulting rivals; carrying concealed weapons in school; using, selling, and stealing drugs; intimidating or assaulting victims and witnesses; and participating in drive-by shootings and homicides than nongang youths, even though the latter may have grown up under similar circumstances.

Exhibit 2   Comparison of Gang and Nongang Criminal Behavior (Cleveland)

Crime (p^1)	Gang N=47	Nongang N=49
Auto Theft (***)	44.7%	4.1%
Assault Rivals (***)	72.3	16.3
Assault Own Members (*)	30.4	10.2
Assault Police (n.s.)	10.6	14.3
Assault Teachers (n.s.)	14.9	18.4
Assault Students (n.s.)	51.1	34.7
Mug People (n.s.)	10.6	4.1
Assault in Streets (*)	29.8	10.2
Theft-Other (***)	51.1	14.3
Intim/Assault Vict/Wit (***)	34.0	0.0
Intim/Assault Shoppers (*)	23.4	6.1
Drive-by Shooting (***)	40.4	2.0
Homicide (**)	15.2	0.0
Sell Stolen Goods (*)	29.8	10.2
Guns in School (***)	40.4	10.2
Knives in School (***)	38.3	4.2
Concealed Weapons (***)	78.7	22.4
Drug Use (**)	27.7	4.1
Drug Sales (School) (n.s.)	19.1	8.2
Drug Sales (Other) (***)	61.7	16.7

Exhibit 2 *continued*

Crime (p[1])	Gang N=47	Nongang N=49
Drug Theft (***)	21.3	0.0
Bribe Police (n.s.)	10.6	2.0
Burglary (Unoccupied) (*)	8.5	0.0
Burglary (Occupied) (n.s.)	2.1	2.0
Shoplifting (n.s.[.058])	30.4	14.3
Check Forgery (n.s.)	2.1	0.0
Credit Card Theft (n.s.)	6.4	0.0
Arson (*)	8.5	0.0
Kidnapping (n.s.)	4.3	0.0
Sexual Assault/Molest (n.s.)	2.1	0.0
Rape (n.s.)	2.1	0.0
Robbery (*)	17.0	2.0

[1] Level of statistical significance: *p<.05; **p<.01; ***p<.001;
n.s. = no significant difference.

Drug Sales

Gang members in all four sites are extensively involved in drug sales, especially cocaine and marijuana (see exhibit 3). The types of drugs sold vary from one region to another. The comparative data from Cleveland showed gang members sell significantly more cocaine than do nongang youths. Across the four sites studied, the relationship between race and whether a gang member sold drugs was statistically nonsignificant.

Researchers asked both gang and nongang interviewees about the dynamics of their drug sales, including how frequently they sell drugs, how much they make each week, how many customers they have each week, how much of their profits is spent on their own drug use, the location of their drug source, and (if known) the type of organization that sells them their drugs. They also asked a tipping point question: How much would the interviewee need to make in legitimate wages (per hour) to stop selling drugs? The data from Cleveland in exhibit 4 are comparable to the findings in the other sites.

Many gang members sell drugs, often daily. The majority of at-risk youths reported that they do not sell drugs. Those who sell, however, do so on a daily basis. Gang members reported earning about $1,000 per week from only 30 customers, while nongang youths earned about $675 per week, based on an estimated 80 customers. Gang members sell more expensive and profitable drugs and are better connected to nonlocal sources than nongang drug traffickers. Neither gang nor nongang drug sellers reported using their profits to buy drugs, except in Broward County, where gang members spent 20 percent of their earnings and nongang interviewees spent 5 percent of their profits to buy drugs.

Both gang members and at-risk youths reported that it would require average wages of $15 to $17 an hour to get them to stop selling drugs. While this figure reflected the median, it should be noted that about 25 percent of those sampled would accept wages of about $6 to $7 per hour—not much more than many fast-food restaurants pay today. They are tired of living with the fear that accompanies drug sales. However, as these young people often pointed out, it is difficult for them to find full-

Exhibit 3   Types of Drugs Gang Members Report Selling

	Aurora N=49	Broward Co. N=50	Cleveland N=47	Denver N=41
Crack Cocaine	57.1%	38.7%	65.9%	63.4%
Powder Cocaine	24.5	51.0	26.1	41.5
Marijuana	57.1	73.5	48.9	62.5
PCP	6.3	14.3	4.3	12.2
LSD/Mushrooms	18.4	38.8	2.1	25.0
Heroin	6.3	17.0	4.3	14.6
Crystal Meth.	10.2	14.6	4.3	9.7

Exhibit 4   Gang and Nongang Descriptions of the Nature of Their Drug Selling (Cleveland)

Responses (p[1])	Gang N=47	Nongang N=49
Median frequency (***)	Daily	Daily[2]
Median earnings/week (*)	$1,000	$675
Median customers/week (**)	30	80
Median percent of earnings kept for own drug use (n.s.)	0	0
Percent of drug sources, local (**)	31.9	50.0
Percent of drug sources, foreign (**)	26.1	12.5
Percent of drug sources, gang (**)	21.7	18.8
Median wages/hour required to stop selling (n.s.)	$15	$17

[1]Level of statistical significance: *$p < .05$; **$p < .01$; ***$p < .001$; n.s. = no significant differences.

[2]Based on subsample who do sell drugs (n = 11).

time work with one employer. It is also true, of course, that once one has a criminal record, it is more difficult to obtain regular employment.

Nevertheless, the evidence shows that drug sales are not controlled by gangs nor do drug sales represent an organized, collective gang activity. Quite to the contrary, research over the past 12 years suggests that most drug sales by gang members are individual or small-clique activities, rather than collective gang efforts.[6]

Guns

Interviewees were also asked about gun ownership among the members of their gang or (for nongang youths) their peers. In all four sites, nearly 75 percent of gang members acknowledged that nearly all of their fellow gang members own guns. Even more alarming, 90 percent of gang interviewees reported that gang members favor powerful, lethal weapons over smaller caliber handguns. Between 25 and 50 percent of nongang youths said their peers own guns, and about 50 percent stated that their friends owned powerful, lethal weapons. The gang/nongang differences were statistically significant across all four sites—that is, gang members are significantly more likely to own guns and more likely to own powerful, lethal weapons.

From "Wannabe" to First Arrest

How long does it take from the initial stage of "hanging out" with a gang (often called the "gang wannabe" stage) before a youngster is arrested for the first time? The findings across all four sites were remarkably consistent, as shown in exhibit 5.

Based on the survey sample taken at the four sites (in three states), youngsters generally begin hanging out with gangs at 12 or 13 years of age, join the gang at 13 or 14 (from 6 months to a year after they first hang out with the gang), and are first arrested at 14. Young adolescents are most vulnerable to the seduction of gang membership at a time when physiological, sociological, and psychological factors, including a strong need for peer acceptance, are acting upon them.

Exhibit 5   Age at First Association with Gang to Age at First Arrest

	Aurora N=49	Broward Co. N=50	Cleveland N=47	Denver N=41
1st Association	13.1	13.3	12.9	12.4
Joined Gang	14.2	14.3	13.4	13.5
1st Arrest	14.0	14.0	14.0	14.0

Gang Resistance and Consequences

Many young people believe they will be physically punished if they refuse an offer to join a gang. At the same time, schools and other social organizations across the country have launched gang resistance education and training programs. Therefore, it seemed important to ask gang interviewees whether they knew of individuals who refused to join the gang and, if so, the consequences of their refusal.

As exhibit 6 shows, reality differs dramatically from the intuitive beliefs held by many young people—consistently across all four sites. Clearly, the cost-benefit ratio favors gang resistance, especially if one resists politely, without "disrespecting" the gang or its members.[7] In instances in which youths resisted gang overtures and suffered physical reprisals, their injuries were seldom serious. Media accounts of gang killings and serious assaults on youths who refuse to join the gang paint an exaggerated picture. The reality is quite the opposite.

Another finding tips the scales even further in favor of resisting gang membership. The most common initiation ritual reported in all four sites involves gang members assaulting ("beating in" or "jumping in") the new recruit to prove that he is "tough," "can take it," and "has heart." Thus, youths who respectfully refuse to join a gang face very good odds that nothing serious will happen to them;[8] on the other hand, those who join a gang usually suffer serious physical assault as an initiation rite. In addition, data indicate that gang involvement significantly increases one's chances of being arrested, incarcerated, seriously injured, or killed. These factors must be presented to youths who may be attracted by the glamour and excitement of gang life.

Exhibit 6   Gang Resistance and Consequences (Percent)[1]

	Aurora N=49	Broward Co. N=50	Cleveland N=47	Denver N=41
Know Someone Who Refused to Join	59.2%	72.0%	71.7%	65.9%
Consequences: Physical Harm	6.1	16.0	12.1	17.5
Consequences: Nothing	36.7	34.0	66.7	30.0

[1] Interviewees were asked, "Do you know someone who refused to join a gang?" They were then asked, "Do you know the consequences of that refusal to join?" The disparity in the percentage figures above reflects the interviewees' lack of knowledge of the consequences for some youths who refused to join a gang.

TRACKING GANG LEADERS AND HARDCORE MEMBERS

The final component of this study focused on the nature and magnitude of the criminal behavior of 83 individuals who in 1986 were key gang leaders and hardcore gang members in Columbus, Ohio. Researchers examined their arrest histories (from 1980 to 1993) to see if their gang involvement triggered their criminal career. Very few arrests occurred prior to the mid-1980s (when gangs emerged in Columbus), but thereafter the frequency and seriousness of gang members' criminal behavior accelerated dramatically, as shown in exhibit 7.

The great majority of these arrests occurred in the 7-year period between 1985 and 1992. An important positive correlation exists between when these individuals joined gangs and when their arrest histories accelerated. The correlation coincides with the data presented in exhibit 5. It is important to note that they were arrested for violent offenses (37 percent), property offenses (29 percent), drug offenses (18 percent), weapons offenses (6 percent), and other offenses (10 percent). Arrests began to decline in 1992, based on the following factors:

- **Incarceration.** Serving jail time temporarily halts new arrests.

- **Death.** At least 7 of the 83 gang leaders had already died. Coroner's records for six of them indicated that all died violent deaths (five by gunshots, one by strangulation).

- **Law enforcement reorganization.** Like many other communities, Columbus experienced a surge in the crack cocaine market during the mid-1980s, prompting the police to consolidate the gang enforce-

Exhibit 7   Total Arrests for 83 Gang Leaders and Members (Columbus)

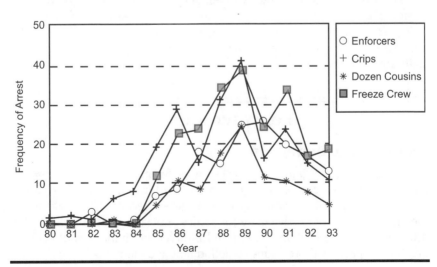

ment unit with the narcotics bureau. Police resources were scarce, and it was perceived that many gang members were selling drugs. As a result, less attention was paid to newly developing gangs, and more intelligence and enforcement activity was directed toward narcotics trafficking, most of which was not gang related.[9]

Finally, the study sought to determine whether these gang leaders committed more serious offenses over time or whether their first offenses were serious. This information is important in assessing the developmental stages of gangs and in developing appropriate prevention, intervention, and suppression strategies. For all four of Columbus's major gangs, evidence showed a clear progression in serious offenses, based on a time series analysis of when each gang's arrests peaked for property crimes, drug offenses, and violence. Exhibit 8 illustrates this pattern for each of the four gangs separately and for an aggregate "progression window" for the four gangs combined.

Exhibit 8   Progression in Seriousness of Offenses (Columbus)

Gang	N	Arrests	Peak Prop.	Peak Drugs	Peak Viol.
Crips	25	219	1988	1989	1989
Freeze Crew	19	227	1988	1989	1989
Enforcers	14	154	1987	1990	1989
Dozen Cousins	9	105	1987	1989	1989

Progression from Property Offenses to Drug Offenses: +1.75 Years
Progression from Property Offenses to Violent Offenses: +1.50 Years
Progression from Drug Offenses to Violent Offenses: –0.25 Years

These data suggest a progression in gang crime from property offenses to violent crimes and drug-related crimes. The progression takes about 1.5 to 2 years, depending on the specific gang and first offense. The data also mirror the close connection between drug trafficking and violence, especially since the mid-1980s.[10]

POLICY IMPLICATIONS

Education and Prevention

Youths who join gangs tend to begin as "wannabes" at about age 13, join about 6 months later, and get arrested within 6 months after joining the gang. By age 14 they already have an arrest record. This underscores the urgent need for effective gang-resistance education programs and other primary and secondary prevention and intervention initiatives directed at preteens, especially those prone to delinquent and violent behavior.[11]

Resisting Overtures

Young people can refuse to join gangs without substantial risk of physical harm. Moreover, they are far better off to resist joining gangs than to expose themselves to the beating they are likely to take upon initiation and the increased chances of arrest, incarceration, injury, and death associated with gang membership.[12]

Windows of Opportunity for Intervening

Because prevention programs will not deter all youths from joining gangs, it is also important to address the brief window of opportunity for intervention that occurs in the year between the "wannabe" stage and the age at first arrest. It is vital that intervention programs that target gang members and successfully divert them from the gang are funded, developed, evaluated, improved, and sustained.[13]

A second opportunity to intervene occurs between the time gang members are first arrested for property crimes and their subsequent involvement in more serious offenses. This period, which lasts about 1.5 to 2 years, affords a chance to divert young offenders from the gang subculture before they further endanger their own lives and victimize other citizens. Gang members are more likely than their nongang peers to sell higher profit drugs, underscoring the need for prevention and early intervention programs designed to divert "wannabes" before they become hooked on illegal earnings. Successful intervention at this stage (with, for example, prosecutorial diversion programs targeting first-time, gang-involved property offenders) can still save lives (of both offenders and victims) and save society the enormous cost of arresting, convicting, and incarcerating serious offenders.

While many gang members and nongang, at-risk youths who sell drugs indicated they would not give up drug selling for less than $15 per hour, a significant number of them told researchers they would accept far lower wages—not much more than is currently being paid in fast-food restaurants—if they could obtain a sufficient number of work hours per week. Employers often split job slots into part-time jobs that offer few or no fringe benefits, a widespread practice within the fast-food industry.

Early Warning Signals

Data suggest that gang members are especially likely to commit the crimes highlighted in exhibits 1 and 2. A sudden increase in these crimes may serve as a "distant early warning signal" that the community needs to consider local gangs in the context of its overall crime problem. Crimes that are especially worth monitoring closely (and can realistically be monitored) include auto theft, bringing weapons to school, and drive-by shootings.[14]

Weapons

Gang members are likely to possess powerful and highly lethal weapons, although many gang members are not old enough to legally drive a car. Efforts to reduce the number of illegal weapons possessed by youths and adults should be emphasized to reduce gun-related crimes.[15]

Notes

[1] Longitudinal cohort studies in Denver; Rochester, New York; and Seattle have provided extensive data that demonstrate the relationship between criminal behavior and gang membership. Youths are more involved in delinquent and criminal behavior while active in gangs than either before they join or after they leave gangs. See Esbensen, Finn-Aage, and David Huizinga, "Gangs, Drugs, and Delinquency in a Survey of Urban Youth," *Criminology* 31(1993): 565–589; Thornberry, Terence P. et al., "The Role of Juvenile Gangs in Facilitating Delinquent Behavior," *Journal of Research in Crime and Delinquency* 30 (1993): 55–87; and Battin, Sara R. et al., "The Contribution of Gang Membership to Delinquency Beyond Delinquent Friends," *Criminology* 36 (1998): 93–115.

[2] Office of Juvenile Justice and Delinquency Prevention, *Highlights of the 1995 National Youth Gang Survey*, Fact Sheet #63, Washington, D.C.: U.S. Department of Justice, Office of Juvenile Justice and Delinquency Prevention, 1997; also see Curry, G. David, Richard A. Ball, and Scott H. Decker, in "Estimating the National Scope of Gang Crime From Law Enforcement Data," *Gangs in America* (2nd edition), Huff, C. Ronald, editor, Thousand Oaks, California: Sage Publications, 1996: 21–36.

[3] Estimates range as high as 1.5 million gang members in the United States. See Knox, G. W., The "1996 National Law Enforcement Gang Analysis Survey," *Journal of Gang Research* 3, (1996): 41–55.

[4] For a more detailed discussion of the stages that communities often go through, see Huff, C. Ronald, editor, *Gangs in America* (1st edition), Thousand Oaks, California: Sage Publications, 1990.

[5] The Ohio sites were originally proposed as part of the NIJ study, but the willingness of Ohio's Office of Criminal Justice Services to fund the additional study permitted researchers to include five sites in the overall research instead of only three.

[6] Klein, Malcolm W., *The American Street Gang: Its Nature, Prevalence, and Control*, New York, New York: Oxford University Press, 1995; Fagan, J. E., "Gangs, Drugs, and Neighborhood Change," in Huff, C. Ronald, editor, *Gangs in America* (2nd edition), Thousand Oaks, California: Sage Publications, 1996: 39–74; Decker, S. H., and B. Van Winkle, *Life in the Gang: Family, Friends, and Violence*, New York: Cambridge University Press, 1996.

[7] Over the past 12 years of interviewing gang members, the author has developed a gang-resistance strategy anchored in the cognitive dissonance theory of psychology—which postulates the difficulty of accepting two competing ideas at the same time. Gang members, who generally state that they love their mothers dearly, frequently recognize that they have disappointed them by their criminal behavior. Youths attempting to resist gang involvement might tell gang members that they respect them and might like to join the gang, but that their mother disapproves, and they do not want to show disrespect to her. Gang members in overwhelming numbers told researchers that they would not join the gang if they could make that decision again, and they do not want their siblings to join gangs. They may recognize in retrospect that the youth, in respecting his mother's wishes, is doing what they themselves wish they had done.

[8] Even when gang members reported that the consequences of gang resistance were physical in nature, they indicated that these nearly always resulted in only minor injuries.

[9] Although many youth gang members sell drugs, youth gangs do not control drug markets in the United States and do not account for most drug sales in major urban areas. For a useful and concise discussion of street gangs and drugs, see Klein, Malcolm W., *The American Street Gang*.

[10] For an extensive discussion of related issues, see Zimring, Franklin E., et al., "Guns and Violence Symposium," *Journal of Criminal Law and Criminology* 86 (1996):1–256.

[11] For an overview and assessment of appropriate intervention and prevention strategies, see Goldstein, Arnold P., and C. Ronald Huff, editors, *The Gang Intervention Handbook*, Champaign, Illinois: Research Press, 1993; Klein, Malcolm W., *The American Street Gang: Its Nature, Prevalence, and Control*; Spergel, Irving A., *The Youth Gang Problem: A Community Approach*, New York: Oxford University Press, 1995; Tonry, Michael, and David Farrington, editors, *Building a Safer Society: Strategic Approaches to Crime*, Chicago, Illinois: University of Chicago Press, 1995; and Sherman, Lawrence W. et al., *Preventing Crime: What Works, What Doesn't, What's Promising*, Washington, D.C.: U.S. Department of Justice, Office of Justice Programs, 1997.

[12] The mortality rate among the study sample of 83 Columbus gang leaders and hardcore members far exceeds the expected death rate for adolescent males of comparable ages.

[13] The key to developing successful intervention programs is to conduct rigorous evaluations that carefully assess what works for whom and under what circumstances.

[14] For additional discussion of crimes that appear to be especially related to gangs and crimes that the media often mistakenly attribute to gangs, see Klein, Malcolm W., *The American Street Gang*.

[15] Recent successful projects to reduce gun violence occurred in both Kansas City and Boston. See Sherman, Lawrence W., James W. Shaw, and Dennis P. Rogan, *The Kansas City Gun Experiment*, Research in Brief, Washington, D.C.: U.S. Department of Justice, National Institute of Justice, 1995 and Kennedy, David M., Anne M. Piehl, and Anthony A. Braga, "Youth Violence in Boston: Gun Markets, Serious Youth Offenders, and a Use-Reduction Strategy," *Law and Contemporary Problems* 59 (1996): 147–196.

Recent Patterns of Gang Problems in the United States
Results from the 1996–2002 National Youth Gang Survey

Arlen Egley, Jr., James C. Howell, & Aline K. Major

INTRODUCTION

Three significant changes in America's gang problem over the past 20 years have been noted: a greater degree of lethality associated with the availability of firearms; a greater amount of diversity in the structure and form of contemporary gangs; and an unprecedented spread of gang problems from large urban areas to many smaller cities and towns, as well as suburban and rural counties—areas atypically associated with gangs (Klein, 2002, p. 243). The wave of gang violence in the early to mid-1990s perhaps best exemplifies the first of these points. And in recent years, the emergence of a "hybrid gang culture"—gangs that do not follow the same rules or methods of operation as their predecessors—continues to redefine the boundaries of the form and behaviors of youth gangs (Howell, Moore, and Egley, 2002; Starbuck, Howell, and Lindquist, 2001).

Prepared especially for *American Youth Gangs at the Millennium* by Arlen Egley, Jr., James C. Howell, and Aline K. Major.

Klein's third observation, the proliferation of gang problems across the United States, serves as the focal point of this article. While it is generally known that many new localities experienced the emergence of youth gang activity in the past two decades, this fact alone raises a whole new series of questions concerning the extent and pattern of this proliferation. In this chapter we explore the spread of youth gang problems across the United States using data obtained annually from a representative sample of law enforcement agencies from 1996 to 2002. We also discuss findings from previous national-level surveys that have provided a foundation of knowledge for understanding the scope of the current gang problem. The following are the relevant questions that we address:

- How extensive is the current youth gang problem?
- Is the likelihood of gang problems the same across all city sizes and county types?
- Where and how did the presence of gang problems vary in the mid- to late 1990s and early 2000s?
- What are the noticeable patterns of gang-problem emergence across cities?
- What characteristics distinguish jurisdictions that have and have not been persistently affected by gang problems in recent years?
- How many gang members have been identified by law enforcement, and how has this number changed over the years?

In addressing these questions, we hope to provide a more concrete and descriptive nationwide portrait of the current youth gang problem and the implication these findings have for the coming years.

PRIOR NATIONAL-LEVEL YOUTH GANG SURVEYS

National-level surveys measuring the scope of the gang problem were initiated around 30 years ago (see Curry and Decker, 2003, pp. 17–30; Howell, 1994). In this section we review earlier surveys and their continuing importance for current national survey efforts. No doubt the reader will notice that these surveys were conducted by a number of different researchers over intermittent years and with various sampling frames. This is largely due to the fact that various research agendas were the impetus for each different survey. The common thread throughout each, however, was the measurement of the presence and magnitude of gang-related problems across many different localities and communities. Due to the pioneering and sedulous work of this group of researchers, our understanding of the nature and extent of the nation's youth gang problem covers more than a quarter of a century.

The first series of efforts to study the nation's gang problem was undertaken by Walter Miller (1975). Six of the twelve cities selected for his initial study were identified as having a "gang problem" in 1975. Miller (1982) subsequently expanded the sample to include 36 metropolitan areas and revealed the widespread presence of gangs that, judging by media accounts, had seemingly disappeared from the nation's landscape. Based on reports from multiple sources across a wider range of cities, Miller estimated that during the late 1970s there were approximately 2,300 gangs with 98,000 members located in approximately 300 U.S. cities and towns. With the exception of cities in California, Miller noted a positive relationship between city population size and reported gang presence. He also calculated the relative proportion of police arrests in the largest gang-problem cities, estimating that 42 percent of all arrests of male youths for serious and violent crimes and about 23 percent of all homicide arrests were gang members. Because of the pervasiveness and seriousness of gang crime, Miller (1976, 1990) recommended a new federal initiative to systematically gather information on youth gangs nationwide. Miller has continued to compile a list of localities with gang problems, culminating in a recent report that finds that cities experiencing youth gang problems increased nearly tenfold between the 1970s and the late 1990s (Miller, 2001).

The next gang survey, conducted in the early 1980s (Needle and Stapleton, 1983), assessed law enforcement responses to youth gangs in 60 cities with populations over 100,000, of which 27 of them reported gang problems. In finding that the majority of police departments operated without written policies and procedures in dealing with youth gangs and with personnel who have little to no formal training in gang intervention techniques, the study authors offered numerous recommendations for improving police responses to youth gangs. Although it was limited in scope, this study established the need for law enforcement training and technical assistance in dealing with youth gangs.

Subsequent youth gang surveys were considerably broader in scope, beginning with the only national assessment of organized community agency and police efforts to combat gangs (Spergel, 1995; Spergel and Curry, 1990, 1993). This landmark 1988 study began with a universe of 101 cities in which the presence of gangs was suspected. Contacts with police, regarding the presence of gangs and the existence of an organized agency or community response, reduced the number to 74 cities. A total of 254 respondents were surveyed in the 45 cities (and 6 institutional sites) that were classified as "chronic" or "emerging" gang-problem cities. Thirty-five of these jurisdictions reported over 1,400 gangs and 120,500 gang members. Gang programs and strategies were examined in detail in the studied cities. This comprehensive study is best known for the foundation it laid for the most sustained federal gang program, the Comprehensive Gang Prevention, Intervention, and Suppression framework (Spergel, 1995; Spergel and Curry, 1990, 1993) that a number of communities continue to implement.[1]

Klein, Maxson, and colleagues established ongoing contact with a number of law enforcement agencies in the 1980s and 1990s. A 1992 survey of law enforcement personnel in approximately 1,100 cities found that "gang member migration, although widespread, should not be viewed as the major culprit in the nationwide proliferation of gangs" (Maxson, 1998, p. 8). By the mid-1990s, Klein (1995a) concluded in his highly regarded book that there were approximately 9,000 gangs and 400,000 gang members in 800 to 1,100 cities in the United States.

Curry, Ball, and Fox (1994) surveyed police departments in 122 cities (including all 79 with populations over 200,000) in 1992. To be counted as having a "gang" problem, agencies had to "identify the group as a 'gang' that was involved in criminal activity and included youths in its membership" (p. 2). Overall, 110 of these agencies (including 72 of the 79 largest police departments) were identified as having a gang problem. Over 4,800 gangs and 249,000 gang members were reported. Additionally, one agency reported a "posse" problem and another reported a "crew" problem, which the authors argue corresponds to the operational definition of a "gang" problem (p. 10).

Curry and colleagues (Curry, Ball, and Decker, 1996a, 1996b) expanded their survey efforts in 1994 (covering the 1993 calendar year) to include all cities with populations over 150,000 and a random sample of 284 cities with populations between 25,000 and 150,000. Using the same measurement technique as before, 57 percent of these agencies were identified as having a "gang problem." Because this sample was representative of all cities over 25,000, the authors could estimate that over 750 cities had gang problems in 1993. A "conservative" nationwide estimate of over 8,600 gangs and 378,500 gang members was also provided (Curry, Ball, and Decker, 1996b, p. 29).

Three main gang survey developments led to federal support from the Office of Juvenile Justice and Delinquency Prevention (OJJDP) for the annual national youth gang surveys of law enforcement that are reported in this chapter. Although it initially was rejected, Miller's (1990) recommendation later stimulated support for a sustained federal youth gang program of research, program development, and survey research. Spergel and Curry's national assessment of gang problems and responses to them increased federal interest in gaining a better understanding of problems youth gangs present and possible solutions. Lastly, the success of two surveys by Curry et al. (1994 and 1996) and the quality of the gang information increased federal officials' confidence in the value of information on youth gangs that could be obtained in surveys of law enforcement agencies.

THE 1996–2002 NATIONAL YOUTH GANG SURVEY

Survey Sample

In 1994, the OJJDP established the National Youth Gang Center (NYGC) to maintain and contribute to the body of critical knowledge about youth gangs and effective responses to them nationwide. Since 1995, NYGC has conducted the National Youth Gang Survey (NYGS).[2] Taken from a nationally representative sample of law enforcement agencies, the NYGS annually assesses the presence and extent of the youth gang problem in jurisdictions throughout the United States. The 1996–2001 survey sample consisted of 3,018 police and sheriffs' departments. An updated sample of 2,563 agencies, based on newly updated information from the U.S. Census Bureau and the Federal Bureau of Investigation (FBI), was selected for the 2002 survey and will be used in subsequent surveys. Agencies included in the two nationally representative NYGS samples are as follows:

1996–2001 NYGS Sample (Former sample):

- All police departments serving cities with populations of 25,000 or more ($n = 1,216$).
- All suburban county police and sheriffs' departments ($n = 661$).
- A randomly selected sample of police departments serving cities with populations between 2,500 and 24,999 ($n = 398$).
- A randomly selected sample of rural county police and sheriffs' departments ($n = 743$).

2002 NYGS Sample (Current sample):

- All police departments serving cities with populations of 50,000 or more ($n = 627$).
- All suburban county police and sheriffs' departments ($n = 745$).
- A randomly selected sample of police departments serving cities with populations between 2,500 and 49,999 ($n = 699$).
- A randomly selected sample of rural county police and sheriffs' departments ($n = 492$).

Sixty-three percent of the agencies in the 2002 NYGS (current) sample were also surveyed from 1996 to 2001, permitting an ongoing longitudinal assessment of gang problems in a large number of jurisdictions. Annual NYGS response rates ranged from 84 to 92 percent across the survey years.

Measurement Issues

One of the most difficult issues encountered in gang research pertains to the definitional dilemma of what constitutes a "gang"—and by extension, a gang member and gang-related incident. A large-scale effort in the late 1980s was unsuccessful in obtaining a consensus among researchers and practitioners for a standardized definition of these concepts (Spergel and Bobrowski, 1989). A similar attempt in the mid-1990s by NYGC, consisting of professionals from local and federal law enforcement agencies, juvenile justice operational and planning agencies, and academia, suffered similar results. In the past ten years, at least 20 states have passed laws explicitly defining "gangs" and "gang members" (Howell, Moore, and Egley, 2002). Some do this to "enhance" or increase the severity of penalties for criminal offenses committed by gang members, while others are more interested in establishing procedures for intelligence gathering. While these codified definitions frequently share commonalities (e.g., identifiable group, pattern of criminal activity), there is also variation in other definitional components. For the purposes of the NYGS, a "youth gang" is defined for the law enforcement agency as:

> A group of youths or young adults in your jurisdiction that you or other responsible persons in your agency or community are willing to identify or classify as a "gang." DO NOT include motorcycle gangs, hate or ideology groups, prison gangs, or other exclusively adult gangs.

Thus, the NYGS measures youth gang activity as an identified problem by interested community agents. This approach is both less restrictive and self-determining, allowing for the observed variation across communities in gang definitions. Across survey years, questionnaire items have examined the characteristics emphasized by law enforcement in defining a gang. Respondents in the 1998 NYGS primarily emphasized involvement in group criminal activity, with varying degrees of emphasis placed on other definitional elements such as having a name, displaying common colors and other symbols, and protecting turf/territory (NYGC, 2000).

Other research has concentrated on evaluating procedures to identify youth gang members. Curry and Decker (2003) argue that the self-nomination technique—asking youths, "Are you now or have you been a gang member?"—is the most powerful and direct measure. To support their contention, the authors point out that support for the self-nomination method has been found across all methodological approaches, including youth surveys, field research, and secondary data analysis of police records. They note that "such convergence across [research] methods is rare indeed" (p. 6). Esbensen, Winfree, He, and Taylor (2001) investigated the impact of using increasingly restrictive definitions of gang membership from a large self-administered survey of middle-school youths and concluded that "the self-nomination technique is a particularly robust measure of gang membership capable of distinguishing gang from nongang youth" (p. 124).

Many law enforcement agencies report relying on self-admission in determining gang membership. In the 2002 NYGS, respondents were provided a list of five commonly used criteria to identify gang membership (e.g., arrested or associates with known gang members, tattoos or other symbols, identified by a reliable source). Sixty-one percent of all gang-problem respondents indicated the most frequently used method (alone or in combination with other factors) by their agency to identify and document individuals as gang members was that "the individual claims to be a gang member." Katz (2003) spent time observing the practices of a midwestern city's gang unit in 1996–97 and found that officers often looked for "other aggravating clues" even though individuals had already met the criteria specified by the department to record them as a gang member. He concludes that "there might be a great deal of underdocumentation that takes place by gang unit officers," cautioning, however, that it is difficult to surmise the extent of this as officers used a "substantial amount of discretion in the collection and documentation of gang-related data" (p. 510–511). In another study, Katz, Webb, and Schaefer (2000) investigated a large, southwestern city's gang-unit file and found that those individuals documented as gang members by the police were more criminally active than a matched sample of nongang youth offenders. The authors conclude these findings demonstrate both the importance of establishing criteria for documenting gang membership and the potential utility of gang intelligence lists.

Thus, law enforcement data represent one methodological avenue for viewing and understanding the nature and extent of local gang problems. Curry, Ball, and Decker (1996b) remind us, however, that a better empirical assessment of the extent of local gang activity can be made by examining gang-related crime statistics rather than numbers of gangs and gang members. Unfortunately, as they also note, this statistic "is the one that has been most neglected in law enforcement record keeping" (p. 36), reflecting the importance of standardized definitions, recording procedures, and reporting practices.

Survey Findings[3]

Prevalence of Youth Gang Problems across Jurisdictions

Figure 1 displays the percent of city law enforcement agencies reporting youth gang problems by service population size from 1996 to 2002. All city law enforcement agencies with a service population above 250,000 affirmatively reported gang problems across all seven of the survey years. A large majority of city agencies in the next largest population group (i.e., 100,000–249,999) reported gang problems as well. For the remaining two population groups, reports of gang problems declined noticeably from 1996 to 2001. Of all city police departments with a service population above 2,500, over 90 percent serve a population below 50,000. Thus, the 16 percent decline from 1996 to 2001 in reported gang problems for this group of agencies importantly influences the estimated number of jurisdictions with gang problems.

Figure 2 displays gang-problem trends for county law enforcement agencies by county type and reveals a high degree of similarity in the shape of their patterns. Nearly 60 percent of the suburban county law enforcement agencies reported gang problems in the first two survey years, and the statistic for this group declined steadily to just over one-third in 2001. For rural counties, around one-fourth reported gang problems in the first two surveys, and just over one in ten have reported gang problems in recent years.

Based on the most recent survey results, it is estimated that youth gangs were active in over 2,300 jurisdictions served by city law enforce-

Figure 1

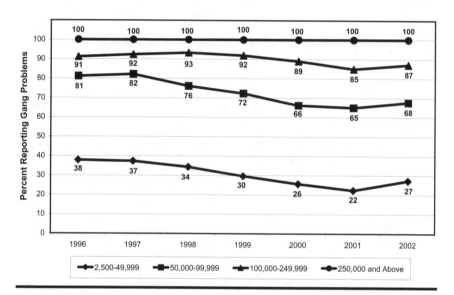

Figure 2

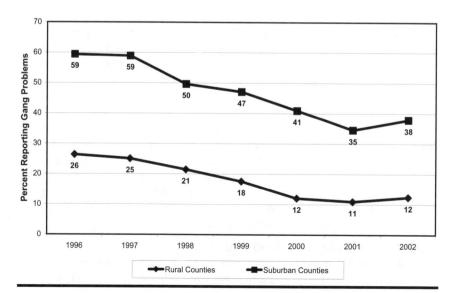

ment agencies with a service population above 2,500 and over 550 jurisdictions served by county law enforcement agencies in 2002. These findings are comparable to recent survey years (accounting for the assumed margin of error for the randomly sampled groups) and provide preliminary evidence that the overall number of jurisdictions experiencing gang problems in a given year has stabilized. Figure 3 displays the more than 1,400 law enforcement agencies in the NYGS in the contiguous 48 states that reported gang problems in one or more years between 1999 and 2001.

Figure 3

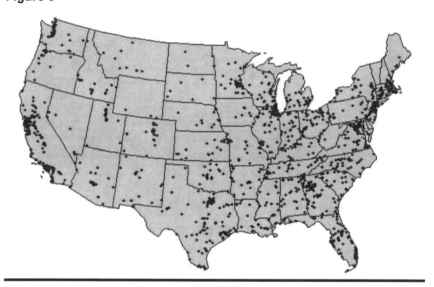

In sum, three patterns are notable in the above examination of reported gang problems. First, prevalence rates of youth gang problems remained very high in the largest cities across the United States. All city agencies with a service population above 250,000 reported gang problems in all survey years, and so did an overwhelming majority of city agencies with a service population of 100,000–249,999. Second, and in stark contrast, reports of gang presence steadily declined in counties and smaller cities over initial survey years. For example, over one-third of the city agencies with a service population of 2,500–49,999 reported gang problems in the first three survey years. This number fell to around one in four in the last three survey years. Third, little change in gang-problem prevalence rates over recent survey years is observed for these counties and smaller cities. This apparent reversal in trend is one to closely observe in future NYGC surveys.

Proliferation of Youth Gang Problems
Undoubtedly, part of the increase in estimated number of cities, towns, and counties experiencing gang problems over the past 30 years

can be attributed to an increasing number of areas studied (i.e., breadth of coverage). In this section, we provide evidence that an equal or greater part of this increase can also be attributed to the proliferation of gang problems nationwide.

To gain insight into the timing of the spread of gang problems across U.S. cities, the 2000 NYGS asked respondents for the approximate year when their current youth gang problem began, more simply referred to as "year of onset." Figure 4 shows the cumulative percent of cities by year of onset for each of the four population groups. For example, among city law enforcement with a service population of 50,000–99,999, the year of gang-problem onset was reported as 2000 or before by 66 percent (which, being the *total* cumulative percent, also reflects the percent reporting youth gang problems in 2000 for this population group). Comparatively, nearly 40 percent of this group of agencies reported both gang problems in 2000 and a year of onset before 1991, and under 10 percent reported the year of onset before 1983. Therefore, both the slope of the trajectory and corresponding time period characterize the growth of youth gang problems across these cities.

Cities with larger population sizes (i.e., 100,000 and above) experienced a much higher and faster rate and earlier onset of gang proliferation than all other cities. Approximately one-third of these cities reported gang problems before 1985, and an additional 50 percent reported an onset of gang problems in the following ten-year period (i.e., from 1985 to the mid-1990s), the most sharply observed increase. These patterns are

Figure 4

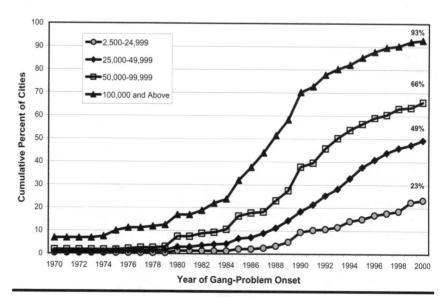

increasingly less pronounced across the remaining population groups, suggesting a cascading pattern of gang proliferation from the larger to smaller populated areas. This is also reflected in the average year of onset across population groups, which was 1985 for cities with populations 100,000 and above, 1988 for cities of 50,000–99,999, 1990 for cities of 25,000–49,999, and 1992 for cities below 25,000.

Patterns of Gang Problems within Jurisdictions

The preceding two sections describe the nation's current gang problem by examining prevalence and proliferation rates across years. However, longitudinal data can offer a more revealing look into the dynamic nature of gang problems by examining within-jurisdiction patterns of gang presence across NYGS years. Data for this analysis pertain to the 1996–2001 NYGS where the same agencies were surveyed annually. One of three patterns are logically possible for each jurisdiction during this six-year period: (1) a persistent gang problem, as indicated by consistent reports of youth gang problems across all survey years; (2) a variable gang problem, as indicated by reported gang problems in at least one survey year and no gang problems in any other year[4]; and (3) an absence of gang problems, as indicated by consistent reports of no youth gang problems in the jurisdiction. To examine within-jurisdiction patterns of gang problems, each agency's reporting record of gang presence was inspected and coded.[5]

Figure 5 displays gang-problem patterns for city law enforcement agencies by service population size. Within each population group, the percent of agencies that reported persistent and variable gang problems are displayed. Not displayed are the percent of agencies that did not report gang problems in any survey year between 1996 and 2001. For example, for city agencies with service populations between 50,000 and 99,999, over half (58 percent) reported persistent gang problems across survey years, and an additional 33 percent reported variable gang problems. Additionally, this indicates that 91 percent of these cities reported gang problems in at least one year between 1996 and 2001, while the remainder (9 percent) experienced no gang problems. A strong relationship between city population size and gang-problem pattern is clearly noticeable in figure 5. As the size of the population group increases, so does the percent of city agencies that report persistent gang problems. Variable gang problems are observed much more frequently in the smaller population groups. Nearly half of the agencies in the two smallest population groups reported a variable gang problem over the six-year period.

Figure 6 displays gang-problem patterns for county law enforcement agencies. Variable gang problems are more frequently observed in both county types. Forty-seven percent of the suburban counties experienced variable gang problems from 1996 to 2001, and just over one-fourth experienced persistent gang problems. For rural counties, these numbers are 37 percent and 4 percent, respectively.

Figure 5

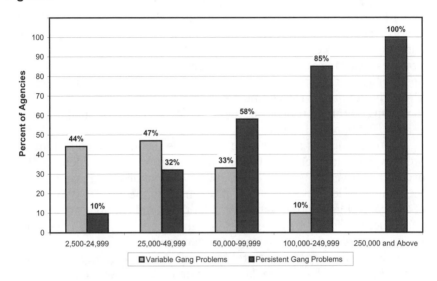

See text for description of "variable" and "persistent" gang problems.

Figure 6

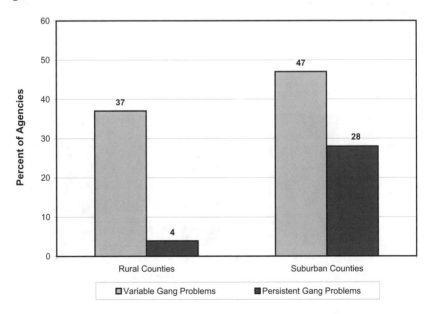

See text for description of "variable" and "persistent" gang problems.

Figure 7 looks more closely at selected characteristics of the city and county agencies that reported a variable gang problem from 1996 to 2001. Remarkably similar features are observed for both agency types. A large majority of agencies in the NYGS sample that reported variable gang problems have a service population below 50,000. Also, a large majority of the agencies reporting variable gang problems report both a relatively recent onset of gang activity and a relatively small number of gang members. These results mirror the comments of one gang researcher: "The bulk of the [gang] proliferation is proliferation of a *relatively* small problem" (Klein, 1995b, p. 233, emphasis added).

Overall, findings from the previous three sections are consistent with Miller's prediction based on his documentation of gang-problem localities over a three-decade period (Miller, 2001), of a possible decreasing trend in the number of localities with gang problems into the late 1990s. Indicative of the cycle of gang proliferation, smaller cities and counties are at greater risk of being affected by gang problems during peak periods of gang activity in the larger areas. Diffusion of the gang culture has been cited as having a "major impact on gang proliferation" (Klein, 1995a, p. 205), along with a growing urban underclass associated with economic restructuring and deindustrialization (Moore, 1998). The cascading pattern of year of gang-problem onset across city sizes presented in figure 4 is notably consistent with these assertions. As the cycle progressed, reports of gang prob-

Figure 7

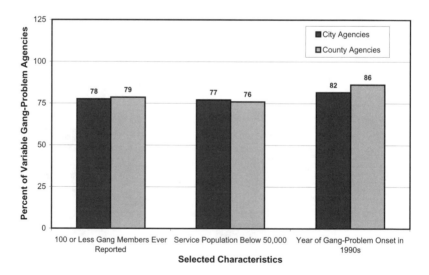

See text for description of "variable" gang problems.

lems began to recede to the larger populated areas, which are characterized by larger numbers of gang members. This cycle highlights the dynamic and sometimes transitory nature of gang problems across smaller jurisdictions. At the time of the 1996 NYGS, prevalence rates of gang problems were the highest observed in NYGS years and, as suggested by the year of gang-problem onset analysis, may have been even greater in the years immediately preceding 1996. Results from the 1996–2002 NYGS are consistent with (1) a relatively stable presence of gang problems across the larger areas, and (2) a recession phase in the cycle of gang proliferation from 1996 to 2001, where many of the more recently affected areas (e.g., smaller cities and counties) contributed only briefly and, comparatively speaking, only minimally to the overall gang problem.

Estimating the Number of Youth Gang Members

Estimating the number of gang members has previously been deemed to be particularly important because, in part, it "reflects individual youths who are either *potential* offenders or victims in gang-related violence" (Curry and Decker, 2003, pp. 28–29, emphasis in original). Research has consistently demonstrated that youths are significantly more criminally involved during periods of active gang membership, particularly in serious and violent offenses (see, for example, Battin, Hill, Abbott, Catalano, and Hawkins, 1998; Esbensen and Huizinga, 1993; Thornberry, Krohn, Lizotte, Smith, and Tobin, 2003). This finding has been noted as "one of the most robust and consistent observations in criminological research" (Thornberry, 1998, p. 147). In this section we provide nationwide estimates of youth gang members from 1996 to 2002 based on reports from the nationally representative sample of law enforcement agencies in the NYGS.

Figure 8 displays "reasonable" estimates[6] of the number of gang members from 1996 through 2002. Approximately 731,500 gang members were estimated to be active in the United States in 2002, an increase of approximately 5 percent from the estimated number in 2001. The percent change in estimated number of gang members from 1996 to 2001 (the largest absolute difference between any two survey years) was –18 percent, while the percent change in the estimated number of gang-problem jurisdictions between these two years was –38 percent. This difference in rates is largely the result of the decline in proportion of smaller cities and counties reporting gang problems that also reported comparatively fewer gang members over the survey years from 1996 to 2001.

In 1998, just over 84 percent of all gang members were estimated to be in larger cities (i.e., populations 25,000 and above) and suburban counties, with the remainder in smaller cities (i.e., populations below 25,000) and rural counties. Since that time, this percentage has steadily risen to the point that approximately 90 percent of all gang members were estimated to be active in larger cities and suburban counties in 2001. This is, of course, in large part a product of the decline in number of smaller cities

Figure 8

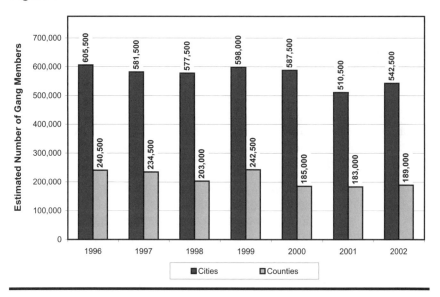

and rural counties reporting gang problems from 1996 to 2001. From 1998 to 2001, these two areas combined reported 43 percent fewer gang members, compared to 5 percent fewer members in larger cities and suburban counties. In fact, the estimated reduction in the *number* of gang members in smaller cities and rural counties over this four-year period is greater than the estimated reduction in the *number* of gang members in larger cities and suburban counties.

CONCLUSION AND DISCUSSION

Results from the 1996 to 2002 NYGS reveal the extensiveness of the current youth gang problem. The latest estimate finds that youth gangs were active in nearly 2,900 law enforcement jurisdictions across the United States in 2002. While the decline in number of areas reporting gang problems might initially appear encouraging, two observations temper this finding. First, among those areas accounting for the overwhelming majority of this decline (i.e., smaller cities and rural counties), fewer gang members were reported and few of these agencies experienced high levels of gang-related violence during their gang-problem periods (Egley, Major, and Howell, forthcoming). Most of these areas, then, contributed only minimally to the overall gang problem. Second, in more recent surveys (i.e., 2000–2002), the overall estimated number of jurisdictions experiencing gang problems in a given year has more or less stabilized. These findings are reflective of the cyclical pattern of gang activity (Klein, 1995b). These cycles occur at multiple levels—within regions, cities, and neighborhoods—and all contribute to the portrait of our nation's gang problem.

Despite the variability of gang problems across the smaller populated areas in the past decade, the size of gang membership has remained formidable. In any given year of the NYGS, over one-half million gang members are estimated to be active in U.S. cities alone. These numbers are comparable to those found by Curry and colleagues (1994) almost a decade ago when gang problems, especially gang violence, were rising to unprecedented heights. They referred to the large number of gang members identified by law enforcement as "a sobering national statistic" (p. 36), a description that is no less accurate today.

In referring to the seeming re-emergence of gang activity in the 1970s, Miller (1982) remarked, "There is no new wave, but rather a continuation of an old wave—a wave that strikes with great fury at one part of the shore, recedes, strikes again at another, ebbs away, strikes once more, and so on" (p. 7). His words were prophetic of the gang problem in the 1990s. How prophetic they will be in this decade will largely be the result of our efforts to proactively respond to our current youth gang problem.

This article is adapted from the *National Youth Gang Survey: 1999–2001* Summary Report (Egley, Major, and Howell, forthcoming) and the *Highlights of the 2002 National Youth Gang Survey* Fact Sheet (Egley and Major, forthcoming). The research on which this chapter is based was conducted under Grant #95-JD-MU-K001 for the Institute for Intergovernmental Research, National Youth Gang Center, from the Office of Juvenile Justice and Delinquency Prevention, U.S. Department of Justice. Points of view or opinions expressed herein are those of the authors and do not necessarily represent the official position or policies of OJJDP or the U.S. Department of Justice.

Notes

[1] The National Youth Gang Center (NYGC) has developed an assessment protocol, based on the framework that Spergel and Curry developed, that any community can use to assess its gang problem (NYGC, 2002a), which guides its development of a gang prevention, intervention, and suppression continuum of programs and strategies. Resource materials that assist communities in developing an action plan to implement the comprehensive gang model are also available (NYGC, 2002b). (These user-friendly resources are available for downloading at www.iir.com/nygc.)

[2] The following publications are the main reports of the National Youth Gang Survey:
1995 survey: National Youth Gang Center (1997) (This was a pilot survey.)
1996 survey: National Youth Gang Center (1999a)
1997 survey: National Youth Gang Center (1999b)
1998 survey: National Youth Gang Center (2000)
1999 survey: Egley (2000)
2000 survey: Egley and Arjunan (2002)
2001 survey: Egley and Major (2003)
2002 survey: Egley and Major (forthcoming)
1999–2001 survey: Egley, Major, and Howell (forthcoming)

For research reports using the NYGS survey data, see Curry, 1999; Howell, Egley, and Gleason, 2002; Howell and Gleason, 1999; Howell and Lynch, 2000; Howell, Moore, and Egley, 2002; Maxson, Curry, and Howell, 2002; Starbuck, Howell, and Lindquist, 2001.

[3] At the time of this writing (July 2003), data collection for the calendar year 2002 NYGS had just recently been completed. The following provides preliminary findings from the 2002 NYGS where available.

[4] This category comprises agencies that report patterns consistent with an emerging or desisting gang problem and agencies who report gang problems intermittently across survey years.

[5] In order to increase confidence in properly interpreting each jurisdiction's pattern, certain classification restrictions were imposed. First, the agency must have responded to three or more surveys, and second, it must have responded to a recent survey (i.e., 2000 or 2001 NYGS). Ninety-two percent ($n = 2766$) of the survey sample agencies were included in the analysis under these restrictions.

[6] In previous national gang surveys of law enforcement, Curry, Ball, and Decker (1996b, p. 31) provide "more 'reasonable' estimates" by using an estimation procedure which substitutes the 5 percent trimmed mean (a more robust measure of central tendency) for missing values. The estimates provided in figure 8 are based on this approach, similarly providing "reasonable" estimates.

References

Battin, S. R., Hill, K. G., Abbott, R. D., Catalano, R. F., and Hawkins, J. D. (1998). The contribution of gang membership to delinquency beyond delinquent friends. *Criminology*, 36(1), 93–115.

Curry, G. D. (1999). Race, ethnicity, and gender issues in gangs: Reconciling police data. In C. S. Brito and T. Allan (Eds.), *Problem-Oriented Policing: Crime-Specific Problems, Critical Issues and Making POP Work* (Vol. 2, pp. 63–89). Fleming, NJ: Police Executive Research Forum.

Curry, G. D., Ball, R. A., and Decker, S. H. (1996a). *Update on Gang Crime and Law Enforcement Recordkeeping: Report of the 1994 NIJ Extended National Assessment Survey of Law Enforcement Anti-Gang Information Resources*. Research Report. National Criminal Justice Reference Service. Washington, DC: U.S. Department of Justice.

Curry, G. D., Ball, R. A., and Decker, S. H. (1996b). Estimating the national scope of gang crime from law enforcement data. In C. R. Huff (Ed.), *Gangs in America* (pp. 21–36). Thousand Oaks, CA: Sage.

Curry, G. D., Ball, R. A., and Fox, R. J. (1994). Gang crime and law enforcement recordkeeping. *Research in Brief*. Washington, DC: U.S. Department of Justice, National Institute of Justice.

Curry, G. D., and Decker, S. H. (2003). *Confronting Gangs: Crime and Community* (2nd ed.). Los Angeles, CA: Roxbury.

Egley, A., Jr. (2000). Highlights of the 1999 National Youth Gang Survey. *Fact Sheet #2000–20*. Washington, DC: U.S. Department of Justice, Office of Juvenile Justice and Delinquency Prevention.

Egley, A., Jr., and Arjunan, M. (2002). Highlights of the 2000 National Youth Gang Survey. *Fact Sheet #2002–04*. Washington, DC: U.S. Department of Justice, Office of Juvenile Justice and Delinquency Prevention.

Egley, A., Jr., and Major, A. K. (2003). Highlights of the 2001 National Youth Gang Survey. *Fact Sheet #2003–01*. Washington, DC: U.S. Department of Justice, Office of Juvenile Justice and Delinquency Prevention.

Egley, A., Jr., and Major, A. K. (forthcoming). Highlights of the 2002 National Youth Gang Survey. Tallahassee, FL: National Youth Gang Center.

Egley, A., Jr., Major, A. K., and Howell, J. C. (forthcoming). *National Youth Gang Survey: 1999–2001*. Summary Report. Tallahassee, FL: National Youth Gang Center.

Esbensen, F., and Huizinga, D. (1993). Gangs, drugs, and delinquency in a survey of urban youth. *Criminology*, 31(4), 565–589.

Esbensen, F., Winfree, L. T., He, N., and Taylor, T. J. (2001). Youth gangs and definitional issues: When is a gang a gang, and why does it matter? *Crime and Delinquency*, 47(1), 105–130.

Howell, J. C. (1994). Recent gang research: Programs and policy implications. *Crime and Delinquency*, 40(4), 495–515.

Howell, J. C., Egley, A., Jr., and Gleason, D. K. (2002). Modern day youth gangs. *Juvenile Justice Bulletin*. Youth Gang Series. Washington, DC: U.S. Department of Justice, Office of Juvenile Justice and Delinquency Prevention.

Howell, J. C., and Gleason, D. K. (1999). Youth gang drug trafficking. *Juvenile Justice Bulletin*. Youth Gang Series. Washington, DC: U.S. Department of Justice, Office of Juvenile Justice and Delinquency Prevention.

Howell, J. C., and Lynch, J. (2000). Youth gangs in schools. *Juvenile Justice Bulletin*. Youth Gang Series. Washington, DC: U.S. Department of Justice, Office of Justice Programs, Office of Juvenile Justice and Delinquency Prevention.

Howell, J. C., Moore, J. P., and Egley, A. Jr. (2002). The changing boundaries of youth gangs. In C. R. Huff (Ed.), *Gangs in America III* (pp. 3–18). Thousand Oaks, CA: Sage.

Katz, C. M. (2003). Issues in the production and dissemination of gang statistics: An ethnographic study of a large midwestern gang unit. *Crime and Delinquency*, 49(3), 485–516.

Katz, C. M., Webb, V. J., and Schaefer, D. R. (2000). The validity of police gang intelligence lists: Examining differences in delinquency between documented gang members and nondocumented delinquent youth. *Police Quarterly*, 3(4), 413–437.

Klein, M. W. (1995a). *The American Street Gang*. New York: Oxford University Press.

Klein, M. W. (1995b). Street gang cycles. In J. Q. Wilson and J. Petersilia (Eds.), *Crime* (pp. 217–236). San Francisco, CA: Institute for Contemporary Studies Press.

Klein, M. W. (2002). Street gangs: A cross-national perspective. In C. R. Huff (Ed.), *Gangs in America III* (pp. 237–254). Thousand Oaks, CA: Sage.

Maxson, C. L. (1998). Gang members on the move. *Juvenile Justice Bulletin*. Youth Gang Series. Washington, DC: U.S. Department of Justice, Office of Juvenile Justice and Delinquency Prevention.

Maxson, C. L., Curry, G. D., and Howell, J. C. (2002). Youth gang homicides in the United States in the 1990's. In W. Reed and S. Decker (Eds.), *Responses to Gangs: Evaluation and Research* (pp. 107–137). Washington, DC: U.S. Department of Justice, National Institute of Justice.

Miller, W. B. (1975). *Violence by Youth Gangs and Youth Groups as a Crime Problem in Major American Cities*. Washington, DC: U.S. Department of Justice, Office of Juvenile Justice and Delinquency Prevention.

Miller, W. B. (1976). New federal initiatives re: serious collective youth crime. In *Hearings before the Subcommittee to Investigate Juvenile Delinquency of the Committee on the Judiciary* (pp. 262–266), United States Senate, 95th Cong. 2d Sess., April 10 and 12.

Miller, W. B. (1982) (Reissued in 1992). *Crime by Youth Gangs and Groups in the United States*. Washington, DC: U.S. Department of Justice, Office of Juvenile Justice and Delinquency Prevention.

Miller, W. B. (1990). Why the United States has failed to solve its youth gang problem. In C. R. Huff (Ed.), *Gangs in America* (pp. 263–287). Newbury Park, CA: Sage.

Miller, W. B. (2001). *The Growth of Youth Gang Problems in the United States: 1970–1998.* Washington, DC: U.S. Department of Justice, Office of Juvenile Justice and Delinquency Prevention.

Moore, J. W. (1998). Understanding youth street gangs: Economic restructuring and the urban underclass. In M. W. Watts (Ed.) *Cross-Cultural Perspectives on Youth and Violence* (pp. 65–78). Stamford, CT: JAI Press.

National Youth Gang Center. (1997). *1995 National Youth Gang Survey.* Washington, DC: Office of Juvenile Justice and Delinquency Prevention.

National Youth Gang Center. (1999a). *1996 National Youth Gang Survey.* Washington, DC: Office of Juvenile Justice and Delinquency Prevention.

National Youth Gang Center. (1999b). *1997 National Youth Gang Survey.* Washington, DC: Office of Juvenile Justice and Delinquency Prevention.

National Youth Gang Center. (2000). *1998 National Youth Gang Survey.* Washington, DC: Office of Juvenile Justice and Delinquency Prevention.

National Youth Gang Center. (2002a). *Guide to Assessing Your Community's Youth Gang Problem.* Washington, DC: Office of Juvenile Justice and Delinquency Prevention.

National Youth Gang Center. (2002b). *Planning for Implementation.* Washington, DC: Office of Juvenile Justice and Delinquency Prevention.

Needle, J., and Stapleton, W. V. (1983). *Police Handling of Youth Gangs.* Washington, DC: U.S. Department of Justice, Office of Juvenile Justice and Delinquency Prevention.

Spergel, I. A. (1995). *The Youth Gang Problem.* New York: Oxford University Press.

Spergel, I. A., and Bobrowski, L. (1989). Minutes from the Law Enforcement Youth Gang Definitional Conference: September 25, 1989. Rockville, MD: Juvenile Justice Clearinghouse.

Spergel, I. A., and Curry, G. D. (1990). Strategies and perceived agency effectiveness in dealing with the youth gang problem. In C. R. Huff (Ed.), *Gangs in America* (pp. 288–309). Newbury Park, CA: Sage.

Spergel, I. A., and Curry, G. D. (1993). The National Youth Gang Survey: A research and development process. In A. Goldstein and C. R. Huff (Eds.), *The Gang Intervention Handbook* (pp. 359–400). Champaign, IL: Research Press.

Starbuck, D., Howell, J. C., and Lindquist, D. J. (2001). Hybrid and other modern gangs. *Juvenile Justice Bulletin.* Youth Gang Series. Washington, DC: U.S. Department of Justice, Office of Juvenile Justice and Delinquency Prevention.

Thornberry, T. P. (1998). Membership in youth gangs and involvement in serious and violent offending. In R. Loeber and D. P. Farrington (Eds.), *Serious and Violent Juvenile Offenders: Risk Factors and Successful Interventions* (pp. 147–166). Thousand Oaks, CA: Sage.

Thornberry, T. P., Krohn, M. D., Lizotte, A. J., Smith, C. A., and Tobin, K. (2003). *Gangs and Delinquency in Developmental Perspective.* New York: Cambridge University Press.

SECTION II

Varieties of Gangs

One thing that gang research has clearly shown is that there are numerous types of gangs and that new types are constantly being formed and recognized. Although traditional studies largely described the characteristics of inner-city, male street gangs, only in the last few decades have researchers acknowledged other types of gangs, such as female gangs, drug gangs, and other specific forms. Even in the last decade we have seen new growth in "hybrid" youth gangs in the suburbs and communities that did not report gang activity prior to the 1980s or 1990s. It seems that the more we study gangs, the more varieties of gangs are found. Furthermore, new forms of gangs are constantly emerging as manifestations of our culture change over time. For instance, it is no surprise that there has been a recent rise in hybrid gangs given the integration of schools and the shift toward suburban sprawl over the last 30 years in the United States. We can expect that new gang types will evolve as our nation inevitably changes, and that these new forms will be as important to study and understand as the ones we recognize and examine now.

Space does not permit this section to include all types of gangs; other categories of gangs are equally important. We have selected certain types of gangs because they represent some of the most important and proliferating gang forms in our society in the new millennium. Our primary intent is for readers to realize the vast array of gangs that exist in our nation and that specific types of gangs may require special forms of intervention. Thus, the need to consider catering intervention efforts toward particular gangs and certain gang characteristics is a common theme across the five selections in this section.

In the first article of this section, Marjorie Zatz and Edwardo Portillos examine the dynamic relationships between Chicano/a gang members and their communities in Phoenix, Arizona. Although the data collected for this study were generally limited to the south Phoenix area, many of the findings parallel those reported in studies of other large cities in the United States, such as Chicago and Los Angeles. Still, the south Phoenix area presents a unique context for gang development due to its proximity to the Mexican border, as well as the heightened sense of isolation and relative deprivation the residents appear to have in contrast to the booming growth and prosperity of north Phoenix. One of the strengths of this piece is that the authors interviewed both gang members and nongang individuals in the neighborhood, providing different perspectives of the phenomenon. Zatz and Portillos effectively employ an ecological framework that emphasizes complex and dynamic processes in the community, which is particularly beneficial due to the apparent contradictions that emerge in the interviews. Importantly, the authors identify some of the links between various types of social control and individual characteristics of gangs and gang members, such as age and gender, highlighting the significance of understanding the types of gangs that are being targeted for intervention.

The importance of racial and ethnic differences that affect various aspects of gang membership is explored in the next article of this section. As authors Adrienne Freng and Thomas Winfree point out, most gang studies that examine racial effects concentrate on ethnically homogeneous groups and usually only look at one or a few sites. In contrast, one key advantage of this study was that the data were collected from 11 sites across the nation based largely on their geographic and demographic diversity. Another important advantage is that this study estimates the influence the gang members' race/ethnicity has on the gang experience. In other words, Freng and Winfree provide one of the first investigations of whether individuals of various racial and ethnic groups have different gang experiences due to their attitudes and motives, as well as organization and criminality. Some of the findings are quite surprising, particularly the significant differences observed between Whites and other groups regarding pro-gang attitudes. Significant differences are also found across racial/ethnic groups for gang organizational characteristics and criminal activities, as well as the reasons for joining, which challenge commonly held perceptions of being forced into a gang. As the authors claim, this study has important implications for policy, primarily for prevention programs, given that the most significant differences across racial groups appeared regarding the reasons for joining a gang in the first place.

In the next selection, Jody Miller and Rod Brunson explore gender dynamics in street gangs with the unique advantage of examining both male and female perceptions of the normative features of gang culture.

This represents an important return to attempting to gain insights of female criminal activity via male accounts, which feminist scholars have been quite critical of in the past. As the authors effectively argue, what male gang members say about female gang members and gender dynamics in gangs is invaluable in providing insight into the organizational and structural aspects of the group, as well as the criminal activities and victimization of gang members. Importantly, Miller and Brunson emphasize female accounts of gender dynamics of youth gangs along with the male perspectives, which should satisfy both the traditional and feminist camps. Results of the study show that all-male gang members' attitudes are quite different and more stereotypical as compared to those in mixed-gender gangs. Although the accounts of males and females in mixed-gender gangs were more similar, a notable exception was the exploitive nature of the male accounts of the gender dynamics in these gangs. The findings of this study demonstrate the importance of understanding the type of gang one is dealing with regarding intervention programs. After all, the attitudes of members of all-male gangs appear to be quite different than those of members of mixed-gender gangs; obviously knowing which of these types a targeted gang is would be important to know before intervention techniques are implemented. Thus, it is important to be attentive to such variations in youth gangs because they shape the contexts in which females (and males) interact.

Analyzing the early risk factors that predispose one to joining a gang is the primary topic of the next article by Karl Hill, Christina Lui, and David Hawkins. The authors use one of the few longitudinal, prospective studies on gang membership: the Seattle Social Development Project (SSDP). One of the key findings of this study was confirming that youths who participate in gangs (regardless of the type of gang) are more likely than their nongang peers to engage in various crimes, particularly violence. Regarding different types of gangs and gang members, the SSDP showed that gang members came from diverse racial/ethnic backgrounds, but the rate for joining a gang differed significantly across groups. Gender and age also played an important role in gang membership, while the duration of gang membership seemed to depend mostly on the degree of behavioral or developmental problems the youth had in childhood, such as aggression and attention disorders. Furthermore, an additive effect was observed in the number of environmental risk factors—neighborhood, family, school, etc.—that were present, especially when coupled with individual developmental disorders. The more risk factors present, the more the risk of gang membership and the longer the duration of membership. Hill, Lui, and Hawkins conclude that prevention programs should begin at an early age and that multifaceted programs should target youths who are exposed to the most risk factors. As some of the previous articles in this section have shown, the individual traits and experiences that members bring to the gang may impact the group dynamics and activities of the gang. Therefore, the risk-factor approach is likely to have implications for what happens in the gang due to the type of membership as well as duration.

The final article of this section deals with one of the fastest growing types of gangs in recent years, which are referred to as "hybrid" gangs. In this piece, David Starbuck, James Howell, and Donna Lindquist claim that although hybrid gangs were identified as early as the 1920s, this type of group has become much more common in the United States due to the societal changes that have occurred. Hybrid gangs are generally characterized by mixed-race or mixed-ethnicity members or individuals participating in multiple gangs, which are often characterized by unclear codes of conduct and ambiguous affiliations. These hybrid gangs are likely to be found in communities that have not experienced gang activity prior to the 1980s or 1990s, and may be hard to define as traditional gangs due to their vague definition of a certain "type" of gang. Still, they should be acknowledged as youth gangs as much as established gangs, such as the traditional Bloods or Crips, because of the consequential criminal activity that results from the formation of such groups. As Starbuck, Howell, and Lindquist claim, the extent to which communities deal with gangs in terms of traditional stereotypes results in erroneously adapting a response that is inappropriate for such hybrid gangs. It becomes clear in their overview that communities must create a specific method for dealing with the particular gang problems that are acute in their area, which varies a great deal based on the types of gangs in that jurisdiction. In other words, the advised model of prevention or intervention should be multifaceted and multilayered, involving the individual youths, the family, local agencies, and the greater community.

If anything becomes clear from the various articles in this section, it should be that each community must acknowledge and understand the gang dynamics that are occurring in their jurisdiction. Only by determining the types of gangs that are functioning in their area can a community attempt to deal with such groups while seeking to reduce the reasons for joining and remaining in gangs.

Voices from the Barrio

Chicano/a Gangs, Families, and Communities

Marjorie S. Zatz & Edwardo L. Portillos

Criminologists have long been fascinated with the problems posed by youth gangs. In recent years, community ecology approaches to gang-related crime and social control have become popular. One strand of research has focused on macrosocial patterns of crime and inequality among the urban underclass (e.g., Sampson and Laub, 1993; Sampson and Wilson, 1996; Wilson, 1987). A second strand has examined the "dual frustrations" facing inner-city parents who fear both gang- and drug-related crime *and* police harassment of young men of color (Meares, 1997:140; see also Anderson, 1990; Madriz, 1997). These concerns converge in research that examines the connections between and among the structural causes and community-level effects of economic deprivation, institutional and personal networks within a community, the capacity of local networks to garner human and economic resources from outside the community, and gang-related crime (Anderson, 1990; Bursik and Grasmick, 1993a, b; Hagedorn, 1998; Moore, 1991; Spergel, 1986; Sullivan, 1989). Bursik and Grasmick (1993a) take this approach the farthest theoretically, incorporating Hunter's (1985) three tiers of local community social control into a reformulation of Shaw and McKay's (1942) social disorganization framework. Their theory of community relations recognizes the relevance of

Zatz, Marjorie S., and Portillos, Edwardo L. "Voices from the Barrio: Chicano/a Gangs, Families, and Communities." *Criminology*, Vol. 38, No. 2, pp. 369–401, copyright © 2000 by the American Society of Criminology.

long-term economic deprivation on and institutional racism for community-based social control at the private, parochial, and public levels.

Bursik and Grasmick suggest that traditional social disorganization theory, sometimes in combination with subcultural theories, placed an emphasis on the private level of systemic control, as reflected in family and friendship dynamics. In underclass neighborhoods characterized by stable, high levels of delinquency, however, parochial (e.g., churches and schools) and public (e.g., police) forms of social control become more apparent. A few researchers, most notably Hagedorn (1998) and Decker and Van Winkle (1996), have applied Bursik and Grasmick's theory to inner-city gang research. Yet, these studies have been limited to midwestern cities. We also draw on this theory of community social control, but focus our research in a Chicano/a and Mexicano/a community in the Southwest.[1] As we will demonstrate, our research site reflects a pocket of poverty in the midst of an almost unprecedented economic boom. Also, the community is close to the Mexican border, allowing perhaps for a greater range of traditionalism than might be found in midwestern cities.

Informed by the gang studies noted above and by other scholarship on the urban poor (e.g., Hernández, 1990; Moore and Pinderhughes, 1993; Wilson, 1996), we see gang members as integral parts of their communities, engaging in some actions that hurt the community and in some that help it. At the same time, we are particularly attentive to the ways in which gender, age, educational status, and degree of traditionalism differentiate the adults' perceptions of the gangs and choice of private, parochial, or public forms of social control.

CONTEXTUALIZING THE PHOENIX GANG PROBLEMS: POCKETS OF POVERTY IN A BOOMING ECONOMY

Our research is set in Phoenix, Arizona, a large, thriving, sunbelt city close to the Mexican border. As we will show, many of our findings parallel those reported by gang researchers in Chicago and Los Angeles, where most of the prominent theories about Chicano gangs were developed (e.g., Moore, 1978, 1985, 1991, 1998; Spergel, 1986; Vigil, 1988). Like those earlier researchers, we find that youths join neighborhood gangs for a variety of reasons, including friendship networks, access to alcohol, drugs, and parties; and wanting to feel included and protected by a group. Some of the youths come from multigenerational-gang families, whereas others do not. The adult men we interviewed, as well as the youths, also talked about gangs and gang-barrio relations in terms similar to those reported by other scholars.

Unlike the other cities, however, Phoenix has experienced a spectacular economic boom in recent years. Phoenix is the sixth largest city in the United States and ranks number one nationally for its job growth. As we discuss later in this paper, the city and state have received high marks on a number of economic indicators, yet parts of the city remain severely depressed. Indeed, South Phoenix, where we conducted our research, was one of President Clinton's stops during his four-day national tour of impoverished sites in July 1999, along with Appalachia, Watts, the Mississippi Delta, and the Oglala Sioux reservation in Pine Ridge, South Dakota. As the White House stated, it is "a classic example of a fast-growing region where some residents are being left behind" (Barker, 1999:A1).

This situation of poverty in the midst of plenty contextualizes our research. For example, the youths and adults we interviewed lamented that the schools in their communities are in terrible states of disrepair. Yet, the state legislature was unwilling to commit resources to poor school districts until the courts intervened, ordering development of a new system for school funding. Similarly, respondents spoke of the need for better public housing, basic city services such as more streetlights and paved roads, and accessible public transportation. Just a mile away from their poverty-stricken neighborhoods, they can see the beautiful new housing developments being built on scenic South Mountain to the south, and the new ballpark to the north, constructed in part out of state and local funds. As a consequence, many residents of South Phoenix barrios feel isolated and alienated, excluded from the boom that surrounds their community. As we will demonstrate, some community members blame gangs for businesses not coming into the barrios. Other residents blame the city for not investing in the barrios, recognizing that economic, educational, and recreational resources might entice businesses *and* give young people something to do besides hang out in gangs. These sometimes divergent perspectives contribute further to tensions within the community. Yet, it is interesting to note that although gangs in other cities have become entrepreneurial, selling drugs as a way for the gang to make money (e.g., Jankowski, 1991; Padilla, 1993), Chicano gangs in Phoenix have not organized around the drug industry. That is not to say that gang members do not use or sell drugs—many do, but the gangs themselves are not organized around drug sales.

A second key factor that distinguishes our study from earlier work on Chicano gangs in Chicago, Milwaukee, and other large cities aside from Los Angeles is Phoenix's proximity to the Mexican border. This factor has a dual effect, contributing both to cultural replenishment and to tensions between Chicanos and Mexican immigrants and migrants. Many of the adults we interviewed commented that the Mexican culture flourishes in Phoenix, although it has been heavily commercialized. Yet, conflicts also develop because many Chicanos and Chicanas are embarrassed by the apparent provincialism of immigrants from rural Mexico and angered that their willingness to work for low wages depresses pay scales for all Latinos. Rivalry between Chicanos and Mexicanos also plays out among the youths, with Chicano/a and Mexicano/a gangs often fighting one another.

Finally, as our interview data demonstrate, the degree of traditionalism and immigration status are also key elements in explaining men's and women's views about gangs and, perhaps more importantly, their abilities to tap parochial and public resources.

The prominence of the Chicano and Mexicano population in Phoenix is a related factor that distinguishes Phoenix from other major sites for gang research. Chicago and Los Angeles, for example, have large African-American and Asian/Asian-American populations. Moreover, in Chicago, the Latino population is divided between Puerto Ricans and Chicanos. In Phoenix, however, the Chicano and Mexicano population is the single largest racial/ethnic minority group, far larger than the African-American, Asian-American, or American Indian populations. This fact, we suggest, alters the urban dynamics considerably. For instance, in Arizona (and California, which has a larger number of immigrants), fierce political attacks on immigrants have occurred, aimed primarily at Latinos (e.g., English Only, Proposition 187). Yet, these attacks were ultimately foiled because the Latino population and supporters had sufficient political clout at the state level and in the courts. Nevertheless, this clout does not extend to poor Latino neighborhoods or individuals; on the contrary, barrio residents seem to have very little ability to challenge economic and political decisions unless a higher court intervenes on their behalf, as was seen in the school-funding situation. We suspect that the relative deprivation felt by individual Latinos is probably aggravated because only one major racial/ethnic minority exists, and thus the comparisons between their economic plight and that of wealthier Whites becomes especially stark.

DATA AND METHODS: OUR YOUTH AND ADULT SAMPLES

If we are to understand the complexities of gang life, it is important that diverse voices and perspectives are heard. Accordingly, we interviewed teenagers involved in gangs and adults active in neighborhood associations or working with local teenagers. Snowball sampling was used to obtain both samples. For the youths, we began with a sample of teenagers on parole and who were participating in a partnership project between our university and the juvenile correctional system. For the adults, we began with a listing of youth services providers and neighborhood association leaders. At the conclusion of each interview, we asked the respondent for names of others whom we might interview to gain a full picture of gang life and of gang and community relations. Given the small samples and our dual focus on youths' and adults' perceptions of gangs and the larger community, this study must be considered exploratory.

Semistructured interviews lasted from 45 minutes to about 2 hours. The youths were interviewed in the summer and fall of 1995, and the adults in the summer of 1995. All of the interviews were taped and transcribed. Thematic content analysis was conducted to explore major themes in the data, as described in later sections (Lofland and Lofland, 1995).

Consistent with our theoretical interest in exploring multiple standpoints, we used an insider-outsider approach in our interviews. This strategy enhances validity and encourages reciprocity between researchers and the people asked to share their lives and thoughts (Baca Zinn, 1975; Frankenburg, 1993; Zavella, 1996). Although ideally both authors would have interviewed the youths and the adults, we recognized that the youths would be very reluctant to talk frankly with the first author, a White, middle-class, middle-aged female professor, seeing her as too removed from their lives. Based on prior experiences in the field, however, we expected that they would be very willing to talk with the second author, a Chicano graduate student in his mid-twenties. Similarly, we expected that the adults might not be willing to carve out much time from their schedules to talk with a graduate student but would be willing to discuss their work with a university professor. Accordingly, we employed two strategies. First, we wanted to situate ourselves to minimize social distances along racial/ethnic, educational, and professional lines, which meant that the first author interviewed the adults and the second author interviewed the youths. Second, we were cognizant of and worked with our insider-outsider statuses, discussing our findings as we went along and offering one another insights and suggestions.

Interviews were conducted with 33 self-identified current or former gang members: 24 males and 9 females. They ranged between 14 and 18 years of age, although they were between 9 and 15 when they joined their gangs. Thus, our focus was on the youths, not the older *veteranos*. Five of the youths were born in Mexico; the other 28 are of Mexican or mixed descent but were born in the United States.[2] Interviews took place in restaurants, their homes, the neighborhood, an alternative school for juvenile parolees, and locked institutions. The second author had already worked with some of the youths and their friends for more than a year in a related ethnographic project and was able to quickly establish rapport with them. Another factor facilitating both rapport and validity was his knowledge of Spanish and of *calo* (Chicano gang slang); otherwise, certain phrases might have been misinterpreted (Marin, 1991).

Very few of the youths had managed to avoid entanglement with the juvenile justice system, and most of them were under parole or probation supervision or incarcerated at the time of the interviews. Respondents were given a choice of receiving $10 or lunch at a restaurant of their choice. For the 12 incarcerated youths, $10 was placed in their account. Youths were asked to discuss their relationships with their families and friends, their own involvement with the gang, and their perceptions of gang life. Some bias could result from respondents' concerns that their comments might be relayed to their parole officers or caseworkers. They might exaggerate the extent to which they are easing out of gang activities and other changes in their lives that caseworkers would view positively. To reduce this risk, we made every effort to convince them that the interviews were confidential and that the transcripts would be anonymous.

Interviews were also conducted with 20 adults. They included youth service providers and social workers active in the Chicano/a and Mexicano/a communities, neighborhood association leaders and other neighborhood activists, city neighborhood services representatives from elected neighborhoods, a parish priest, a paid activist from Mothers Against Gangs, and a representative of the Phoenix Police Department. Seven of the adults self-identify as Chicano or Chicana, four as African American, two as Puerto Rican, four as White, one as Hispanic, and one as mixed Hispanic-African American. Our final respondent was born in Mexico. All but one of the adults spoke at least some Spanish. Two interviews were conducted solely in Spanish; in others, the conversations wove between languages. Most of the interviews were conducted in the respondents' offices, although one took place in a cemetery, next to the grave where the respondent's son was buried.

None of the adults saw the South Phoenix community as simply a site where they worked. Ten of the adults grew up in South Phoenix. Some still reside there; others have moved across town but continue to work with neighborhood youths and visit family and friends in the community. Most of those adults who have moved now live in more affluent areas, but a few made economically lateral moves to other, equally depressed neighborhoods. For example, five of the adult respondents live on the Westside, a largely African-American area bordering South Phoenix. Eleven of the respondents lived in South Phoenix when we interviewed them.

All of the adult respondents living in South Phoenix or Westside see the very real possibility of death for their children, as well as for their nieces, nephews, and neighbors. This possibility had become a reality for three of the respondents, whose children had died in gang-related incidents in recent years. The three children are buried near one another, in the same section of a local cemetery. The adults had been active in neighborhood affairs before their children's deaths and continue this work, sometimes being paid for it and sometimes as volunteers. Thus, the issues of gangs and violence touched their lives in special ways.

In addition to offering their own impressions, the adults were asked for their expert opinions about how others in the community perceived gangs and efforts to control gang-related crime within the barrio. They were asked to consider variation within the community along lines of gender, age, number of generations the family had lived in the United States, and nationality. Thus, the adult respondents were also both insiders and outsiders, speaking in their own voices in some instances, and for other adults in the neighborhoods where they lived and worked at other times. These multiple standpoints allowed us to explore the intersection of race, class, and gender within the community, and then to take the analysis a step further to tease out the ways in which acculturation and traditionalism cross-cut nationality and age in gendered ways.

Finally, we should note that the validity of qualitative research rests on the researchers' abilities to accurately and fully understand the phenomena under study. Although it is always possible that individuals have lied in telling their stories, we are confident that the 53 interviews we conducted, in combination with the ethnographic research and interviews with juvenile justice officials in the larger study of which this is a part, have afforded us a reasonably nuanced understanding of the relationship between gang youths and their communities. Respondents present a multitude of perspectives on this relationship. Some respondents reinforce popular images of gangs as terrible and support police efforts to rid the neighborhoods of organized gang activity. Other respondents tell what Ewick and Silbey (1995) have called more "subversive" tales about police brutality, politicians ignoring poor parts of town, and lack of resources. Among and within these voices lies a complex set of experiences, fears, and hopes.

THEORETICAL FRAMEWORK: SYSTEMIC APPROACH TO NEIGHBORHOOD AND GANG DYNAMICS

Most gang research in the United States has been grounded in social disorganization theory, subcultural theories, or, most recently, economic marginalization theories derived from Wilson's (1987) work on the underclass. Bursik and Grasmick (1993a) offer a theoretical framework that combines key elements of Shaw and McKay's (1942) social disorganization theory with recent work on gangs in underclass communities. The central problem with social disorganization theory for gang research, they suggest, is that it overemphasizes family dynamics, focusing on individualized resources and constraints to the exclusion of larger structural concerns. Accordingly, social disorganization approaches cannot adequately account for ongoing patterns of gang behavior in stable neighborhoods where families may live in the same houses or on the same block for many years, often spanning several generations. The gangs in these neighborhoods are often multigenerational, with several members of the extended family belonging to the gang in each generation.

Although initially subcultural theories became popular because of the inability of traditional social disorganization approaches to explain these multigenerational gangs, Moore (1978, 1985, 1991, 1998), Vigil (1988), Hagedorn (1991, 1998), and Sullivan (1989), among others, have offered an alternative explanation that refocuses attention at structural factors, including, especially, the economic marginalization of underclass communities. These scholars point to the crucial importance of whether, and to what extent, residents of poor but stable neighborhoods have access to public resources. Bursik and Grasmick (1993a) weave these concerns into a larger, more encompassing framework that examines access to private, public, and parochial resources. Drawing from Hunter's (1985) typology of local community social control, they suggest that these three dimensions operate simultaneously and that gang activity is most likely to emerge "in areas in which the networks of parochial and public control cannot effectively provide services to the neighborhood" (Bursik and Grasmick, 1993a:141).

Private social control refers to the influences and actions of family and close friends; which could be the nuclear family, the extended family, or the interwoven networks of family and friends that characterize stable barrio communities. Through the family's actions supporting or disdaining particular behaviors, social control is exerted. Parochial social control reflects "the effects of the broader local interpersonal network and the interlocking of local institutions, such as stores, schools, churches and voluntary organizations" (Bursik and Grasmick, 1993a:17). Control is exerted through residents supervising activities within the neighborhood and the integration of local institutions into many aspects of everyday life. Individuals and neighborhoods will vary in the extent to which they can harness parochial forms of social control. For example, monolingual Spanish-speaking parents may encounter difficulties and be easily intimidated when they try to communicate with their children's teachers or school authorities. Public social control, in turn, focuses "on the ability of the community to secure public goods and services that are allocated by agencies located outside the neighborhood" (Bursik and Grasmick, 1993a:17). As Moore and Hagedorn have noted most pointedly, poor barrio communities often do not have access to or alliances with key urban institutions. For instance, although many barrio residents must interact regularly with health care, education, welfare, criminal justice, and immigration authorities, they do so from a position of little or no individual or institutional power. The absence of people who might serve as power brokers, interceding between community residents and institutional authorities, means that residents of economically marginal communities cannot effectively use public systemic control. One example that surfaced often in our interviews was access to police. Although many residents perceived the police to be omnipresent, the same residents complained that the police did not respond quickly when they called for help.

Combining these three forms of social control into a fully systemic model enables a more complete understanding of gang-community dynamics. Following Bursik and Grasmick (1993a), we apply this model to Chicano/a and Mexicano/a gangs in Phoenix. We draw from interviews with gang youths and with adults active in the communities to explore how they perceive gang-neighborhood dynamics. One of the unique contributions of our research to this theoretical agenda is our recognition that access to parochial and public resources is very much gendered. Moreover, as we shall show, recent immigrants and parents with more traditional Mexicano beliefs and values may be more intimidated by key societal institutions and by their children. Thus, we suggest that gender and traditionalism cross-cut age, educational level, and income to influence the extent to which individual parents and neighborhoods can draw on private, parochial, and public social control.

The Phoenix Economy and Public Social Control In Latino/a Communities

Most of the research on gangs that draws from political economic and community ecology perspectives has been conducted in cities that have experienced severe economic decline (e.g., Anderson, 1990; Decker and Van Winkle, 1996; Fagan, 1996; Hagedorn, 1998; Horowitz, 1987; Spergel, 1986; Sullivan, 1989). Chicago, St. Louis, and Milwaukee, for example, all faced structural dislocations with the movement of factories out of central cities. The political, social, and economic plight of poor blacks in these urban ghettos led to Wilson's (1987) depiction of them as the "underclass." We draw from this theoretical and empirical body of research to explore gang-community dynamics in a very different context, that of a pocket of poverty within spectacular economic growth. From 1993 to 1998, Arizona had the nation's second highest job growth rate, and the Phoenix area ranked first in the nation among the 22 largest metropolitan areas, with a 5.8% job growth rate in 1997–1998. The years 1993–1997 were the strongest five-year period of job growth in Arizona history, with more than 400,000 private-sector jobs created during these years. Unemployment rates in Arizona are consistently among the lowest in the nation, and in the 1990s they were at their lowest levels since the early 1970s. By September, 1998, unemployment in metropolitan Phoenix had dropped to 2.9% (Arizona Economic Development Update, 1998; Arizona Department of Economic Security, 1998).

In the midst of this economic boom sits South Phoenix. The unemployment rate for 18 census tracts in the South Phoenix area in 1990 was 13.34, almost triple the unemployment rate of 5.3 for Arizona and 5.6 for the United States (U.S. Council of Economic Advisors, 1998), and quadruple that of the rest of metropolitan Phoenix. Elementary schools in the inner city are woefully underfunded. In 1998, the Arizona Supreme Court finally intervened, declaring Arizona's system of school funding to be unconstitutional. The high school serving South Phoenix had a 51.9% graduation rate in 1994 (White, 1995:Appendix A). Broken down by race/ethnicity, 66% of the White youths attending this high school graduated, compared with 48% of the Latino students (White, 1995:Appendix D).

Between 1980 and 1990, the percentage of the county's children living in poverty increased from 12.9% to 17.5%, rising to 19.1% in 1993 (Morrison Institute for Public Policy, 1994:69). In 1993, 20.7% of the families in the county received food stamps, up from 12.7% in 1990. Although only

26% of the county's juvenile population was Latino/a, 40% of the children in Aid to Families with Dependent Children in 1993 were Latino (Morrison Institute for Public Policy, 1994:69, 73), indicating that Latino youths participate in poverty programs at about double their population rate. Also, although 24% of the children 19 years or younger in the state were enrolled in its indigent health care program (up from 19.1% in 1991), 43% of the children enrolled in the program were Latino (Morrison Institute for Public Policy, 1994:69, 73). Finally, Latinos composed 46% of the firearm-related deaths of youths aged 0–19 years, and 32% of juvenile arrests (aged 8–17 years). These statistics paint a bleak picture for Latinos and Latinas in the Phoenix metropolitan area, particularly in South Phoenix. The pockets of poverty appear especially stark, given the strong economic indicators for the state and for the city as a whole.

Like the neighborhoods Hagedorn (1998, 1991) studied in Milwaukee, South Phoenix is a "checkerboard" of stable working-class families living next door to crack houses and abject poverty. Some houses are nicely maintained with fresh paint and flowers growing in the gardens, but others are shacks lacking such basic services as electricity and running water. Air conditioning is unusual, although temperatures in the summer regularly rise above 110 degrees Fahrenheit. The barrio receives few municipal resources. Public transportation is practically nonexistent, and roads are poorly maintained. Few streetlights illuminate the darkness at night, lending an eeriness to the neighborhood that exacerbates residents' fears of crime.

The war on drugs waged across the nation can be felt here as well. Grandparents and aunts are often left raising children when their parents are incarcerated for drug offenses, or too strung out to care for their children (see further Donziger, 1996; Lusane, 1991; Mann and Zatz, 1998; Miller, 1996). Drugs are commonplace, especially marijuana, glue, and paint, and drug houses appear to be doing a thriving business.

Yet, the blight cannot be blamed solely on drugs and the drug business. Few economic resources have been invested in the community. No factories or other large businesses are located in the area. Convenience stores and liquor stores abound, but residents must go elsewhere if they want to shop at major chain grocery stores or retail outlets. No shopping malls, movie theaters, or skating rinks are nearby, leaving the streets as the only viable place for teens to hang out.

Thus, in the midst of a remarkable economic boom caused by the surge in the computer microprocessor industry and tourism, residents of South Phoenix have been excluded, marginalized, and isolated. They have been excluded from participation in the mainstream labor market because they lack the necessary training and skills for the jobs that do exist and because public transportation is woefully inadequate; marginalized politically because they have little clout and fewer resources that might make politicians listen to them; and isolated socially because of cultural and linguistic barriers (see, similarly, Moore, 1998:7). As we have noted, poverty and unemployment are rampant in South Phoenix, schools are under-funded, and graduation rates for Latino/a students are horrid. Residents have minimal access to political and economic power brokers, and little exists for young people to do except hang out on the streets. In this context, Bursik and Grasmick's (1993a, b) attention to the possibilities and difficulties of parochial and public social control contributes substantially to our understanding of gang-community dynamics (see, similarly, Hagedorn, 1998; Spergel, 1986).

ADULT PERSPECTIVES ON GANGS AND THE COMMUNITY

The adults expressed a wide range of views, from seeing gangs as a normal part of adolescence to viewing them as social parasites that must be routed from the neighborhoods. This contrast is not surprising, given the heterogeneity of life experiences among barrio residents. Jankowski (1991), Moore (1991), Hagedorn (1998), Decker and Van Winkle (1996), Sullivan (1989), Padilla (1993), and Venkatesh (1996) also report contradictory or ambivalent stances toward gangs in the communities they studied. In the discussion that follows, we attempt to tease out these different perspectives and to account for some of the divergent opinions.

Gangs, the Neighborhood, and the Local Economy

According to a neighborhood specialist for the city, the major problems that surfaced in a survey of South Phoenix residents were crime, homes and landscaping not being well maintained, graffiti, and a shortage of streetlights, followed by the lack of recreational opportunities for young people. Similarly, community leaders repeatedly voiced the fear that graffiti, combined with the threat of drugs and violence, contributes to urban decay by making the neighborhood less attractive to businesses.[3] Yet, gang activity is only one factor affecting the local economy and can as easily be seen as an outcome of economic dislocation as its cause. The weak linkages to centers of economic and political power, in turn, reduce residents' abilities to exercise public systemic control very effectively (Bursik and Grasmick, 1993a:146; Moore, 1985; Moore and Pinderhughes, 1993). It is in precisely such contexts that Bursik and Grasmick suggest gang activity is most likely to develop.

One of the most important and visible forms of public social control is the police. Although a substantial portion of the community is very willing to work with local police in at least some limited ways to eradicate gangs and crime, another portion sees the police, courts, and similar institutions as unable or unwilling to adequately protect them. Tensions between Latino community members and the police have historically been high, the result of years of institutionalized racism in police and court processing (Escobar, 1999; Mirandé, 1987; National Minority Advisory Council on

Criminal Justice, 1980; U.S. Commission on Civil Rights, 1970; Vigil, 1988). Allegations of police use of excessive force often lie at the heart of these strained relations. In Phoenix, community anger with the police has centered around the violent deaths of three young men: Rudy Buchanan, Jr., Edward Mallet, and Julio Valerio. Buchanan was African American and Latino. A member of the Crips gang who had reputedly threatened that he was going to kill a police officer, Buchanan was shot at 89 times in January of 1995, with 30 bullets entering his body. His family was awarded $570,000 in a settlement with the City of Phoenix in March 1998. Edward Mallet was a 25-year-old African-American double amputee who died in 1994 after being placed in a neck hold by police officers. In March 1998, a jury awarded Mallet's parents $45 million, finding that the police used excessive force that resulted in his death. The city later settled with Mallet's family, paying about $5 million. Finally, 16-year-old Julio Valerio's case is still pending. He was holding a butcher knife when he was pepper sprayed and then shot at 25 times in 1996 by police (Fiscus and Leonard, 1999).

Access to public social control goes beyond policing to encompass the range of agencies and actors who can provide public goods and services. The South Phoenix community did not perceive itself as well situated with regard to such access. Respondents criticized state and local politicians and other city officials for reducing the community's resource base and for placing it low on the priority list for revitalization, and businesses for taking money from the community but not investing in it. Finally, 19 of the 20 adults condemned sensationalist and biased reporting by the television and print media, particularly, exaggerated reports of gang violence that create the impression that violence is rampant in South Phoenix. Many of the adult respondents pointed out that much of the violence occurs north of the Salt River bed, in what is *not* formally South Phoenix. Nevertheless, South Phoenix continues to bear the stigma of a violent part of town, making it less attractive to businesses that might otherwise relocate there. This reputation, in turn, contributes further to the economic devastation of the community. A local resident and neighborhood activist whose son died in a gang-related shooting described the contradiction.

> It's a chicken and egg thing. What do we need first? Jobs and businesses that really care, or to clean up our community of drugs and gangs? How do we do this without jobs and educational opportunities?

Some neighborhood residents work directly with the youths to curtail gang activities. Exercising both private and parochial social control, some residents tutor neighborhood teens with their studies and help them to find jobs; other residents work with voluntary organizations and local churches, organizing block watches to prevent violence, burglaries, graffiti, and drug sales in the neighborhood. One youth service provider criticized block watches, however, for excluding gang members. She argued that neighborhood organizations would be far more effective if they brought the youths in, saying, "What are you going to do?" rather than making them feel like outcasts with little stake in the community. In her words:

> The community refuses—*will not*—include them in organizing block watches [and] neighborhood associations for the betterment of the community. Instead, the strategy is to attack them, so gang kids become meaner, more defensive. They claim ownership of the community, and we need to make them a part of it, and instead they're pushed off. Gangs are defined as the enemy, not as part of the community. We need to say to kids, "Hey, we need you to help with the block watch. What's your part going to be?" They could clean up graffiti, whatever.

In the past, our respondents noted, "Mexican gangs were tied closely to the community. This has changed." Today, gangs "rob people of their sense of security. They barricade themselves in their homes because they feel so vulnerable." Another adult respondent told us:

> If a gang is neighborhood based, they protect their neighborhoods and one another, and to the extent they can, their families and the families of other gang members. But that doesn't always work.

These quotes reinforce one of the central contradictions inherent in neighborhood gangs. The youths see themselves as protectors of their communities and the police as abusive interlopers, regardless of whether this imagery appears exaggerated to outsiders. The protection gangs offer may be reduced today to simply making sure that competing gangs do not gain a foothold in the neighborhood, but the youths are adamant that protection of the community is still one of their primary responsibilities. In this sense, they are an integral component of parochial social control. Nevertheless, gangs also wreak havoc in their communities, both by their actions and by the lure they present to rival gangs. In particular, neighborhood residents are at greater risk of injury today than they were a generation ago because of the increase in drive-by shootings. A youth service provider expressed the views of many adults:

> A lot of innocent people get hurt in drive-bys. They're just there in the wrong place at the wrong time and get killed or shot when they don't have anything to do with the problem.

Similarly, a Chicano social worker commented,

> Neighbors feel they can't go out at night, can't sit on the porch. There's violence and crime. Many gang members may hang out in the neighborhood and not be involved in violence, but they're targets. Somebody will drive by and verbally abuse them, throw things in their yard, or shoot them.

Thus, two different, though interrelated, perspectives surface within the community. Some residents blame the gangs, seeing "the stigma of having gang problems" as contributing to businesses and middle-class families leaving the neighborhood. Other residents focus on the city's and the media's willingness to ignore economic problems in parts of town where poor people of color live. When city officials and reporters do pay attention to the area, they focus only on the negative aspects of life there without doing much to improve the infrastructure. To better understand these varied perspectives, we looked for structural patterns in the data. As we will demonstrate, much of the variation can be explained by gender, age, number of generations in the United States, educational level, traditionalism, and the extent to which the person's family is gang identified.

The Men's Voices

We asked all of the adult respondents to tell us not only their own opinions about the relationships among gang kids, their families, and the community, but also how they thought other adults in the community perceived these issues. We expected men and women to differ somewhat in their views, consistent with the extant literature on fear of crime and neighborhood-based crime control efforts (Bursik and Grasmick, 1993a:91; Madriz, 1997; Skogan and Maxfield, 1981). Considering first how men in South Phoenix viewed gangs, the neighborhood activists and service providers saw men's opinions as determined primarily by whether they are gang identified. For example, one woman observed:

> Fathers don't have a big problem with gangs. They were involved in one way or another when they were younger. They always had a homie-type camaraderie.

Other respondents tied acceptance of gangs to prison life, and pointed to the difficulty of private, familial social control of youths with incarcerated parents. From this perspective,

> [some men] are accepting of [gangs] and are in prison gangs themselves. We have a gang problem because the adult male population is in prison, so the kids are in street gangs.

Regardless of whether they ever formally joined gangs themselves, adults whose families belong to multigenerational gangs appear to be more accepting of their children's involvement in them, may gain prestige from their children's acts, and see the gang as a barrio institution through which cultural norms of personal and family honor are played out. This finding is consistent with similar research in other cities (Harris, 1994; Horowitz, 1983; Horowitz and Schwartz, 1974; Moore, 1978, 1991; Padilla, 1993; Vigil, 1988). A neighborhood specialist for the city said,

> It's multigenerational. The grandfather may have been in a gang. Grandfathers of 40 could still have ties with the gang. You could have a great-grandfather with ties to old gangs!

As they get older, the men ease out of gang life. Yet, as a Latina director of a youth service center commented,

> The oldsters, old gangsters, sit back and watch what's happening. They are very aware. They are learning they have to pull away if they want to live, but those are strong friendships that last forever.

An African-American male police officer expressed a similar opinion:

> In areas with multi-generational gangs, it is difficult for older males to understand why society comes down so hard on the young ones. The degree of criminal activity has not hit them upside the head until they lose a loved one to a shooting. . . . If the men get a reality slap, they see the differences over time. Or they'll say to the kids, "Why don't you have a gang like we had? We had a good gang."

Yet, some differences of opinion surface among the men. The neighborhood specialist quoted above continued,

> Some men view the gangs with disdain, seeing them as a blight on the community and a threat to community life, and others feel it provides a sense of fraternity, an opportunity to become involved with others who think and act like they'd like to; it provides them with an outlet.

An African-American woman working closely with neighborhood residents drew similar distinctions:

> Some of them are from multigenerational gang families. The parents are hardcore members supportive of the life, and they're raising their kids in it. Others are very hardcore in opposition to it, saying to make prisons tougher. They are harder, more judgmental, saying, "if you do the crime, do the time." . . . They say, "I'm gonna stop it by buying a .45 and blowing away the first motherfucker who comes in my door."

Thus, for some adult men in the community, gangs are perfectly normal, acceptable parts of life. They take pride in their children following in their footsteps. Other adult men abhor today's gangs. Key factors accounting for these differences of opinion include the extent to which the men hold traditional Mexican values, the length of time they have spent in the United States, and educational achievements. A man born in South Phoenix, still living in the area and working with local teens both as a volunteer and in his job as a probation officer, sees these factors as intertwined.

> The first generation, the traditionalists, see the second generation as lazy, as not pursuing the education and opportunities they are seeking for their children. . . . They try to prevent their children from getting involved. . . . The Chicanos who are traditional and have held ground (in the neighborhood) don't see the gangs as so much of a threat. They have raised their children to be successful. They can see the other folks and say, "Hey, there's a problem there and I wish they'd take care of it!" . . . Of those in the second generation of gangs, the dads have limited educations. They take care of things physically, instead of rationally. They are starting to be supportive of changing the system, though, because they are seeing too much violence. For the second

generation, bicultural men, and I count myself as one, success depends on how much education they have.

According to the adults we interviewed, men born in Mexico generally hold the most traditional values and tend to disapprove of the gang life. Yet, they are stymied by their inability to control their children or grandchildren, and if public resources exist that they might employ to better control the youths, these immigrant men do not know how to access them. They are also uncomfortable requesting help from parish priests, school teachers, or social workers. The women, as we shall see, are somewhat more willing to reach out for these parochial forms of social control.

A middle-aged woman directing a neighborhood association providing educational and employment-related services and training for youths noted, "Grandfathers disapprove, see them as lazy and shiftless." A Puerto Rican social worker stated similarly:

> A grandfather will say, "I worked in the fields, why can't you?" Kids killing one another is not readily understood by the more traditional older generation.

Yet, another man working closely with boys in the neighborhood said:

> For the *abuelos* (grandfathers), they have a firm grasp of life, they've lived through many tragedies so they appreciate life and the foolish wasting of it in gangs.

Our data indicate that substantial changes have occurred over time in the perceived extent to which gangs protected the larger community, the dangers to gang members and others in the community posed by today's more lethal weapons, and, generally, the respect with which gang members were and are held by others in the community. We were told,

> The general consensus is gangs are negative. This is especially from grandparents who are used to gangs, from the Zoot Suits. They were respected, they were not a danger to the community. They say, "I don't understand these punks, why are they doing these things, not taking care of us, of the neighbors. They talk all the time about being part of the neighborhood but they don't take care of us."

> [What about the fathers?]

> When I was a kid we had gangs, but we never used guns. We used chains. When we had a problem and fought, it was one-on-one, or a gang on a gang, but never three, five, six to one. That sounds cowardly to them [the fathers]. This generation gap is a problem. The kids say, "Your way wasn't better, it didn't work. I have more money than you, so how can you tell me it's not right, that your way is better?" This is a big issue. They make money! And they [fathers] can't make money in society.

Another local social worker also reminisced about the "old days" when he was involved in gangs:

> In the past, we weren't out to kill each other. Maybe there'd be fist fights or knives, but we weren't out to kill each other. Guns and drugs are the problem, and they're easily bought on the streets.

Thus, educational level, age, and the recency of their family's immigration to the United States structure barrio men's views about gangs and the range of resources they see as available to them. Grandfathers and fathers who immigrated to the United States may be leery of public forms of social control, such as the police and the juvenile justice system, and more hesitant than their wives to call on the Catholic Church for aid. They rely most heavily on the extended family to control youths, often unsuccessfully. In contrast, men raised in the gang life and still tied to it are more accepting of their children's involvement. Finally, the men raised in the barrio but now successful in local businesses and social services (e.g., probation, clinical psychology) have greater access to political and economic brokers in the metropolitan area and, perhaps for this reason, are more willing to rely on public as well as parochial and private forms of social control. Our data suggest that less variation exists within women's perspectives, with the key distinguishing factor being whether they were raised in a traditional Mexican family, either in the United States or in Mexico.

The Women's Voices

The consensus among our adult respondents was that most women disapprove of gangs. A Puerto Rican male working with families of gang members had the impression that "nine out of ten mothers despise gangs." Some of the women were members themselves when they were younger and may remain at least peripherally involved, but as they become mothers many grow increasingly fearful that their children could die in a gang-related shooting.

Gendered cultural expectations of child-rearing responsibilities appear to have contributed to mothers becoming more active than fathers in opposing gang activities. Also, many of the barrio's adult men are incarcerated, or for other reasons do not interact much with their children. Neighborhood leaders, both male and female, commented that it is primarily the women who come forward to work with them. One neighborhood activist said:

> [The women] are pretty fed up with it . . . 60% of those who come to community meetings are female. They are very vocal, fed up, afraid to lose their children. Some have already lost their children, or their nephews and nieces, at the hands of guns. They want to bring the neighborhood back under control.

Some of these mothers take a very strong line and "won't let daughters date boys who look like cholos." Neighborhood women are also well represented at funerals. A parish priest with the dubious honor of burying the neighborhood's children told us, "At wakes you will see 400 kids, 50 mothers, and maybe 10 fathers." Mothers Against Gangs, a grassroots organization begun by a mother after her 16-year-old son died in a gang shooting, is a prime example of women organizing to reduce gang violence. Again, we see a link between private and parochial forms of social control. When parents and grandparents are not able to control the youths, they often turn to community organizations, such as Mothers Against Gangs (see, similarly, Fremon, 1995). Moreover, we see that these examples of private and parochial social control are very much gendered.

Mothers and grandmothers raised with traditional values were less likely to be out on the streets and so did not themselves live the gang life. These traditional women often do not know what to do about their children's involvement with gangs. As an activist knowledgeable about gangs said of the mothers who moved here from Mexico,

> [They] feel helpless. It's something new for them. Many of them have problems with language. The kids speak English better than they [the mothers] do and better than they speak Spanish, so the parents can't communicate with the kids. It's not like in Mexico, where the *abuelos* can say and do things. Here, it depends on the parents.

Similarly, a Chicano social worker stated that for mothers,

> The general feeling is powerlessness. They have to care for them and love them and wish they weren't involved. They may feel guilty. It must be their fault, what did they do wrong. . . . It is *very* painful if the girls are in the gangs.

The sense of individual, rather than societal, responsibility for gang violence was stressed by many of our respondents. Specifically, they suggested that young mothers often have inadequate parenting skills. A probation officer raised in the barrio commented:

> These kids intimidated their parents way before this. The hardline mothers and grandmothers who really push their kids to stay out [of gangs] are winning the battle. Those who are afraid, and they're mostly the 18–20 year olds, are afraid because they didn't put their foot down enough. It comes down to parenting skills, taking a hard line.

Social workers and neighborhood activists suggest that some mothers are unwilling to believe that their children are involved in gangs, even when signs are all around them. We were told that traditional women, in particular,

> [See gangs as] a danger to the family unit. They don't want their kids involved in it, are very protective. But they also may have blinders when it comes to their own kids, saying, "My kid isn't into that" when he is.

A South Phoenix parish priest related a story about a mother who wanted her son to be buried in a red shirt and the pallbearers to wear red, claiming it was always her son's favorite color. Another mother insisted that her son was not involved with gangs, until the priest turned to the young man and asked him to explain the significance of his red shoelaces to his mother.

In conclusion, then, our data suggest that whether and when adults rely on private, parochial, or public forms of social control depends on their access to economic and political resources and their position within the family and neighborhood power structures. One of our contributions to this literature is to show that this access may also be gendered, with women evidencing more indicators of powerlessness, such as not speaking English, and less experience dealing with businesses, courts, and the like. These women are most likely to advocate for a mix of parochial and public social control. They fear for their children's lives, but they tend to be among the most intimidated by their sons and daughters. Many of these women have organized within their communities and work with the police to at least a limited extent, hoping that these efforts will help to keep their children alive. This combination of private, parochial, and public social control is the premise of groups such as Mothers Against Gangs. In contrast, women who were in gangs as teenagers and who maintained that identity are generally the most accepting, and perhaps the least fearful, of gang violence and the least willing to let the police into their communities. Even these women, however, express fears of losing their children to gang violence and may draw on parochial forms of social control within the community.

The perceptions held by adult service providers and residents may be plagued by faulty, perhaps romanticized, recollections of what gangs were like in earlier generations. Also, many of the adults we interviewed had vested interests in the gang problem. Reliance solely on their perceptions ignores how young people see their own lives and the relationship between their gangs and other community members. Consistent with our emphasis on multiple standpoints, we turn now to the thoughts and concerns of the youths.

YOUTH PERSPECTIVES ON GANGS AND THE COMMUNITY

Historically, gangs have been important neighborhood institutions offering disenchanted, disadvantaged youths a means of coping with the isolation, alienation, and poverty they experience every day (Decker and Van Winkle, 1996; Hagedorn, 1991, 1998; Horowitz, 1983; Jackson, 1991; Joe and Chesney-Lind, 1995; Moore, 1978, 1985, 1991; Padilla, 1993; Sullivan, 1989; Vigil, 1988). Yet, gangs are dynamic, responding to transformations in the larger social order. Sometimes, changes in the social and economic structures also cause cracks in what we call the gang-family-barrio equality. It is not so unusual today to find families living in two different neighborhoods and, thus, often participating in two or more gangs. When this situation occurs, fissures appear in the cement bonding the community's social structure together.

Gangs as Neighborhood Institutions

Regardless of what other neighborhood residents may think of them, the youths identify strongly with their neighborhoods, consider themselves to be integral parts of their barrios, and view their gangs as neighborhood institutions. They see themselves as protectors of their neighborhoods, at least against intrusion by rival gangs. A few youths take pride in their care of elderly residents. However, most youths acknowledge that they do not contribute much to their neighborhoods, excluding community service stipulated as part of their probation or parole agreements.[4] For example, one youth stated:

> We spray paint the walls and stuff like that, stealing cars, shooting people when we do drive-bys and stuff like that.

Moreover, some youths recognize that innocent bystanders are occasionally shot in drive-bys or other revenge killings.

> People are getting smoked everyday and you don't even hear about it on the news, only if it is crazy and shit.

Chicano/a gangs often take the name of their barrio as their gang name. With few exceptions, the youths must live in the neighborhood and be of Mexican origin to become a member of the neighborhood gang.[5] These membership requirements hold whether the youth is "born into" the gang or "jumped" in. Some, particularly the young women, are simply "born" into the gang because they live in the neighborhood. They do not need any more formal initiation rites: It is their neighborhood, so it is their gang. If they want to be taken seriously as a gang member, though, being "born" in is not enough. The youths—male and female—must endure a serious beating by a group of their homeboys or homegirls (Portillos, 1999).

Beyond feeling ties to the physical boundaries of the barrio, the youths feel strong emotional ties because neighbors are often family members. If we contextualize the term "family" more broadly to include the nuclear family, the extended family, and the fictive family (*compadres* and *comadres*), gang-family ties become even stronger. All of the youths in our sample claimed that at least one other family member was involved in gangs. For example, a youth informed us:

> I got two aunts that were in a gang, my dad was in a gang, my grandpa was in a gang, and I got a lot of cousins in gangs. Most of them are in my barrio but some of them aren't.

Siblings, cousins, and family friends so close as to be considered cousins are frequently members of the same gang, resulting in what often appears to be a gang-family-barrio equality. Although these overlapping social relationships have characterized Chicano/a gangs in the past (Moore, 1991; Vigil, 1988; Zatz, 1987), and in large part continue to define them today, we find that geographic dispersion has altered the tight bonds among the gang, the family, and the barrio.

Communities in Turmoil: Family Fighting Family

Family mobility was another issue that came up frequently in our interviews and provides insights into some of the ways in which public social control and, to a lesser extent, parochial control shape and constrain private forms of social control. Sometimes, families moved because of divorce or job opportunities elsewhere in the valley. Other times, they moved because the parents were so fearful of gang activity in the neighborhood. Children also went to live with grandparents or aunts when their parents were incarcerated. Finally, teenagers unable to get along with their parents sometimes moved in with relatives. An unfortunate and ironic side effect of this mobility is that it may lead to gang rivalries cross-cutting families. That is, if gang warfare erupts between these different neighborhoods, families may literally be caught in the cross-fire. This phenomenon of family fighting family is anathema to more traditional Chicanos/as and Mexicanos/as, challenging existing notions of private, familial social control.[6] A 15-year-old female commented that more than 50 members of her extended family are or were in gangs:

> We can't have family reunions or anything because they are always fighting, like my *tíos* (uncles) fight. At the funerals they fight, or at the park, or at a picnic when we get together, they just fight. So sometimes the family don't get together, only for funerals, that's the only time.

Similarly, a 16-year-old male reported that his dad was mad because

> I am from westside; they are from eastside. See, I was supposed to be from eastside, but I didn't want to be from there. He don't want me to be his son because I'm not from eastside.

For the family that is split across two feuding gangs, cycles of revenge killings are particularly devastating. A 17-year-old male described the conflicts within his family:

> And it's crazy because we are like from different gangs, only me and my cousin are from the same gang. Like my brother, I always disrespect him because he's from Camelback and shit, they did a drive-by on my house and shit, and then he called me. I was like, "Fuck you, motherfucker, fuck your barrio and shit," and he was like, "Don't disrespect," and I was like, "Fuck you." That's the only thing bad about it, if you decide to join the wrong gang.[7]

Similarly, a young Mexicano-Indian clarified his relationship with his uncles:

> They are from different gangs, though . . . but I don't care about them because they be trying to shoot at us all the time. My own uncle shot at me, one of them tried to kill me already, but that's alright.

He explained further that although most members of his family, including brothers, sisters, aunts, uncles, his dad, his mom, his grandfather, and numerous cousins were in the same gang, a few claimed different neighborhoods. He noted rather matter-of-factly,

> I got about two uncles in a gang. I had four of them, but one is dead. My uncles killed him for some reason, I don't know, different barrio maybe.

As this youth noted, it is sometimes difficult to assess the basis for fighting within and across gang families. He was not certain why his uncle was killed, whether it was over gang issues or identities or for some other reason unrelated to gang membership. Yet, his assumption, perhaps because of the centrality of gangs in his own life, was that the intrafamilial homicide was gang related. When family feuds become entwined with gang rivalries, it is clear that the private system of social control has broken down. Family and friendship dynamics are no longer able to keep peace within a community. Under these conditions, parochial and public forms of social control typically come into play. Because one of the major public institutions of social control is the juvenile court, in a related study we asked a sample of juvenile court judges and probation officers whether they perceived gang-related violence within families to be a significant problem. Most of the court officials responded that intrafamily gang conflicts were not a problem in their courts, although a few had seen such conflicts within extended families. Where intrafamily conflicts developed, the judicial officials attributed them either to the gang becoming a stronger psychological force than the family for particular youths or to youths moving into neighborhoods with strong gangs. As one judicial officer stated,

> I think it would depend on the neighborhood that you live in and who was in control of that neighborhood. . . . A lot of these kids join gangs for their own protection. And if this is the gang that is going to afford me the most protection, I don't care what gang José on Oak St. belongs to just because he's my cousin. I don't live over there. I live over here, and I have to do what's best for me.

Not To Die For

Gang members are supposed to be willing to do anything for their homeboys and homegirls, even to die for them. The importance of demonstrating one's "heart," or willingness to be "down" for the gang, is the major reason for jumping in new members and the basis for extolling acts of bravery and craziness *(locura)* by gang members (Portillos et al., 1996). To assess the relative importance of gangs and families as predominant institutions in the youths' lives, Decker and Van Winkle (1996) explicitly asked gang members to choose between their family or the gang. The overwhelming majority, 89%, of the youths chose their families. As Decker and Van Winkle explain their finding, "For most gang members, the gang was a place to find protection, companionship and understanding. Their family, however, represented something deeper, a commitment that most saw as transcending life in the gang" (1996:251). As we have shown, often gang members *are* family members.

Given the assumed importance of gangs and historically close ties among the gang, the family, and the barrio, one of our most interesting findings was that more than half of the youths would *not* willingly die for all of their homeboys and homegirls. About a third were willing to die for specific individuals who were in their gang, but not for everyone. Another third straightforwardly stated that they would not willingly die for their gangs. The reason, they said, was "because I know they wouldn't die for me, they ain't that stupid."

In response to the direct query, "For whom would you willingly die?" all of the youths claimed that they would die for their families. When probed, they named their mothers, their children, their siblings, maybe an aunt or grandmother, and specific friends and relatives. Some of these family members belonged to the gang, but others did not. The distinction between someone who is simply a member of one's gang and someone who is family (including fictive kin) was clarified for us by a 16-year-old male who, a few days previously, had been struck by a bullet that, had he not gotten in the way, would have hit a friend's grandmother. He said, "I will die for my *true* homeboy; he would die for me."

We suggest that affirming one's willingness to die for a friend takes on new meaning when easy access to guns makes death a real possibility. When asked about the bad parts of gang life, "death" was typically the first factor named by both the gang members and adults. Probing indicated that the youths have a very real sense that they could die if they remain in *la vida loca*.[8] In earlier generations of gangs, when death was not so common a feature, it may have been far easier to claim, with plenty of bravado, that one would die for one's gang.

The responses to our question reinforce the gendered nature of gang life. Even though female gang members prided themselves on their fighting skills, none of the young women declared a willingness to die for her gang. A few confessed that they might have done so when they were younger, but their tone suggested that this was a phase they had outgrown. These gendered responses are consistent with the general findings in the literature of lower rates of violence and lesser acceptance of violence among females than males (Chesney-Lind and Sheldon, 1998; Curry, 1998; Joe and Chesney-Lind, 1995), but they may also reflect the greater relevance of the family and private social control for young women than for young men.

It is difficult to determine at this point whether we are simply seeing an aging or maturation effect, in which as youths become older and perhaps leave the gang life behind, they see the gang in less romantic terms. They may be maturing into a more adult way of taking care of the barrio, which, as we have maintained, *is* their extended family; or we may be seeing evidence of a crack in the gang-family-barrio equality.

Of particular interest to our thesis, we suggest that the apparent contradiction between intrafamily fighting and a willingness to die only for one's family may be explained by a more careful analysis of variation in the forms that private social control may take. That is, family fighting family suggests a *reduction* in the amount of private social control, but when youths report that they would die for their families, but not for their gangs (excepting gang members who are family or close family friends), this indicates that the family remains a potent force in their lives. Thus, we do not see a complete breakdown in private social control, but rather what appear to be some changes in the form that private social control takes as we move from more traditional families to more acculturated families. When we add economic stresses and political disenfranchisement, we also see few opportunities for courting public social control on the community's terms. In the section that follows, we return to our earlier theme of economic and political dislocations and what these imply for local youths.

Gangs, Multiple Marginalities, and Urban Dislocations

The final theme that emerged from interviews with the youths brings us back to Vigil's concept of multiple marginalities and urban dislocations. The immediate world within which these youths live is marked by poverty, racial discrimination, cultural misunderstandings, and gendered expectations. As one young man stated, "We are a bunch of project kids, always on the move."

All of the youths in our sample were either kicked out or dropped out of school, and many had not completed ninth grade. This lack of education makes it exceedingly difficult to leave their marginal positions in the inner city and the gang life in their neighborhoods behind (see, similarly, Anderson, 1990; Padilla, 1993; Spergel, 1986). They spoke at length about problems they faced in school. For example,

> I use to go to Lincoln Middle School. The teachers, fuckin' White teachers. The gym teacher, you know just because I was messin' around, threw me up against the locker and I reported him. And nobody said shit about it. I told them, "fuck that, I ain't coming to this school no more" and they didn't even call the damn police. When they did call the police, they said they were going to take me to jail. So I just took off, I was like what the fuck, the motherfucker, he was the one pushing me.

It is interesting to note that the only times when the youths spoke about what we might call parochial and public forms of social control, it was to complain about them. As the above quote indicates, teachers were not viewed as a resource by most of these youths, but rather as authority figures who reinforced their daily experiences of racism, marginality, and alienation. Moreover, their sense was that the police regularly sided with the teachers, rather than protecting the youths against what they perceived to be assaults and other forms of aggression on the part of the teachers.

The teens we interviewed are cognizant of the barriers confronting them. They recognize that their criminal and academic records make it almost impossible for them to move up the socioeconomic ladder. Yet, they still hold very mainstream aspirations. They see themselves as settling down to life with a steady partner or spouse and children, and they hope to be able to find a decent job. They want to become jet pilots, police officers, and firefighters, and they aim someday to purchase their own homes. For example, a young man expressed high hopes for his future but recognized the sad reality of life in the barrio:

> I want to become an Air Force pilot, that wouldn't be a bad thing to be. The only fucked up thing is that I can't become a pilot because I have already been convicted of a felony in adult court.

Thus, although these youths may aspire to very mainstream futures, they recognize that poor schooling, inadequate job training, felony records, and racial/ethnic discrimination limit their potential for success.

CONCLUSIONS

In closing, we must stress that ours is an exploratory study, and our conclusions are based on only 53 interviews. Also, we did not set out to test Bursik and Grasmick's thesis; thus, our study does not constitute a full test of their model. We found, however, that attention to private, parochial, and public social control helped us to better understand the complexities of the relationship between gang members and other community residents.

We urge further research examining the perspectives of adults living and working with the youths. They know a lot about the youths' lives. Some adults are very sad and jaded, having watched their own children die in gang-related incidents. Other adults remain hopeful of making small changes in their worlds, with or without the help of police, business leaders, or politicians. Many adults are themselves former gang members and can shed light on historical shifts in the relationship between the gang, the family, and the neighborhood. Their insights, we suggest, should be incorporated into future studies of neighborhood-based gangs.

In conclusion, our study contributes to the growing body of research on gangs as situated socially and politically within poor urban communities of color. Like many other gang researchers (e.g., Curry and Decker, 1998; Curry and Spergel, 1988; Decker and Van Winkle, 1996; Hagedorn, 1991, 1998; Horowitz, 1983,1987; Jankowski, 1991; Joe and Chesney-Lind, 1995; Klein, 1995; Moore, 1978, 1985, 1991; Padilla, 1993; Vigil, 1988), we assert that the social, economic, and political contexts within which gang life is set help to explain the complex and often contentious relations among gang members, their families, and the larger communities of which they form a part.

The gang was, and is, composed of brothers, sisters, cousins, and neighbors. The gang gives them a sense of community, a place where they belong. Kicked out of school, assumed to be troublemakers, looking tough and feeling scared, these young people are well aware that their options in life are very much constrained by poverty, racial discrimination, cultural stereotyping, and inadequate education.

Within this context, we suggest that Bursik and Grasmick's (1993a) theory of neighborhood dynamics helps explain the complex and often contradictory relations among the gang, the family, and the barrio. Their attention to private, parochial, and public levels of community-based social control are evident in the barrio we studied, and they point further to the difficulties facing community residents when they try to garner political and economic resources from outside their communities. It is, perhaps, to these political and economic linkages and disconnections that gang researchers and others concerned with crime in poor urban communities should look next.

Notes

[1] For purposes of this paper, Chicano/a refers to men (Chicano) and women (Chicana) of Mexican descent living in the United States. Mexicano/a refers to men (Mexicano) and women (Mexicana) who were born in Mexico. While the Mexicano and Mexicana youths must be living in the United States to become part of our sample, they may or may not be U.S. citizens or permanent residents.

[2] Of the 33 youth, 11 self-identified as Mexican, 2 as "wetback," 1 as "wetback" and Indian, 7 as Chicano or Chicana, 2 as Chicano and American Indian, 1 as Chicano and White, and 7 as Hispanic. Two respondents, both of whom were born in the U.S., did not self-identify their ethnicity. It is worth noting that "wetback" has two meanings in this context. It is a derogatory term for an undocumented Mexican immigrant, yet it is also used with pride by members of the Wetback Power gang. Similarly, some of the youth who call themselves "Hispanic" are members of Hispanic Varrio Homeboys, and thus may have selected this term as both an ethnic and a gang identifier.

[3] Neighborhood vehemence against gangs defacing the community was highlighted in October of 1995, while we were conducting our field work. More than 40 angry residents appeared at a juvenile court hearing, hoping to convince the judge that two 16-year-olds should be prosecuted in adult court. The youths had gone on a rampage, spray painting 32 houses and some cars (Whiting, 1995).

[4] Members of the gangs we studied sell drugs, steal cars, and commit other crimes as both individual and gang-related activities. Unlike the gangs discussed by Padilla (1993) and Jankowski (1991), however, these gangs are not organized as criminal enterprises.

[5] The major exception is a predominantly Mexicano gang that accepts some White youths as members.

[6] The theme of inter-gang conflicts within families arose during the course of our interviews with the youths. Because interviews with adults were taking place at the same time, we were not able to systematically ask the adults for their perceptions of how extensive this problem had become. We did, however, ask samples of probation officers and juvenile court judges whom we later interviewed for a related project to discuss this issue, and we incorporate their views here.

[7] With the exception of the gangs named in note two, pseudonyms are used in place of individual and gang names throughout this analysis. Street names have also been changed so as not to identify particular neighborhoods.

[8] According to one of our respondents, a machine gun cost about $35 in 1996, when we were collecting our data. While guns may have been used in the past, in recent years they have become exceedingly cheap and easy for teenagers to obtain.

References

Anderson, Elijah. 1990. *Street Wise*. Chicago, IL: University of Chicago Press.

Arizona Department of Economic Security. 1998. *Arizona Economic Indicators*. Spring. Tucson: The University of Arizona.

Arizona Economic Development Update. 1998. *The Gold Sheet*. http://www.commerce.state.az.us/general/gold.html

Baca Zinn, Maxine. 1975. Political familism: Toward sex role equality in Chicano families. *Aztlan* 6:13–26.

Barker, Jeff. 1999. Phoenix forgotten get Clinton's notice; prosperity's shortfall to be focus of visit. *Arizona Republic* (June 29):A1.

Bursik, Robert J. Jr. and Harold G. Grasmick. 1993a. *Neighborhoods and Crime: The Dimensions of Effective Community Control*. New York: Lexington Books.

Bursik, Robert J. Jr. and Harold G. Grasmick. 1993b. Economic deprivation and neighborhood crime rates, 1960–1980. *Law and Society Review* 27(2):263–283.

Chesney-Lind, Meda and Randall G. Sheldon. 1998. *Girls, Delinquency, and Juvenile Justice*. 2nd ed. Belmont, CA: Wadsworth.

Curry, G. David. 1998. Female gang involvement. *Journal of Research in Crime and Delinquency* 35(1):100–118.

Curry, G. David and Scott H. Decker. 1998. *Confronting Gangs: Crime and Community*. Los Angeles: Roxbury Publishing Co.

Curry, G. David and Irving A. Spergel. 1988. Gang homicide, delinquency, and community. *Criminology* 26:381–405.

Decker, Scott H. and Barrik Van Winkle. 1996. *Life in the Gang: Family, Friends, and Violence*. New York: Cambridge University Press.

Donziger, Steven R. (ed.). 1996. *The Real War on Crime: The Report of the National Criminal Justice Commission*. New York: HarperPerennial.

Escobar, Edward J. 1999. *Race, Police, and the Making of a Political Identity: Mexican Americans and the Los Angeles Police Department, 1900–1945*. Berkeley: University of California Press.

Ewick, Patricia and Susan S. Silbey. 1995. Subversive stories and hegemonic tales: Toward a sociology of narrative. *Law and Society Review* 29(2):197–226.

Fagan, Jeffrey. 1996. Gangs, drugs, and neighborhood change. In Ronald C. Huff (ed.), *Gangs in America*. 2nd ed. Beverly Hills, CA: Sage.

Fiscus, Chris and Christina Leonard. 1999. Phoenix, Buchanans settle suit. *Arizona Republic* (March 18):B1–B2.

Frankenberg, Ruth. 1993. *The Social Construction of Whiteness: White Women, Race Matters*. Minneapolis: University of Minnesota Press.

Fremon, Celeste. 1995. *Father Greg and the Homeboys*. New York: Hyperion.

Hagedorn, John M. 1991. Gangs, neighborhoods, and public policy. *Social Problems* 38(4):529–542.

Hagedorn, John M. 1998. *People and Folks: Gangs, Crime and the Underclass in a Rustbelt City*. 2nd ed. Chicago, IL: Lake View Press.

Harris, Mary G. 1994. Cholas, Mexican-American girls, and gangs. *Sex Roles* 30(3/4):289–301.

Hernández, José. 1990. Latino alternatives to the underclass concept. *Latino Studies Journal* 1:95–105.

Horowitz, Ruth. 1983. *Honor and the American Dream*. New Brunswick, NJ: Rutgers University Press.

Horowitz, Ruth. 1987. Community tolerance of gang violence. *Social Problems* 34:437–450.

Horowitz, Ruth and Gary Schwartz. 1974. Honor, normative ambiguity and gang violence. *American Sociological Review* 39:238–251.

Hunter, Albert J. 1985. Private, parochial and public school orders: The problem of crime and incivility in urban communities. In Gerald D. Suttles and Mayer N. Zald (eds.), *The Challenge of Social Control: Citizenship and Institution Building in Modern Society.* Norwood, NJ: Ablex Publishing Co.

Jackson, Pamela Irving. 1991. Crime, youth gangs, and urban transition: The social dislocations of postindustrial economic development. *Justice Quarterly* 8:379–398.

Jankowski, Martín Sanchéz. 1991. *Islands in the Street: Gangs and American Urban Society.* Berkeley: University of California Press.

Joe, Karen and Meda Chesney-Lind. 1995. Just every mother's angel: An analysis of gender and ethnic variation in youth gang membership. *Gender and Society* 9:408–430.

Klein, Malcolm W. 1995. *The American Street Gang: Its Nature, Prevalence, and Control.* New York: Oxford University Press.

Lofland, John and Lyn H. Lofland. 1995. *Analyzing Social Settings: A Guide to Qualitative Observations and Analysis.* Belmont, CA: Wadsworth.

Lusane, Charles. 1991. *Pipe Dream Blues: Racism and the War on Drugs.* Boston, MA: South End Press.

Madriz, Esther. 1997. *Nothing Bad Happens to Good Girls: Fear of Crime in Women's Lives.* Berkeley: University of California Press.

Mann, Coramae Richey and Marjorie S. Zatz (eds.). 1998. *Images of Color, Images of Crime.* Los Angeles: Roxbury Publishing Co.

Marin, Marguerite D. 1991. *Social Protest in an Urban Barrio: A Study of the Chicano Movement 1966–1974.* Lanham, MD: University Press of America.

Meares, Tracey L. 1997. Charting race and class differences in attitudes toward drug legalization and law enforcement: Lessons for federal criminal law. *Buffalo Criminal Law Review* 1:137–174.

Miller, Jerome G. 1996. *Search and Destroy: African-American Males in the Criminal Justice System.* New York: Cambridge University Press.

Mirandé, Alfredo. 1987. *Gringo Justice.* South Bend, IN: Notre Dame Press.

Moore, Joan W. 1978. *Homeboys: Gangs, Drugs, and Prison in the Barrios of Los Angeles.* Philadelphia: Temple University Press.

Moore, Joan W. 1985. Isolation and stigmatization in the development of an underclass: The case of Chicano gangs in East Los Angeles. *Social Problems* 33:1–10.

Moore, Joan W. 1991. *Going Down to the Barrio: Homeboys and Homegirls in Change.* Philadelphia: Temple University Press.

Moore, Joan W. 1998. Introduction. Gangs and the underclass: A comparative perspective. In John Hagedorn (ed.), *People and Folks.* 2nd ed. Chicago: Lake View Press.

Moore, Joan W. and Raquel Pinderhughes (eds.). 1993. *In the Barrios: Latinos and the Underclass Debate.* New York: Russell Sage.

Morrison Institute for Public Policy. 1994. *Kids Count Factbook: Arizona's Children 1994.* Tempe: Arizona State University.

National Minority Advisory Council on Criminal Justice. 1980. *The Inequality of Justice.* Washington, DC: U.S. Department of Justice.

Padilla, Felix. 1993. *The Gang as an American Enterprise*. New Brunswick, NJ: Rutgers University Press.

Portillos, Edwardo L. 1999. Women, men and gangs: The social construction of gender in the barrio. In Meda Chesney-Lind and John Hagedorn (eds.), *Female Gangs in America: Girls, Gangs and Gender*. Chicago: Lake View Press.

Portillos, Edwardo L., Nancy C. Jurik, and Marjorie S. Zatz. 1996. Machismo and Chicano/a gangs: Symbolic resistance or oppression? *Free Inquiry in Creative Sociology* 24(2):175–183.

Sampson, Robert J. and John H. Laub. 1993. Structural variations in juvenile court processing: Inequality, the underclass, and social control. *Law and Society Review* 27(2):285–311.

Sampson, Robert J. and William J. Wilson. 1996. Toward a theory of race, crime and urban inequality. In John Hagan and Ruth D. Peterson (eds.), *Crime and Inequality*. Stanford, CA: Stanford University Press.

Shaw, Clifford R. and Henry D. McKay. 1942. *Juvenile Delinquency and Urban Areas*. Chicago, IL: University of Chicago Press.

Skogan, Wesley G. and Michael G. Maxfield. 1981. *Coping with Crime: Individual and Neighborhood Reactions*. Beverly Hills, CA: Sage.

Spergel, Irving A. 1986. The violent gang problem in Chicago: A local community approach. *Social Service Review* (March):94–131.

Sullivan, Mercer. 1989. *"Getting Paid": Youth Crime and Work in the Inner City*. Ithaca, NY: Cornell University Press.

U.S. Commission on Civil Rights. 1970. *Mexican Americans and the Administration of Justice in the Southwest*. Washington, DC: U.S. Government Printing Office.

U.S. Council of Economic Advisors. 1998. *Economic Indicators. July*. Prepared for the Joint Economic Committee. Washington, DC: U.S. Government Printing Office.

Venkatesh, Sudhir Alladi. 1996. The gang in the community. In Ronald C. Huff (ed.), *Gangs in America*, 2nd ed. Beverly Hills, CA: Sage.

Vigil, James Diego. 1988. *Barrio Gangs: Street Life and Identity in Southern California*. Austin: University of Texas Press.

White, Jonathan B. 1995. *Dropout Rate Study 1993–94: Annual Dropout Rates in Arizona Public Schools Grades Seven Through Twelve*. Phoenix: Arizona Department of Education.

Whiting, Brent. 1995. Adult justice sought for two teenage "taggers." *Arizona Republic* (October 19):131–136.

Wilson, William Julius. 1987. *The Truly Disadvantaged*. Chicago: University of Chicago Press.

Wilson, William Julius. 1996. *When Work Disappears: The World of the New Urban Poor*. New York: Random House.

Zatz, Marjorie S. 1987. Chicano youth gangs and crime: The creation of a moral panic. *Contemporary Crises* 11:129–158.

Zavella, Patricia. 1996. Feminist insider dilemmas: Constructing ethnic identity with Chicana informants. In D. L. Wolf (ed.), *Feminist Dilemmas in Fieldwork*, Boulder, CO: Westview Press.

Exploring Race and Ethnic Differences in a Sample of Middle School Gang Members

Adrienne Freng & L. Thomas Winfree, Jr.

Minority-group membership has long been tied to explanations of gang membership. This observation is curious given the fact that most contemporary gang researchers have focused on racially homogeneous groups and specific gangs in particular sites. One consequence of this approach has been a paucity of research that examines the role of gang members' race or ethnicity on the gang experience. This article explores the extent to which gang members from various racial and ethnic groups report differences or similarities in their attitudes, behaviors, and gang characteristics, regardless of their specific minority-group membership, and examines the implications of these findings for gang researchers and policy makers.

INTRODUCTION

Gang research in urban America began in the early twentieth century. During the last three decades, however, the topic has attracted newfound interest, coinciding with a rise in youth gangs in rural areas, higher levels

Prepared especially for *American Youth Gangs at the Millennium* by Adrienne Freng and L. Thomas Winfree, Jr.

of female gang involvement, and more violent offenses and drug offenses within gangs (Battin-Pearson, Thornberry, Hawkins, and Krohn, 1998; Decker, 2000; Deschenes and Esbensen, 1999; Esbensen and Winfree, 1998; Howell, 1998; Howell and Decker, 1999; Klein, Maxson, and Cunningham, 1991; Winfree, Fuller, Vigil, and Mays, 1992). This heightened interest in youth gangs has led to more detailed information on the gang experience, including the following consensus view of gang members when contrasted to their nongang counterparts: gang members tend to be males, younger, urban residents, lower in socioeconomic status, minority group members, engaged in more delinquent activity, and possessed of less pro-social attitudes (Bowker and Klein, 1983; Brewer, Hawkins, Catalano, and Neckerman, 1995; Covey, Menard, and Franzese, 1997; Curry, Ball, and Decker, 1996; Curry and Spergel, 1992; Esbensen and Huizinga, 1993; Esbensen and Winfree, 1998; Howell, 1998; Klein, 1995; Moore, 1978, 1991; Short, 1968, 1990; Thornberry, Krohn, Lizotte, and Chard-Wierschem, 1993).

One limitation of most gang research to date—including the classic studies of urban gangs conducted at the start of the twentieth century—is an almost single-minded focus on particular gangs, specific racial or ethnic groups, or single geographic locations. Moreover, while much gang research has focused on the demographic, attitudinal, and behavioral differences between nongang and gang members, variations among gang members have not been as thoroughly examined. Furthermore, minority group membership has long been associated with gang membership, and gang members from certain racial or ethnic groups are often associated with specific forms of delinquency and types of gang organization.

Little available research actually explores the differences in attitudes, orientations, and behavior within a group of past or present gang members and, in particular, addresses the role either race or ethnicity plays in these relationships. More specifically, researchers have tended to neglect the question of whether gang membership cancels out the effects of either race or ethnicity. It is toward this important issue—the extent to which race and ethnicity distinguish between the attitudes, orientations, and behavior of individuals within a sample of youths claiming prior or current involvement with youth gangs—that the current research turns. Before exploring whether race and ethnicity are integral or unessential elements in youth gang membership, it is helpful to review the literature on the core concepts.

LITERATURE REVIEW

The extant literature suggests a relationship between race and delinquency that has not yet fully been examined. For example, early researchers linked gang membership to White ethnic groups, while over the past 35 years more emphasis has been placed on racial minority group membership (cf., Campbell, 1991; Chin, 1996; Decker and Van Winkle, 1996; Hagedorn, 1988; Moore, 1978, 1991; Thrasher [1927], 1963; Vigil, 1988; Whyte [1955], 1981). Race has come to be recognized as a secondary variable in gang research. Indeed, the alleged relationship between race and gangs is based largely on ethnographic studies of racially homogeneous groups (Campbell, 1991; Decker and Van Winkle, 1996; Hagedorn, 1988; Moore, 1978, 1991; Vigil, 1988). This body of qualitative research provides valuable information on characteristics of gang members from particular groups, but it neglects to answer whether and how race or ethnicity influences gang membership beyond that particular group.

The emphasis on race and ethnicity found in ethnographic studies—as well as in the popular media—has led researchers to conclude that gang membership is a minority issue. This conclusion is supported by law-enforcement data that mirror much of the ethnographic data, including statements about the over-involvement of minorities in street gangs (Curry et al., 1996; Curry, Ball, and Fox, 1994; Maxson and Klein, 1990; Spergel, 1990). However, several factors limit law-enforcement conclusions, including how they define gang members and gang-related crimes, differences in purposes and policies in various jurisdictions, and the actions of law-enforcement agents in determining who is targeted (Bursik and Grasmick, 1995b; Curry et al., 1996). While gang researchers' current methods include surveys, they are still unable to address the issue completely. Most surveys sample relatively homogeneous populations, and they tend to include only a single geographic location (Bjerregaard and Smith, 1993; Esbensen and Huizinga, 1993; Thornberry et al., 1993). The relatively small body of research that employs fairly heterogeneous samples in multiple locations tends to support the conclusion that minority group status is often highly correlated with gang membership; however, Whites are not excluded from gang membership, and in fact their levels of membership may be on the rise (Covey et al., 1997; Curry et al., 1996; Esbensen and Winfree, 1998).

The available studies paint only a partial picture of the relationship between race or ethnicity and gang membership. Nonetheless, the single-site nature of most such research means that the data cannot address whether the characteristics of gang members from certain racial and ethnic groups vary across geographic locations. Furthermore, the research examining the impact of race and ethnicity on gang membership has largely been limited to the examination of particular gangs in very specific geographic locations. Finally, researchers rarely address the issue of differences in attitudes, orientations, and behaviors between gang members from various racial and ethnic groups. That these issues have seldom been addressed further restricts our ability to find solutions to this significant social problem.

Delinquency Theories, Race, Ethnicity, and Youth Gangs

In order to understand the gang issue, we propose to ascertain the reasons that juvenile gangs form, the characteristics of those gangs, and whether those reasons and characteristics vary by racial or ethnic group. We have many explanations for the development of gangs, and a number of these theories combine several related explanations (e.g., Cloward and Ohlin, 1960; Cohen, 1955; Hagedorn, 1988; Klein, 1971, 1995; Miller, 1958, 1975; Moore, 1991; Short and Strodtbeck [1965], 1974, 1968, 1973; Spergel, 1964, 1969; Thrasher [1927], 1963; Vigil, 1988; Whyte [1955], 1981; Yablonsky [1962], 1970). Few of these theories, however, consider the variables of race and ethnicity. The few available theories that provide a race- or ethnicity-sensitive explanation point to the underclass and social disorganization theories proposed by Wilson (1978, 1980, 1987) and Shaw and McKay ([1942] 1969). These theories emphasize the changing economic structures of urban areas and the consequences of this change, including the loss of jobs.

For example, Moore (1991) and Hagedorn (1988) proposed that the loss of jobs prevents adolescents from aging out of the gang because aging-out opportunities no longer exist. The image of an intransigent underclass has become a permanent fixture in the urban landscape. The resulting economic segregation affected minorities more often than non-minorities, and, as a result, the number of minority gang members in these areas began to increase (Hagedorn, 1988). In a related vein, Vigil (1988) stated that economic stratification combines with other factors such as discrimination, family and school issues (including language barriers for Hispanics), and structural conditions found in minority communities to create what he described as "multiple marginality." That is, racial and ethnic minorities residing in disorganized areas were victims of multiple disadvantages, a condition that eventually led to gang formation. Decker and Van Winkle (1996) expanded this theory in their examination of primarily African-American gang members in St. Louis. They proposed that in disorganized communities, threats to community stability result from the pandemic violence. As individuals involved themselves in higher levels of personal violence, they became isolated from the local community. This isolation, in turn, led to the further perpetuation of violence and gang membership (Decker and Van Winkle, 1996).

Based on these theories, one might assume that gang members should report economic reasons for joining gangs. However, evidence suggests that money or economics is only one reason given for joining gangs. African-American gang members reported that they joined a gang because their family or peers were already in the gang (Curry and Spergel, 1992; Decker and Van Winkle, 1996). Other reasons that African-American gang members gave for joining gangs consisted of: protection, support, companionship, and impressing people (Decker and Van Winkle, 1996). Among

Hispanics, the community environment and peer relationships represented the reasons given for joining the gang (Moore, 1991). Curry and Spergel (1992) suggested that Hispanics joined the gang due to educational frustration and poor self-esteem and academic performance. Contrary to some media depictions of gangs, very few members, whatever their particular race or ethnicity, reported joining due to violence or the threat of violence (Decker and Van Winkle, 1996; Padilla, 1992; Vigil, 1988).

Gangs: Attitudes, Orientations, and Behavior

Another central issue is how and when gang members develop gang-related attitudes. Gang members tend to have less pro-social attitudes and more pro-gang attitudes than nongang members (Esbensen, Huizinga, and Weiher, 1993; Winfree, Mays, and Vigil-Backstrom, 1994; Wyrick, 2000). The question of whether certain gang members hold more delinquent attitudes—and more pro-gang attitudes—than other gang members, or, more importantly for the current study, whether these conditions vary by racial or ethnic identification, has not been addressed in gang literature.

Beyond knowing why individuals join gangs, appreciating the characteristics and the activities of both the gangs themselves and individual gang members is imperative for a more complete understanding of the gang issue. One important gang characteristic is the level of structural organization found in gangs. Several researchers have reported that gangs tend to be highly structured organizations with rules, roles, and symbols (Esbensen et al., 1993; Padilla, 1992; Sanchez-Jankowski, 1991), while others characterized gangs as loosely structured peer groups with little or informal organization and leadership (Decker and Van Winkle, 1996; Fleisher, 1998; Yablonsky [1962], 1970). The amount of structure does not seem to vary by racial or ethnic groups except for the observation that high levels of organization tend to be associated with Asian gangs (Chin, 1996; Klein, 1995), which also are linked with organized crime more often than other gangs (Chin, 1996).

Regardless of their structure, gangs are associated with increased levels of delinquent activity by their active members. Additionally, gangs are often associated with certain types of delinquent activities depending on the race or ethnicity of their members. For example, drug-related offenses and fighting distinguish African-American gangs, while Hispanic gangs are more likely to be involved in turf-related violence (Decker and Van Winkle, 1996; Howell, 1998). White and Asian gangs, on the other hand, are more often identified with property crimes (Chin, 1996; Howell, 1998; Klein, 1995).

In a manner similar to the delinquency found in gangs, the delinquency *and victimization* of *individual* gang members is also of special concern to policy makers and social control agents. This distinction—contrasting group behavior and the behavior of individuals who happen to share membership in a group—is a highly contentious area when examining the role of race and ethnicity in delinquency level and type. The debate involves the largely indisputable fact that racial and ethnic minorities are overrepresented in the criminal justice system. What is in dispute is whether this overrepresentation results from discrimination in the criminal justice system or an actual tendency of minorities to commit more crime (e.g., Gibbons, 1997; Russell, 1998; Walker, Spohn, and DeLone, 2000; Wilbanks, 1987). Self-report data suggest that the levels of delinquency between racial and ethnic groups are far more similar than official statistics would lead one to believe (Elliott and Ageton, 1980; Huizinga and Elliott, 1986; Pope, 1979; Short and Nye, 1958; Snyder and Sickmund, 1999; Walker et al., 2000; Williams and Gold, 1972).

Criminologists rarely dispute the differences in the delinquency and victimization levels found among nongang and gang members. Although gang members' involvement in delinquent activity exceeds that of nongang members (Battin-Pearson et al., 1998; Esbensen et al., 1993; Huff, 1998; Klein, 1995), the primary activities of both groups are nondelinquent in nature (Decker and Van Winkle, 1996; Fleisher, 1998; Hagedorn, 1988; Klein, 1995; Padilla, 1992). Gang members' delinquent behavior is largely characterized as cafeteria-style delinquency (Klein, 1995), which is illustrated by participation in a variety of activities rather than specializing in particular activities (see, e.g., Decker and Van Winkle, 1996; Esbensen and Huizinga, 1993; Huff, 1998). Although one common perception of gangs is involvement in drug sales, such illicit activities are actually more a form of individual behavior than of collaborative group conduct (Decker and Van Winkle, 1996; Huff, 1998; Klein, 1995).

Victimization by gangs and victimization of gang members are topics that have received even less attention from gang researchers. When victimization by gangs is considered at all, the emphasis typically has been the victimology of females within the gang context (Chesney-Lind, 1997; Deschenes and Esbensen, 1999; Miller, 1998; Miller and Decker, 2001). Race and ethnicity present an even more problematic research topic. Regarding the relationship between race, ethnicity, and victimization, various racial groups tend to victimize people of their own race or ethnicity at higher rates than they do racial/ethnic out-group members (Pope, 1979). While general victimization levels might actually be higher within gangs, African-American gang members did not think that gang membership increased victimization (Decker and Van Winkle, 1996).

Research Questions

In summary, our intent is to expand the current gang literature by descriptively exploring the role of race and ethnicity in gang membership. Specifically, we explore the following three questions related to the characteristics and experiences of gang members:

1. Do gang members hold different attitudes about gangs and join for different reasons, based on their racial/ethnic background?

2. Do these gangs share similar characteristics, such as type and level of organization and criminal activity?

3. Do gang members differ in terms of rates and types of criminality and victimization, based on their race/ethnicity?

Using data from a multi-site, national survey of eighth graders, this research investigated differences between gang members from various racial or ethnic groups on demographic, attitudinal, behavioral, and gang characteristic questions.

Methods

The data used in this study were collected as part of the cross-sectional component of the National Evaluation of the Gang Resistance Education and Training program (G.R.E.A.T.), a school-based gang-prevention program; consequently, the site and sampling selection of the original evaluation shaped the data set. The cross-sectional component was conducted during the spring of 1995 in 11 geographically and demographically diverse sites across the nation (Kansas City, MO; Las Cruces, NM; Milwaukee, WI; Omaha, NE; Orlando, FL; Philadelphia, PA; Phoenix, AZ; Pocatello, ID; Providence, RI; Torrance, CA; and Will County, IL). These sites were purposively selected based on three characteristics: (1) their geographic and demographic diversity, (2) the presence of a G.R.E.A.T. law enforcement officer at the site, and (3) implementation of the G.R.E.A.T. program during the 1993–1994 school year (for more information on the sampling and site selection, see Esbensen and Winfree, 1998).

Schools chosen for inclusion in the cross-sectional study had students who participated in the G.R.E.A.T. program as seventh graders. Surveying them in the eighth grade provided a one-year follow-up and also guaranteed that no students were still participating in the program (Esbensen and Winfree, 1998). Those surveyed included all students in attendance on the data collection day, or a total of 5,935 eighth graders.

In comparison to most previous surveys of public school children, this data set presents a unique picture of gang members for several reasons. First, the diversity of the sample allows the examination of gang members from multiple racial and ethnic groups, as contrasted with the racially homogeneous focus of most previous gang research. Additionally, the ages of the respondents in the present study, while quite narrow in range, created a younger age cohort than is traditionally included in gang research, offering interesting insights into the characteristics and behaviors of this particular age group. Finally, this data set is not restricted to high-risk individuals or to gang members but instead provides a relatively diverse sample of eighth graders.

Measures

The G.R.E.A.T. research questionnaire sought a wide array of demographic, attitudinal, and behavioral data. Race or ethnicity, a measure central to the current study, was measured by self-identification: students could indicate whether they viewed themselves as White/not Hispanic, Black/African American, Hispanic/Latino, American Indian/Native American, or Asian/Pacific Islander/Oriental. Students could also report belonging to another racial group not presented, while those circling more than one race or ethnicity were categorized as having a mixed-race background.

The questionnaire also included scales designed to assess possible differences in attitudes towards gangs. For example, with respect to the first research question, students were asked about the good and bad things they associated with gangs, and their level of attachment to their particular gang. Gang attachment was measured by questions such as: being in my gang makes me feel important, my gang members provide a good deal of support and loyalty for one another, and being a gang member makes me feel respected. A similar measure examined the reasons students joined a gang; this measure allowed them to indicate several reasons, such as protection, having friend a or sibling in the gang, being forced to join, respect, and monetary reasons.

The second research question centers on the illegal activities of the gang and the level of hierarchy present in the specific gangs in which the youths claimed membership. The questionnaire included questions about the illegal activities of the gangs, including fighting other gangs, property theft, robbery, auto theft, selling marijuana and other illegal drugs, and vandalism. In order to estimate the structure and hierarchical nature of the gangs in which sample members claimed membership, a series of questions explored such things as whether the gang had initiation rites, established leaders, rules, roles, symbols/colors, and roles for females.

The third research question focused on personal (and self-reported) criminal participation and victimization. The available measures of delinquency included whether the respondent had ever participated in any of the following activities: carried a hidden weapon, attacked someone, robbed someone, shot at someone, sold marijuana, and sold illegal drugs. Students were also asked whether they had been hit, attacked, robbed, or had something stolen to assess their level of victimization.

One of the issues plaguing gang research is how to define gang membership. Definitional issues surrounding the concept of gang membership have led to widely varying estimates of the number of gang members and the actual scope of the gang problem (see, e.g., Bursik and Grasmick, 1995a; Decker and Kempf-Leonard, 1995; Maxson and Klein, 1990; W. Miller, 1958; Short, 1968; Spergel, 1995; Winfree et al., 1992). In this paper, we measured gang membership using answers to the following two-step filter process: (1) "Have you ever been a member of a gang?" and (2) "Is your gang involved in one or more of the following activities: fighting other gangs, stealing cars, stealing in general, or robbing people?" Affirmative answers to both questions resulted in a respondent's designation as a present or former gang member. The use of delinquency as measurement criterion is still debated among researchers, but its inclusion in this research limited the current analyses specifically to delinquent-gang members (see, e.g., Ball and Curry, 1995; Bursik and Grasmick, 1995a; Curry and Decker, 1998; Esbensen, Winfree, He, and Taylor, 2001; Klein, 1995). This definition resulted in 613 self-identified gang members. (There were a total of 623 individuals who fit the definition of gang members, but 10 were eliminated owing to incomplete data on the gang and race variables.)

Analysis

We used chi-square comparisons and one-way ANOVA with Tukey's Studentized Range Test (HSD) to compare means between the racial/ethnic groups on the different measures. Since the study questionnaire included no specific items regarding the racial or ethnic composition of gangs, the analyses were limited to the individual level rather than to gang-level data. Furthermore, we restricted the analyses to the three largest ethnic and racial groups (i.e., Whites, African Americans, and Hispanics). The remaining racial or ethnic groups (i.e., American Indian, Asian, and Other) were quite small, precluding any meaningful comparisons with the other groups. Consequently, this report is based on a subsample of 491 youth gang members.

Results

Before addressing the specific research questions, we turn to a brief review of the demographic description of the gang members (see table 1). Few differences existed between the percentages of each of the groups that reported gang members. Thirty-eight percent of gang members reported being African American, while equivalent numbers of gang members reported being White or Hispanic (31%). Most gang members, regardless of race or ethnicity, reported being 14 years of age. A larger percentage of White gang members reported being 13 or younger, while a larger percent of African American and Hispanic gang members were 15 years or older. However, the relatively narrow range of ages is expected given the sampling method employed. The majority of gang members from all racial/ethnic groups were males (62%). A high level of female involvement in gangs was reported regardless of racial or ethnic background. In fact, female involvement in gangs was almost 45% for Latinas. The majority of White and Hispanic gang members reportedly came from intact families, while the single-parent family was the most common (51%) arrangement among African-American gang members.

Gang Attitudes and Reasons for Joining the Gang

The first research question explored the gang-related attitudes and reasons for joining gangs expressed by the various racial and ethnic groups. More specifically, the attitudinal measures addressed the question of whether delinquent attitudes among gang members differed, based on particular racial or ethnic groups. Table 2 reports the means for scales measuring gang attitudes. White gang members reported significantly more positive attitudes about gangs *and* saw more good things about gangs than African Americans (i.e., the higher the scale score, the more positive the attitudes toward gangs). Gang members from all three racial and ethnic groups saw the bad things about gangs in roughly the same terms. Regardless of racial or ethnic group membership, gang members

Table 1　Gang Member Demographics

Racial Composition of Gang Members:

	N	% of Sample	Number of Gang Members	% of Gang Members
White	2337	47%	150	31%
African American	1527	31%	188	38%
Hispanic	1077	22%	153	31%
Total	4941		491	

Demographics of Gang Members:

	White	African American	Hispanic
Age:			
<13	20%	12%	12%
14	68%	56%	63%
>15	12%	32%	25%
Sex:			
Male	65%	66%	56%
Female	35%	34%	44%
Family Structure:			
Intact	56%	35%	51%
Single Parent	37%	51%	40%
Other	7%	14%	9%

Table 2　Youth Gang Member Attitudes by Race (Mean Scores with Standard Deviations in Parentheses)

	Attitudes about Gangs*	Good Things about Gangs*	Bad Things about Gangs	Gang Attachment
OVERALL	3.48 (.83)	1.58 (.30)	1.43 (.30)	3.68 (.78)
White	3.60 (.84)	1.65 (.27)	1.44 (.30)	3.77 (.80)
African American	3.34 (.85)	1.55 (.31)	1.42 (.31)	3.67 (.76)
Hispanic	3.52 (.76)	1.56 (.31)	1.42 (.30)	3.61 (.76)

ANOVA
* Significant differences between Whites and African Americans ($p < .05$).

reported moderate levels of gang attachment. In short, on only two of four dimensions of gang attitudes—and out of 12 possible two-group comparisons—did the members of two groups differ significantly from one another, and in those two cases, the differences were between White and African-American gang members.

Another measure used to indicate gang-related orientations consisted of the reasons members cited for joining gangs. As is evident from even a cursory look at table 3, gang members join gangs for a wide variety of reasons. In this instance, significant differences appeared between the racial and ethnic groups in terms of all the given reasons, except for "forced to join." In general, Whites endorsed all reasons for joining gangs at significantly higher levels than African Americans or Hispanics. The lone exception was having a sibling in the gang, which was given more often by African Americans as a reason. The highest percentage of African Americans reported joining because of money, although they did not differ significantly from the other gang members on this dimension. Similarly, the highest proportion of Hispanic gang members indicated that they joined the gang for protection, which placed them ahead of African Americans but behind Whites on this dimension. Interestingly, very few gang members joined because they felt forced into it, a finding that contradicts the general social perception. In summary, according to the Chi-square comparisons, the various racial and ethnic groups exhibited significantly different support for five of the six reasons for joining gangs, and Whites were in the highest agreement category in four of the five reasons, with African Americans highest on the fifth.

Table 3   Reasons for Joining the Gang

	For Protection*	Friend in Gang*	Sibling in Gang*	Forced to Join	For Respect*	For Money*
OVERALL	52%	46%	30%	8%	48%	46%
White	65%	66%	20%	11%	58%	53%
African American	43%	34%	39%	8%	45%	49%
Hispanic	51%	42%	31%	4%	41%	36%

Chi-Square
*$p < .05$

Gang Organization and Illegal Activities of Gangs

The second research question explored structural characteristics of gangs and the illegal behaviors in which they routinely engage. Overall, gang members' answers suggested reasonably high levels of organizational structure in their gangs (see table 4). The only significant differences appeared for initiation rites, symbols/colors, and the roles assigned within the gang to females. Hispanic gang members reported symbols/colors and roles for females most often, followed by Whites and then African Americans. Whites, on the other hand, were more likely to report having initiation rites as part of the organizational structure of their gangs. Regardless of race or ethnicity, over 73% of gang members stated their gangs had initiation rites, established leaders, and rules; and almost 90% of gang members said that their gangs had symbols/colors. The overall results *suggest* that White gang members had a higher level of organization compared to gang members of other racial or ethnic categories, as this pattern held for all organizational questions except symbols/colors and female roles in the gang. Nonetheless, it is also important to observe that only on initiation rites, symbols/colors, and the roles assigned to females did significant differences exist by race or ethnicity.

Table 5 summarizes the results of racial or ethnic differences for reported illegal gang activities. Regardless of race or ethnicity, participants stated that their gangs were involved in a variety of different illegal activities. Fighting other gangs, property theft, and vandalism were the only illegal activities where gang members of the various ethnic groups differed significantly with one another. Whites indicated the highest levels of par-

Table 4 Gang Characteristics by Race

	Initiation Rites*	Established Leaders	Rules	Roles	Symbols/ Colors*	Roles for Females*
OVERALL	78%	78%	76%	68%	92%	55%
White	86%	85%	78%	72%	91%	57%
African American	73%	73%	75%	63%	89%	46%
Hispanic	76%	79%	74%	71%	97%	62%

Chi-Square
*$p < .05$

Table 5 Illegal Activities of Gangs by Race

	Fighting Other Gangs*	Theft*	Robbery	Auto Theft	Selling Marijuana	Selling Illegal Drugs	Vandalism*
OVERALL	93%	73%	60%	70%	82%	64%	79%
White	92%	86%	63%	68%	81%	61%	89%
African American	91%	61%	57%	70%	78%	66%	67%
Hispanic	97%	73%	61%	71%	86%	65%	84%

Chi-Square
*$p < .05$

ticipation in property theft and vandalism, while Hispanics were more likely to report fighting other gangs. In all three of these cases, African Americans reported the lowest levels. Additionally, Whites reported the highest percentage of involvement in robberies but did not differ significantly from the other groups for this activity. Compared to the other groups, African-American gang members reported the lowest percentage of gang involvement in all illegal activities except auto theft and selling illegal drugs. Hispanic gang members described higher involvement for their gangs in fighting other gangs, auto theft, and selling marijuana. Almost 95% of all gang members stated that their gangs fought with other gangs, and marijuana sales was reported by close to 80% of all gang members, irrespective of race or ethnicity. More than 60% of all gang members reported the involvement of their respective gangs in each illegal activity. Again, significant differences existed in only three of seven possible comparisons by race or ethnicity.

Consequences of Gang Membership

Individual gang members—irrespective of race or ethnicity—indicated involvement in many different forms of delinquent activity, as evidenced by the fact that there were no significant differences for the racial and ethnic group comparisons summarized in table 6. Between 70% and 80% of gang members reported carrying hidden weapons, and about one-third reported shooting at someone. In addition, about one-half of gang members reported attacking someone. Although African Americans are often stereotypically associated with selling illegal drugs, White gang members reported higher percentages of individuals participating in this activity. But even these differences were not significantly different. Judged by the self-reported delinquency in table 6, many—and in some cases most—youth gang members are quite busily engaged in illicit conduct.

The gang members in this study indicated relatively high rates of certain types of victimization; significant differences between the racial and ethnic groups, however, were absent (see table 7). Gang members reported fairly high levels of having been hit and having been victims of theft, ranging from around 60% to 80%. About one-fourth of gang members indicated they had been robbery victims, and approximately 40% reported being attacked by someone trying to hurt them. While there are some differences between racial/ethnic groups, they are small and not statistically significant. Those claiming to have been robbed, however, were absolutely in the lowest response categories, ranging from only 16% to less than 30%. African-American gang members reported the highest percentages of being robbed and having something stolen. Violent personal victimizations seemed to impact Whites and Hispanics more often, and a higher percentage of Whites reported being hit, but a higher percentage of Hispanics reported being attacked. Again, none of these latter differences were statistically significant, even if they are substantively interesting.

Table 6 Self-Reported Delinquencies of Gang Members by Race

	Carried Hidden Weapon	Attacked Someone	Robbed Someone	Shot at Someone	Sold Marijuana	Sold Illegal Drugs
OVERALL	76%	51%	28%	29%	57%	33%
White	76%	49%	33%	28%	60%	37%
African American	74%	49%	27%	32%	51%	34%
Hispanic	78%	54%	24%	27%	59%	28%

Table 7 Victimization by Race

	Been Hit	Been Robbed	Been Attacked	Had Something Stolen
OVERALL	66%	24%	40%	74%
White	74%	26%	39%	75%
African American	63%	28%	40%	78%
Hispanic	64%	16%	42%	69%

DISCUSSION

In order to understand the gang issue fully and to develop responsive public policy, we must ascertain the characteristics and activities of gang members. While gang research proliferated in the 1980s and 1990s, the differences between gang members of various racial or ethnic groups received little attention. The present study addressed this issue by answering three research questions related to reported differences by racial/ethnic groups in attitudes, gang organization, and behaviors.

Since gang researchers have shown that gang members tend to report less pro-social attitudes than nongang members (Esbensen et al., 1993; Winfree et al., 1994; Wyrick, 2000), the first research question explored whether certain gang members harbor more delinquent attitudes than other gang members. The results clearly indicate an inconsistency in this important aspect of "gang belonging." On the one hand, White gang members actually reported more pro-gang attitudes than African Americans and Hispanics did, contradicting the perception that minorities become involved in gangs due to the positive aspects of the gang. On the other hand, regardless of racial/ethnic background, gang members declared equal attachment to the gang and bad things about the gang.

To further test gang-related orientations, we next considered reasons for joining the gang. This area of exploration resulted in the most significant differences between gang members by race/ethnicity, a finding that supports Curry and Spergel (1992), who found that African Americans and Hispanics join gangs for different reasons. Differences appeared for all the reasons examined except for "forced to join." While African Americans joined because a sibling belonged to the gang, Whites were more likely to report joining for the remaining reasons. The largest percentage of Hispanics reported joining for protection. Furthermore, recently the press has perpetuated the idea that in certain parts of society, gangs force juveniles to join and, if given the choice, juveniles would not belong to the gang. These results challenge that perception: very few gang members reported coercion as the reason for joining the gang.

The second and third research questions investigated the characteristics of gangs and the consequences of gang membership. Are gangs highly structured entities or loose peer affiliations? The results clearly point to the fact that gangs tend to have characteristics associated with structured organizations. The only organizational factors that vary by racial or ethnic group are initiation rites, symbols/colors, and roles assigned to females. Significantly more Hispanics report symbols/colors and female roles as being more characteristic of their gangs, while Whites are more likely to have initiation rites.

This research is important for two reasons. First, the findings contradict several common perceptions of gang membership and provide more in-depth information about gang members from different racial or ethnic groups. The current analysis supports a contrasting view of gang membership from previous literature and widely held stereotypes. Since policy reflects current understanding of the issues, this emergent picture of gang members has the potential to influence future policy and programs.

Some of the more interesting contradictions revealed in this research are based on the gang members' demographic characteristics. For example, even though this was a relatively young cohort, gang members tended to be older; thus a nine- or ten-year-old gang member would be an exception rather than the rule. Furthermore, while the perception has been that gang membership is largely a male phenomenon, the current study supports other recent research that indicates a higher level of female involvement in gangs than has previously been believed; in fact, some racial/ethnic groups include considerably higher rates of female involvement, specifically Hispanics (Bjerregaard and Smith, 1993; Chesney-Lind and Shelden, 1992; Chesney-Lind, Shelden, and Joe, 1996; Esbensen and Deschenes, 1998; Esbensen and Winfree, 1998; Miller, 2001). Additionally, while a considerable amount of research links single-parent families and gang membership (see, e.g., Bowker and Klein, 1983; Decker and Van Winkle, 1996; Esbensen, Deschenes, and Winfree, 1999; Hill, Howell, Hawkins, and Battin-Pearson, 1999; Vigil, 1988), even more recent gang studies suggest results that vary by racial or ethnic group (Esbensen and Winfree, 1998; Maxson, Whitlock, and Klein, 1998; Winfree et al., 1992). In a manner consistent with these latter studies, our analyses illustrate that a higher percentage of White and Hispanic gang members reported coming from intact families, while more African-American gang members stated they came from single-parent families.

Regardless of race or ethnicity, gang members reported individual and gang involvement in a variety of delinquent activities, with significant differences appearing only for fighting other gangs, theft, and vandalism. Participants stated that their gangs were involved in a variety of different illegal activities, supporting Klein's (1995) notion of cafeteria-style delinquency. You will recall that Klein (1995) proposed that most delinquency is not specialized in a certain type of activity but instead consists of involvement in many different activities. This contention was supported by the findings of this study, which contradicts some common perceptions—for example, that African-American gang members are largely responsible for the illegal drug market. Furthermore, no differences appeared regarding victimization of gang members, indicating that the consequences of gang membership do not vary for gang members based on racial or ethnic group identification.

The second implication of this research deals with the fact that past research linking race and ethnicity with gang membership resulted in the development of different programs to address gang membership based on racial or ethnic identity (Curry and Spergel, 1992). If few differences exist between gang members on attitudes, behaviors, and other gang factors, it seems likely that race-specific programs are unnecessary. This research largely supports the contention that general gang-prevention programs will meet the challenge of addressing the gang issue. Although some differences between the gang members appeared, more similarities than differences emerged. Furthermore, programs addressing individual issues where differences appeared probably would be beneficial to all gang members, not just those of certain groups. For example, examine the reasons for joining a gang, where the most differences appeared (see table 3). Although there were differences between the groups, over 30% of members from each racial and ethnic group responded affirmatively to each of the reasons for joining the gang, with the exception of forced membership. Thus, programs directed at each of the reasons for joining the gang would target not only the individual group most affected by each reason but also a considerable number of gang members from other groups.

Although these research findings extend the current gang literature, restricting the survey to the three major racial and ethnic groups (Whites, African Americans, and Hispanics) constituted one of several limitations of this study. It is possible that the mechanisms for gang membership might differ for racial or ethnic groups not considered. The limitations of survey research such as memory bias, exaggeration or concealment of answers, loss of high-risk students, and students missing school also apply to this data (Esbensen and Osgood, 1997; Loeber, Farrington, and Waschbusch,

1998). Furthermore, the sample consisted of only eighth graders; it is possible that a different picture would emerge if our sample represented other age groups, specifically older students.

While this is only one picture of the broad phenomenon of gangs in America, the current research suggests that many of the common stereotypes are not supported and maintains the idea that the gang experience is largely homogeneous. Since the policy implications of this research are considerable, further research, especially research utilizing racially and ethnically diverse samples, is needed. Further exploration into the reasons for joining the gang—where the most differences appeared in the present analyses—seems especially important for prevention researchers. Knowing why individuals become involved in the gang and whether the reasons differ by racial or ethnic group will determine if separate gang-prevention programs, such as those proposed by Curry and Spergel (1992), are necessary. For a better understanding of the role of race and ethnicity in gang membership, researchers need to explore this area in more detail in order to better inform public policy.

An earlier version of this article was presented at the 2002 Western Society of Criminology Meetings in San Diego, CA. The original research was supported under award #94-IJ-CX-0058 from the National Institute of Justice, Office of Justice Programs, U.S. Department of Justice. Points of view expressed in this document are those of the authors and do not necessarily represent the official position of the U.S. Department of Justice. The authors thank Dr. Finn Esbensen for comments on an earlier draft.

References

Ball, Richard and G. David Curry. 1995. "The Logic of Definition in Criminology: Purposes and Methods for Defining 'Gangs.'" *Criminology* 33:225–45.

Battin-Pearson, Sara, Terence Thornberry, J. David Hawkins, and Marvin Krohn. 1998. "Gang Membership, Delinquent Peers, and Delinquent Behavior." Washington, DC: Office of Juvenile Justice and Delinquency Prevention, Juvenile Justice Bulletin.

Bjerregaard, Beth and Carolyn Smith. 1993. "Gender Differences in Gang Participation, Delinquency, and Substance Use." *Journal of Quantitative Criminology* 9:329–55.

Bowker, Lee and Malcolm Klein. 1983. "Etiology of Female Juvenile Delinquency Gang Membership: A Test of Psychological and Social Structural Explanations." *Adolescence* 72:739–51.

Brewer, Devon, J. David Hawkins, Richard F. Catalano, and Holly Neckerman. 1995. "Preventing Serious, Violent, and Chronic Juvenile Offending: A Review of Evaluations of Selected Strategies in Childhood, Adolescence, and the Community." Pp. 61–141 in *Serious, Violent, and Chronic Juvenile Offenders*, edited by J. Howell, B. Krisberg, J. D. Hawkins, and J. Wilson. Thousand Oaks, CA: Sage Publications.

Bursik, Robert and Harold G. Grasmick. 1995a. "Defining Gangs and Gang Behavior." Pp. 8–13 in *The Modern Gang Reader*, 1st ed., edited by M. Klein, C. L. Maxson, and J. Miller. Los Angeles, CA: Roxbury Publishing.

Bursik, Robert and Harold G. Grasmick. 1995b. "The Collection of Data for Gang Research." Pp. 154–57 in *The Modern Gang Reader*, 2nd ed., edited by M. Klein, C. L. Maxson, and J. Miller. Los Angeles, CA: Roxbury Publishing.

Campbell, Anne. 1991. *The Girls in the Gang*, 2nd ed. Cambridge, MA: Basil Blackwell.

Chesney-Lind, Meda. 1997. *The Female Offender: Girls, Women, and Crime*. Thousand Oaks, CA: Sage Publications.

Chesney-Lind, Meda and Randall G. Shelden. 1992. *Girls: Delinquency and Juvenile Justice*. Pacific Grove, CA: Brooks/Cole.

Chesney-Lind, Meda, Randall G. Shelden, and Karen A. Joe. 1996. "Girls, Delinquency, and Gang Membership." Pp. 185–204 in *Gangs in America*, 2nd ed., edited by C. R. Huff. Thousand Oaks, CA: Sage Publications.

Chin, Ko-Lin. 1996. "Gang Violence in Chinatown." Pp. 157–81 in *Gangs in America*, 2nd ed., edited by C. R. Huff. Thousand Oaks, CA: Sage Publications.

Cloward, Richard and Lloyd Ohlin. 1960. *Delinquency and Opportunity: A Theory of Delinquent Gangs*. New York: Free Press.

Cohen, Albert. 1955. *Delinquent Boys: The Culture of the Gang*. New York: Free Press.

Covey, Herbert, Scott Menard, and Robert Franzese. 1997. *Juvenile Gangs*. Springfield, IL: Charles C. Thomas.

Curry, G. David, Richard A. Ball, and Scott H. Decker. 1996. "Estimating the National Scope of Gang Crime From Law Enforcement Data." Washington, DC: National Institute of Justice, Research in Brief.

Curry, G. David, Richard A. Ball, and Robert Fox. 1994. "Gang Crime and Law Enforcement Recordkeeping." Washington, DC: National Institute of Justice, Research in Brief.

Curry, G. David and Scott H. Decker. 1998. *Confronting Gangs: Crime and Community*. Los Angeles, CA: Roxbury Publishing Company.

Curry, David and Irving A. Spergel. 1992. "Gang Involvement and Delinquency among Hispanic and African-American Adolescent Males." *Journal of Research in Crime and Delinquency* 29:273–91.

Decker, Scott H. 2000. "Legitimizing Drug Use: A Note on the Impact of Gang Membership and Drug Sales on the Use of Illicit Drugs." *Justice Quarterly* 17:393–410.

Decker, Scott H. and Kimberly Kempf-Leonard. 1995. "Constructing Gangs: The Social Definition of Youth Activities." Pp. 14–23 in *The Modern Gang Reader*, 1st ed., edited by M. Klein, C. L. Maxson, and J. Miller. Los Angeles, CA: Roxbury Publishing.

Decker, Scott H. and Barrik Van Winkle. 1996. *Life in the Gang: Family, Friends, and Violence*. New York: Cambridge University Press.

Deschenes, Elizabeth Piper and Finn-Aage Esbensen. 1999. "Violence and Gangs: Gender Differences in Perceptions and Behavior." *Journal of Quantitative Criminology* 15:63–69.

Elliott, Delbert S. and Suzanne S. Ageton. 1980. "Reconciling Race and Class Differences in Estimates of Delinquency." *American Sociological Review* 45:95–110.

Esbensen, Finn-Aage and Elizabeth Deschenes. 1998. "A Multisite Examination of Youth Gang Membership: Does Gender Matter?" *Criminology* 36:799–827.

Esbensen, Finn-Aage, Elizabeth Deschenes, and L. Thomas Winfree, Jr. 1999. "Differences between Gang Girls and Gang Boys: Results from a Multisite Survey." *Youth and Society* 31:27–53.

Esbensen, Finn-Aage and David Huizinga. 1993. "Gangs, Drugs, and Delinquency in a Survey of Urban Youth." *Criminology* 31:565–89.

Esbensen, Finn-Aage, David Huizinga, and Anne Weiher. 1993. "Gang and Non-gang Youth: Differences in Explanatory Factors." *Journal of Contemporary Criminal Justice* 9:94–116.

Esbensen, Finn-Aage and Wayne Osgood. 1997. "National Evaluation of G.R.E.A.T." Washington, DC: National Institute of Justice, Research in Brief.

Esbensen, Finn-Aage and L. Thomas Winfree, Jr. 1998. "Race and Gender Differences between Gang and Nongang Youths: Results From a Multisite Survey." *Justice Quarterly* 15:505–25.

Esbensen, Finn-Aage, L. Thomas Winfree, Jr., Ni He, and Terrence Taylor. 2001. "Youth Gangs and Definitional Issues: When is a Gang a Gang, and Why Does It Matter? *Crime and Delinquency* 47:105–30.

Fleisher, Mark S. 1998. *Dead End Kids: Gang Girls and the Boys They Know*. Madison, WI: University of Wisconsin Press.

Gibbons, Don C. 1997. "Review Essay: Race, Ethnicity, Crime, and Social Policy." *Crime and Delinquency* 43:358–80.

Hagedorn, John M. 1988. *People and Folks: Gangs, Crime and the Underclass in a Rustbelt City*. Chicago, IL: Lakeview.

Hill, Karl, James Howell, J. David Hawkins, and Sara Battin-Pearson. 1999. "Childhood Risk Factors for Adolescent Gang Membership: Results from the Seattle Social Development Project." *Journal of Research in Crime and Delinquency* 36:300–22.

Howell, James C. 1998. "Youth Gangs: An Overview." Washington, DC: Office of Juvenile Justice and Delinquency Prevention, Juvenile Justice Bulletin.

Howell, James C. and Scott H. Decker. 1999. "The Youth Gangs, Drugs, and Violence Connection." Washington, DC: Office of Juvenile Justice and Delinquency Prevention, Juvenile Justice Bulletin.

Huff, C. Ronald. 1998. "Comparing the Criminal Behavior of Youth Gangs and At-Risk Youths." Washington, DC: National Institute of Justice, Research in Brief.

Huizinga, David and Delbert S. Elliott. 1986. "Reassessing the Reliability and Validity of Self Report Delinquency Measures." *Journal of Quantitative Criminology* 2:293–327.

Klein, Malcolm. 1971. *Street Gang and Street Workers*. Englewood Cliffs, NJ: Prentice-Hall.

Klein, Malcolm. 1995. *The American Street Gang: Its Nature, Prevalence, and Control*. New York: Oxford University Press.

Klein, Malcolm, Cheryl Maxson, and Lea C. Cunningham. 1991. "'Crack,' Street Gangs, and Violence." *Criminology* 29:623–49.

Loeber, Rolf, David P. Farrington, and Daniel Waschbusch. 1998. "Serious and Violent Juvenile Offenders." Pp. 13–29 in *Serious and Violent Juvenile Offenders: Risk Factors and Successful Interventions*, edited by R. Loeber and D. Farrington. Thousand Oaks, CA: Sage Publications.

Maxson, Cheryl L. and Malcolm Klein. 1990. "Street Gang Violence: Twice as Great, or Half as Great?" Pp. 71–102 in *Gangs in America*, 1st ed., edited by C. R. Huff. Newbury Park, CA: Sage Publications.

Maxson, Cheryl L., Monica Whitlock, and Malcolm Klein. 1998. "Vulnerability to Street Gang Membership: Implications for Practice." *Social Service Review* March:70–91.

Miller, Jody. 1998. "Gender and Victimization Risk Among Young Women in Gangs." *Journal of Research in Crime and Delinquency* 35:429–53.

Miller, Jody. 2001. *One of the Guys: Girls, Gangs, and Gender.* New York: Oxford University Press.

Miller, Jody and Scott H. Decker. 2001. "Young Women and Gang Violence: Gender, Street Offending, and Violent Victimization in Gangs." *Justice Quarterly* 18:115–40.

Miller, Walter B. 1958. "Lower Class Culture as a Generating Milieu of Gang Delinquency." *Journal of Social Issues* 14:5–19.

Miller, Walter B. 1975. *Violence by Youth Gangs and Youth Groups as a Crime Problem in Major American Cities.* Washington, DC: U.S. Government Printing Office.

Moore, Joan. 1978. *Homeboys: Gangs, Drugs, and Prison in the Barrios of Los Angeles.* Philadelphia, PA: Temple University Press.

Moore, Joan. 1991. *Going Down to the Barrio: Homeboys and Homegirls in Change.* Philadelphia, PA: Temple University Press

Padilla, Felix. 1992. *The Gang as an American Enterprise: Puerto Rican Youth and the American Dream.* New Brunswick, NJ: Rutgers University Press.

Pope, Carl E. 1979. "Race and Crime Revisited." *Crime and Delinquency* 25:347–57.

Russell, Katheryn. 1998. *The Color of Crime.* New York: New York University Press.

Sanchez-Jankowski, Martin. 1991. *Islands in the Street.* Berkeley, CA: University of California Press.

Shaw, Clifford and Henry D. McKay. [1942] 1969. *Juvenile Delinquency in Urban Areas.* Chicago, IL: University of Chicago Press.

Short, James F., Jr. 1968. "Introduction to Gang Delinquency and Delinquent Subcultures." Pp. 1–21 in *Gang Delinquency and Delinquent Subcultures,* edited by J. F. Short. New York: Harper and Row.

Short, James F., Jr. 1990. *Delinquency and Society.* Englewood Cliffs, NJ: Prentice Hall.

Short, James F., Jr. and F. Ivan Nye. 1958. "Reported Behavior as a Criterion of Deviant Behavior." *Social Problems* 5:207–13.

Short, James F., Jr. and Fred Strodtbeck. [1965] 1974. *Group Process and Gang Delinquency.* Chicago, IL: University of Chicago Press.

Short, James F., Jr. and Fred Strodtbeck. 1968. "Why Gangs Fight?" In *Gang Delinquency and Delinquent Subcultures,* edited by J. F. Short. New York: Harper and Row.

Short, James F., Jr. and Fred Strodtbeck. 1973. "Why Gangs Fight." In *Modern Criminal,* edited by J. F. Short. New Brunswick, NJ: Transaction Books.

Snyder, Howard and Melissa Sickmund. 1999. "Juvenile Offenders and Victims: 1999 National Report." Washington, DC: Office of Juvenile Justice and Delinquency Prevention.

Spergel, Irving. 1964. *Racketville, Slumtown, Haulberg.* Chicago, IL: University of Chicago Press.

Spergel, Irving. 1969. *Community Problem Solving: The Delinquency Example.* Chicago, IL: University of Chicago Press.

Spergel, Irving. 1990. "Youth Gangs: Continuity and Change." Pp. 171–275 in *Crime and Justice: A Review of Research,* vol. 12, edited by M. Tonry and N. Morris. Chicago, IL: University of Chicago Press.

Spergel, Irving. 1995. *The Youth Gang Problem: A Community Approach.* New York: Oxford University Press.

Thornberry, Terence, Marvin Krohn, Alan Lizotte, and Deborah Chard-Wierschem. 1993. "The Role of Juvenile Gangs in Facilitating Delinquent Behavior." *Journal of Research in Crime and Delinquency* 30:55–87.

Thrasher, Frederic M. [1927] 1963. *The Gang: A Study of One Thousand Three Hundred Thirteen Gangs in Chicago.* Chicago, IL: University of Chicago Press.

Vigil, James D. 1988. *Barrio Gangs: Street Life and Identity in Southern California.* Austin, TX: University of Texas Press.

Walker, Samuel, Cassia Spohn, and Miriam DeLone. 2000. *The Color of Justice.* Belmont, CA: Wadsworth.

Whyte, William Foote. [1955] 1981. *Street Corner Society.* Chicago, IL: University of Chicago Press.

Wilbanks, William. 1987. *The Myth of a Racist Criminal Justice System.* Monterey, CA: Brooks/Cole.

Williams, Jay and Martin Gold. 1972. "From Delinquent Behavior to Official Delinquency." *Social Problems* 20:209–29.

Wilson, William Julius. 1978. "The Declining Significance of Race." *Society* 15:56–62.

Wilson, William Julius. 1980. *The Declining Significance of Race: Blacks and Changing American Institutions.* Chicago, IL: University of Chicago Press.

Wilson, William Julius. 1987. *The Truly Disadvantaged.* Chicago, IL: University of Chicago Press.

Winfree, L. Thomas, Jr., Kathy Fuller, Teresa Vigil, and G. Larry Mays. 1992. "The Definition and Measurement of 'Gang Status': Policy Implications for Juvenile Justice." *Juvenile and Family Court Journal* 43:29–38.

Winfree, L. Thomas, Jr., G. Larry Mays, and Teresa Vigil-Backstrom. 1994. "Youth Gangs and Incarcerated Delinquents: Exploring the Ties Between Gang Membership, Delinquency, and Social Learning Theory." *Justice Quarterly* 11:229–55.

Wyrick, Phelan A. 2000. "Vietnamese Youth Gang Involvement." Washington, DC: Office of Juvenile Justice and Delinquency Prevention.

Yablonsky, Lewis. [1962] 1970. *The Violent Gang.* Baltimore, MD: Penguin Books.

7

Gender Dynamics in Youth Gangs
A Comparison of Males' and Females' Accounts

Jody Miller & Rod K. Brunson

Feminist scholars have long criticized traditional gang research for its reliance on male gang members to gain information about young women (Campbell, 1984, 1990a, 1990b). As recently as a decade ago, we had only sketchy information about girls' gang involvement; only a handful of studies were based on interviews or observations with young women themselves (see Bowker and Klein 1983; Campbell 1984; Giordano 1978; Quicker 1983). This is not the case today: a substantial and growing body of literature on girls in gangs addresses a wide variety of issues (for overviews, see Chesney-Lind and Hagedorn 1999; Curry 1998a). These issues include young women's perceptions of how gender shapes their gang involvement, particularly with regard to their relationships with other gang members, participation in delinquency, and other gang activities (Curry 1997; Fleisher 1998; Hagedorn and Devitt 1999; Joe and Chesney-Lind 1995; J. Miller 1998a, 2001; Moore 1991; Portillos, Jurik, and Zatz 1996; Swart 1991).

Miller, Jody and Brunson, Rod K., "Gender Dynamics In Youth Gangs: A Comparison of Males' and Females' Accounts." *Justice Quarterly*, Vol. 17, No. 3, pp. 420–488, 2000. Copyright © 2000 by the Academy of Criminal Justice Sciences. Reprinted with permission of the Academy of Criminal Justice Sciences.

The agenda for studying female gang involvement is in place. We suggest that it is useful, drawing on these recent insights, to revisit male gang members' accounts of gender dynamics in youth gangs. The impetus for our study is twofold. First, although researchers have emphasized the gendered nature of girls' gangs, they have hardly examined how gender shapes young men's gang involvement. For instance, young women's gangs are routinely classified according to their gender composition such as autonomous, mixed-gender, or "auxiliary" (see W. Miller 1975). In contrast, young men's gangs are defined more broadly in terms of their activities, structures, and criminal endeavors (see Hagedorn and Devitt 1999). This difference reproduces the erroneous notion that gender is relevant only for understanding young women's experiences in gangs.

Second, as noted above, recent research has shown that young women emphasize the prominence of gender in their gangs. This is not surprising in view of ample evidence that gender inequality is a salient feature of most delinquent and criminal subcultures (Maher 1997; Maher and Daly 1996; J. Miller 1998c; Steffensmeier 1983; Steffensmeier and Terry 1986), as in American society more broadly (Connell, 1987). Research with young women has shown consistently that youth gangs—with the exception of autonomous female gangs—are largely male-dominated in structure, status hierarchies, and activities, even while young women are able to carve meaningful niches for themselves (see Fleisher 1998; Hagedorn 1998; J. Miller 1998a, 2001; Moore 1991). Even young women in all-female gangs must operate within male-dominated street networks (see Lauderback, Hansen, and Waldorf 1992; Taylor 1993). Thus comparisons of young men's and young women's statements about gender provide important information for understanding more clearly the milieu in which young women in gangs must negotiate.

To address these issues, we draw from in-depth interviews with 31 male gang members and compare their discussions of gender dynamics in gangs with those of 27 female gang members from the same city. Specifically, we examine how these dynamics are shaped by the gendered structures of gangs: single-sex, mixed-gender, or affiliated male and female groups.[1]

GENDER AS AN ORGANIZING PRINCIPLE OF GROUP LIFE

Several strands of sociological thought clarify why gang structures and group processes may influence gender dynamics in gangs. Gender is an important organizational feature of groups. In a seminal article, Kanter (1977:965) suggests that the "*relative* numbers of socially and culturally different people in a group are . . . critical in shaping interactional dynamics" (author's emphasis). She distinguishes between skewed groups, in which (for instance) women are "tokens," and tilted or balanced groups, in which women have a larger, sizable representation. Where women are tokens in primarily male groups, they attempt to adopt "honorary male" status; when they belong to more gender-balanced groups, they have a greater ability to "affect the culture of the group" (Kanter 1977:966). Thus we would expect all-male gangs, and gangs with only a handful of young women, to adopt the most "hypermasculine" cultural norms (also see Martin and Hummer 1989).

Moreover, a number of studies have illustrated the importance of male peer groups in shaping young men's normative beliefs about gender and the treatment of young women (see Schwartz and DeKeseredy 1997 for an overview). Group processes are important. Young men in fraternities, for instance, behave differently towards women when they are in exploitative normative contexts than in non-exploitative normative contexts (Boswell and Spade 1996). When they are part of a larger peer group in a culture where the exploitation of women is favorable, group norms supersede individual beliefs about right and wrong (Martin and Hummer 1989).

Previous research provides evidence on the significance of group processes in gangs. With regard to delinquency, for example, longitudinal evidence suggests that gang membership facilitates delinquency: that is, youths' participation in delinquency increases dramatically when they join gangs, and it declines significantly once they leave their gangs (Thornberry 1997; Thornberry et al. 1993). Something unique about being in a gang increases the likelihood that youths will be involved in crime, such that "the norms and group processes of the gang . . . facilitate involvement in delinquency" (Thornberry 1997:160; also see Battin et al. 1998; Decker 1996; Esbensen and Huizinga 1993). In view of evidence that similar group processes regarding gender dynamics operate in youth groups such as fraternities and sports teams (Boswell and Spade 1996; Lefkowitz 1997; Martin and Hummer 1989; Schwartz and DeKeseredy 1997), it makes sense to conclude that group processes in gangs shape normative constructions of gender and thus influence the gender dynamics of these groups. Moreover, as the research on gender and organizations suggests, gender composition and ratios within gangs will influence constructions of gender in these groups.

GENDER AND GANG STRUCTURES

Recent survey research has shown, contrary to law enforcement figures (see Curry, Ball, and Fox 1994), that young women are involved in gangs in fairly large numbers. Drawing on a sample of grade 8 pupils in 11 cities, Esbensen and Deschenes (1998) report a 14% prevalence rate of gang membership for boys and an 8% rate for girls (also see Bjerregaard and Smith 1993). Moreover, researchers examining the gender ratio of gang members estimate that young women account for approximately 20 to 46% of gang members (Esbensen and Huizinga 1993; Esbensen and Winfree 1998; Winfree et al. 1992). Only a few studies, however, have investigated the gender structure of gangs beyond young women's proportion of involvement, and we are aware of no studies that examine the gender structure of young men's gangs.

Walter Miller (1975) classifies female gangs into the three types mentioned above: (1) mixed-gender gangs with both female and male members, (2) female gangs that are affiliated with male gangs, which he calls "auxiliary" gangs, and (3) independent female gangs. Although several case studies of these various gang types exist (see Fleisher 1998; Harris 1988; Lauderback et al. 1992; Quicker 1983), there is little evidence on the prevalence of each. Curry's (1997) study of female gang members in three cities found that only 6.4% of girls reported membership in autonomous female gangs, while 57.3% described their gangs as mixed-gender, and another 36.4% said they were in female gangs affiliated with male gangs. Dana Nurge (1998), though critical of Miller's typology, found that the majority of girls she interviewed in Boston belonged to groups that were in some way mixed-gender rather than female-only. Similarly, Jody Miller's (2001) comparative study of female gang members in St. Louis and Columbus, Ohio found that mixed-gender gangs were predominant (88%). In fact, most young women resisted the label female gang, calling it "stupid," "silly," and "laugh[able]."

Miller's research suggests that both the gender structure of girls' gangs and the gender ratio within mixed-gender gangs (i.e., the number and percentage of female versus male members) shape girls' experiences and perceptions of gender in their gangs. She reports:

> Young women who were members of independent female gangs, female gangs that affiliate with male gangs, and mixed-gender gangs with a large portion or substantial number of female members appeared, on the whole, to have more favorable attitudes about girls in general, and described close and supportive relationships among themselves and their female gang peers. Young women in mixed-gender gangs with a small number or percentage of female members clearly articulated the most misogynist attitudes about other young women, did not describe any "sisterhood" within the gang, and instead preferred the company of young men. (1998b:27)

To date we have little information about the gender structures of young men's gangs. Miller's research, along with some recent work on variations among male gang members (see Hagedorn 1997; Lynskey, Esbensen, and Miller 2000), suggests that this topic deserves attention. Before moving on to the current research, we review previous studies about gender dynamics in gangs.

GENDER DYNAMICS IN YOUTH GANGS

As aptly summarized by Campbell (1990a), early discussions of girls' involvement in youth gangs, based on male gang members' accounts, placed young women into one of two roles: the "tomboy" or the "sex object." Campbell notes that the tomboy role appeared to be less accepted by males because it was viewed as outside the realm of appropriate female behavior (also see Swart 1991). On the other hand, young women's "use" as sexual objects was beneficial for male gang members, both because young women were available as sex partners and because they could be used to entrap rival gang males and to conceal weapons and drugs from the police (Campbell 1990a:167–68; also see Fishman 1995). In one of the few studies comparing male with female perspectives, Moore suggests that some young men viewed young women as sexual objects or "possessions" (1991:53); meanwhile young women, though they recognized gender inequalities in their gangs, on the whole wanted to regard themselves as respected by male members. More recent accounts also emphasize the entrenched gender inequality in many gangs (Fleisher 1998; J. Miller 1998a). On the other hand, recent research based on interviews with young women often emphasizes the "sisterhood," support, and companionship that young women find among their female gang peers (Campbell 1990b; Joe and Chesney-Lind 1995; Lauderback et al. 1992). This topic was much neglected in earlier accounts.

As research on young women's gang involvement has increased, so has information about two important elements of gang life: the effects of gender on participation in delinquency and on risk of victimization. Recent research on delinquency suggests several patterns. First, young women in gangs have higher rates of delinquency than their nongang peers, both male and female (Bjerregaard and Smith 1993; Esbensen and Winfree 1998; Thornberry et al. 1993). Second, despite gang girls' greater involvement in delinquency, gang boys still are involved more extensively in the most serious of gang crimes (Fagan 1990). In fact, several studies have noted "a bimodal distribution [for girls], with nearly as many multiple index offenders as petty delinquents" (Fagan 1990:201; also see J. Miller 2001). Researchers have suggested two reasons for gang girls' lesser involvement in serious gang crime. Bowker, Gross, and Klein (1980:516) found evidence of "the structural exclusion of women from male delinquent activities," whereby male respondents reported that they purposely kept girls from participating in activities such as drive-by shootings and gun assaults on rivals. Miller (1998a) found evidence of this as well, but also suggested that young women themselves often use gender as a means of avoiding involvement in activities they find dangerous or morally troubling.

Gender also shapes the risk of victimization within gangs. Part of this relationship is self-evident. Because of the association between participation in delinquency and victimization risk (Lauritsen, Sampson, and Laub 1991), girls' lesser involvement in serious gang crimes makes them less likely to encounter the types of retaliatory gang violence that face the young men involved in these crimes. Hagedorn (1998:197), for instance, states that, on average, the female gang members in his sample report having been shot at .33 times, compared with 9.1 for the males. Findings from the St. Louis Homicide Project offer similar documentation: from 1990 to 1996, 229 gang homicides occurred in the project's study area. Only 19 (8%) of these involved female victims; moreover, the great majority of the young women killed were not the intended targets (Miller and Decker forthcoming 2001). Miller's (1998a) work, however, suggests that young women are at greater risk for particular types of victimization within gangs, particularly sexual abuse and exploitation, routine physical violence at the hands of male peers, and sexual assault (also see Fleisher 1998). In all of the literature cited, certain questions remain unanswered: whether and how these gendered elements of gang life vary across different types of gangs, particularly gangs with different gender structures and ratios. The current study addresses these questions.

METHODS AND SETTING

Our research is based on in-depth interviews with 58 gang members in St. Louis, Missouri. Although St. Louis is typically classified as an emergent gang city (i.e., a city in which gangs have appeared since the 1980s), gangs actually have waxed and waned there for the last century (Decker and Van Winkle 1996). St. Louis gangs appeared most recently in 1985. There is no evidence that these contemporary groups have ties to the gangs that last surfaced there, in the mid-1960s (Maxson, Woods, and Klein 1995). Instead the most recent gang proliferation in the city appears to be linked to recent socioeconomic trends and to urban distress. St. Louis, like many other midwestern cities, has been harmed by considerable deindustrialization and population loss in recent decades; these problems are exacerbated by extreme racial inequality and segregation (Decker and Van Winkle 1996; see Wilson 1996 for an overview). As a number of researchers have shown, such conditions are ripe for the emergence of street gangs (Hagedorn 1998; Hein 1995).

On the basis of their response to a survey by the National Youth Gang Center, the St. Louis Police Department reports approximately 75 active street gangs with 1,300 members (Curry 1998b). With regard to young women's gang involvement, their estimates are not helpful. Law enforcement data is widely known to underreport girls' gang involvement, in part because the data weigh heavily toward older members and members involved in more serious crimes (Curry 1998c). In addition, however, official policies and/or bias exclude young women from consideration (Curry et al., 1994). Although we found it relatively easy to locate young women to participate in our study, the St. Louis Police Department characterizes gangs there as 100% male.

Our sample includes 31 young men and 27 young women. The respondents ranged in age from 12 to 20; most (83%) ranged from 14 to

17. The mean age was 16.1 for boys and 15.6 for girls. We found more age variation among young women: Nine of the 27 girls were 14 or younger, compared with only one young man. This is not unexpected: girls tend to become involved in gangs at younger ages and to exit earlier (see Esbensen and Huizinga 1993). The great majority of participants were African American (54 of 58, or 93%); four (7%) described themselves as multiracial. The interviews with young women were drawn from a larger comparative study that included both gang and nongang girls in two cities. As that project produced data about gender dynamics in gangs, the research was supplemented with the inclusion of male gang members.

Interviewing began in St. Louis in spring 1997 and was completed in early 1998. Most of the interviews were conducted by the second author, including all of the interviews with young men and three-quarters of those with young women. We found no discernible differences in the type or quality of information acquired from his interviews and from those conducted by others. The second author is an African-American man who grew up in north St. Louis, in a neighborhood similar to those the respondents called home. Given his familiarity with life in their communities, he had little difficulty establishing rapport with the youths.

Respondents were recruited to participate in the project with the cooperation of several organizations working with at-risk youths. Once we decided to include young men in the sample, they were drawn from the same agencies as the young women. These included a street outreach program, several additional community agencies that provided drop-in programs for youths, and a local public high school serving youths suspended or expelled from other schools. In addition, eight youths (13%) were interviewed at the local detention center. The interviews were voluntary, and respondents were promised strict confidentiality. Interviews were conducted primarily in private offices, empty classrooms, interview rooms, or secluded spots in visiting rooms. Respondents were paid $10 to $20 for participating, depending on the site.

Because the total population of gang members is unknown, the sampling was purposive; thus the representativeness of our sample is unknown (see Decker and Van Winkle 1996; Glassner and Carpenter 1985). Cooperation by agency personnel generally is useful in providing access to gang members (see Bowker et al. 1980; Fagan 1989). These referrals, however, pose the problem of targeting only officially labeled gang youths. We were able to counteract this problem for the young women in the sample through the comparative design of the original research. Though the sample came from agencies working with young women, we did not target agencies working explicitly with gang members, nor did we attempt to generate a pool of "known" gang members. Instead we asked agency workers to refer us both to girls they believed were involved with gangs and to girls living in neighborhoods where they might have contact with gangs. The young men also were not drawn from agencies working with gang members as such, although we asked agency work-ers to refer us to young men they believed were involved with gangs.

All of the respondents were identified as gang members through self-nomination: that is, when they said they were gang members, we classified them as such. An extensive body of evidence suggests that self-nomination is a robust measure of gang membership (Bjerregaard and Smith 1993; Esbensen, Huizinga, and Weiher 1993; Esbensen and Huizinga 1993; Thorn-berry et al. 1993; Winfree et al. 1992). Nonetheless, as with any method, self-nomination is not foolproof. One potential problem is "wannabes" who claim gang membership although they are not actually involved. To contend with this possibility, we compared youths' accounts and their depth of knowledge with other youths' descriptions of their gangs and other available information. An additional benefit of self-nomination was that it provided a means of applying a limited definitional criterion to capture what may be a varied phenomenon (see Horowitz 1990). Ultimately, finding no blatant inconsistencies in the youths' accounts, we took them at their word.

The youths first were administered a survey, in which they were asked a series of questions about their gang: what the gang was like, how it was structured, what members did (including the kinds of delinquent activities they engaged in), and how and why they became involved. All but two respondents participated in a follow-up interview, which was conducted either just after the survey or within a few days.

The in-depth interviews were semistructured with open-ended ques-tions and were audiotaped. They were organized around several groups of questions and allowed for considerable probing. We discussed the struc-ture of the gang—its history, size, leadership, and organization, and the respondent's place in the group. We asked the youths general questions about their gang involvement and activities, as well as a series of questions on gender in the gang. For example, we asked whether they believed that females and males got involved for similar or for different reasons and in similar or in different ways, what activities males and females engaged in together and separately, and what kinds of males and females had the most status and the greatest influence in the gang. We also asked about issues of safety and danger in the gang, whether the respondents per-ceived these to be gendered, and (if so) in what ways. We followed this basic guideline for each interview, although when additional topics arose, we often departed from the interview guide to pursue them.

The in-depth interviews in particular allowed us to learn more about gang life from the members' viewpoints (see Glassner and Loughlin 1987; Miller and Glassner 1997). Although out-of-context reports may present a more exaggerated, more glamorous, or smoother picture than is war-ranted (see Agar 1977), interviews are not inherently less "trustworthy" than data gathered in other contexts. Instead they reveal particular *sorts* of information, which was quite useful for our purposes. Gangs have particu-lar stories, which are refined through conversation. These stories are part of the gangs' normative structures, even when they are not enacted consistently in behaviors. The stories told by gang members are shaped both by larger cultural standards and by the normative features of the gang itself (see Miller and Glassner 1997; Richardson 1990). For instance, Klein (1971:85) observed that violence is a "predominant 'myth system'" within gangs, even though there is often much more talk about violence than actual violent behavior. Viewed in this way, youths' accounts are significant for what they reveal about constructed norms and values in their gangs. Thus they actually provide two sets of findings: evidence on the nature of their gangs and the cultural frames they use to talk about them. Here we are interested in youths' normative statements about gender, and how these are used to describe their experiences in gangs.

Perhaps the greatest limitation of our data is that, to ensure the youths' confidentiality, we did not record the names of their gangs. Thus we cannot determine whether girls and boys were reporting information on the same gangs. Hagedorn and Devitt (1999) suggest that different members of the same gangs sometimes describe their groups differently with regard to composition and activities. Fortunately we found consistency in the reports of the few youths we could identify as members of the same gangs (youths who revealed their gangs' names without being prompted). On the whole, however, our data cannot address this question.

Nonetheless, throughout the interviews the youths provided overlapping discussions about gender dynamics in their gangs. These issues form the core of the discussion that follows. Though our research is exploratory, it offers insights into variations in young men's and young women's experiences of gang life, and into the ways in which gender inequality shapes these experiences. Throughout we provide discussions of young men's and young women's accounts. Yet because the research on girls has appeared in other venues (see J. Miller 1998a, 2001), we focus here primarily on the young men to avoid too much overlap, and highlight how their perceptions compare with those of the young women.

GENDER AND GANG LIFE

The goal of this study is to examine and compare young men's and young women's accounts of gender dynamics in youth gangs. We concentrate on the varied nature of gender hierarchies in gangs to understand more fully the milieu in which female gang members must negotiate, as well as how normative beliefs about gender shape young men's gang involvement. We begin with a discussion of gang structure, comparing how youths describe males' and females' positions in their gangs. Specifically, we examine how young men define their gangs as masculine groups and yet account for the involvement of girls, and how these accounts are shaped by the structures and gender ratios in their gangs. Next we examine gang members' everyday activities and delinquency, focusing on how these are explained in the context of accounts about gender. Finally, we discuss victimization and risk, investigating how youths perceive victimization risk to be shaped by gender.

Gender Structures in Youth Gangs

Recent work suggests that gang structure, including the gender ratio in gangs, influences girls' experiences in these groups (J. Miller 2001; Nurge 1998). Here we examine how young men's descriptions of their gangs' gender composition compare with those of young women. Table 1 provides an overview of the gender composition of youths' gangs in St. Louis. As this table shows, the majority of both girls and boys describe their gangs as mixed-gender (41 of 58, or 71%). Young women were more likely to say their gangs had both male and female members (81%), while a substantial minority of young men (39%) described their gangs as all-male. Moreover, among youths in mixed-gender gangs, young men were much more likely to describe their gangs as composed primarily of other males, while young women characterized their gangs as containing a larger percentage of females.[2]

What accounts for this difference? As we stated in the discussion of methods, it may well be that we simply sampled youths from different gangs, and thus our numbers represent differences across gangs. This is most likely to be the case with youths who describe their gangs as single-sex. Although this may be a partial explanation, it is likely that other dynamics are present as well. Table 2 provides youths' characterizations of several organizational features of their gangs: notably, girls and boys described these aspects of their gangs in essentially the same ways.[3] We call attention to gang initiations: the majority of youths (37 of 58, or 64%) said their gangs use initiations to induct new members. The initiation is often an important rite of passage, establishing the initiate as a "real" member in the eyes of the gang.[4]

In St. Louis, Decker and Van Winkle (1996) report greater latitude in what counts as a gang initiation for young women than for young men. Though we did not ask young men about their own initiations, we found differences in the youths' descriptions. Young men who described their initiations said that they were beaten into the gang by its members, assaulted a rival gang member, and/or participated in a drive-by shooting. Eleven girls (41%) reported that they went through such an initiation, but the other six girls (22%) who said their gangs held initiations listed an array of other activities. Vickie[5] was tattooed, committed a carjacking, and punched a girl on the street; Marie said she was "blessed in" the gang (members said a gang "prayer" over her); Sheila received gang tattoos; Dionne received a gang tattoo and "snatch[ed] a lady's purse"; Brenda indicated she was "sexed in" (engaged in sexual intercourse with a number of male members); and Wanda said that although her gang typically held initiations, she wasn't required to go through one.

Table 1   Gender Composition of Gangs (*N* = 58)

	Females	Males
Gang Type	(*n* = 27)	(*n* = 31)
Mixed-gender	22 (81%)	19 (61%)
Male-only	0 (0%)	12 (39%)
Female-only	2 (8%)	0 (0%)
Female/associated with male gang	3 (11%)	0 (0%)
Gender Ratio, Mixed-Gender Gangs	(*n* = 22)	(*n* = 19)
Majority male	14 (64%)	19 (100%)
Half or more female	8 (36%)	0 (0%)
Females one-fifth or fewer members	7 (32%)	13 (68%)
Females one-third or fewer members[a]	11 (50%)	18 (95%)

[a] Cumulative figure; includes youths who report one-fifth or fewer female members.

Table 2   Gang Characteristics (*N* = 58)

	Females (*n* = 27)	Males (*n* = 31)
Initiation rites or rituals	17 (63%)	20 (65%)
Established leaders	14 (52%)	16 (52%)
A territory that it claims	25 (93%)	30 (97%)
Specific rules or codes	19 (70%)	18 (58%)
Special colors, symbols, signs, clothing	27 (100%)	29 (94%)

It could be that young women are more likely than young men to count these alternative activities as "initiations." Several young men reported, for instance, that they knew girls who thought of themselves as members of the boys' gang, although the young men did not classify them as such. Curtis explained:

> There ain't no girls in our gang. Like the girls that we talk to, *they'll try to say they from our 'hood, but . . . they ain't from our gang.* Some is raised up over there [in the 'hood] but they just, like, hang with us every day. We wouldn't consider them as no members, but they just be around sometimes. (our emphasis)

All of the young men in our sample said that girls whom they didn't define as members hung around their gang. Many of these young women probably didn't define themselves as members either, but probably some of them did so. Possible gender differences in definitions of a "member" thus may explain some of the difference in youths' perceptions of their groups' gender composition.

Accounts of Girls' Place in Gangs

In regard to gender composition and how it shapes young men's perspectives, it is useful to compare the way boys in all-male gangs account for the absence of young women with the way boys in mixed-gender gangs account for their presence. Most of the boys who classified their gangs as all-male were adamant that gangs, by their nature, were masculine groups. Asked why there were no girls in his gang, Frank replied, "What can a female do in gangs? What can a female do? It's just for fellas for real." Carlos agreed: "I like hangin' out with the homeys full-time. Hangin' out with a female and doin' the same thing dudes do, that ain't for me." And Lamont said:

> Females, I just don't see it. I couldn't respect a female in a gang. I couldn't respect it. . . . With a female, she plays like a backbone, she supposed to just support the male. I don't think she supposed to be out there on the field with him, [but] just have his back. You ain't supposed to be out there hanging and banging. I don't think so.

Obviously, one explanation that these young men gave for females' lack of involvement in their gangs was that it was inappropriate for girls to participate in (and encroach on) "the fellas'" thing: girls shouldn't behave like boys. In addition, several young men suggested that having girls in the gang would pose a risk for members because girls were less reliable and couldn't be counted on to be "down" when the gang really needed them. Mike explained, "We don't want to take a chance of them getting soft for real." Lamont agreed: "Females really can't handle drama . . . . A female can't fight. I can't say all females can't fight males, but you just don't want to take that chance." He elaborated: "Males, if they have something they living and dying for, I mean they go to the fullest with it. What I've seen with females, I mean they so sometime [about their commitment], they can switch up [change loyalties] at any time."

Doug said that one girl who hung with his group received a lot of respect because "she got a male's mentality. She acts like a male, she just be down for whatever." On the whole, however, he suggested that having girls in the gang would obligate boys to watch out for them, distracting them from the business at hand and damaging others' perceptions of the strength of their group:

> RB: You said before that there aren't any females in your gang. Why is that?
>
> Doug: I don't know. We're not gonna be strong, you know what I'm saying, we don't want no girls. I mean it could be some girls in there, but [we] don't want a lot for real 'cause we're about strictly money and down for ourselves.

RB: And how would girls affect that?

Doug: People would look at us. . . . Letting a girl in your gang is like, well, you would let them get in there but you would have to watch them like if they was your sister.

Young men in mixed-gender gangs also viewed gangs as a primarily "male thing," but in doing so, they had to account for the presence of young women. All of the boys in these gangs said their gangs were mostly males; as shown in table 1, however, the gender composition varied. At the low end, Robert said his gang included only one female member; at the high end, Eric's gang was nearly gender-balanced, with approximately 20 males and 15 females. Depending on the number of girls in their gang, young men accounted for female involvement somewhat differently.

Robert's gang, for instance, was essentially all-male. The one young woman in his gang was given "honorary male" status. He explained, "Tia's not a regular girl, she like a boy for real. She act like a boy and work around the boys. Other girls, I don't think they should be in no gang, they soft for real." Asked why there weren't more girls in his gang, Robert replied emphatically, "Because don't nobody let them. 'Cause Tia, she grew up, she like us for real. She just like the dudes for real, that's why." He said that the only time Tia was excluded from the boys' activities was "when we trying to get on other girls, 'cause she'll mess it up sometimes." As an added benefit, however, Tia "bring a lot of new girls to the clique, so we can always have a girl to talk to."

Most young men in gangs with a small number of female members gave similar accounts. James explained, "Most people look at the girls in our neighborhood [with respect] because they [are] mostly like us. They don't do mostly things that girls do, they do what we do." Kevin agreed: "People know about Terri. They say she ain't no joke. [She] beat up dudes, do everything. . . . She don't really fight girls, she don't like fighting girls 'cause she say they too weak. She fights dudes."

Young men in gangs with a sizable number of girls described their gangs in somewhat different terms. Although they clearly emphasized its masculine endeavors, they also left space for young women's involvement, mostly by highlighting their gangs' social elements. Many St. Louis gangs have strong neighborhood ties (also see Decker and Van Winkle 1996; J. Miller 2001). Being from the 'hood and "being down" for the 'hood were important prerequisites for membership. These young men described girls' gang membership as occurring in much the same way as young men's: because they grew up in the neighborhood, around the gang, and wanted to be a part of it. Asked how girls got involved, Arthur explained, "The same way males do, they just grow up around there and just join." In addition, these young men said that girls got involved as a result of their ties to male members. For instance, Maurice observed, "They got big cousins, big brothers that showed them a lot of stuff, stuff they can get from being in the gang."

Being from the neighborhood and/or having ties to other members, girls were an accepted part of these gangs. Nonetheless, these young men described girls as essentially different from, and lesser than, the boys in the gang. For instance, although Reggie said that girls joined his gang "the same way I did, hangin' out with 'em," he also explained that with the possible exception of "a gal that's been raised, they mother been a dope fiend or something, they know all about the ghetto, I wouldn't even, see what I'm saying, consider [girls] as being like me because they ain't been through stuff I've been through." Consequently, as we show below, although males and females in these gang spent much of their social time together, gender segregation increased when it was time to "get down to business": girls did their own thing, and boys did theirs.

We found similar variation in young women's accounts. Young women in gangs with only a few female members differentiated themselves from other girls, and instead described themselves as one of the guys (see J. Miller 2001). As Toni explained, "I don't really hang out with girls." Her role models in the gang were "dudes . . . [that] got a nice car, money just coming out, and got all gals." She explained, "They just ball like that . . . just have money coming out the butt . . . and I'm gonna be up there one day eventually." Of other young women, she commented, "Ain't no girl over there doing it like the dudes."

In contrast, young women in gangs with a sizable number of female members did not characterize girls as lesser members. Yvette explained, "The boys, the girls are no different for real, we all the same." Like the boys, however, they emphasized the social aspects of their time with male and female gang members, and also indicated that there were differences between boys and girls when it came to confrontations with rival gangs and others on the streets (also see J. Miller 1998a, 2001). Pam, a member of a mixed-gender set that was half female, remarked, "Most of the girls for real is family and friends. We went to school together, grew up together." She said her friendships were the most valuable benefits she gained from being in the gang, despite the group members' ongoing involvement in drug sales and other criminal endeavors and the economic benefits she derived from these. In comparison, the two young women in an all-female gang stated their dislike of gender inequality in mixed-gender gangs, and saw it as distinguishing those gangs from their own. They also defined their gang as being more about "friendship" and less about the typical criminal endeavors of other St. Louis gangs. As noted, young women in predominantly male gangs did not emphasize these relational elements, but focused instead on status and economic benefits.

Gang Activities, Delinquency and Everyday Life

Although the criminological literature emphasizes gangs' delinquent activities, much of youths' time with their gangs tends to be relatively mundane. Occasional acts of serious crime become the material for much ongoing conversation and discussion (see Fleisher 1998; Jensen 1995; Klein 1995). Gang members spend much of their time in the same activities as other adolescents—hanging out, talking and laughing, playing sports or games, listening to music, watching television, and having parties. As discussed above, all of our male respondents indicated that they spent part of their time hanging out with girls, whether or not the girls were members of the gang. Here we examine gang members' accounts of how gender shapes gang members' activities. These accounts were influenced by the gender composition of the young men's gangs.

Along with their belief that the gangs are "a male thing," young men in all-male gangs were those most likely to describe girls primarily as sexual objects or individuals to be exploited. Curtis summed this up succinctly: "Most girls are just for pleasure, fun and pleasure for real. We don't see girls like we see dudes." He said that members of his gang hung out with girls to "have sex with them and stuff like that." Mike said that girls who hung out with his gang were "freaked on. Just getting touched on everywhere. It gets pretty nasty." Asked why girls would hang out with them, he surmised, " 'Cause they like thugs, that's all it is. Being around money." Carlos said that when they hung out with girls, they had "sleepovers and parties, just sex and all that. . . . They ain't . . . hangin' with us, they just there for whoever want to do something with 'em." Similarly, Frank described some of the girls who hung out with his gang as "nothing but . . . freaks."

> RB: What makes a girl that hangs out with the gang a freak?

> Frank: Everybody done had her, everybody done been with her. Tricking her, giving up [her] money, and stuff like that.

On the whole, these young men suggested that girls had no place in their gangs except to provide sex. In fact, Lamont said that other than being available for sex, girls caused problems for the gang:

> Girls tend to just bring a lot of bad, bad vibes. I mean because they be with us one day, they be with the next gang the next day, this gang, that gang, and when they with our gang, they tell us about a different gang, so when they with a different gang they telling about us. So we hit 'em [have sex with them] or you got to go. We don't really kick it with women.

Young men in these gangs engaged in a variety of criminal activities, mostly centered around drug sales and disputes with rival gangs. The young women who hung around them were not included in these activities. Frank said the girls could "come and buy what they want [drugs] and leave, that's it." Doug said, "We bang with other sets . . . whoever's tripping with us. [But] they don't do that." Several young men in all-male gangs observed, however, that one benefit of having girls around was that they tempered young men's actions, particularly with regard to violence.

Carlos explained, "[Girls] keep people from doin' things, 'cause when a girl ain't around they just get crazy." Jon agreed: "Dudes would go places and be the ones that usually fight . . . and sometimes girls usually break it up. If it wasn't for them, we would have gotten in a whole lot of trouble." Mike described one such incident: "I had this one little girl that I used to talk to, and my partner Walter got shot by some dudes and we was gonna go and get 'em. She hid my gun from me and I couldn't even go do it." Young women's presence gave these young men an excuse for avoiding violence, even though they depicted girls as good only for sex.

Because of the composition of their groups, young men in mixed-gender gangs spent more time with young women, particularly the girls in their gangs. Not surprisingly, the young men with only one or a few "honorary males" in their gangs described these young women as active participants in many of their criminal endeavors. Recall that Robert's gang had one female member, Tia. Robert said, "[We] go to parties and drink together, sling [sell drugs] together, all that." Tia was an integral part of her gang's drug selling: Robert commented, "Nobody gonna mess with her for real." The only difference Robert noted was that "drive-bys, shootings, and stuff—Tia don't too much get into that." In fact, this was the general pattern across all of the mixed-gender gangs: young women hung out and partied with the young men in the gang, and like the young men they were routinely involved in street-level drug sales, but they tended not to be involved in the most serious forms of gang crime, such as confrontations with rivals that entailed shooting. Instead, girls' confrontations were usually fights with other girls, which typically involved fists or, less frequently, knives (also see J. Miller 1998a, 2001).

For instance, although James said that males and females in his gang "do a lot of things together" socially, they typically did not get involved in each other's fights. In fact, he said that when "guns and stuff" were involved, young men excluded the girls from their activities "'cause we didn't want nobody to blame us because something happen to them, if something would have happened to them." Other young men told much the same story. Dwayne explained, "Robbery and stuff like that, we don't want no girls with us doing stuff like that. . . . We don't want no girls with us, period, when we got to go to work." Ray said, "Girls, they usually do all the drug selling and all that. We do more than all the girls do, but we just give them what they can do. They don't do no hard, you know, shooting nobody or drive-bys." Jermaine commented, "Girls ain't no punks. They ain't gonna kill nobody though."

Differences in the use of violence also appeared in the survey portion of the interviews. When asked whether and how the gang provided protection for its members, the majority of both males and females said that a primary means was providing members with guns. All but one of the girls simply said "Guns"; in contrast, many of the boys described particular types of guns: 9mms, AK-47s, Mac 11s, Tech 9s, 44 mags, rifles, gauges. In addition, the young women emphasized that guns were primarily the boys' domain. Explaining why girls used fists and knives rather than guns, Pam suggested that it was because "we ladies, we not dudes for real." In fact, when the young women were asked whether they carried weapons, 19 (70%) said they carried knives or similar instruments, while only seven (26%) reported carrying guns. Of these, only four carried guns as their weapon of choice.[6]

Most of the youths in mixed-gender gangs, male and female, also said that members sometimes had casual sexual relationships or dated one another. Shawn characterized these simply as "getting high and having sex." Debra explained that girls in her gang went with boys in the same gang "all the time," but she said they "don't write about it"—that is, they don't "tell everybody in the 'hood." Several young men, however, said that they chose to avoid dating within the gang. Kenny said, "We strictly sisters and brothers." And James explained that he didn't date girls in his gang because "I can't have a girl that's the same way as me. I want to find me a young lady, not a tomboy." Others pointed to conflicts that arose when gang relationships were mixed up with romantic relationships. Kevin said that it was the source of fights between males and females: "Crazy stuff, sleeping with each other and stuff, telling people [about it]." Several young women also described fights that arose between girls over their relationships with particular boys, or between boys and girls.

In contrast to the young men in all-male gangs, even when young men in mixed-gender gangs spoke about dating or sexual relationships, very few described gang girls exclusively in these terms. (With the exception of serious girlfriends, however, they described nongang girls who hung with the gang in primarily sexual terms.) Instead they also related to gang girls in nonsexual ways. Nonetheless, their descriptions of this aspect of their relationships were quite similar to those of boys in all-male gangs, as illustrated in the following conversation with Jamal:

> Jamal: I don't really date none of the girls from the 'hood. I done hit 'em but we ain't never, say, went with them. That would cause some problems.
>
> RB: So explain what hitting is.
>
> Jamal: Have sex with them.
>
> RB: You don't think that causes any problems, so if you actually had a relationship with them you think that would cause a problem?
>
> Jamal: Yeah, 'cause we out there chilling, getting high, trying to get up on some more babes, they be like, "You got me bumped [disrespected me]," wanna fight, wanna argue.
>
> RB: So do they go for that? You just hitting it every now and then, do they go for that?
>
> Jamal: It depends . . . how your game is, you got to have a game.

Dwayne said that although males in his gang don't "go out with" or date girls in the gang, they will "just talk to them, hit 'em, this and that, like female dogs . . . just fuck 'em." Asked how the girls react to this treatment, he continued, "Some of them out for what we out for . . . just to fuck or get they stuff or whatever." For some girls, this might be true: they might take the same attitude about their relationships with boys as the boys take toward them. Many young women, however, complained about young men's attitudes about sex and what they saw as young men "running games" on girls. Moreover, for some girls these experiences are clearly exploitative, and set the stage for further exploitation (also see J. Miller 1998a).

The clearest illustration is the practice of "sexing" girls into the gang. Describing this initiation, Jermaine explained that the girl has to have sex with "anybody that wants to." The conversation continued:

> RB: Suppose everybody wants to?
>
> Jermaine: She ain't gonna let everybody do it. Half probably get in it, though.

Once these girls have gone through a sexual initiation, they are denigrated by other members of the gang, male and female, and are widely viewed by the males as sexually available. As Jermaine continued, "If they get sexed in, they don't really get no respect."

Young men in mixed-gender gangs remained wedded to narrow accounts of gender and sexuality, and this attitude shaped their relation-ships with young women in their gangs. As a result, young women acknowledged that male-female relationships were often a source of strife between and among gang members. Nonetheless, belonging to a mixed-gender gang, as opposed to hanging out with members of male gangs (or with members of mixed-gender gangs), appears to offer young women more room to negotiate interactions with other gang members, which extend beyond the sexual. On the whole, young men in these gangs described the girls in their gangs in ways that were less single-minded and less disparaging than in the accounts given by young men in all-male gangs. In fact, girls received status and protection in the gang as well; these benefits may be regarded as worth such a trade-off (see J. Miller 1998a, 2001).

Victimization and Risk in Gangs

Despite the differences we reported above when comparing the accounts of young men in all-male and mixed-gender gangs, we found consistency in their perceptions of victimization risk and how it was shaped by gender. Three themes emerged in young men's interviews; these were equally likely to be articulated by young men in all-male and in mixed-gender gangs. First, they argued that young men faced dangers that young women did not, both because rival male gang members were more likely to target males than females, and because young men placed themselves at greater risk through their own behaviors. Second, they argued that young women faced dangers because they were weaker than young men and less capable of handling themselves. Finally, a number of young men suggested that young women were at risk of being kidnapped and sexually assaulted by rival gang members who wished to send a message or retaliate against the gang.

With regard to the dangers faced by young men, Dwayne explained that rival gang members targeted males rather than females: "If the enemy over there, unless you got a crowd over here and a crowd over here with girls and us, they'll shoot at us first. They'll just ride through and see the girls there, probably keep on rolling, but if they see one of the dudes, they'll shoot." James agreed: "Most of the time they be trying to get on us before they try to get on the girls." Carlos said that "a man's gonna take it hard on another man," but he'll "take it more easy" on a female. Several young men noted that girls often simply were unnoticed by rivals. Maurice explained, "[Girls] ain't got to worry about no nigger coming up to them 'cause the nigger don't always see them in the hood, they always seeing us." And Mark noted, "If you look at a girl, you won't be thinking about is she in a gang. But if you look at a dude, he could just have on a wrong color and you will label him as a gang member."

Overall, young men felt that males faced greater limitations on their movement and activities because of the constant threat that they would be recognized by a rival and attacked. Rick stated, "Girls, they can wear any color they want to without another girl worried about them being in a gang. Dudes can't wear any color they want to." Wayne said, "You got to constantly keep your head up looking over your shoulder, worried about what time you got to be here, . . . worried about who trying to set you up." In fact, some of the young men felt that they were trapped in gang life because their enemies would always remember them, even after they quit their gang involvement. Will explained, "Being in a gang ain't a life. It's not like getting in no bathtub. You can't get in and get out so easy. Once you a member, you stuck being a gang member, and you got these enemies knowing that you a gang member. I mean, you a gang member forever to them." Travis agreed: "It ain't gonna be like, you out of the gang. It be like, he was in it then, he still in it."

Although they sometimes felt "stuck," young men said that they often brought the risk on themselves because of their actions toward other gangs. As Jermaine explained, "The men, they always the ones that get shot at, and start trouble and stuff. The girls don't too much start it unless it's with another female." Curtis similarly observed,

> The dudes . . . they get into static with other dudes, but girls, they'll get into static, they'll fight, and then it'll be over with. But . . . dudes, when you in a gang, you get into a fight. After you done beat them up with your hands, then it's time for them to go get they guns 'cause they got to win.

Although they believed that males were more likely than females to be targeted most of the time, young men believed that girls were also at risk, as Lamont explained, because "females are more weaker." Ray agreed: "Girls don't really have [as] much power as dudes have except for the real big ones." Ronald said, "Man got courage but a woman don't." And James noted, "It's dangerous [for girls] because they ain't as strong as we is and most of the time they can't take the things we can take." Wayne argued that men not only had greater physical strength but also more street smarts. He explained, "It's more dangerous for women, 'cause it ain't a spot for them. Because I think, to me, I think a man thinks more than a woman. Some things a woman think, a man done already thought of." Similarly, Reggie noted that "men can handle theyself more than women." And Travis said:

> It's more easier to get the girls 'cause they be showing they face more than we do. If we know we got enemies, we gonna stay where we at in our territory. They be going outside to other people's territory. That's what's getting them caught up, what's getting them whipped and stuff. So if you know you got some enemies over there, you can't go over there. That's dumb.

Because females were described as easier targets than males, a number of young men stated that rival gangs sometimes targeted females, not by simply shooting at them, as they did with males, but by kidnapping, beating, and sexually assaulting them. Lamont explained, "Say my home-boys, when we need to, gang members will kidnap women who you associate with to get information or even to send a message. They won't kidnap no male, they'll kidnap a female to send a message, beat her up, rape her, do whatever to send a message." Travis described the same scenario: "If she in a gang and I know her, say I'm in this one gang and I'm on her, I'll probably know her brother and I'll know she in a gang. Like if I can't get to him and you in a gang, the same gang, I'm gonna get to you first. You more easier to get to, you a female." Will described the emotional turmoil such a retaliation might entail:

> If it's a girl Blood right here and a boy Blood right here, if the boy Crip think that the boy Blood more tougher than the girl, he might go off on the girl just to hurt the other gang member. . . . It be the same way if somebody catch your cousin. It's gonna hurt you more than killing you—that's your cousin. You gonna have the same feelings.

We found little evidence that such incidents occur routinely. These events are atypical, but nonetheless they occur.[7] Regardless of how widespread such practices are, they feature prominently in young men's accounts and illustrate how girls in gangs are viewed in regard to sexuality and sexual vulnerability.

When young women spoke about victimization risk, they described many of the same issues raised by young men, with one important exception. Young women agreed that the threats they faced were different than those faced by young men. In contrast with the boys, however, the young women did not regard themselves as particularly vulnerable because they were weak or not strong enough to take care of themselves. Instead they noted the danger of being targeted by male gang members because they were viewed as easy targets. Marie said she knew of young men "taking a female just because it's a female, he think she can't do nothing because she's a female."

Although the girls generally believed that gangs were dangerous, they did not view themselves as facing the same threats as young men, partly because some girls chose not to be involved in particularly risky endeavors. Brittany explained that she didn't worry much about violence "because when they do stuff I scatter, I ain't nowhere around. When they do their little dirt, Brittany is at home." Thus, while boys described themselves as excluding girls from dangerous activities, many girls said they excluded themselves (also see J. Miller 1998a).

Most girls didn't say they were afraid of being shot by rival gang members. Instead they focused on the threat of being jumped and beaten up. Because they did not perceive themselves as facing life-threatening situations, they were more likely to emphasize the strength of their fighting skills to get them out of risky situations. When young women mentioned the danger of being shot, they described their fear of being in a group situation when someone opened fire—being in the wrong place at the wrong time, rather than being a specific target. Girls were more likely to describe the devastating effects when young men they cared about were killed in gang violence. Marie recalled, "My partner, my best friend, he got shot, was sixteen years old. He was a Blood. He shouldn't have gone out like that."

In combination, girls' and boys' accounts suggest that both groups face a series of gender-specific victimization risks, shaped as well by variations in gang type. Young women face risks tied to their perceived sexual vulnerability; young men are at greater risk for lethal violence. Again, Miller and Decker's (forthcoming, 2001) analysis of gang homicides in St. Louis bear out these youths' descriptions. One-quarter of St. Louis homicides in the 1990s were gang-related; only 8% of those involved female victims, who almost always were not the intended targets. Moreover, Decker's (1999) follow-up of the gang members in Decker and Van Winkle's (1996) research on gangs in St. Louis supports that young men's descriptions of the dangers they face are not mere "bravado." Of the 99 youths in their study, 19—nearly one-fifth—are now dead. This is a conservative estimate: Decker has succeeded in tracking only about half of the original sample. These findings highlight the importance of victimization risk among young men in gangs. Our research suggests that the normative features of gang masculinity are important in shaping that risk.

DISCUSSION

The goal of this paper has been to compare young men's and young women's perspectives on gender dynamics in youth gangs, with an eye toward variations that result from differences in the gender composition of these groups. Our findings are exploratory, but they raise important issues for future research. To more clearly understand gender dynamics in youth gangs, we must examine both young women's and young men's perspectives, and we must recognize that gender is as relevant for young men as for young women. Research with young women has shown us that the dichotomous tomboy/sex object categories are insufficient to account for girls' gang involvement. Although these characterizations are present in young men's discussions of girls' roles in gangs, they are also inadequate for capturing the range of young men's accounts. Young men's depictions of girls appear to be shaped by the types of gangs to which young men belong, and by the number of females in their groups.

Young men who characterize their gangs as all-male hold the most stereotypical and most derogatory views of girls, while young men in mixed-gender gangs apparently have a wider variety of interactions with girls and a broader conceptualization of girls' place in gangs. In many ways, girls' and boys' accounts of young women's place in mixed-gender gangs are quite similar, with a notable exception: young men often hold exploitative views of their sexual interactions with girls in their gangs. It is evident, however, that girls in mixed-gender gangs are not treated *only* as "sex objects," and that in certain circumstances girls whom the young men view as "tomboys" are accepted as one of the boys. This is not the case with young men in all-male gangs; they state clearly that young women don't belong in gangs, and that the young men do not want girls around doing the things that "the fellas" do.

These findings suggest that it is important to be attentive to variations in gangs because these shape the contexts in which young women in and around gangs must negotiate. For instance, it is likely that young women who hang around all-male gangs are at greatest risk for ongoing sexual mistreatment. On the other hand, young women who are one of only a few females in primarily male gangs may be at the greatest risk for participation in serious delinquency, and thus may face greater physical dangers at the hands of rival gangs. Finally, young women in gangs with a substantial number of female members have more supportive relationships with other young women and with young men, and are better able to moderate their participation in risky activities. Even these young women, however, are likely to vary in the nature of their gang involvement and the extent to which young men view them as hard-core gang members or as sexually available (see J. Miller 1998a).

Our research cannot address why youths join one type of gang rather than another. For instance, do young men choose all-male or mixed-gender gangs in part on the basis of their attitudes about girls? Recall that Carlos said, "Hangin' out with a female and doin' the same things dudes do, *that ain't for me*" (our emphasis). We don't know how strongly this belief influenced Carlos to join an all-male gang, or whether he adopted the attitudes of the other young men around him as a result of his involvement in such a gang. The same question applies to young women. Do girls who perceive themselves as different from other females, as more like "one of the dudes," choose gangs that fit their beliefs, or does involvement in particular types of gangs facilitate the construction of this belief? Some of this variation may not be a matter of substantial choice: because gangs tend to be neighborhood-based, especially in St. Louis (see Decker and Van Winkle 1996), it may depend partly on the gangs available to youths. At this point, this question remains unanswered.

Moreover, we cannot say how fully the youths' accounts about gender are the result of attitudes they acquire while in the gang or how much they are due to attitudes they bring to the gang. We know that the larger community and societal beliefs about gender teach young women and young men how to think and act in normatively scripted ways (see West and Zimmerman 1987). Consider Lefkowitz's (1997) sophisticated analysis of a gang rape by a group of high school athletes in suburban New Jersey. He deftly shows how community attitudes, shaped by traditional family values and by the valorization of high school athletics, created a social context in which this group of privileged boys gained a sense of entitlement and acquired attitudes about women that allowed the gang rape to occur. Larger community norms also taught girls to fit themselves into scripted roles as "mothers" or as "sex objects." Within gangs as well, these larger community and societal contexts must be examined and considered (see Pyke 1996).

Nonetheless, abundant evidence points to the importance of the organizational features of groups and indicates the strength of male peer dynamics in maintaining gender hierarchies and supporting the exploitation of young women (Kanter 1977; Lefkowitz 1997; Martin and Hummer 1989; Schwartz and DeKeseredy 1997). In addition, research suggests that less exploitative norms regarding girls, such as those we found in mixed-gender gangs, exist in some groups (Boswell and Spade 1996; Kanter 1977). All of this work, however, points to the importance of group processes, which we know are evident in other features of gang norms and activities (Decker 1996; Klein 1995).

Finally, our research has focused primarily on youths' accounts of *young women's* place in gangs. Future research also must be more attentive to male gang members' constructions of masculinities in their interactions with one another, and with the police and others in their communities (see Anderson 1990). Several studies have attempted this (Jankowski 1991; Messerschmidt 1993; Portillos, et al. 1996); however, we need more nuanced accounts that examine variations in young men's masculine identities in gangs (see Connell 1995; Hagedorn 1997). This is particularly important for understanding the interlocking relationship between gang crime and the risk of gang-related victimization among young men (also see J. Miller 1998a).

In addition, future research on youth gangs must focus on other aspects of gangs that may shape gender relations. We concentrated here on gender structures and ratios in gangs, but other important factors exist as well. Nurge's (1998) research on gangs and cliques in Boston, for instance, raises other significant issues that shape girls' gang involvement, including leadership, duration, territoriality, and the primary activities and goals of these groups. By teasing out these complexities, we can achieve a full, rich account of contemporary youth gangs.

Notes

[1] Several scholars have pointed out that this tripartite division misses some of the complexity of gang formations (Hagedorn and Dewitt 1999; Nurge 1998). In her research in Boston, Nurge found four distinct types of mixed-gender groups; these were differentiated further by whether the groups were territorial, and by whether they referred to themselves as gangs or as cliques. Nonetheless we maintain our focus on the three-way comparison, paying attention to the gender ratio within these groups but not to other organizational features.

[2] Because of the small number of girls in all-female gangs, these are not a primary focus of the analysis.

[3] We found few differences here according to gang type. A smaller proportion of young men in all-male gangs (50%, versus 74% in mixed-gender gangs) said their gangs held initiations; they also were less likely to characterize their gangs as having rules or codes (42% versus 68%), and fewer (83% versus 100%) described their gangs as adopting gang colors, symbols, or signs. Among girls, only the two in an all-female gang described their gang as nonterritorial, although it was neighborhood-based.

[4] Gang initiations vary across sites. Ethnographic work in traditional gang cities suggests that males initiate males, while females initiate females. Yet because of the proliferation and diffusion of "gang culture," youths adapt to their own settings what they have learned about gangs. Miller's (2001) work suggests that this is the case with regard to initiations as well as other features of gangs. For instance, Columbus gangs are influenced strongly by the traditional Chicago gang style; they attach more importance to initiations than do gangs in St. Louis, which are influenced more strongly by Los Angeles gang style. Reports on both places include descriptions of males initiating females and females initiating females, but no descriptions of females initiating males. In the current study, though youths were disdainful toward girls who had been "sexed in" (also see J. Miller 1998a, 2001), both males and females nonetheless classified them as members because this was a standard (though gender-specific) initiation practice in some mixed-gender gangs.

[5] All names are fictitious.

[6] Unfortunately, because the scope of the interviews with young men was narrower, we did not ask about their weapon-carrying practices. Even so, when the young men were asked about fights with rivals and/or the gang's protective functions, 26 (84%) described their gangs as using guns.

[7] In St. Louis, one recent case received a great deal of press coverage. A woman was kidnapped, sexually assaulted, and tortured by a group of male and female gang members for her perceived transgressions against the group (Bryan 1998). In Miller's (2001) study, three young women reported that they had been gang-raped by gang members. Another young woman described her participation in the kidnapping and beating of a rival gang girl, and then her role as a witness while her fellow gang members gang-raped the girl.

References

Agar, M. H. 1977. "Ethnography in the Streets and in the Joint: A Comparison." Pp. 143–56 in *Street Ethnography: Selected Studies of Crime and Drug Use in Natural Settings*, edited by R. S. Weppner. Beverly Hills, CA: Sage.

Anderson, E. 1990. *Streetwise: Race, Class, and Change in an Urban Community.* Chicago: University of Chicago Press.

Battin, S. R., K. G. Hill, R. D. Abbott, R. F. Catalano, and J. D. Hawkins. 1998. "The Contribution of Gang Membership to Delinquency Beyond Delinquent Friends." *Criminology* 36:93–115.

Bjerregaard, B. and C. Smith. 1993. "Gender Differences in Gang Participation, Delinquency, and Substance Use." *Journal of Quantitative Criminology* 4:329–55.

Boswell, A. A. and J. Z. Spade. 1996. "Fraternities and Collegiate Rape Culture: Why Are Some Fraternities More Dangerous Places for Women?" *Gender & Society* 10:133–47.

Bowker, L. H., H. S. Gross, and M. W. Klein. 1980. "Female Participation in Delinquent Gang Activities." *Adolescence* 15:509–19.

Bowker, L. H. and M. W. Klein. 1983. "The Etiology of Female Juvenile Delinquency and Gang Membership: A Test of Psychological and Social Structural Explanations." *Adolescence* 18:739–51.

Bryan, B. 1998. "Woman Is Beaten, Tortured by Gang Members, Police Say." *St. Louis Post-Dispatch*, March 26, p. 1B.

Campbell, A. 1984. *The Girls in the Gang.* New York: Basil Blackwell.

Campbell, A. 1990a. "Female Participation in Gangs." Pp. 163–82 in *Gangs in America*, edited by C. R. Huff. Newbury Park, CA: Sage.

Campbell, A. 1990b. "On the Invisibility of the Female Delinquent Peer Group." *Women & Criminal Justice* 2:41–62.

Chesney-Lind, M. and J. M. Hagedorn, eds. 1999. *Female Gangs in America: Essays on Girls, Gangs and Gender.* Chicago: Lakeview.

Connell, R. W. 1987. *Gender and Power.* Stanford, CA: Stanford University Press.

Connell, R. W. 1995. *Masculinities.* Berkeley: University of California Press.

Curry, G. D. 1997. "Selected Statistics on Female Gang Involvement." Presented at the fifth Joint National Conference on Gangs, Schools, and Communities, September, Orlando, FL.

Curry, G. D. 1998a. "Female Gang Involvement." *Journal of Research in Crime and Delinquency* 35:100–18.

Curry, G. D. 1998b. Personal correspondence, August 13.

Curry, G. D. 1998c. "Proliferation of Gangs in the U.S." Presented at the Eurogang Workshop, October, Schmitten, Germany.

Curry, G. D., R. A. Ball, and R. J. Fox. 1994. "Gang Crime and Law Enforcement Recordkeeping." Washington, DC: National Institute of Justice.

Decker, S. H. 1996. "Collective and Normative Features of Gang Violence." *Justice Quarterly* 13:243–64.

Decker, S. H. 1999. Untitled paper on future directions of gang research. Presented at gang research cluster meeting, Office of Juvenile Justice and Delinquency Prevention and National Institute of Justice, October, Washington, DC.

Decker, S. H. and B. Van Winkle. 1996. *Life in the Gang.* Cambridge, UK: Cambridge University Press.

Esbensen, F. and E. P. Deschenes. 1998. "A Multi-Site Examination of Gang Membership: Does Gender Matter?" *Criminology* 36:799–828.

Esbensen, F. and D. Huizinga. 1993. "Gangs, Drugs, and Delinquency in a Survey of Urban Youth." *Criminology* 31:565–89.

Esbensen, F., D. Huizinga, and A. W. Weiher. 1993. "Gang and Non-Gang Youth: Differences in Explanatory Factors." *Journal of Contemporary Criminal Justice* 9:94–116.

Esbensen, F. and L. T. Winfree. 1998. "Race and Gender Differences Between Gang and Non-Gang Youth: Results from a Multi-Site Survey." *Justice Quarterly* 15:505–25.

Fagan, J. 1989. "The Social Organization of Drug Use and Drug Dealing Among Urban Gangs." *Criminology* 27:633–67.

Fagan, J. 1990. "Social Processes of Delinquency and Drug Use Among Urban Gangs." Pp. 183–219 in *Gangs in America*, edited by C. R. Huff. Newbury Park, CA: Sage.

Fishman, L. T. 1995. "The Vice Queens: An Ethnographic Study of Black Female Gang Behavior." Pp. 83–92 in *The Modern Gang Reader*, edited by M. W. Klein, C. L. Maxson, and J. Miller. Los Angeles: Roxbury.

Fleisher, M. S. 1998. *Dead End Kids: Gang Girls and the Boys They Know*. Madison: Wisconsin University Press.

Giordano, P. C. 1978. "Girls, Guys and Gangs: The Changing Social Context of Female Delinquency." *Journal of Criminal Law and Criminology* 69:126–32.

Glassner, B. and C. Carpenter. 1985. "The Feasibility of an Ethnographic Study of Property Offenders." Unpublished report prepared for the National Institute of Justice, Washington, DC.

Glassner, B. and J. Loughlin. 1987. *Drugs in Adolescent Worlds: Burnouts to Straights*. New York: St. Martin's.

Hagedorn, J. M. 1997. "Frat Boys, Bossmen, Studs and Gentlemen: A Typology of Gang Masculinities." Pp. 152–67 in *Masculinities and Violence*, edited by L. Bowker. Thousand Oaks, CA: Sage.

Hagedorn, J. M. 1998. *People and Folks: Gangs, Crime and the Underclass in a Rustbelt City*. 2nd ed. Chicago: Lakeview.

Hagedorn, J. M. and M. Devitt. 1999. "Fighting Female: The Social Construction of Female Gangs." Pp. 256–76 in *Female Gangs in America: Essays on Girls, Gangs and Gender*, edited by M. Chesney-Lind and J. M. Hagedorn. Chicago: Lakeview.

Harris, M. G. 1988. *Cholas: Latino Girls and Gangs*. New York: AMS.

Horowitz, R. 1990. "Sociological Perspectives on Gangs: Conflicting Definitions and Concepts" Pp. 37–54 in *Gangs in America*, edited by C. R. Huff. Newbury Park, CA: Sage.

Jankowski, M. S. 1991. *Islands in the Streets: Gangs and American Urban Society*. Berkeley: University of California Press.

Jensen, E. L. 1995. "An Interview with James F. Short, Jr." *Journal of Gang Research* 2:61–68.

Joe, K. A. and M. Chesney-Lind. 1995. "'Just Every Mother's Angel': An Analysis of Gender and Ethnic Variations in Youth Gang Membership." *Gender & Society* 9:408–30.

Kanter, R. M. 1977. "Some Effects on Proportions of Group Life: Skewed Sex Ratios and Responses to Token Women." *American Journal of Sociology* 82:965–90.

Klein, M. W. 1971. *Street Gangs and Street Workers*. Englewood Cliffs, NJ: Prentice-Hall.

Klein, M. W. 1995. *The American Street Gang: Its Nature, Prevalence and Control*. New York: Oxford University Press.

Lauderback, D., J. Hansen, and D. Waldorf. 1992. "'Sisters Are Doin' It For Themselves': A Black Female Gang in San Francisco." *Gang Journal* 1:57–70.

Lauritsen, J. L., R. J. Sampson, and J. H. Laub. 1991. "The Link Between Offending and Victimization Among Adolescents." *Criminology* 29:265–92.

Lefkowitz, B. 1997. *Our Guys: The Gled Ridge Rape and the Secret Life of a Perfect Suburb.* Berkeley: University of California Press.

Lynskey, D., F. Esbensen, and J. Miller. 2000. "The Impact of Gender Composition on Gang Member Attitudes and Behavior: Results from a Multi-Site Survey." Presented at the annual meetings of the American Society of Criminology. November, San Francisco, CA.

Maher, L. 1997. *Sexed Work: Gender, Race and Resistance in a Brooklyn Drug Market.* Oxford: Clarendon Press.

Maher, L. and K. Daly. 1996. "Women in the Street-Level Drug Economy: Continuity or Change?" *Criminology* 34:465–92.

Martin, P. Y. and R. A. Hummer. 1989. "Fraternities and Rape on Campus." *Gender & Society* 3:457–73.

Maxson, C. L., K. Woods, and M. W. Klein. 1995. "Street Gang Migration in the United States." Final report to the National Institute of Justice, Washington, DC.

Messerschmidt, J. W. 1993. *Masculinities and Crime: Critique and Reconceptualization of Theory.* Lanham, MD: Rowman and Littlefield.

Miller, J. 1998a. "Gender and Victimization Risk Among Young Women in Gangs." *Journal of Research in Crime and Delinquency* 35:429–53.

Miller, J. 1998b. "One of the Boyz? Girls' Gender Strategies in Youth Gangs." Presented at the annual meetings of the American Sociological Association, August, San Francisco.

Miller, J. 1998c. "Up It Up: Gender and the Accomplishment of Street Robbery." *Criminology* 36:37–66.

Miller, J. 2001. *One of the Guys: Girls, Gangs and Gender.* New York: Oxford University Press.

Miller, J. and S. H. Decker. Forthcoming, 2001. "Young Women and Gang Violence: An Examination of Gender, Street Offending and Violent Victimization in Gangs." *Justice Quarterly* 18.

Miller, J. and B. Glassner. 1997. "The 'Inside' and the 'Outside': Finding Realities in Interviews." Pp. 99–112 in *Qualitative Research*, edited by D. Silverman. London: Sage.

Miller, W. 1975. *Violence by Youth Gangs and Youth Groups as a Crime Problem in Major American Cities.* Washington, DC: U.S. Government Printing Office.

Moore, J. 1991. *Going Down to the Barrio: Homeboys and Homegirls in Change.* Philadelphia, PA: Temple University Press.

Nurge, D. 1998. "Female Gangs and Cliques in Boston: What's the Difference?" Presented at the annual meetings of the American Society of Criminology, November, Washington, DC.

Portillos, E., N. Jurik, and M. Zatz. 1996. "Machismo and Chicano/a Gangs: Symbolic Resistance or Oppression?" *Free Inquiry in Creative Sociology* 24:175–84.

Pyke, K. D. 1996. "Class-Based Masculinities: The Interdependence of Gender, Class, and Interpersonal Power." *Gender & Society* 10:527–49.

Quicker, J. C. 1983. *Homegirls: Characterizing Chicana Gangs.* San Pedro, CA: International University Press.

Richardson, L. 1990. *Writing Strategies: Reaching Diverse Audiences.* Newbury Park, CA: Sage.

Schwartz, M. D. and W. S. DeKeseredy. 1997. *Sexual Assault on the College Campus: The Role of Male Peer Support.* Thousand Oaks, CA: Sage.

Steffensmeier, D. J. 1983. "Organizational Properties and Sex-Segregation in the Underworld: Building a Sociological Theory of Sex Differences in Crime." *Social Forces* 61:1010–32.

Steffensmeier, D. J. and R. Terry. 1986. "Institutional Sexism in the Underworld: A View from the Inside." *Sociological Inquiry* 56:304–23.

Swart, W. J. 1991. "Female Gang Delinquency: A Search for 'Acceptably Deviant Behavior.'" *Mid-American Review of Sociology* 15:43–52.

Taylor, C. 1993. *Girls, Gangs, Women and Drugs.* East Lansing: Michigan State University Press.

Thornberry, T. P. 1997. "Membership in Youth Gangs and Involvement in Serious and Violent Offending." Pp. 147–66 in *Serious and Violent Juvenile Offenders: Risk Factors and Successful Interventions*, edited by R. Loeber and D. P. Farrington. Thousand Oaks, CA: Sage.

Thornberry, T. P., M. D. Krohn, A. J. Lizotte, and D. Chard-Wierschem. 1993. "The Role of Juvenile Gangs in Facilitating Delinquent Behavior." *Journal of Research in Crime and Delinquency* 30:75–85.

West, C. and D. H. Zimmerman. 1987. "Doing Gender." *Gender & Society* 1:125–51.

Wilson, W. J. 1996. *When Work Disappears: The World of the New Urban Poor.* New York: Knopf.

Winfree, L. T., Jr., K. Fuller, T. Vigil, and G. L. Mays. 1992. "The Definition and Measurement of 'Gang Status': Policy Implications for Juvenile Justice." *Juvenile and Family Court Journal* 43:29–37.

Early Precursors of Gang Membership
A Study of Seattle Youth

Karl G. Hill, Christina Lui, & J. David Hawkins

Gang members engage in more delinquent behavior than their peers who are not in gangs. The Seattle Social Development Project (SSDP) study shows that compared with youth who are not gang members, those who are gang members more often commit assault, robbery, breaking and entering, and felony theft; indulge in binge drinking; use and sell drugs; and are arrested (see figure 1). Other studies also show that gang members are more likely to commit violent crimes and property crimes and use drugs (Spergel, 1995; Thornberry, 1998). They are more than twice as likely to carry guns and three times as likely to sell drugs (Bjerregaard and Lizotte, 1995).

Why do some youth join gangs while others do not? Understanding what predicts gang membership is vital for preventing youth from joining gangs. The SSDP study is especially valuable for understanding the predictors of gang membership. As a longitudinal project that has tracked a sample of more than 800 youth from 1985 to the present, SSDP affords the opportunity to trace the effect of factors present in youth's lives at ages 10 to 12 on the likelihood of their joining and remaining in gangs between the ages of 13 and 18. Although numerous other studies have focused on gang membership (see Howell, 1998, for a review), their cross-sectional design makes it difficult to disentangle predictors of gang membership from the

Hill, Karl G., Lui, Christina, and Hawkins, J. David. 2001, December. "Early Precursors of Gang Membership: A Study of Seattle Youth," *Office of Juvenile Justice and Delinquency Prevention*. Washington, DC: U.S. Department of Justice.

191

Figure 1   Prevalence of Delinquency among Gang and Nongang Youth Ages 13 to 18, SSDP Sample

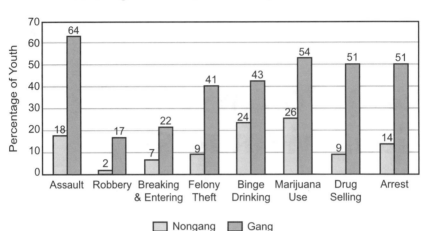

Note: Youth were interviewed at ages 13 to 16 and 18. In each interview, youth reported activities for the past month (except for drug selling and arrest, which were reported for the past year). For gang members, prevalence reflects only the year(s) of membership.

effects. Only two other projects—the Rochester Youth Development Study (Thornberry, 1998; Thornberry and Burch, 1997; Browning, Thornberry, and Porter, 1999) and the Denver Youth Survey (Esbensen and Huizinga, 1993; Esbensen, Huizinga, and Weiher, 1993)—have reported prospective data on gang membership. (These projects are funded by OJJDP as part of its Program of Research on the Causes and Correlates of Delinquency.) This article presents SSDP data on youth who join gangs. It summarizes findings on gender, race/ethnicity, age at joining, and duration of membership; analyzes the relationship between risk factors present at ages 10 to 12 and the likelihood of joining a gang between ages 13 and 18; and discusses prevention-related implications of the risk factor analysis.

SSDP SAMPLE AND METHODOLOGY

SSDP has tracked a sample of 808 persons since 1985, when the participants were fifth-grade students at 18 Seattle, WA, public schools that serve high-crime neighborhoods. Approximately half of the participants are female (396, or 49 percent of the sample). The sample is also ethnically diverse: 372 (46 percent) of the participants identified themselves as European American, 195 (24 percent) as African American, 170 (21 percent) as Asian American, 45 (6 percent) as Native American, and 26 (3 percent) as other ethnicities. Roughly half of the participants are from low-income families. Parents of 46 percent of the participants reported a family income of less than $20,000 a year. Fifty-two percent of the participants took part in the National School Lunch/School Breakfast Program at some point in the fifth, sixth, or seventh grade.

Data on the SSDP participants were collected annually from age 10 through age 16 and then were collected again at age 18. The participants responded to a wide range of questions on family, community, school, peers, gangs, alcohol and drug use, drug selling, violence, weapon use, and victimization. Data were also collected from the participants' parents or guardians, teachers, and school, police, and court records. Collection of data on gang membership began when the participants were 13 years old.

DEMOGRAPHICS OF GANG MEMBERSHIP

Of the 808 SSDP participants, 124 (15.3 percent) reported that they joined a gang at some point between the ages of 13 and 18. Of the 124 participants who joined gangs, the majority (90) were male. Whereas 8.6 percent of all female participants joined gangs, 21.8 percent of all male participants joined (figure 2).Gang members came from diverse racial/ethnic backgrounds—European American, African American, Asian American, Native American, and Hispanic and other ethnicities. However, the

Figure 2   Percentage of Youth Ages 13 to 18 Who Joined a Gang, SSDP Sample

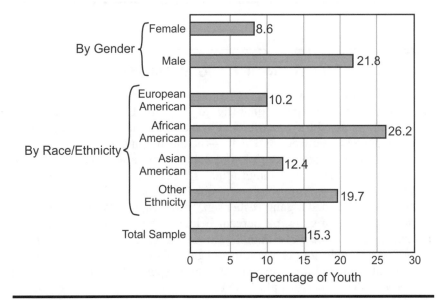

rate for joining a gang was highest among African American SSDP participants. As figure 2 shows, 26.2 percent of all African American participants
reported joining a gang, compared with 10.2 percent of all European
American participants, 12.4 percent of all Asian American participants,
and 19.7 percent of other ethnicities.

Youth in the Seattle sample joined gangs throughout adolescence. Figure 3 shows the cumulative percentage of youth at each age who reported
ever joining a gang. Youth were at risk of joining every year, but the risk
rose most sharply at age 15—the age at which most students make the
transition to high school.

**Figure 3   Cumulative Percentage of Youth Reporting Ever Joining a
Gang, Ages 13 to 16 and 18, SSDP Sample**

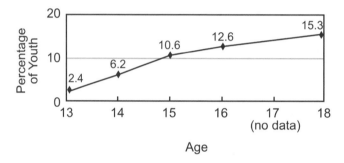

Note: Youth were at risk of joining every year, but the risk rose most
sharply at age 15, at the transition to high school.

Duration of Gang Membership

Of the SSDP participants who became gang members, most belonged to
the gang for a short period of time (figure 4). Of the 124 who joined gangs,
69 percent belonged for 1 year or less and 31 percent belonged for longer.
Only 0.8 percent belonged for 5 years—the maximum period studied.

The SSDP findings on duration of membership are comparable to the
findings of the two other longitudinal studies on gang members mentioned above. Denver Youth Survey researchers reported that 9–11 percent
of their sample joined a gang (Esbensen, Huizinga, and Weiher, 1993). Of
those who joined a gang, 67 percent belonged for 1 year or less and 33
percent belonged for more than 1 year. In the Rochester Youth Development Study sample, 25 percent joined a gang. Of those who joined a gang,
53 percent belonged for 1 year or less and 47 percent belonged for more
than 1 year (Thornberry et al., 1993).

Figure 4   Duration of Gang Membership, SSDP Sample

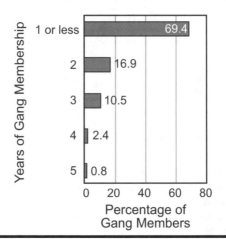

CHILDHOOD RISK FACTORS THAT PREDICT
JOINING AND REMAINING IN A GANG

The table on page 196 shows risk factors present when the SSDP participants were ages 10 to 12 (fifth and sixth grades), with odds ratios that indicate the extent to which each factor predicted whether the participants would join a gang between ages 13 and 18. (For example, the odds ratio of 3.6 for "availability of marijuana" means that youth from neighborhoods where marijuana was most available were 3.6 times more likely to join a gang, compared with other youth.) The table shows that the predictors of gang membership are found in the neighborhood, family, school, peer group, and individual. Having an elevated score for a statistically significant risk factor (i.e., one reliably related to subsequent gang membership) increased the odds of joining a gang about two to three times. The finding of multiple predictors suggests that no single overriding factor explains gang membership. Not all factors tested were reliably related to subsequent gang membership. Although low bonding with parents and low religious service attendance were examined as possible predictors of gang membership, neither was found to predict membership.

Risk Factors and Duration of Gang Membership

These findings suggest that youth join gangs as a result of antisocial influences in neighborhoods, antisocial tendencies in families and peers, failure to perform well in school, and early initiation of individual problem behaviors. All of these factors distinguish youth who join gangs from those

Childhood Predictors of Joining and Remaining in a Gang, SSDP Sample

Risk Factor	Odds Ratio*
Neighborhood	
Availability of marijuana	3.6
Neighborhood youth in trouble	3.0
Low neighborhood attachment	1.5
Family	
Family structure[†]	
One parent only	2.4
One parent plus other adults	3.0
Parental attitudes favoring violence	2.3
Low bonding with parents	ns[‡]
Low household income	2.1
Sibling antisocial behavior	1.9
Poor family management	1.7
School	
Learning disabled	3.6
Low academic achievement	3.1
Low school attachment	2.0
Low school commitment	1.8
Low academic aspirations	1.6
Peer group	
Association with friends who engage in problem behaviors[§]	2.0 (2.3)
Individual	
Low religious service attendance	ns[‡]
Early marijuana use	3.7
Early violence[§]	3.1 (2.4)
Antisocial beliefs	2.0
Early drinking	1.6
Externalizing behaviors[§]	2.6 (2.6)
Poor refusal skills	1.8

* Odds of joining a gang between the ages of 13 and 18 for youth who scored in the worst quartile on each factor at ages 10 to 12 (fifth and sixth grades), compared with all other youth in the sample. For example, the odds ratio for "availability of marijuana" is 3.6. This means that youth from neighborhoods where marijuana was most available were 3.6 times more likely to join a gang, compared with other youth.

[†] Compared with two-parent households.

[‡] ns = not a significant predictor.

[§] These factors also distinguished sustained gang membership (i.e., more than 1 year) from transient membership (1 year or less). For each factor, the number in parentheses indicates the odds of being a sustained gang member (compared with the odds of being a transient member) for youth at risk on that factor.

who do not. What distinguishes youth who remain in gangs for more than 1 year from those who remain for only 1 year or less? The Seattle study indicates that youth who were the most behaviorally and socially maladjusted in childhood were most likely to be gang members for several years. In particular, youth who exhibited early signs of violent and externalizing behavior (e.g., aggression, oppositional behavior, and inattentive and hyperactive behaviors) and those who associated with antisocial peers were more than twice as likely to remain in a gang for more than 1 year than for just 1 year or less.

Multiple Risk Factors

Not only do predictors of gang membership exist in various elements of a youth's environment, but the predictors add up. The more risk factors a youth experienced, the more likely he or she was to join a gang. To assess the effect of multiple risk factors on the likelihood of joining a gang, SSDP researchers divided participants into four groups (each representing one-fourth of the sample), based on the number of risk factors for gang membership they experienced at ages 10 to 12. "No-risk" youth experienced either no risk factors or only one, "low-risk" youth experienced two to three risk factors, "medium-risk" youth experienced four to six risk factors, and "high-risk" youth experienced seven or more risk factors. As figure 5 shows, compared with no-risk youth, low-risk youth were 3 times more likely to join a gang, medium-risk youth were 5 times more likely to join, and high-risk youth were 13 times more likely to join. The more risk factors present in a youth's life, the higher his or her odds of joining a gang.

Figure 5 Odds of Joining a Gang at Ages 13 to 18, by Number of Childhood Risk Factors Present at Ages 10 to 12, SSDP Sample

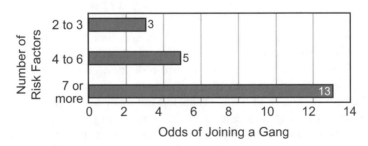

Note: The odds are expressed as comparisons with youth who had no risk factors or only one factor.

IMPLICATIONS FOR PREVENTION

These findings from the SSDP study have three implications for efforts to prevent youth from joining gangs:

Prevention efforts should begin early. Although the SSDP study found that the peak age for joining a gang was 15, this does not mean that prevention efforts should be aimed at 14-year-olds. The risk factors that predicted gang membership in this study were measured when the participants were ages 10 to 12 (fifth and sixth grades)—well before the peak age for joining a gang. Prevention efforts can target these risk factors during the late elementary grades. Some predictors of gang membership, such as marijuana use and violence, are problems in themselves and should be prevented (Ellickson et al., 1998; Ellickson and Morton, 1999; Loeber and Farrington, 2001). SSDP study findings suggest that efforts to prevent these precursors of gang membership may benefit from starting even before the fifth grade.

Prevention efforts should target youth exposed to multiple risk factors. This study has shown that the more risk factors present in a youth's environment, the higher his or her odds of joining a gang. Compared with youth who experienced none or only 1 of the 21 risk factors discussed in this study, youth who experienced 7 or more of the risk factors were 13 times more likely to join a gang. Decreasing the number of risk factors in the environments of youth should help to reduce the prevalence of gang membership.

Prevention efforts should address all facets of youths' lives. As noted earlier, factors that influence youth to join gangs occur in the neighborhood, family, school, peer group, and individual. Efforts to prevent youth from becoming gang members must address the different aspects of their lives. There is no single solution, no "magic bullet" that will prevent youth from joining gangs. Although the thought of combating the 21 predictors of gang membership discussed here may seem daunting, anyone—a parent, brother, sister, teacher, friend, or member of the community—can find ways to reduce the chances that a youth will become a gang member. If these efforts are coordinated, the reduction of risk for gang membership will be even greater.

Taken together, the findings reported in this article suggest some clear guidelines for new strategies to prevent youth from joining gangs. Prevention efforts should start early, focus on youth with multiple risk factors, and take a comprehensive approach that addresses multiple influences.

References

Battin, S. R., Hill, K. G., Abbott, R. D., Catalano, R. F., and Hawkins, J. D. 1998. The contribution of gang membership to delinquency beyond delinquent friends. *Criminology* 36(1):93–115.

Bjerregaard, B., and Lizotte, A. J. 1995. Gun ownership and gang membership. *The Journal of Criminal Law and Criminology* 86(1):37–58.

Browning, K., Thornberry, T. P., and Porter, P. K. 1999. *Highlights of Findings from the Rochester Youth Development Study.* Fact Sheet. Washington, DC: U.S. Department of Justice, Office of Justice Programs, Office of Juvenile Justice and Delinquency Prevention.

Ellickson, P. L., Bui, K., Bell, R., and McGuigan, K. A. 1998. Does early drug use increase the risk of dropping out of high school? *Journal of Drug Issues* 28(2): 357–380.

Ellickson, P. L., and Morton, S. C. 1999. Identifying adolescents at risk for hard drug use: Racial/ethnic variations. *Journal of Adolescent Health* 25(6):382–395.

Esbensen, F. A., and Huizinga, D. 1993. Gangs, drugs, and delinquency in a survey of urban youth. *Criminology* 31(4):565–589.

Esbensen, F. A., Huizinga, D., and Weiher, A. W. 1993. Gang and non-gang youth: Differences in explanatory variables. *Journal of Contemporary Criminal Justice* 9:94–116.

Hill, K. G., Howell, J. C., Hawkins, J. D., and Battin-Pearson, S. R. 1999. Childhood risk factors for adolescent gang membership: Results from the Seattle Social Development Project. *Journal of Research in Crime and Delinquency* 36(3):300–322.

Howell, J. C. 1998. *Youth Gangs: An Overview.* Bulletin. Washington, DC: U.S. Department of Justice, Office of Justice Programs, Office of Juvenile Justice and Delinquency Prevention.

Loeber, R., and Farrington, D. P., eds. 2001. *Child Delinquents: Development, Intervention and Service Needs.* Thousand Oaks, CA: Sage.

Spergel, I. 1995. *The Youth Gang Problem.* New York: Oxford University Press.

Thornberry, T. P. 1998. Membership in youth gangs and involvement in serious and violent offending. In *Serious & Violent Juvenile Offenders: Risk Factors and Successful Interventions*, edited by R. Loeber and D. P. Farrington. Thousand Oaks, CA: Sage Publications, pp. 147–166.

Thornberry, T. P., and Burch, J. H., II. 1997. *Gang Members and Delinquent Behavior.* Bulletin. Washington, DC: U.S. Department of Justice, Office of Justice Programs, Office of Juvenile Justice and Delinquency Prevention.

Thornberry, T. P., Krohn, M. D., Lizotte, A. J., and Chard-Wierschem, D. 1993. The role of juvenile gangs in facilitating delinquent behavior. *Journal of Research in Crime and Delinquency* 30(1):55–87.

Hybrid and Other Modern Gangs

David Starbuck, James C. Howell, & Donna J. Lindquist

INTRODUCTION

"Hybrid" youth gangs[1] have existed in the United States at least since the 1920s (Thrasher, 1927). Early hybrid gangs were described mainly as mixed-race or mixed-ethnicity gangs; modern-day hybrid gangs, however, have more diverse characteristics. "Hybrid gang culture" is characterized by members of different racial/ethnic groups participating in a single gang, individuals participating in multiple gangs, unclear rules or codes of conduct, symbolic associations with more than one well-established gang (e.g., use of colors and graffiti from different gangs), cooperation of rival gangs in criminal activity, and frequent mergers of small gangs.

As the new millennium begins, hybrid gangs are flourishing and their changing nature is making it more difficult to study and respond to them. Today, many gangs do not follow the same rules or use the same methods of operation as traditional gangs such as the Bloods and Crips (based in Los Angeles, CA) or the Black Gangster Disciples and Vice Lords (based in Chicago, IL). These older gangs tend to have an age-graded structure of subgroups or cliques. The two Chicago gangs have produced organizational charts and explicit rules of conduct and regulations, including detailed punishments for breaking gang rules (Spergel, 1995:81). They have developed coalitions with other gangs, forming what are called gang

Starbuck, David, Howell, James C., and Lindquist, Donna, J. 2001, December. "Hybrid and Other Modern Gangs," *Juvenile Justice Bulletin*. Washington, DC: Office of Juvenile Justice and Delinquency Prevention.

"nations," such as Folks (including the Black Gangster Disciples) and People (including the Vice Lords).

Although many communities have gangs that bear the names of earlier gangs that originated in Los Angeles and Chicago, the actual membership of these newer gangs is often locally based and has little or no real national affiliation. These hybrids—new gangs that may have the names but not the other characteristics of older gangs—are one of the new types of gangs most frequently found in communities that had no gang culture prior to the 1980s or 1990s. Because gangs, gang culture, and gang-related activities are dynamic, affected communities need to recognize the new faces of these groups and avoid popularly held, media-influenced misconceptions (see Best and Hutchinson, 1996; Decker, Bynum, and Weisel, 1998; Fernandez, 1998; Fleisher, 1995, 1998; Klein, 1995; Miethe and McCorkle, 1997; McCorkle and Miethe, 1998).

The public continues to perceive youth gangs and gang members in terms of the media stereotype of the California Crips and Bloods rather than in terms of current scientific data (Klein, 1995:40–43, 112–135). Some jurisdictions may erroneously adapt a response that is appropriate for well-publicized Los Angeles or Chicago gang problems but not for gang issues in their own jurisdictions (Miethe and McCorkle, 1997). For example, misreading local gangs as drug trafficking enterprises rather than neighborhood conflict groups could render interventions ineffective. Because the characteristics of local gangs and their criminal involvement may differ from the features of gangs in distant cities, different strategies may be required to address the local gang problem effectively.

This article addresses youth gangs in the 21st century by considering what constitutes a hybrid gang, whether gangs and individual members are migrating across the country, and how new coalitions such as hybrid gangs differ from stereotypical and traditional gangs. The article brings together survey data, recent research results, and firsthand reports from the field to examine today's gangs and their members. For reports from the field, the article draws heavily on insights shared by author David Starbuck, formerly a Sergeant in the Kansas City Police Department's Gang Unit, whose contributions are incorporated throughout the article, especially in the sidebars that give the law enforcement practitioner's point of view.

The broad range of modern or contemporary gangs, as depicted in research studies and survey data, is discussed in the first section of this article. The growth of modern gangs provides a social context for the emergence of hybrid gangs. Hybrid gangs are discussed in the second section, and conclusions and policy implications are highlighted in the final section.

CHARACTERISTICS OF MODERN YOUTH GANGS

Location

Once a problem primarily in large cities, youth gangs are now present in suburbs, small towns, and rural areas (Miller, W.B., 2001). In 1999, law enforcement agencies reported active youth gangs in 100 percent of the nation's largest cities (those with populations of 250,000 or more), 47 percent of suburban counties, 27 percent of small cities (those with populations below 25,000), and 18 percent of rural counties (Egley, 2000; Howell, Moore, and Egley, forthcoming). The average year of gang problem onset was 1989 for large cities, 1990 for suburban counties, 1992 for small cities, and 1993 for rural counties (National Youth Gang Center, 1999). The localities reporting later onset of gang problems are most likely to be in rural counties, small cities, and suburban counties with populations of less than 50,000 (Howell, Egley, and Gleason, forthcoming).

Gangs are also becoming commonplace in institutions, including schools, that had been considered safe havens. For many students, school has become a gathering place for gangs. More than one-third (37 percent) of a nationally representative sample of students reported gang presence in their schools in 1995, a 100-percent increase over 1989 (Howell and Lynch, 2000). Gang presence is being reported even in the military (Hasenauer, 1996).

Member Diversity

Although many gangs continue to be based on race or ethnicity, gangs are increasingly diverse in racial/ethnic composition. Law enforcement agencies responding to the 1998 National Youth Gang Survey estimated that more than one-third (36 percent) of youth gangs had a significant mixture of two or more racial/ethnic groups (National Youth Gang Center, 2000). Small cities had the largest proportion of gangs with mixed race/ethnicity. The Midwest had a larger proportion of mixed gangs than any other region.

Recent student surveys and field studies of local gangs also report significant gender mixtures (Esbensen, Deschenes, and Winfree, 1999; Fleisher, 1998; Miller, J.A., 2001). For example, 92 percent of gang youth in one student survey (Esbensen, Deschenes, and Winfree, 1999:42) said both boys and girls belonged to their gang.

Gangs in suburban areas, small towns, and rural areas show more membership diversity than gangs in large cities. Gangs in these areas have more racially/ethnically mixed membership (National Youth Gang Center, 2000:22–23) and include more females, Caucasians, and younger members than gangs in larger cities (Curry, 2000; Howell, Egley, and Gleason, forthcoming).

Organization

Although a fixed definition has not been established, youth gangs are often presumed to be highly organized groups that engage in some level of criminal activity. Several studies challenge the notion that youth gangs are highly organized. Decker and colleagues (1998) compared the two most highly organized gangs (as reported by police) in Chicago, IL, and San Diego, CA. They found that the Chicago gangs were far more organized than the San Diego gangs but levels of organization were not necessarily linked to increased involvement in crime (Decker, Bynum, and Weisel, 1998:408). Their observation that the San Diego gangs were disorganized mirrors Sanders' (1994) findings. Other studies have questioned the extent of youth gang organization in emerging gang cities such as Denver, CO (Esbensen, Huizinga, and Weiher, 1993); Cleveland and Columbus, OH (Huff, 1996, 1998); Kansas City, MO (Fleisher, 1998); Milwaukee, WI (Hagedorn, 1988); Pittsburgh, PA (Klein, 1995); San Francisco, CA (Waldorf, 1993); Seattle, WA (Fleisher, 1995); and St. Louis, MO (Decker and Van Winkle, 1996; Decker and Curry, 2000).

Modern youth gangs are generally less territory based than gangs of the past (Klein, 1995; Miller, 1992; National Youth Gang Center, 2000). In the older gang cities and the Southwest, gangs traditionally were tied strongly to their neighborhoods or barrios. The Mexican-American "turf gang" pattern, transmitted across generations and ethnicities, has given way to autonomous gangs as the predominant pattern (Klein, 1995:102). These autonomous gangs consist of single, named groups occupying smaller territories and may be based in a neighborhood, a public housing project, or another community location (such as a schoolyard or shopping mall).

Some gang research in the 1960s suggested that youngsters were pressured to join gangs by peers who used strong-arm tactics (Yablonsky, 1967). Community (adult) representatives view peer pressure to join gangs as irresistible (Decker and Kempf-Leonard, 1991). However, it is not as difficult for adolescents to resist gang pressures as is commonly believed. In most instances, adolescents can refuse to join gangs without reprisal (Decker and Kempf-Leonard, 1991; Fleisher, 1995; Huff, 1998; Maxson, Whitlock, and Klein, 1998).

Perpetuating the myth of lifetime membership helps sustain a gang, because the group's viability depends on the ability of active members to maintain the perception that leaving the gang is nearly impossible (Decker and Lauritsen, 1996:114). The reality is that members (especially marginal members) typically can leave a gang without serious consequences (Decker and Lauritsen, 1996; Decker and Van Winkle, 1996; Fleisher, 1995). In fact, most adolescents do not remain in gangs for long periods of time—particularly in areas with emerging gang problems. Studies in three cities that developed gang problems fairly recently—Denver, CO; Rochester, NY; and Seattle, WA—show that from 54 to 69 percent of adolescents who joined gangs in the three cities stayed in them for 1 year or less and 9 to 21 percent belonged for 3 years or more (Thornberry, 1998).

Practitioner's View: The Challenges of Hybrid Gangs

Law enforcement officers from communities unaffected by gangs until the 1980s or early 1990s often find themselves scrambling to obtain training relevant to hybrid gangs. When gang-related training first became widely available in the early 1990s, it often emphasized historical information, such as the formation of the Los Angeles Crips and Bloods in the late 1960s or the legacy of Chicago-based gangs (the Black Gangster Disciples, Latin Kings, and Vice Lords). As law enforcement officers learned about the origins of these influential gangs, they sometimes attempted to apply this outdated information in their efforts to deal with hybrid gangs in their jurisdictions. The assumption that new gangs share the characteristics of older gangs can impede law enforcement's attempts to identify and effectively counter local street gangs, and actions based on this assumption often elicit inappropriate responses from the community as a whole. Citizens may react negatively to law enforcement efforts when they sense that gang suppression actions are geared to a more serious gang problem than local gangs appear to present.

Because of uncertainty in reporting on problem groups such as "cliques," "crews," "posses," and other nontraditional collectives that may be hybrid gangs, some police department staff spend an inordinate amount of time trying to precisely categorize local groups according to definitions of traditional gangs. When training law enforcement groups on investigative issues surrounding drug trafficking or street gangs, instructors must resist the tendency to connect gangs in different cities just because the gangs share a common name. If the groups engage in ongoing criminal activity and alarm community members, law enforcement officers should focus on the criminal activity, regardless of the ideological beliefs or identifiers (i.e., name, symbols, and group colors) of the suspects. This practical approach would circumvent the frustration that results from trying to pigeonhole hybrid gangs into narrow categories and would avoid giving undue attention to gangs that want to be recognized as nationwide crime syndicates.

Onset of Local Gang Problems

It appears that the emergence of gangs in new localities[2] in the 10-year period 1986–96 has contributed to the growth of hybrid gangs. For example, the use of names and symbols of traditional gangs may provide a sense of "legitimacy" to new groups, but the context of the new localities may produce adaptations that lead to divergence from the traditional patterns. Data from the 1996 National Youth Gang Survey show that nearly 9 in 10 (87 percent) of the localities reporting gang problems said that onset occurred during the 1986–96 period (National Youth Gang Center, 1999).

An analysis of National Youth Gang Center (NYGC) survey data on early-onset (before 1990) versus late-onset (during the 1990s) localities (Howell, Egley, and Gleason, forthcoming) found that gangs in the newer gang-problem localities were distinctly different in their demographic characteristics from traditional gangs in jurisdictions where gang problems began much earlier. Gangs in late-onset localities had younger members, slightly more females, more Caucasians, and more of a racial/ethnic mixture. Caucasians were the predominant racial/ethnic group in the latest onset (1995–96) localities. Gangs in localities where gang problems began in the 1990s also tended to have a much larger proportion of middle-class teens.

Gang members in late-onset localities also were far less likely to be involved in violent crimes (homicide, aggravated assault, robbery, and use of firearms) and property crimes than gang members in early-onset localities. For example, about 8 in 10 gang members in localities with the earliest onset of gang problems (before 1986) were said to use firearms in assault crimes "often" or "sometimes," compared with fewer than 3 in 10 gang members in localities with the latest onset (1995–96).

A comparison of drug trafficking patterns in areas with early and late onset of gang problems found that both gang member involvement in drug sales and gang control of drug distribution were much less likely to be significant problems in jurisdictions where gang problems emerged in the past decade (Howell and Gleason, 1999). In the newer gang problem localities, gang control of drug distribution was less likely to be extensive than was gang member involvement in drug sales.

Gang member involvement in drug sales was less extensive in the oldest gang jurisdictions (onset of gang problems before 1980) than in jurisdictions where onset occurred between 1981 and 1990 (Howell and Gleason, 1999). Gang member involvement in drug sales was most extensive in jurisdictions with onset between 1981 and 1985 and then decreased consistently in subsequent onset periods through 1995–96. Thus, gang members in the newest gang problem jurisdictions were much less likely to be involved in drug sales than gang members in jurisdictions where gang problems began during the early to mid-1980s.

Gang Stereotypes

The characteristics of modern gangs contrast sharply with the stereotypical image of gangs that emerged in the 1980s and continues to predominate. From the 1920s through the 1970s, gang members were characterized mainly as young (11–22 years old) Hispanic or African American males who lived in lower class ghetto or barrio sections of the inner city (Klein, 1995; Miller, 1992; Spergel, 1995). In that period, gangs usually were viewed as racially and ethnically homogeneous, spontaneously organized, and authoritatively controlled fighting groups (Miller, 1992). Classic "rumbles" historically were the major form of gang fighting, but they gave way in the 1970s to forays by small armed and motorized bands.

Most gang violence was motivated by honor or local turf defense and, to a lesser extent, control over facilities and areas and economic gain (Miller, 1992:118). Gang violence was not a major social concern (Klein, 1969).

In the mid- to late 1980s, this predominant gang stereotype was modified significantly by a California study in which researchers contended that the two major Los Angeles gangs, the Crips and Bloods, had become highly organized and entrepreneurial and were expanding their drug markets to other cities (Skolnick et al., 1988). Where these drug operations appeared, presumably, so did violent crime.

Gang Migration

The expanded presence of gangs is often blamed on the relocation of members from one city to another, which is called gang migration. Some gangs are very transient and conduct their activities on a national basis. However, the sudden appearance of Rollin' 60s Crips graffiti in a public park in rural Iowa, for example, does not necessarily mean that the Los Angeles gang has set up a chapter in the community. Gang names are frequently copied, adopted, or passed on. In most instances, there is little or no real connection between local groups with the same name other than the name itself (Valdez, 2000:344).

Gang migration does occur, however. According to the 1999 National Youth Gang Survey, 18 percent of all youth gang members had migrated from another jurisdiction to the one in which they were residing (Egley, 2000). Although gang migration is stereotypically attributed to illegal activities such as drug franchising, expansion of criminal enterprises is not the principal driving force behind migration (Maxson, 1998). The most common reasons for migration are social considerations affecting individual gang members, including family relocation to improve the quality of life or to be near relatives and friends. Moreover, in the 1999 National Youth Gang Survey, the vast majority (83 percent) of law enforcement respondents agreed that the appearance of gang members outside of large cities in the 1990s was caused by the relocation of young people from central cities (Egley, 2000). Thus, the dispersion of the urban population to less populated areas contributed to the proliferation of gangs in suburban areas, small towns, and rural areas.

Law enforcement professionals may not be able to differentiate among local gangs that have adopted names of the same well-known gangs from other locales but have no real connection with each other until they begin to interact with gang members through interviews, debriefings, and other contacts. "Hybrid" versions will begin to display variations of the original gang, such as giving different reasons for opposing rival gangs or displaying certain colors. Investigators who take the time to cross-check their local gang intelligence with that of other agencies concerning gangs with identical names are likely to find some subtle and some glaring differences.

Practitioner's View: Gang Migration and Hybrid Gangs in Kansas City

Gangs began moving into the Midwest in the early 1980s, with Kansas City, MO, emerging as a textbook example of a locality experiencing gang migration. Located in almost the geographical center of the continental United States, Kansas City has approximately 5,000 documented gang members and affiliates and numerous Chicago- and California-style gangs in the metropolitan area.[1] No single group has achieved dominance.

The Kansas City Police Department's Drug Enforcement Unit first encountered gang migration while investigating a new wave of drug entrepreneurs in the 1980s. By 1988, these trafficking suspects included confirmed members of the Crips and Bloods sets (subgroups) from the Los Angeles, CA, area. As the presence of the Crips and Bloods became increasingly pronounced in Kansas City, other law enforcement agencies in the Midwest began sharing similar gang intelligence information. Suddenly, Los Angeles Crips and Bloods were known to be dealing cocaine in most major midwestern cities, including Des Moines, IA; Minneapolis, MN; Oklahoma City, OK; Omaha, NE; and Wichita, KS. By 1990, the arrival of Chicago-based gang members in Kansas City was also confirmed through routine investigations of drug trafficking and homicides.

Although Kansas City has experienced gang migration, the area's larger gangs continue to be locally based hybrids that may not have any affiliations with migrant gang members. These groups exemplify the evolving modern gangs that are now increasingly common throughout the United States, particularly in suburban areas, small cities, and rural communities. In the past decade or more, Kansas City's hybrid gang members have adopted traditional gang culture, modified it with personal interpretations and agendas, and become much more of a criminal and societal problem to the community than any of the groups that have migrated into the area.

For example, in two sections of Kansas City, two different gangs operate as the Athens Park Boys (APB). These groups share the name with the original Athens Park Boys, a well-established Bloods set originating in Los Angeles County. Although both of the Kansas City APB gangs engage in criminal activities and antisocial behavior, they have no connection other than the shared name: one set is composed of African American teens on the east side of the city, and the other consists of Caucasian teens, primarily from affluent families in the suburbs. Each group seems to be unaware of its Kansas City counterpart, and neither set is connected to APB in California or any other jurisdiction. Because of their increasing membership and unique characteristics and culture, hybrid gangs (like Kansas City's APBs) warrant further examination.

[1] According to 2000 U.S. Census projections, the total population of Kansas City, MO, is 443,277 and the population of the Kansas City metropolitan area is approximately 1.2 million.

EMERGING INFORMATION ON HYBRID GANGS

Hybrid gangs are more frequently encountered in communities in which gang problems emerged during the 1990s than in localities that reported onset of gang problems in the 1980s. According to law enforcement respondents in the 1998 National Youth Gang Survey, gangs with a significant mixture of two or more racial/ethnic groups represent a larger proportion of all reported gangs in localities that said their gang problem began in the 1990s (Howell, Moore, and Egley, forthcoming). A more specific question was asked about hybrid gangs in the 1999 survey. The survey questionnaire noted: "Some contend that there are youth gangs 'that don't fit the mold' of any particular gang category. These gangs may have several of the following characteristics: a mixture of racial/ethnic groups, male and female members, display symbols and graffiti of different gangs, or have members who sometimes switch from one gang to another." Respondents were asked if they had gangs that fit this description. Six in ten respondents (61 percent) said they had such gangs. However, the average number of such gangs in a given locality—four—is small (Howell, Moore, and Egley, forthcoming).

Hybrid gangs tend to have the following nontraditional features:

- They may or may not have an allegiance to a traditional gang color. In fact, much of the hybrid gang graffiti in the United States is a composite of multiple gangs with conflicting symbols. For example, Crip gang graffiti painted in red (the color used by the rival Blood gang) would be unheard of in California but has occurred elsewhere in the hybrid gang culture.

- Local gangs may adopt the symbols of large gangs in more than one city. For example, a locally based gang named after the Los Angeles Bloods may also use symbols from the Chicago People Nation, such as five-pointed stars and downward-pointed pitchforks.

- Gang members may change their affiliation from one gang to another.

- It is not uncommon for a gang member to claim multiple affiliations, sometimes involving rival gangs. For example, in Kansas City, MO, police may encounter an admitted Blood gang member who is also known in the St. Louis, MO, area as a member of the Black Gangster Disciples gang.

- Existing gangs may change their names or suddenly merge with other gangs to form new ones.

- Although many gangs continue to be based on race/ethnicity, many of them are increasingly diverse in both race/ethnicity and gender. Seemingly strange associations may form, such as between Skinheads, whose members frequently espouse racist rhetoric, and Crips, whose members are predominantly African American.

- Gang members who relocate from California to the Midwest may align themselves with a local gang that has no ties to their original gang.
- Members of rival gangs from Chicago or Los Angeles frequently cooperate in criminal activity in other parts of the country.

Youth often "cut and paste" bits of Hollywood's media images and big-city gang lore into new local versions of nationally known gangs with which they may claim affiliation. Other hybrids are homegrown and consider themselves to be distinct entities with no alliance to groups such as the Bloods/Crips or Folks/People. Because these independent gangs can be the most difficult to classify, they frequently pose the biggest problems for local law enforcement.

Practitioner's View: Gang Trends in the Midwest

Hybrid gangs are particularly prevalent in the Midwest region of the United States. Three features of the Midwest hybrid gangs are troublesome for law enforcement officers: new alignments the hybrid gangs may make, Hispanic gang patterns, and Asian gang criminal activity.

New Alignments. Los Angeles gang members relocating to the Midwest may align themselves with a local gang that has no real ties to the California members' original gang set. In certain cases, gang members relocating from Chicago or Los Angeles conduct criminal activity in cooperation with their former rivals. For example, a recent Kansas City investigation identified multiple defendants in a drug trafficking operation. Checking the suspects' backgrounds through Los Angeles law enforcement files, investigators discovered that some of the defendants were affiliated with the 135 Compton Pirus Bloods, and others were affiliated with the rival Los Angeles gang, the 5 Deuce Hoover Crips. This coalition surprised investigators in Los Angeles, but cooperation often occurs when drug alliances form in "neutral" parts of the country, such as the Midwest. Frequently, profit potential outweighs traditional gang loyalties.

Hispanic Gang Patterns. Factions of Hispanic gangs are becoming increasingly prominent in much of the United States, including the Midwest. It is crucial for law enforcement to know the origins and rivalries of Hispanic gangs, including the Surenos, Nortenos, and Sinaloan Cowboys, because officers increasingly encounter these and other factions. Transient Hispanic gangs may continue their animosity with rivals in other parts of the country and engage in violent encounters with local Hispanic gangs. This phenomenon is more common with Hispanic gangs than with other types of gangs. Hispanic gang members tend to be more loyal and traditional in supporting their gang, even when in transit or when relocating to other parts of the country.

Asian Gang Criminal Activity. In the Midwest, Asian gang criminal activity, much of which is perpetrated by transient gangs, continues to have a great impact. Problems for law enforcement include cultural misunderstandings, identification issues, language barriers, and the transient nature of these gangs (who travel out of State to commit crimes).

Migrating gang members appear to have contributed to the growth of hybrid youth gangs in newer gang problem localities in the 1990s. Migrant gang members may act as cultural carriers of the folkways, mythologies, and other trappings of more sophisticated urban gangs (Maxson, 1998:3).

Movies and "gangsta" lyrics also have contributed to the proliferation of bits and pieces of gang culture. Law enforcement agencies began to notice hybrid gangs after one such gang was depicted in the movie *Colors* (Valdez, 2000:13). Gang migration, movies, and gangsta music work together to introduce local gangs to large-city gang culture. The lack of an existing gang culture allows for modification and adaptation of the culture of urban gangs.

A field study of the Fremont Hustlers in Kansas City, MO, illustrates a unique form of hybrid gang (Fleisher, 1998). The gang had no written set of rules, no membership requirements, and no leader or hierarchy that might pull all 72 members into a coherent organization. By hanging out and establishing ties with Fremont Hustlers, an outsider is slowly assimilated into the gang's social life (Fleisher, 1998: 39). Fremont gang youth did not use the term "member"; their closest expression was "down with Fremont" (Fleisher, 1998: 41). Because the Fremont Hustlers was not a cohesive organization and youth did not talk about the group's structure or operation, the gang structure was difficult to recognize at first. In the study, Fremont gang youth said they were Folks, but they did not know why, except that they liked to draw the pitchfork symbol used by the Folks (Fleisher, 1998:26). Fleisher described this gang as "a haphazardly assembled social unit composed of deviant adolescents who shared social and economic needs and the propensity for resolving those needs in a similar way" (1998:264).

POLICY AND PROGRAM IMPLICATIONS

To devise an appropriate response to hybrid gangs, law enforcement and other community agencies must understand that hybrids do not operate by traditional rules but they often follow general patterns that distinguish them as a new type of gang. That is, they often have members of different racial/ethnic groups, members may claim multiple gangs, codes of conduct may be unclear, graffiti may contain a mixture of symbols, and they may be involved in criminal activity alongside other gangs. In other instances, exemplified by the many cities that have factions of Black Gangster Disciples or Rollin' 60s Crips, there may be differing levels of true connection to the original gang, or the tie may be primarily related to criminal activities such as drug trafficking. This melting pot of gangs and gang culture can confuse concerned agencies, including those in the juvenile and criminal justice systems, as they struggle to separate gangs into neat categories that often do not exist. It is vitally important for law enforcement to concentrate on gang-related criminal activity rather than on more ephemeral aspects of gang affiliation or demographics.

When addressing local gang problems, communities need to understand ongoing changes in the nation's gang dynamics, provide and participate in updated gang-related training, and monitor the specific gangs and associated cultures within their own jurisdictions. Unfortunately, one thing has not changed with the advent of the hybrid gang. There is no universal formula for a patently successful response, and what works in one city may have little impact in another. An effective strategy must be based on an accurate assessment of the local problem, updated information about local gang activities, an examination of resources in the community, and a realistic appraisal of how to gauge the impact of the response. As many agencies as possible, particularly local government and police administration, must be included early in the process of developing a strategy for gang prevention and intervention. The more resources and partners that are involved, especially those with authority to respond directly to gangs, the greater a community's chances for success.

All jurisdictions experiencing gang problems need to assess their problems carefully in light of the gang characteristics reviewed in this article. NYGC (2001a) has developed a protocol that communities can use to guide the assessment of their gang problem. This assessment protocol is applicable in communities of all sizes and characteristics.

The U.S. Department of Justice's Office of Juvenile Justice and Delinquency Prevention (OJJDP) has invested considerable resources in the development and testing of a Comprehensive Community-Wide Approach to Gang Prevention, Intervention, and Suppression (Spergel et al., 1994). This model, based on a national assessment of youth gang policies and programs (Spergel and Curry, 1990), is a general framework that addresses the youth gang problem through the following five interrelated strategies:

- Community mobilization.
- Social intervention, including prevention and street outreach.
- Provision of opportunities.
- Suppression/social control.
- Organizational change and development.

The model is multifaceted and multilayered, involving the individual youth, the family, the gang structure, local agencies, and the community. NYGC (2001b) has prepared a planning guide to assist communities in developing a plan to implement OJJDP's Comprehensive Gang Model.

CONCLUSION

Although hybrid gangs are not new to the United States, they clearly have flourished in the past decade. This article stresses the "culture" of modern hybrid gangs. This concept means that they are characterized by more than simply a mixture of age, gender, and racial/ethnic membership—although the diverse membership of gangs in newer gang problem localities certainly contributes to a wide diversity of gang forms. The hybrid gang culture sharply distinguishes modern gangs from traditional gangs. Modern hybrid gangs do not operate by traditional gang rules. Their affiliation with gangs based in Chicago or Los Angeles is likely to be in name only. They tend to "cut and paste" gang culture from traditional gangs, and they may display symbols traditionally associated with several gangs. They may form alliances with rival gangs to carry out criminal activity, but their independent mode of operating makes them difficult for law enforcement to classify. Thus, it is very important for law enforcement agencies to recognize the diverse gang culture of hybrid gangs, to approach them without any preconceived notions, and to concentrate on their gang-related criminal activity rather than on their presumed affiliations with traditional gangs. Every community—regardless of the presence or absence of hybrid gangs—should conduct a thorough assessment of its unique gang problem before devising strategies for combating it.

Endnotes

[1] In the remainder of this article, unless otherwise noted, the term "gang" refers to youth gangs.
[2] The term "locality" refers to the major types of named place units found in the United States (Miller, W. B., 2001:15). It includes cities, suburban areas, and counties in the National Youth Gang Survey.

References

Best, J., and Hutchinson, M. M. 1996. The gang initiation rite as a motif in contemporary crime discourse. *Justice Quarterly* 13:383–404.

Curry, G. D. 2000. Race, ethnicity, and gender issues in gangs: Reconciling police data. In *Problem Oriented Policing*, vol. 2. Washington, DC: Police Executive Research Forum.

Decker, S. H., Bynum, T. S., and Weisel, D. L. 1998. A tale of two cities: Gangs as organized crime groups. *Justice Quarterly* 15:395–423.

Decker, S. H., and Curry, G. D. 2000. Addressing key features of gang membership: Measuring the involvement of young gang members. *Journal of Criminal Justice* 28:473–482.

Decker, S. H., and Kempf-Leonard, K. 1991. Constructing gangs: The social definition of youth activities. *Criminal Justice Policy Review* 5:271–291.

Decker, S. H., and Lauritsen, J. L. 1996. Breaking the bonds of membership: Leaving the gang. In *Gangs in America*, 2nd ed., edited by C. R. Huff. Thousand Oaks, CA: Sage Publications, Inc., pp. 103–122.

Decker, S. H., and Van Winkle, B. 1996. *Life in the Gang: Family, Friends, and Violence.* New York: Cambridge University Press.

Egley, A., Jr. 2000. *Highlights of the 1999 National Youth Gang Survey.* Fact Sheet. Washington, DC: U.S. Department of Justice, Office of Justice Programs, Office of Juvenile Justice and Delinquency Prevention.

Esbensen, F., Deschenes, E. P., and Winfree, L. T. 1999. Differences between gang girls and gang boys: Results from a multi-site survey. *Youth and Society* 31(1):27–53.

Esbensen, F., Huizinga, D., and Weiher, A. W. 1993. Gang and non-gang youth: Differences in explanatory variables. *Journal of Contemporary Criminal Justice* 9(1):94–116.

Fernandez, M. E. 1998. An urban myth sees the light again. *Washington Post* (November 15):B2.

Fleisher, M. S. 1995. *Beggars and Thieves: Lives of Urban Street Criminals.* Madison: University of Wisconsin Press.

Fleisher, M. S. 1998. *Dead End Kids: Gang Girls and the Boys They Know.* Madison: University of Wisconsin Press.

Hagedorn, J. M. 1988. *People and Folks: Gangs, Crime and the Underclass in a Rustbelt City.* Chicago: Lakeview Press.

Hasenauer, H. 1996 (October). Gang awareness. *Soldiers Online* www.dtic.mil/soldiers

Howell, J. C., Egley, A., Jr., and Gleason, D. K. Forthcoming. *Modern Day Youth Gangs.* Youth Gang Series Bulletin. Washington, DC: U.S. Department of Justice, Office of Justice Programs, Office of Juvenile Justice and Delinquency Prevention.

Howell, J. C., and Gleason, D. K. 1999. *Youth Gang Drug Trafficking.* Youth Gang Series Bulletin. Washington, DC: U.S. Department of Justice, Office of Justice Programs, Office of Juvenile Justice and Delinquency Prevention.

Howell, J. C., and Lynch, J. P. 2000. *Youth Gangs in Schools.* Youth Gang Series Bulletin. Washington, DC: U.S. Department of Justice, Office of Justice Programs, Office of Juvenile Justice and Delinquency Prevention.

Howell, J. C., Moore, J. P., and Egley, A., Jr. Forthcoming. The changing boundaries of youth gangs. In *Gangs in America*, 3rd ed., edited by C. R. Huff. Thousand Oaks, CA: Sage Publications, Inc.

Huff, C. R. 1996. The criminal behavior of gang members and non-gang at-risk youth. In *Gangs in America*, 2nd ed., edited by C. R. Huff. Thousand Oaks, CA: Sage Publications, Inc., pp. 75–102.

Huff, C. R. 1998. *Comparing the Criminal Behavior of Youth Gangs and At-Risk Youth.* Research in Brief. Washington, DC: U.S. Department of Justice, Office of Justice Programs, National Institute of Justice.

Klein, M. W. 1969. Violence in American juvenile gangs. In *Crimes of Violence*, vol. 13, edited by D. J. Mulvihill and M. M. Tumin. Washington, DC: National Commission on the Causes and Prevention of Violence, pp. 1427–1460.

Klein, M. W. 1995. *The American Street Gang.* New York: Oxford University Press.

Maxson, C. L. 1998. *Gang Members on the Move.* Youth Gang Series Bulletin. Washington, DC: U.S. Department of Justice, Office of Justice Programs, Office of Juvenile Justice and Delinquency Prevention.

Maxson, C. L., Whitlock, M. L., and Klein, M. W. 1998. Vulnerability to street gang membership: Implications for practice. *Social Service Review* 72(1):70–91.

McCorkle, R. C., and Miethe, T. D. 1998. The political and organizational response to gangs: An examination of "moral panic" in Nevada. *Justice Quarterly* 15(1):41–64.

Miethe, T. D., and McCorkle, R. C. 1997. Evaluating Nevada's anti-gang legislation and gang prosecution units. Unpublished report. Washington, DC: U.S. Department of Justice, Office of Justice Programs, National Institute of Justice.

Miller, J. A. 2001. *One of the Guys: Girls, Gangs, and Gender.* New York: Oxford University Press.

Miller, W. B. 1992 (Revised from 1982). *Crime by Youth Gangs and Groups in the United States.* Washington, DC: U.S. Department of Justice, Office of Justice Programs, Office of Juvenile Justice and Delinquency Prevention.

Miller, W. B. 2001. *The Growth of Youth Gang Problems in the United States: 1970–98.* Report. Washington, DC: U.S. Department of Justice, Office of Justice Programs, Office of Juvenile Justice and Delinquency Prevention.

National Youth Gang Center. 1999. *1996 National Youth Gang Survey.* Summary. Washington, DC: U.S. Department of Justice, Office of Justice Programs, Office of Juvenile Justice and Delinquency Prevention.

National Youth Gang Center. 2000. *1998 National Youth Gang Survey.* Summary. Washington, DC: U.S. Department of Justice, Office of Justice Programs, Office of Juvenile Justice and Delinquency Prevention.

National Youth Gang Center. 2001a. Assessing your community's youth gang problem. Unpublished report. Tallahassee, FL: National Youth Gang Center. Copies are available from NYGC.

National Youth Gang Center. 2001b. Planning for implementation of the OJJDP Comprehensive Gang Model. Unpublished report. Tallahassee, FL: National Youth Gang Center. Copies are available from NYGC.

Sanders, W. 1994. *Gangbangs and Drive-Bys: Grounded Culture and Juvenile Gang Violence.* New York: Aldine de Gruyter.

Skolnick, J. H., Correl, T., Navarro, E., and Rabb, R. 1988. *The Social Structure of Street Drug Dealing.* Report to the Office of the Attorney General of the State of California. Berkeley: University of California, Berkeley.

Spergel, I. A. 1995. *The Youth Gang Problem.* New York: Oxford University Press.

Spergel, I. A., Chance, R., Ehrensaft, C., Regulus, T., Kane, C., Laseter, R., Alexander, A., and Oh, S. 1994. *Gang Suppression and Intervention: Community Models.* Research Summary. Washington, DC: U.S. Department of Justice, Office of Justice Programs, Office of Juvenile Justice and Delinquency Prevention.

Spergel, I. A., and Curry, G. D. 1990. Strategies and perceived agency effectiveness in dealing with the youth gang problem. In *Gangs in America*, edited by C. R. Huff. Newbury Park, CA: Sage Publications, Inc., pp. 288–309.

Thornberry, T. P. 1998. Membership in youth gangs and involvement in serious and violent offending. In *Serious and Violent Juvenile Offenders: Risk Factors and Successful Interventions*, edited by R. Loeber and D. P. Farrington. Thousand Oaks, CA: Sage Publications, Inc., pp. 147–166.

Thrasher, F. M. 1927. *The Gang—A Study of 1,313 Gangs in Chicago.* Chicago: University of Chicago Press.

Valdez, A. 2000. *Gangs: A Guide to Understanding Street Gangs*, 3rd ed. San Clemente, CA: LawTech Publishing.

Waldorf, D. 1993. When the Crips invaded San Francisco: Gang migration. *Journal of Gang Research* 1:11–16.

Yablonsky, L. 1967. *The Violent Gang*, revised ed. New York: Penguin.

SECTION III
Gang Activities

In the previous two sections, we attempted to provide a better definition of what constitutes a gang and attend to the varieties of gangs that exist. Section II, Varieties of Gangs, demonstrates that there are substantial differences among gangs in terms of organization, ethnic and gender makeup, and social setting. The social and ecological factors that envelop a gang to some extent affect how the members of the gang act and interact with their environment. Although there is a core of gang activities that can be identified, significant differences remain across gangs. Thus, we should be interested in gang activities.

The media, law enforcement, and citizen spokespersons all have espoused varying descriptions of gangs built largely on real and perceived gang activities. To a great extent, we have socially constructed a mythical idea of gangs and their activities; a mythical idea that is both dark and dangerous (Best and Hutchinson, 1998). This is not to say that gangs generally do not pose a threat to society, but that our understanding of gangs and their activities has largely been spun into gigantic proportions. This section consists of a series of readings that attempt to objectively examine gang activities and place them in a proper perspective. If criminal justice policymakers have a realistic understanding of the gang problem, then they are better prepared to develop strategies and policies that will more effectively counteract gang problems.

In the first article in this section, James Vigil examines the initiation rites of a Chicano gang. Vigil examined a number of Chicano gangs in the Los Angeles area, a city that historically has had a large number of both Chicano and African-American gangs. It is important to examine gang initiation rites because there is substantial myth surrounding them. Some of the myths surrounding gang initiation postulated that an initiate had to kill someone before becoming a member. Vigil's description of the initiation rites shows that they are violent, but they are not a life-and-death situation and they do not involve death or injury to citizens who are not members of gangs.

Although not addressed in this volume in detail, many have believed that once someone joins a gang, they could never leave it. However, our knowledge of gangs shows that exiting gangs is a fairly common event. Gangs tend to be large, loosely organized cliques with a small core of members who oversee its activities (see Weisel, 2002; Sanders, 1994). Those who are at the core of the gang generally maintain a lasting relationship with the gang, even when arrested and sent to prison. Those outside the core, the bulk of a gang's membership, are more transient. In some cases, members may enter and exit a gang several times. Gangs tend not to take retributive action against a member who voluntarily leaves the gang.

Next, Geoffrey Hunt and Karen Joe Laidler examine the relationship of alcohol and violence in the gang setting. Many people not familiar with gang research, including government policymakers, have long perceived that the root of gang violence has been drugs and drug trafficking. Hunt and Laidler examine the role of alcohol in gangs and gang violence. They see alcohol as the catalyst for violent behavior. This should not be unexpected. For example, Auerhahn and Parker (2003) note that alcohol, not drugs, is associated with a larger portion of violence in American society. Thus, gang violence simply mirrors larger society. In essence, alcohol consumption has become normative behavior within the gang, and it is a driving force behind several types of violent behavior.

A number of years ago, Skolnick, Correl, Navarro, and Rabb (1990) examined California gangs and classified them as being either "cultural" or "entrepreneurial." Entrepreneurial gangs were those that formed with the specific intent to sell drugs or make money (e.g., some of the Bloods' and Crips' sets in the Los Angeles area). Cultural gangs, on the other hand, identified with a geographical area or neighborhood and were seen to some extent as an "extended family" (e.g., many of the Chicano gangs in southern California). They noted that the distinction between these two types was blurred as a number of cultural gangs moved into drug trafficking as a method of making money. Skolnick's and his colleagues' research spurred researchers to examine the financial activities of gangs. In the third article of this section, Sudhir Venkatesch examines the financial activities of the modern gang. Venkatesch notes that gangs, especially those deeply enmeshed in drug trafficking and other crimes, have a significant cash flow. Yet, at the same time, they have a number of expenses and they tend to squander large amounts of money. This description of organized gangs and their involvement in drug trafficking stands in sharp contrast to the relationship between gangs and drug dealing described by the authors of the next two articles.

In the fourth article, Scott Decker, Tim Bynum, and Deborah Weisel examine gangs to see if they have evolved or assumed some of the attributes of organized crime by examining an African-American gang and a Hispanic gang. They interviewed a number of gang members who were imprisoned or on probation and found the Hispanic gang to have acquired a number of organized-crime attributes, while the African-American gang remained quite disorganized. The Hispanic gang developed relations with prison gangs and gangs in other cities. It also had more structure than the African-American gang. Even so, there was no evidence that the Hispanic gang had moved into traditional organized-crime types of activities.

The final article in this section by Cheryl Maxson examines the nature of gang homicides. Over the past several decades there has been a great deal of hyperbole and claims making in the media about the nature and extent of gang homicides (Brownstein, 2000, 1991). The media concentrated their coverage on innocent bystanders who were killed by gangs and the violence associated with gang drug dealing. Media and political misrepresentations of the problem created moral panic and fear among many citizens. Maxson examines gang homicides in the United States and finds that contrary to popular thought, most are not associated with drug trafficking and there are relatively few homicides involving innocent bystanders. Most of the homicides involve turf battles, showing disrespect for other gangs' members, and intra-gang disputes and rivalries.

This section examines several gang activities, including initiation rites, the role of alcohol in gangs, gang finances, their evolution toward organized-crime models, and the types of homicides associated with gangs. It also attempts to shed light on some of the more controversial gang activities. The articles show that there has been substantial misunderstanding about how many gangs operate, as well as pointing to important policy considerations.

References

Auerhahn, K., & Parker, R. N. (2003) Drugs, Alcohol, and Homicide. In L. Gaines & P. Kraska (Eds.), *Drugs, Crime, and Justice: Contemporary Perspectives*. Prospect Heights, IL: Waveland Press.

Best, J., & Hutchinson, M. M. (1998) The Gang Initiation Rite as a Motif in Contemporary Crime Discourse. In G. Potter & V. Kappeler (Eds.), *Constructing Crime: Perspectives on Making News and Social Problems*. Prospect Heights, IL: Waveland Press.

Brownstein, H. (2000) *The Social Reality of Violence and Violent Crime*. Needham Heights, MA: Allyn and Bacon.

Browstein, H. (1991) The Media and the Construction of Random Drug Violence. *Social Justice* 18:85–103.

Sanders, W. B. (1994) *Gang-bangs and Drive-bys: Grounded Culture and Juvenile Gang Violence*. New York: Walter de Gruyter.

Skolnick, J., Correl, T., Navarro, E., & Rabb, R. (1990) The Social Structure of Street Drug Dealing. *American Journal of Police* 9:1–42.

Weisel, D. L. (2002) The Evolution of Street Gangs: An Examination of Form and Variation. In W. Reed & S. Decker (Eds.), *Responding to Gangs: Evaluation and Research*. Washington, DC: Office of Justice Programs.

10

Street Baptism
Chicano Gang Initiation

James Diego Vigil

Street gangs in Chicano *barrios* (neighborhoods) have regularized a gang initiation ordeal which serves several functions. While long and deep exposure to street socialization has made many youths at risk to become gang members, this "street baptism" of gang initiation has become a clear marker and accelerator of gang behavior. For the gang,[1] the baptism functions as a ritual ceremony to show admittance and dedication to the gang. For the initiate, the baptism is an introduction to the gang and "sanctifies" him (or less often, her) as a true member. This event represents different facets of the gang subculture, such as group membership, social solidarity, ritualistic behavior, ceremonial processes, gender clarification, and symbolic changes.

Data and information for this analysis have been gathered over several years, from 1978 to 1982 and again from 1989 to the present (Vigil 1988a, 1988b, 1993a, 1993b, 1994), in a continuing ethnographic investigation of more than two dozen different barrios of Mexican Americans in the greater Los Angeles area. Old and more recently established gangs in urban and suburban neighborhoods were examined. In all, more than sixty life histories and three hundred questionnaire-guided interviews were gathered along with many pages of ethnographic observation notes. Although female gang members were included in the study, the emphasis usually (as here) was on males. The focus was the *cholo* (marginalized) gang youth, from 12 to 19 years of age, who belonged to and identified with the barrio

Vigil, James Diego. "Street Baptism: Chicano Gang Initiation." *Human Organization*, Vol. 55, No. 2, copyright © 1996 by the Society for Applied Anthropology.

street gang. These gangs have been fixtures in some communities for over 40 years (Vigil 1988a) and recently have spiraled out of control with gang violence—drive-by shootings, random shootings, school ground fights, and so on—daily capturing the attention of the media and law enforcement.

Most of the older Southern California barrios, both urban and (originally) rural, came into being as visibly distinct, spatially bounded neighborhoods separated from other neighborhoods, located, e.g., "across the tracks," in a government-owned housing development or in ravines, hollows, etc.—what Bogardus (1926) called the area's interstices. Families of unskilled and semi-skilled workers settled into the small houses or apartments, which were often located near major worksites—railroad yards, brickyards, or concentrations of small factories. Socioeconomic and cultural barriers reinforced the physical boundaries. Later, most of the rural enclaves were incorporated into the suburbs that grew up around them, but they remained visibly distinct from the surrounding tract home neighborhoods. Newer urban and suburban barrios arose in once prosperous, but now rundown, neighborhoods as the Mexican American population continued to grow. In these, as in the older barrios, relatively low skill levels of the workforce led to recurrent joblessness and poverty for many households.

For example, the White Fence barrio is located across a river and freeway from downtown Los Angeles. It was first settled in the 1920s by Mexicans who worked nearby and built their houses in the ravines alongside an affluent Anglo neighborhood. Centered on its small Catholic church, the community remains one of the poorest in the county and still features empty lots on many blocks. On the other hand, the Cucamonga barrio began, also in the 1920s, as a Mexican farm laborers' settlement. It was located in a vineyard and close to the citrus groves near the boundary between San Bernardino and Los Angeles counties. By the 1970s, it was surrounded by middle-class housing tracts, but still had many unpaved roads and no sewers (Moore and Vigil 1993). While these barrios have distinctive differences, they and most others in the region share a history of sociocultural marginality, poverty, crowded living conditions, and institutional neglect (Vigil 1988a).

An age-graded cohorting tradition in each barrio ensures a fairly steady, if small (usually no more than 10%), supply of youths (often the brothers, nephews, cousins, and sons of older members) to carry on the gang reputation for fighting and defending its "turf." Even though the adolescent group that constitutes the gang participates in normal youthful activities such as socializing, playing sports, and driving cars, it is the more destructive habits that reflect the troubled and deeply disturbed lives of its members. Poverty, stressed families, insensitive schools, intergenerational strife, and culture conflict are among the precursors to the creation of gangs and gang members (e.g., Covey et al. 1992). Moore (1991), for example, found that more than a third of the gang members in her systematic sampling of two East Los Angeles gangs had been raised in father-absent households. Similarly, in an ongoing study of the families of gang members in an East Los Angeles public housing development, I found that these families were significantly more often headed by single females than a control sample of randomly selected households from the same project (Vigil 1994); moreover, the "gang family" households also contained more household members. Children seeking respite from crowded, unsettled households spend increasing amounts of time outside in the streets. There, in an often dangerous but also exciting environment, they come under the influence of similarly displaced peers and older street toughs.

Thus, such youths are often pre-conditioned for gang participation while they are still in elementary school. Junior high school "is where intensive gang membership activity typically begins. It is . . . where street youths from different barrios come into regular contact with one another . . . [and] with other children also willing to experiment and flirt with new role behaviors" (Vigil 1993a:97). Home conditions have not been conducive to completing assigned homework, and by now the street-socialized youth have lost interest in school, "ditching" often to hang out with youths with similar inclinations. With more time on their hands, the youths begin to get into minor (and subsequently more serious) illicit behaviors, drawing them into contact with the criminal justice authorities. Many are incarcerated for varying lengths of time in youth camps or even prisons. Thus, over the generations, the gang has become a social group with cultural rules and values derived from "street socialization," which has replaced what was lost when parents, schools, and police failed.

Gang baptism occurs especially during the adolescent status shift when age and sex development and assertion are most crucial. The gang initiation ordeal of "jumping-in" a new member (a timed affair in which two or three gang members beat up a novitiate) is a "shock" treatment for many personal and group objectives. At its simplest level, the ordeal is a mechanism wrought by street youth to recruit, test, and turn out more gang conflict-oriented youth and thus perpetuate the existence and purpose of the gang. In many ways it is a tradeoff: we'll protect you if you help protect us from our enemies. At its most profound level, however, it is a surreal coming of age under the auspices of the street. The streets, with their dark, overwhelming, fear-inspiring threats, have left many youths unprotected and unsupervised. Where there is the need for protection and escape from fear, there is also the need to vent pent-up aggression born of trauma and rage. In such a context, the initiation is an inverted "gang-bang" (Klibaner 1989), where the gang members get to do to a new member what they do to rival gang members.

THE INVERTED GANG-BANG: TYPE, TIME, AND PLACE

For most individuals, the path toward becoming a gang member begins early, and initiation into it for the most part simply formalizes membership;

some can even avoid such trials. Specific routines of induction do exist, however, and how these are practiced varies with particular gangs and individuals. Generally, although details of the initiation vary, its ceremonial character and function have been much the same from one site to another and over time. In any event, these routines indicate the public nature of membership in the gang and provide insights into the psychological underpinning of gang behavior. An initiation is commonly viewed and accepted as an ordeal that entails a physical beating by several other gang members. Gang entrance ceremonies are most commonly prescribed for peripheral and temporary members, less often for regular gang members whose early experiences have tended to lock them into the gang subculture.

In nearly all cases, the initiation occurs when the individual is in junior high school, at the age of 12 or 13. A much smaller number are initiated in grammar school. Each of such early initiates the author has encountered came from long-established barrios and had older relatives who were already gang members. Only a handful of initiations occur when the individual is already in high school. Such individuals that the author encountered lived in established barrios, however, and they had refrained from joining until peer pressure overwhelmed them. Before high school is over, they usually quit the group.

Most initiations take place somewhere in the barrio, usually near the "hangout" or at the home of one of the initiators. Geronimo, from Barrio Nuevo Estrada, described his initiation (which occurred when he was in junior high school):

> If you wanted to get in, one, two, three guys, you go against them, so I went up against them. It was in the front yard of one of the guys' homes. It was during the afternoon. They surrounded me. If you just stood there and let them hit you and they whip your ass and you don't do nothing, you're going to get an ass whipping for nothing. I guess I took an ass whipping to be able to back up the barrio. They would go about thirty seconds. They would count like this: one [5 seconds elapse], two [4 or 5 seconds elapse], and so on.

It is usually a spontaneous affair. Some are initiated at a party when most of the initiators are under the influence of alcohol or other substances. One 18-year-old from White Fence, who had grown up in the barrio, recalled his initiation at age 14:

> They came up to me at a party, all at one time. It was a big party. . . . They told me if I want to get into the barrio. I said I don't know, *ese* [guy], I want to get in, but I want to think about it. They said, when you get into the barrio you have to be *trucha* [alert, prepared], for you're taking a big risk and you can get killed by anyone just by being from White Fence. I thought about it, and said: "*Orale* [O.K.], I'll get in." . . . It was about 2:00 in the morning. I was loaded, but I knew what I was doing. I went out into the alley and eight homeboys followed me. Like, there was a big crowd, you know, a lot ran out after

> them, but eight of them did the thing. "Orale," one of the homeboys said, "take a *trago* [a drink], ese, before you do it." I drank the rest of the bottle, about half of it. Then one of the homeboys hit me in the mouth. I kept on going for about twenty seconds, I was going head on, throwing with one of them. Throwing mine in and they would get theirs in. All the eight guys were coming at me at the same time. I never got a second of a break, for every moment was a serious hit. They downed me about four times, and I kept getting up. I was all fucked up, I had a broken nose and everything.

When the onlookers, especially the homegirls who by now pitied him, thought he had enough, they said, "He's a homeboy now." He shook hands with everybody to confirm the fact.

Some describe the initiation as a gauntlet trial of running through two lines of gang members. For others, however, especially among members of younger contemporary cliques, it is a timed affair, from thirty seconds to two minutes, with two to eight gang members doing the pummeling. Whether the initiation is administered by a small or large group, or timed or untimed, the severity of the beating is dependent on a number of other factors. If members are intoxicated at the time they decide to initiate someone, which often happens spontaneously and typically is aimed at a younger, weaker youngster, the beating can be intense and open-ended, as in the example cited above. There are even instances where a nonresident of the barrio has had to undergo a stabbing to show his mettle, as this account from the Chicano Pinto Research Project (1979) shows:

> They stabbed him and threw him into the bushes. The dudes that got him in were loaded and were *muy locos* (real crazy), and he kept getting up and he kept saying he was from the neighborhood. They kept getting him in and getting him out and finally they just stabbed him.

More commonly, however, the beating is merely a formality, especially for a long-term barrio resident. As one youth said,

> When they would jump us in, they would start a fight. Some other guy jumps in, then another. They would get me down, then start hitting and kicking me, to see if I had *huevos* [balls; literally, eggs]. They're not out to really hurt you, you know, they just want to see if you can take the punches.

Individuals already known as "able to take it" are accordingly subjected to briefer *pro forma* attacks.

Whatever the circumstances, the initiate must accept the group's determination of where and how the ordeal takes place. The beating must also be endured without complaint (although this does not preclude fighting back); the slightest whimper or other expressed sign of pain could result in rejection of membership. The initiation thus acts as a prerequisite to weed out the weak and uncommitted. Successful endurance of the ordeal also reinforces the attraction of gang membership. Even those informants who admit to substantial trepidation prior to initiation assert that it enhances their desire to belong to the gang. In fact, the desire to belong, prove oneself, gain respect, and show loyalty are all intertwined with the appropriate (by gang standards) role behaviors expected of the initiate.

THE ROLE OF INITIATION IN GANG LIFE

More than three and a half decades ago, Bloch and Niederhoffer likened gang initiations generally with "puberty rites in primitive societies" and added that "we may conceive of much of gang practice and the spontaneous, informal rituals of gang behavior as arising because our culture has been unable, or has refused, to meet the adolescent's needs during a critical juncture in his life" (1958:30). In the same work they noted that, for the new member of a gang, "once having succeeded in passing through the ceremony with honor, the psychological aftermath of the experience contributes towards creating bonds of solidarity with those other initiates who have shared this vital experience with him" (1958:123).

Structurally, the barrio gang exists in part to provide psychological support for youths who have not received adequate reinforcement from family and other social caretaker institutions. Initiation can additionally be viewed as affirming one's ethnic orientation. Some of the street solidarity and ethnic loyalty is based on defiance of school and law enforcement authorities, which many adult residents and nearly all the resident disaffected youth consider insensitive to low-income Mexican barrios. Thus, the event also tends to affirm one's ethnic identification as well, showing they are "Chicano." (On a psychological level, of course, it may also satisfy sadomasochistic urges, opportunities to intimidate and coerce, and even simply a sense of excitement in aggressive, socially sanctioned—by street standards—combat.)

In tribal societies, initiation practices aid in building social cohesiveness and sexual differentiation. This is especially the case "in tribal societies, where equality of status among adults of the same sex is emphasized" (Barry and Schlegel 1980:134; Schlegel and Barry 1991). While egalitarianism among gang members is also valued, there are other elements in the gang subculture which the gang initiation emphasizes. For instance, because many gang members come from households that are female-centered and the streets are dominated by males, the initiation serves to mark passage to a new status. In their crosscultural survey, Burton and Whiting (1961) pointed out how initiation serves to clarify such cross-sex ambiguities, and the gang subculture serves this same purpose. Thus, gang baptism jointly marks passage to a new status, enhances social cohesiveness, creates a ceremonial atmosphere, encourages ritualistic behavior, and serves practical gang goals.

Marking Passage and Sex Role Differentiation

As with the two examples of gang initiation noted above, marking passage for these members meant that they now were expected to abide by gang rules and routines and perform acts in the name of the gang. There are clear ego, group, and role psychological aspects to the baptism. The initiation itself is charged with symbolic, rite of passage messages which signal a rebirth of an individual as a gang member who adheres to the street subculture. When a beating is administered, at least two signs emerge: the act of gang members pummeling an initiate under the purview of other gang members who witness it, and the actual imprints of the beating (i.e., the bruises, abrasions, blackened eyes, nicks, etc.) left on the novitiate.

These two signs symbolize that established gang members recognized the newcomer as a "homeboy." The new homeboy also carries that evidence, the street imprimatur, upon him and proudly displays the wounds as a badge of honor wherever he may go. Moreover, the act marks a key period of puberty, the childhood to adult (or more appropriately, "manhood") transition, where a new affiliation is formalized. Such a group event has tremendous personal ramifications. Typically, gang initiates (of both grammar school and junior high ages) mentioned a desire for group acceptance or to "prove oneself," that is, to demonstrate manliness, as motivation for undergoing the ritual.

The rite of passage, with all its new gang role expectations and symbolic qualities, operates at the personal level to assuage the "psychosocial moratorium" that Erikson (1968) spoke of as occurring during the adolescence transition when a new age/sex identity is sought. This is especially important for those youth who come from female-centered households and have lacked adult male role models. Where ambivalence and ambiguity of one's sex identity may have reigned before, the initiation helps dramatize a clarification, even if it is an ephemeral, superficial personal adjustment, to announce that a boy has been transformed into a "man." A significant event related by a 16-year-old youth who just underwent the baptism illustrates this point:

> I remember my Mom used to comb my hair . . . she used to comb it to the sides. So one day I took the comb from her and started combing it back. That's when I started thinking I was all *chingón* [in control; literally, fornicator].

Thus, with gang baptism, street gang swagger, slang cholo talk, and a *locura* (quasi-crazy, wild behavior) mind-set are expected and enhanced. The new gang member is now ready to perform gang tasks. Among these "manliness" tasks are to join in forays and raids against rival barrio gangs and to more habitually ingest alcohol and drugs, like *un hombre con huevos* (a man with balls).

SOCIAL SOLIDARITY

Social cohesiveness and solidarity is strengthened by the initiation. Each time a new member is "jumped-in," all the witnesses reexperience their own baptism to connect with the newcomer. Thus, the event acts as a reaffirmation to solidify the group psychology of the gang. This mental leap entails that the individual surrenders his identity and allegiance to the barrio gang. Now, the person can affix his nickname (most gang members are given a moniker, like "Loco," "Wino," "Puppet," for example, by fellow gang members, reflecting a personal habit, quirk, or feature) to that of the barrio name. The joint personal and group logo, such as "Loco de White Fence," becomes another type of imprint, more observable for all to see. Indeed, central to this newfound identity is the affixing of personal tattoos and graffiti signatures with nickname and barrio name: El Loco de White Fence. It is the plague of public authorities and home and business owners, but to gang members, it is a public demonstration of an intent to be "famous all over town" (Santiago 1984). Thoughts and actions emanate from this group psychology, as a person claims *por mi barrio todo* (for my neighborhood, or gang, everything).

As an affair viewed and sanctioned by the group, it is also a ceremonial celebration. It happens at a fixed point in one's life (roughly, junior high school) to commemorate that the controllers of the street now control you and have affixed a "branding" for all to see, especially you. In one instance cited above, other members of the large party, including homegirls who usually are excluded from such events, followed the initiators outside and became the audience to the ceremony. One of the homegirls, in fact, stepped in to end the affair with her proclamation, "He's a homeboy now."

GANG TRADITION AND PRACTICAL IMPLICATIONS

Because the gang requires fearless fighters, and the streets are such a fear-inspiring place, there is a need to recruit and retain "tough" gang members. The initiation is a way that gangs developed to help screen, test, and authenticate gang members. Most of the earliest gangs did not have an initiation because they were formed spontaneously and unevenly. Over the decades, as the street conditions which spawned gangs persisted and there was intergenerational continuity, a gang subculture evolved with norms and values. Initiation ordeals are one of the gang's subcultural traditions.

It has become a ritualistic affair that is interwoven with the "psychosocial moratorium" and the group psychology of the gang in that a new member is subjected to a type of gang "magic." Because toughness is associated with manliness, or *machismo*, one of the expected outcomes of this magic is that the novitiate is endowed with huevos or that kind of physical and mental power in order to be allowed into the gang. If the test proves him worthy, he gains the approval of the gang members. He is accepted and can now count on gang members to offer protection and friendship.

However, there is a practical side to this tradition. While gangs serve many purposes, for most of their time is spent in the usual adolescent and youth socializing and partying (cf. Vigil 1988a:Ch. 7), one important and highly publicized activity is gang conflict. Gang-banging, as the gang members refer to it, entails ongoing fights and shootings with rival barrio gangs. There is a traditional aspect in these conflict activities, as some of these gang rivalries span several generations, sometimes son following father amassing battles in a long, protracted "turf" war.

The initiation allows for the selection and screening of good "battlers." It is a type of ritual homicide in that the former person (pre-initiation) is killed and a new person (post-initiation) created. As noted, many of the initiators revel in this opportunity to mete out punishment, as personal aggressions help let off steam in a controlled way (e.g., a type of ritualized *locura* binge). This, in many ways, keeps them in shape for the real battles which await them, sometimes on a daily basis; like training and practice before fights with rivals.

CONCLUSION

The gang baptism is a remarkable phenomenon. While many of their neighbor non-gang peers respond to the role expectations of parents and school teachers and learn to behave accordingly, the gang members "jump hoops" for established gang members. Since the gang, and the subculture that is a part of it, have taken over where other caretaker units (i.e., parents and schools) have failed, there has evolved a gang initiation ceremony to assert the gang's claim on newcomers. The ostensible purpose for this "inverted gang-banging" is to test the physical and mental mettle of novitiates and weed out the weak and uncommitted. Then the new "street baptized" homeboy can join to help against enemy barrio gangs.

The latter is the practical goal, but there are other objectives to the initiation event and different messages which reflect it. As an example, the gang imprimatur becomes an element in one's tattoos, a public announcement of one's new status. Scrawling gang graffiti of one's nickname and the barrio gang's name is further advertisement that the initiation "took." Providing new gang members with a set of role expectations and behaviors is also something that is encouraged and accelerated in the aftermath. Many of the symbolic outcomes are focused on aggression and masculinity: the signs of the beating, the sullen, defiant stare of "I can take it," a witnessed public "ritual homicide" to match the "soul murder" a person willingly submits to because of a sense of self-worthlessness, and the nonverbal, body-language "pats-on-the-back" one receives from gang members as they welcome a new member of the "select group."

Until such time that major social institutions, such as the family and schools, are able to win over social control from the street gangs, the latter will continue to socialize and enculturate large numbers of barrio youth and subject them to a street baptism. Street baptisms, of course, are culminating events that usually succeed a long, deep series of experiences that compel a youngster to join a gang. I have elsewhere discussed these background experiences leading to and accompanying gang participation as "multiple marginality" (Vigil 1988a), which constitutes a set of ecological, economic, sociocultural, and psychological forces, and events.

In large measure, the initiation is a "boyish" inclination to mark a "manly" passage under the pressures of the street. Personal and social factors are intertwined in understanding this process. It is notable that gangs have spontaneously formulated this initiation in such a way that it resembles what many pre-industrial tribal societies have followed as tradition. Gender differentiation and clarification and social solidarity and cohesiveness are both served by the gang initiation, just as they frequently are in such groups.

Note

[1] Over the years, the term "gang" has been defined and redefined many times (cf. Covey et al. [1992] for a recent review). In Chicano barrios in the U.S., gang has generally meant a territorially affiliated group of youths (typically organized into age-graded cliques) dedicated at least in part to fighting other, similar groups.

References

Barry, Herbert, and Alice Schlegel. 1980. Early Childhood Precursors of Adolescent Initiation Ceremonies. *Ethos* 8(2): 132–145.

Bloch, H. A., and A. Niederhoffer. 1958. *The Gang: A Study in Adolescent Behavior.* New York: Philosophical Library.

Bogardus, Emory. 1926. *The City Boy and His Problems.* House of Ralston: Rotary Club of Los Angeles.

Burton, R. V., and J. W. M. Whiting. 1961. The Absent Father and Cross-Sex Identity. *Merrill-Palmer Quarterly* 7:85–95.

Chicano Pinto Research Project (CPRP). 1979. *A Model for Chicano Drug Use and for Effective Utilization of Employment and Training Resources by Barrio Addicts and Ex-Offenders.* Los Angeles: Final Report for the Department of Labor and National Institute of Drug Abuse.

Covey, Herbert C., Scott Menard, and Robert J. Franzese. 1992. *Juvenile Gangs.* Springfield: Charles C. Thomas.

Erickson, Erik H. 1968. *Psychosocial Identity. International Encyclopedia of the Social Sciences*, 7:61–67. New York: Macmillan and the Free Press.

Klibaner, Aaron K. 1989. Concepts of Initiation. Unpublished Student Paper, University of Wisconsin–Madison.

Moore, Joan W. 1991. *Going Down to the Barrio.* Philadelphia: Temple University Press.

Moore, Joan W., and Diego Vigil. 1993. Barrios in Transition. In *In the Barrios: Latinos and the Underclass Debate*, eds. J. W. Moore and R. Pinderhuges, pp. 27–49. New York: Russell Sage Publications.

Santiago, Danny. 1984. *Famous All Over Town*. New York: Penguin Press.

Schlegel, Alice, and Herbert Barry. 1991. *Adolescence: An Anthropological Inquiry.* New York: The Free Press.

Vigil, James Diego. 1988a. *Barrio Gangs: Street Life and Identity in Southern California*. Austin: University of Texas Press.

Vigil, James Diego. 1988b. Group Processes and Street Identity: Adolescent Chicano Gang Members. *Ethos* 16(4): 431–445.

Vigil, James Diego. 1993a. The Established Gang. In *Gangs: The Origins and Impact of Contemporary Youth Gangs in the United States*, eds. S. Cummings and D. Monti, pp. 95–112. New York: State University of New York Press.

Vigil, James Diego. 1993b. Gangs, Social Control, and Ethnicity: Ways to Redirect. In *Identity and Inner-City Youth: Beyond Ethnicity and Gender*, eds. S. B. Heath and M. W. McLaughlin. New York: Teachers College, Columbia University.

Vigil, James Diego. 1994. Gang Families in a Public Housing Project. Unpublished report to the Department of Health and Human Services.

11

Alcohol and Violence in the Lives of Gang Members

Geoffrey P. Hunt & Karen Joe Laidler

Social commentators have had a long-standing interest in and preoccupation with youth groups and violence. Even in Victorian England in the late 19th century, commentators were preoccupied with the apparent escalation in disorder among young violent working-class youth gangs in the industrial cities of Birmingham, Liverpool, and Manchester (Davies 1999, p. 72). In the United States, the first major social science study of youth gangs dates back to the 1920s with the publication of Thrasher's monumental study of 1,313 Chicago gangs (Thrasher 1927). Since then, the interest in gangs from a research perspective, as well as from a media and criminal justice standpoint, has periodically surfaced. The latest wave and, without a doubt, the peak of public concern over gangs began in the mid-1980s and has continued to the present.

Spurred on by the media, law enforcement officials started to take a renewed interest in gangs because of their involvement in drug use and drug sales and because of the belief that gangs were the breeding ground for serious delinquency. The development of the drug trade in the 1980s signaled a transformation from the idea of gangs as "transitory adolescent social networks to nascent criminal organizations" (Fagan 1990, p. 183). Gang researchers began to argue that a new type of youth gang had devel-

Hunt, Geoffrey P., and Laidler, Karen Joe. 2001. "Alcohol and Violence in the Lives of Gang Members," *Alcohol Research & Health*, Vol. 25, No. 1, pp. 66–71. Bethesda, MD: National Institute on Alcohol Abuse and Alcoholism.

oped which was qualitatively different from gangs in earlier periods. The new type of gang possessed a "raison d'être" no longer based on cultural factors, such as attachment to a neighborhood and notions of individual as well as collective honor, but instead centered on the economic rationale of profit making (Goldstein 1989; Skolnick et al. 1989).

In spite of the importance of drugs within the social life of gangs, the recent preoccupation of research on illicit drugs has overshadowed the importance of drinking within youth gangs and its possible relationship to violent behavior. To date, little research has been done specifically on the role of alcohol within the social life of gangs, and consequently, it is a relatively unexplored area. The available research data on the role of alcohol in youth gangs has been, to paraphrase Dwight Heath (1975), a "felicitous by-product" of other interests. This is in spite of the fact, as Fagan (1993) has noted, that alcohol is still the most widely used substance by both gang and nongang youth. This absence of research on the role of alcohol within gang life is particularly striking in the available work on the violent behavior of gang members.

Over the past decade, researchers and public health officials have become increasingly concerned with the increased involvement of youth in violent crime. The juvenile male arrest rate for violent crime offenses increased steadily during the first half of the 1990s, peaking in 1994 with a rate of 880, and then beginning to drop, with an arrest rate of 545 in 1999. Among females, the juvenile arrest rate for violent crime also has risen, peaking in 1995 at 158 and then leveling off at 122 in 1999 (Office of Juvenile Justice and Delinquency Prevention [OJJDP] 2000*a*). Within this growing concern, considerable attention has focused on youth gangs as a key factor. Currently, more than 90 percent of the Nation's largest cities report youth gang problems, and police estimates now put the number of gangs at 28,700 and the number of gang members at approximately 780,200 (OJJDP 2000*b*). As a result, public concern about the involvement of young people in gang activity, and the perceived violence associated with this lifestyle, has soared.

Violence is endemic to gang life. As Sanchez-Jankowski (1991) has noted, it is the "currency of life" within gangs, so much so that it can be taken as normative behavior (Collins 1988). Violence within gang life includes both intragang violence—for example, ritualistically violent initiations (Vigil and Long 1990)—and intergang violence—for example, turf battles (Sanchez-Jankowski 1991). In order to explain the daily occurrence of violence within the social life of gangs, both researchers and criminal justice officials have tended to focus their recent attention on the role of illicit drugs as a crucial explanatory factor (Fagan 1989; Klein and Maxson 1989; Moore 1991; Reiss and Roth 1993). This preoccupation with gangs and drug-related violence has tended to overshadow the significant role of alcohol in gang life and its possible relationship with violent behavior.

In the same way that violent behavior is a common currency within gang life, so also is drinking. Although few researchers have looked specifically at the role of alcohol within the social life of gangs, some gang researchers have noted that drinking is a major component of the social life of gangs and a commonplace activity (Fagan 1993; Hagedorn 1988; Moore 1991; Padilla 1992; Vigil and Long 1990). Therefore, given the extent to which drinking has been implicated in a wide range of interpersonal violence (Parker 1995; Pernanen 1991; White et al. 1993) and the extent to which alcohol problems have been found to occur disproportionately among both juveniles and adults who report violent behaviors (Collins 1986; Jacob and Leonard 1994), an examination of the possible relationship between alcohol and violence in gang life is an important area of investigation. Such an investigation can highlight both the extent to which drinking is present in "violence prone situations" within gang life (Steadman 1982) and the way in which drinking and normative violence are everyday features of gang life. This article examines the arenas in which drinking is present in the life of gangs and reviews existing literature on the situations and contexts in which drinking is associated with violent behavior.

ALCOHOL AND GANG LIFE

To understand the role of alcohol in the lives of gang members, we must begin our analysis by considering the characteristics and dynamics of street life. As many researchers have noted, being on the streets is a natural and legitimized social arena for many working-class, minority male adolescents. For many of these young men, life is "neither the workplace nor the school; it is the street" (Messerschmidt 1993, p. 102). Life on the streets is governed by rules of masculinity, in which notions of honor, respect, and status afford outlets for expressing and defending one's masculinity. The entry to life on the street is through a street gang. The gang epitomizes masculinity and ensures male bonding. Once in the gang, young men gain status and respect through their ability both to assert themselves by being "street smart" and to defend their fellow gang members (i.e., homeboys) by "being down," or being ready to come to the aid of fellow gang members should they need assistance. Working-class, minority gang members can gain respect through their ability to fight (Anderson 1999). Not only must they be prepared to defend themselves and their fellow gang members, they also must be prepared to defend the reputation of their gang. Given the masculine culture of street life, what role does alcohol play?

Hanging Around

Gang members spend the majority of their day "hanging around" (Corrigan 1976), or "just chilling," and typically describe this activity in the very mundane terms of "doing nothing." Although adults perceive this as a waste of time, the everyday practice of "doing nothing" is often an intense and busy period, and the activities that occur include talking, recounting details from previous events, joking, discussing business, defending one's honor, maintaining one's respect, fending off insults, keeping the police at bay, "cruising" around in a car, doing a few deals, defending turf, and getting high. During most of these activities, drinking is endemic, and the consumption of alcohol occurs continually throughout the course of everyday social activities. As with many other social groups, drinking can be said to act as a social "lubricant," or "social glue," working to maintain cohesion and group solidarity (Vigil and Long 1990).

Partying

Partying is a focal event in the life of gang members in which binge drinking is an integral component (Moore 1991; Moore et al. 1978; Vigil 1988). Partying overlaps with gang members "hanging out," and gang members "party" both at public dance places, bars, and parks in the neighborhood or at private parties held in hotel rooms or at someone's home or garage. Sometimes private parties are arranged formally, organized either for celebrations or, on some occasions, for grieving. Like hanging out, partying also operates to maintain and enhance the cohesion of the group (Moore 1991).

Symbolic Drinking

Drinking works in several symbolic ways in the gang. Because drinking is an integral and regular part of socializing within gang life, as the table illustrates, drinking works as a social lubricant, or social glue, to maintain not only the cohesion and social solidarity of the gang but also to affirm masculinity and male togetherness (Dunning et al. 1988). Comparisons across the different ethnic gangs, however, suggest that drinking affirms masculinity in culturally defined ways. Existing research on Latino gangs suggests that drinking plays a key role in the creation of a "macho" identity. "Machismo" includes demonstrations of strength and toughness as well as "locura" (i.e., acting crazy or wild) (Moore 1991; Padilla 1992; Vigil and Long 1990). As Vigil and Long (1990) have noted, alcohol can work as a "facilitator" in the observance of ritually wild or crazy behavior, especially in violent conflicts with outsiders.

Studies of African-American gang life suggest the construction of a different cultural identity, one in which "the overall street style and the desired approach to projecting an individual's personal image can be summed up in the word 'cool'" (Feldman et al. 1985, p. 124; see also Hagedorn 1988; Taylor 1989). In this subculture, occasional drinking is the norm (MacLeod 1987) in both public and private settings. Although the African-American gang members in our sample reported relatively higher alcohol use than the other ethnic groups, the style of drinking and the behavior associated with it stress that intoxicated drinking undermines

Amount of Alcohol Use During Specific Social Situations by Ethnicity

Social Context	Amount of Alcohol Use by Ethnicity		
	Never (%)	Sometimes (%)	Most of the Time (%)
African-American (*n* = 173)			
Cruising	19.7	52.6	27.7
Group parties	4.0	30.1	65.9
Hanging out with group at night	3.5	38.7	57.8
Hanging out with group during day	11.6	52.0	36.4
School	60.1	12.7	2.3
Before fight	44.5	36.4	19.1
After fight	12.7	39.9	47.4
At home with family	51.4	34.7	13.9
Alone	19.1	60.7	20.2
Latino (*n* = 88)			
Cruising	21.6	59.1	19.3
Group parties	3.4	14.8	80.7
Hanging out with group at night	6.8	37.5	55.7
Hanging out with group during day	20.5	53.4	26.1
School	55.7	29.5	1.1
Before fight	54.5	28.4	15.9
After fight	19.3	35.2	43.2
At home with family	58.0	36.4	4.5
Alone	40.9	43.2	14.8
Asian/PI (*n* = 53)			
Cruising	52.8	34.0	13.2
Group parties	0.0	30.2	69.8
Hanging out with group at night	3.8	45.3	50.9
Hanging out with group during day	28.3	47.2	24.5
School	69.8	26.4	3.8
Before fight	45.3	45.3	9.4
After fight	24.5	49.1	26.4
At home with family	64.2	30.2	5.7
Alone	45.3	49.1	5.7
Other (*n* = 38)			
Cruising	42.1	44.7	13.2
Group parties	0.0	15.8	84.2
Hanging out with group at night	5.3	28.9	63.2
Hanging out with group during day	26.3	55.3	18.4
School	57.9	31.6	2.6
Before fight	42.1	44.7	13.2
After fight	13.2	39.5	47.4
At home with family	55.3	31.6	13.2
Alone	31.6	57.9	10.5

n = number of participants within each ethnic category indicated; PI = Pacific Islander.

the "cool" image and is likely to be interpreted as a sign of "being out of control." In the case of Asians and Pacific Islanders, the available research suggests different attitudes to drinking. On the one hand, Chin (1990) suggests that Chinese gangs frown upon intoxication. On the other hand, other work on both Asian and Pacific Islander and Southeast Asian gangs (Toy 1992; Waldorf et al. 1994) suggests that although drinking is not heavy among these groups, it is nevertheless widespread.

In addition to its role as a cohesive mechanism, particular drinking styles within gangs may operate, as with other social groups (Cohen 1985), as a mechanism to maintain group boundaries, thereby demarcating one gang from another. In this way, particular drinking styles can be seen as similar to other symbolic insignia, including tattoos, dress colors, and codes (Miller 1995).

Other examples of internal gang violent activities associated with drinking include fighting between members because of rivalries, tensions, or notions of honor or respect. Tensions may arise when two gang members or cliques compete for power or status within the gang or when two members compete over the affection of another. After bouts of drinking, these simmering rivalries may erupt, and fighting often occurs. In such cases, as other researchers have noted, alcohol works to create a ritualized context for fighting and violent confrontations, whether physical or verbal (Szwed 1966; MacAndrew and Edgerton 1969), in which in-built tensions can be released or disputes settled within a contained arena. Once resolved through alcohol-related violence, the group can maintain its cohesion and unity. In fact, on some occasions, once the conflict has ceased, the antagonists seal their unity by sharing a beer.

At a more manifestly symbolic level, drinking is associated with two important ritual events in gang life. For many gangs, new members are expected to go through an initiation, often referred to as "jumping in." This induction process, or rite of passage, is important, because it is designed to symbolically test the newcomer's toughness and his ability to defend himself and withstand physical violence. The ritualized physical testing of potential group members is a common occurrence in many societies and has been described and analyzed by many anthropologists. As Heald (1986) has noted, group initiations are similar to examples of "battleproofing" in military training, in which the new recruits experience a situation of stress that allows them ". . . to develop confidence in their ability to face danger" (Heald 1986, p. 78). Within the gang, as Vigil and Long (1990) have noted, this process can serve "to test member's toughness and desire for membership . . . and to enhance loyalty to the group" (Vigil and Long, p. 64). Once the initiation has been accomplished and the newcomers accepted, their new status is confirmed by a bout of drinking and getting drunk. The association of alcohol and violent behavior is confirmed. The act of drinking and getting drunk after being "jumped in" also can help to deaden the pain resulting from the violence of the initiation.

Funerals are the second ritual event in gang life in which alcohol and violence are associated. Here, gang members in mourning use alcohol to represent their connectedness to the dead homeboy. They pour alcohol over the grave or leave alcohol at the graveside to symbolize their unity. For example, Campbell describes an incident in which each gang member, during a drinking session, ritually poured alcohol onto the floor prior to drinking from a bottle of rum, which was being passed around: ". . . he pours a little of the rum on the ground in memory of those who are dead or who are in jail" (Campbell 1991, p. 55). After the funeral has taken place, the group may begin heavy drinking. At this time, the gang members may again symbolize their connectedness to the dead by pouring some of their beer or alcohol on the ground. Drinking also may lead the group to decide on taking revenge, either on those responsible for the death of their homeboy or, in some cases, on innocent individuals. In addition to those violent activities internal to the gang, violence between opposing gangs is another frequent and common activity that is associated with drinking. Different types of activities include the following: violence targeting a member or members of a rival gang, violence against residents of the gang's own neighborhood, and violence against gangs or residents of another neighborhood (Sanchez-Jankowski 1991). The reasons for such conflict are varied and include such issues as gang members testing others, gang members' perceptions that they or their territories have been "disrespected," gang members' fears that their turfs are under threat, gang members' attempts to expand their turf, and fighting over the affections of another. In many of these types of external violent activities, drinking prior to the event is common.

Although gang members expressed no overall agreement on the issue of whether alcohol improved their ability to fight, two features were clear. First, confrontations between rival gang members frequently took place while gang members were drinking. Second, in spite of disagreements as to the precise effects of alcohol, many of our respondents admitted that drinking assisted them to develop a sense of "locura" (Vigil and Long 1990), or "pumped them up," making them ready to fight. In these cases, alcohol works not as the literature would suggest, as an excuse or deviance disavowal mechanism (Heath 1978; MacAndrew and Edgerton 1969), but, instead, as an enabling mechanism.

Thus, alcohol may be perceived as the catalyst for violent incidents, either because drinking was more likely to lead to fighting or because, once drunk, the gang members did not care what happened. Violent confrontation with another group may be senseless and provoked by a drunken fellow homeboy; nevertheless, because of their notions of respect and honor, the members must still defend their homeboy. These violent activities, which are encouraged by the young men drinking, work to bind the group together (Sanders 1994). The identity of the group is continually reinforced by these conflicts with other gangs or with other individuals, while enforcing the gang's separateness.

While alcohol and group drinking can work to maintain and confirm group cohesion, it also can operate in a divisive manner (Hunt and Satterlee 1986). These internal conflicts occur because honor and respect have been questioned or previous rivalries and tensions have come to the surface. Fighting often occurs because of a supposed slight, an accident, an unfortunate remark, or paying too much attention to somebody's girlfriend—any action that might be interpreted as showing disrespect. Fortunately, conflicts within the gang do not appear to lead to long-lasting rifts; once the fighting is over, the group reconvenes. In such cases, alcohol works to create a "time-out" period, or a ritualized context for fighting and violent confrontations, whether physical or verbal (MacAndrew and Edgerton 1969), in which in-built tensions can be released or disputes settled within a contained arena. Once the tensions are resolved through alcohol-related violence, the group can again regain its cohesion and unity.

SUMMARY

Few researchers have examined the interconnections between two endemic features of gang life: violence and drinking. To date, most gang researchers have focused on violence and its relationship to illicit drugs and have largely neglected the importance of alcohol in gang life. This article provides a brief review of the extent to which drinking is a pervasive feature of gang life and the ways in which drinking connects with different types and settings of violent behavior.

In focusing on drinking and violence among youth gangs, researchers can begin to explore the social processes that occur in the development of violent behavior after drinking (Pernanen 1991). This focus is important, because many researchers (Roizen 1993) have noted that in spite of the ". . . hundreds of studies that have addressed aspects of the relationship between drinking and violence" (Collins 1988, p.108), little is known about alcohol's role in violent behavior.

References

Anderson, E. *Code of the Street: Decency, Violence and the Moral Life of the Inner City.* New York: Norton and Company, 1999.

Campbell, A. *The Girls in the Gang.* 2d/ed. New Brunswick: Rutgers University Press, 1991.

Chin, K. *Chinese Triad Societies, Tongs, Organized Crime and Street Gangs in Asia and the United States.* Westport, CT: Greenwood Press, 1990.

Cohen, A. Symbolism and social change: Matters of life and death in Walsay, Shetland. *Man* (New Series) 20(2):307–324, 1985.

Collins, J. J. The relationship of problem drinking to individual offending sequences. In: Blumstein, A.; Cohen, J.; Roth, J. A.; and Visher, C. A., eds. *Criminal Careers and "Career Criminals."* Vol. 2. Washington, DC: National Academy Press, 1986.

Collins, J. J. Suggested explanatory frameworks to clarify the alcohol use/violence relationship. *Contemporary Drug Problems* 15:107–121, 1988.

Corrigan, P. Doing nothing. In: Hall, S., and Jefferson, T., eds. *Resistance Through Rituals: Youth Subcultures in Post-War Britain.* London: Hutchinson, 1976.

Davies, A. "These viragoes are no less cruel than the lads": Young women, gangs and violence in late Victorian Manchester and Salford. *The British Journal of Criminology* 39(1):72–89, 1999.

Dunning, E., Murphy, P., and Williams, J. *The Roots of Football Hooliganism.* New York: Routledge Kegan Paul, 1988.

Fagan, J. The social organization of drug use and drug dealing among urban gangs. *Criminology* 27: 633–669, 1989.

Fagan, J. Social processes of delinquency and drug use among urban gangs. In: Huff, C. R., ed. *Gangs in America.* Newbury Park, CA: Sage, 1990. pp. 183–219.

Fagan, J. Set and setting revisited: Influences of alcohol and illicit drugs on the social context of violent events. In: Martin, S. E., ed. *Alcohol and Interpersonal Violence: Fostering Multidisciplinary Perspectives.* NIAAA Research Monograph No. 24. NIH Pub. No. 93–3496. Bethesda, MD: National Institute on Alcohol Abuse and Alcoholism, 1993. pp. 161–191.

Feldman, H. W., Mandel, J., and Fields, A. In the neighborhood: A strategy for delivering early intervention services to young drug users in their natural environments. In: Friedman, A. S., and Beschner, G. M., eds. *Treatment Services for Adolescent Substance Abusers.* Rockville, MD: National Institute on Drug Abuse, 1985.

Goldstein, P. J. Drugs and violent crime. In: Weiner, N. A., and Wolfgang, M. E., eds. *Pathways to Criminal Violence.* Beverly Hills: Sage, 1989. pp. 16–48.

Hagedorn, J. *People and Folks: Gangs, Crime and the Underclass in a Rustbelt City.* Chicago: Lakeview Press, 1988.

Heald, S. The ritual use of violence: Circumcision among the Gisu of Uganda. In: Riches, D., ed. *The Anthropology of Violence.* Oxford: Basil Blackwell, 1986. pp. 70–85.

Heath, D. A critical review of ethnographic studies of alcohol use. In: Gibbins, R. J., Israel, Y., Kalant, H., et al., eds. *Research Advances in Alcohol and Drug Problems.* Vol. 1. New York: John Wiley and Sons, 1975. pp. 1–92.

Heath, D. The sociocultural model of alcohol use: Problems and prospects. *Journal of Operational Psychiatry* 9:655–661, 1978.

Hunt, G., and Satterlee, S. Cohesion and division: Drinking in an English village. *Man* (New Series) 21(3):521–537, 1986.

Jacob, T., and Leonard, K. Family and peer influences in the development of adolescent alcohol abuse. In: Zucker, R., Boyd, G., and Howard, J., eds. *The Development of Alcohol Problems: Exploring the Biopsychosocial Matrix of Risk.* NIAAA Research Monograph No. 26. NIH Pub. No. 94–3495 Bethesda, MD: National Institute on Alcohol Abuse and Alcoholism, 1994.

Klein, M. W., and Maxson, C. L. Street gang violence. In: Wolfgang, M. E., and Weiner, N., eds. *Violent Crime, Violent Criminals.* Beverly Hills: Sage, 1989.

MacAndrew, C., and Edgerton, R. *Drunken Comportment: A Social Explanation.* Chicago: Aldine, 1969.

Macleod, J. *Ain't No Makin It: Leveled Aspirations in a Low-Income Neighborhood.* Boulder: Westview Press, 1987.

Messerschmidt, J. W. *Masculinities and Crime: Critique and Reconceptualization of Theory.* Lanham, MD: Rowman and Littlefield, 1993.

Miller, J. A. Struggles over the symbolic: Gang style and the meaning of social control. In: Ferrell, J., and Sanders, C. R. *Cultural Criminology.* Boston: Northeastern University Press, 1995.

Moore, J. *Going Down to the Barrio: Homeboys and Homegirls in Change.* Philadelphia: Temple University Press, 1991.

Moore, J. W., Garcia, R., Garcia, C., Cerda, L., and Valencia, F. *Homeboys: Gangs, Drugs and Prison in the Barrios of Los Angeles.* Philadelphia: Temple University Press, 1978.

Office of Juvenile Justice and Delinquency Prevention (OJJDP). *Statistical Briefing Book* (December).Washington, DC: Office of Justice Programs, OJJDP, 2000a.

Office of Juvenile Justice and Delinquency Prevention (OJJDP). *1998 National Youth Gang Survey.* Washington, DC: Office of Justice Programs, OJJDP, 2000b.

Padilla, F. *The Gang as an American Enterprise.* New Brunswick, NJ: Rutgers University Press, 1992.

Parker, R. N. *Alcohol and Homicide: A Deadly Combination of Two American Traditions.* Albany: State University of New York Press, 1995.

Pernanen, K. *Alcohol in Human Violence.* New York: Guilford, 1991.

Reiss, A., and Roth, J. *Understanding and Preventing Violence.* Washington, DC: National Academy Press, 1993.

Roizen, J. Issues in the epidemiology of alcohol and violence. In: Martin, S. E., ed. *Alcohol and Interpersonal Violence: Fostering Multidisciplinary Perspectives.* NIAAA Research Monograph No. 24. NIH Pub. No. 93–3496. Bethesda, MD: National Institute on Alcohol Abuse and Alcoholism, 1993. pp. 3–36.

Sanchez-Jankowski, M. *Islands in the Street.* Berkeley: University of California Press, 1991.

Sanders, W. B. *Gangbangs and Drive-Bys: Grounded Culture and Juvenile Gang Violence.* New York: Aldine de Gruyter, 1994.

Skolnick, J., Correl, T., Navarro, E., and Rabb, R. *The Social Structure of Street Drug Dealing.* Sacramento, CA: Office of the Attorney General, State of California, 1989.

Steadman, H. J. A situational approach to violence. *International Journal of Law and Psychiatry* 5:171–186, 1982.

Szwed, J. F. Gossip, drinking and social control: Consensus and communication in a Newfoundland parish. *Ethnology* 5, 1966.

Taylor, C. *Dangerous Society.* East Lansing: Michigan State University, 1989.

Thrasher, F. *The Gang.* Chicago: University of Chicago Press, 1927.

Toy, C. Coming out to play: Reasons to join and participate in Asian gangs. *The Gang Journal* 1(1): 13–29, 1992.

Vigil, J. D. *Barrio Gangs: Street Life and Identity in Southern California.* Austin: University of Texas Press, 1988.

Vigil, J. D., and Long, J. M. Emic and etic perspectives on gang culture: The Chicano case. In: Huff, C. R., ed. *Gangs in America.* Newbury Park: Sage Publications, 1990. pp. 55–68.

Waldorf, D., Hunt, G., and Joe, K. *Report of the Southeast Asian Gangs and Drugs Study.* National Institute on Drug Abuse. San Francisco: Institute for Scientific Analysis, 1994.

White, H. R., Hansell, S., and Brick, J. Alcohol use and aggression among youth. *Alcohol Health & Research World* 17(2):144–150, 1993.

The Financial Activity of a Modern American Street Gang

Sudhir Venkatesh

The street gang has been a part of the social life of American cities for more than 150 years. In the mid-1970s, through a dramatic transformation known as corporatization, street gangs became systematically involved in underground income-generating activities such as drug distribution and extortion.[1] The effects of corporate gang activity, including increased violence and decreased safety of public spaces, are unmistakable and have received significant attention in the popular and social scientific communities. However, only a handful of studies on the financial activities of the corporate street gang have been conducted.[2] Although their findings are valuable, these studies have provided minimal quantitative information on the financial dealings of the gang or the earnings of its individual members.

THE ETHNOGRAPHIC APPROACH

Quantitatively oriented researchers generally have experienced great difficulty in procuring information about the financial activities of gangs and other underground entrepreneurs. The time necessary to gain the trust of informants and to protect one's role as a researcher makes a

Venkatesh, Sudhir. 1999, November. "The Financial Activity of a Modern American Street Gang," *Looking at Crime From the Street Level*, Vol. 1, pp. 1–11. Washington, DC: U.S. Department of Justice, Office of Justice Programs.

"quick-and-dirty" survey interview difficult to carry out. In this context, participant-observation techniques—sometimes called ethnography—have served as a powerful social scientific tool in researching marginal groups. Classic ethnographic objects of study have included street gangs, victims of crime and natural disaster, and the homeless.

Ethnographers use close-up observations of, and lengthy discussions with, gang members to provide answers that statistical surveys cannot capture. Ethnographic studies may be distinguished by their interest in the meaning of a given lifestyle for the participants—for example, why individuals join gangs has been an issue of great concern.

By "hanging out" with people for extended periods of time, ethnographers have been able to acquire information on gang activity outside not only the public eye but also the gaze of many researchers. It is not surprising, therefore, that much of the conceptual and theoretical insight into gang activity is produced by ethnographic studies. Information produced by qualitatively oriented ethnographers also has been valuable for survey researchers in constructing questionnaires and interview protocols.

The particular value of ethnography in street gang studies resonates with the larger use of ethnography in the social sciences. Ethnography has been useful in giving "voice to the voiceless"—in making information publicly known about people, groups, and social processes that are ignored, marginalized, or silenced by the state and media. Ethnography also has served as a means to provide a more complex, richer portrait than can be produced using only quantitative data.

The qualitative information produced by ethnographers is no panacea, however. It is the view of one person (the ethnographer) and is, therefore, subject to his or her biases. Because of time and monetary constraints, ethnographers can study only a small group of people; thus, they are often forced to draw conclusions about gangs in general based on their knowledge of one or two gangs.

Thus, ethnographic information has not been particularly well integrated into social science policy—how can national policy be based on the observations of only one person observing one or two gangs in only one context?

"QUANTITATIVE ETHNOGRAPHY"

In this study of the financial activity of a street gang, ethnographic research techniques were used to obtain quantitative information. Specifically, numerical data on the economic practices of a street gang (including wage and nonwage expenditures) were gathered through the use of participant-observation techniques. The project captured not only qualitative information on gang members' views, daily activity patterns, household relations, and other variables but also information on how much they earned, how their earnings changed as they "aged" in the gang, and other quantitative data.

Ethnography was helpful in gathering two data sets that may assist in the policy arena. In developing the first data set, the ethnographer contacted a former gang member who had access to the financial records maintained by a single gang for a 4-year period between 1988 and 1995 (to protect confidentiality, the exact dates cannot be revealed). These "books" recorded the price and quantity of drugs sold; other sources of revenue; and gang expenditures for wages, weapons, funerals, and other items. The gang leader had updated the data monthly to manage the gang's financial activities.

In developing the second data set, the ethnographer worked with a macroeconomist to conduct longitudinal tracking of nearly one dozen gangs in a large city. Data on wages and expenditures were periodically collected from many different drug dealers in the city. This ongoing observation of gangs was intended to produce a taxonomy of the various organizational structures in which drug trafficking takes place (and to identify the most lucrative and successful) and a model of how gang members age throughout their tenure in the gang. Questions answered included when and why members left the gang and how much they earned over the course of their involvement.

FINDINGS: GANG REVENUES AND EXPENDITURES

Results indicated that ethnography can be a productive technique to study criminal processes. It can provide extremely valuable observations of difficult-to-reach social groups and also can be used with survey and interview protocols to yield quantitative information.

The financial books kept by a large, now-defunct street gang reveal that the gang sustained a lucrative operation. The gang, consisting of several hundred members, included a leadership class (typically, a leader and 3 officers); a "foot soldier" class (ranging from 25 to 100 members aged 16 to 25 years) that sold drugs; and "rank and file" members (usually 200 persons younger than high school age) who were not allowed to conduct entrepreneurial activities. More than 70 percent of the gang's total annual revenue of approximately $280,000 was generated from the sale of crack cocaine. Dues provided some additional gang revenue (approximately 25 percent), and extortion directed at local businesses and entrepreneurs represented a small fraction of revenues (about 5 percent). The gang operated in a neighborhood of roughly four city blocks (eight blocks to a mile).

Costs were subdivided into nonwage and wage expenses. The single greatest nonwage expenditure was the purchase of wholesale powder cocaine. Tribute payments by the leader to the central gang leadership holding authority over the gang represented the local gang's second greatest nonwage expenditure, accounting for nearly $50,000 annually (more than 15 percent of the total revenue).

In return for this payment, local gang members received protection on the streets and, more critically, in prison; some help in finding and maintaining supplier networks; and the opportunity to rise in the organization and extract tribute from other local gangs. Another nonwage gang expense was payment to mercenary fighters (known as warriors), who performed some of the most dangerous tasks (such as drive-by shootings and guarding key drug-selling locations during gang wars). These warriors, typically former gang members with reputations for bravery and violence, were held on retainer by the gang. Funerals and payments to families of the deceased were a nontrivial expense for the gang. When a gang member was killed, the gang paid funeral expenses and typically provided compensation to the slain member's family. The total average cost to the gang was $5,000 per funeral, a large amount compared with the annual wage payment to the typical foot soldier (averaging less than $2,000 per year).

Wage costs were divided into two categories: expenditures for officers and those for foot soldiers. The gang leader retained between $4,200 and $10,900 per month, for an annual wage of $50,000 (year 1) to $130,000 (year 4). Officers (for example, the runner, enforcer, or treasurer) earned roughly $1,000 per month working full time, and most did not work in legitimate jobs simultaneously. The typical foot soldier was paid about $200 per month and worked approximately 20 hours per week, implying an hourly wage well below the Federal minimum. But foot soldiers also were allowed to sell marijuana and heroin outside the gang structure—the gang sold only crack cocaine. Calculations indicated that the average foot soldier's hourly wage ranged from $5.90 to $11.10 during the 4-year period.

On the surface, the wage range available to foot soldiers was substantially greater than the minimum wage available to these poorly educated inner-city youths through legitimate employment. However, as shown in the table below, risk calculations based on the gang's own tally of injuries, deaths, and arrests, combined with ethnographic observations, indicate, not surprisingly, that street-level drug distribution is an extremely risky business. The annual death rate among the gang's foot soldiers was 4.2 percent—more than 40 times the national average for African-American males in the 16- to 25-year-old age group. On average, a drug seller could expect 0.59 wounds (virtually all from bullets) and 1.43 arrests each year. The most alarming statistic is that gang members who were active for the entire 4-year period had roughly a 25-percent chance of dying. Furthermore, there was an average of more than two nonfatal injuries (mostly gunshot injuries) per member and nearly six arrests for the 4-year period.

By comparison, homicide victimization rates for black males aged 14 to 17 in the United States are roughly 1 in 1,000 per year, or about 100 times lower than observed in this sample. Even among rank-and-file members of this gang (for example, those affiliated with the gang but not actively engaged in the drug trade), homicide rates are only 1 in 200 annually in this sample.

Adverse Events Experienced by Gang Members*

	Number in Sample	Annualized Rate per Member
Violent death	3	0.042
Nonfatal wound or injury	42	0.590
Arrests	102	1.433

*Data on adverse events were gathered during ethnographic study of the gang and correspond to the 26 months for which financial data were available (financial data were not available for each month of the entire 4-year period). Annualized rates are based only on the experiences of gang officers and foot soldiers (excluding rank-and-file members who did not actively participate in the drug trade). On average, there were approximately 30 foot soldiers at any given time during the study period.

The nonofficer stratum within the corporate gang endures risky work conditions for the opportunity to move up in the gang's hierarchy and to earn a more significant salary. In economics, this situation is referred to as a "tournament"—an opportunity structure similar in some respects to that of medical residents or associates in law firms. However, even when factoring in the probability of moving up in the gang organization, the expected wage of the average gang member during his tenure in the gang is only $7 per hour. This wage does not seem high enough to counter the tremendous risks of injury, arrest, and death inherent in the drug trade.

WHAT MOTIVATES GANG PARTICIPATION?

Given the findings that the majority of individuals in the gang are poorly compensated and face grave risks, the clear question is, Why would gang members choose to participate in such activities? Those studying corporate gang activity tend to explain gang involvement by emphasizing either economic attractions or symbolic factors. In the economic model, gang members are entrepreneurs who rely on the gang for material benefits because they are unwilling to accept the mainstream opportunities available to them or because they have not encountered much success in the legitimate labor force. In this study, most gang members never realize significant material gain, so an economic-based explanation is not sufficient in itself. Symbolic theories emphasize the role of ideologies such as "family" that afford gang members a basis for personal and collective identity in social ecologies of impoverishment and minimal mainstream resources. Gang members do find in corporate gang activity a measure of peer group support and a sense of belonging to a larger community; however, these symbolic benefits alone also seem to be incapable of sustaining motivation in gang-based entrepreneurialism over an extended time period, perhaps because gang members eventually find social support from peers who are not affiliated with gangs.

Indeed, the life-course appears to be the best perspective from which to understand the interaction of symbolic and economic incentives. Ethnographic observations of several gangs over an extended period of time indicate an aging-out pattern. For example, at the most basic level, the successful corporate gang will provide for all of its members an immediate wage and a direct sense of community and identity. The significance of these two benefits changes, however, as the individual member ages. In his role as an entering foot soldier, the member has few financial commitments, and so gang involvement makes possible fairly continuous consumption and provides an alternative to menial work in the service sector, along with the fellowship of one's peers. The younger foot soldier is motivated to stay in the gang by the prospect of a potentially lucrative salary as an officer. However, for the older, more experienced drug trader, one with perhaps a growing number of financial and familial commitments, the immediate economic wage is no longer sufficient; similarly, while the benefits of the peer group continue to exist, opportunities for high income and promotion in the gang diminish. It is at this point that most of the gang members in this sample abdicated their involvement in the gang's entrepreneurial activities and chose instead to direct their energies to the mainstream labor market. While many continued to participate in the gang's social activities, the symbolic attraction of dramatic future material rewards appeared to lose its motivating capacity.

Faced with continuous turnover, the gang brings aboard new recruits who are sustained by the objectively very slim—but symbolically very powerful—belief that they will achieve substantial earnings while working for the gang. In this manner, the individuals composing the gang are continually changing while the overall structure of the gang remains constant. Nearly every other corporate, metropolitan area variant examined is characterized by this basic structure—there exist both a young cohort motivated by the remote possibility of substantial earnings and an older adult contingent that grows disillusioned with the gang as an adequate employment prospect but relies on the gang for supplemental income (until a full-time legitimate job at a competitive wage is found) and for peer group support. Preliminary study results suggest that both younger and older gang members are motivated by material attractions as well as the benefits of membership in a company of like-minded peers. Further research is clearly necessary, however, to understand the precise role of symbolic and economic motivations.

DATA AUTHENTICITY, VALIDITY, AND USEFULNESS

Never before have such detailed financial data from a street gang been available for scholarly inspection. The existence of such data raises important questions regarding authenticity and validity. On the question of authenticity, there is no reason to doubt that these records actually reflect data that the gang compiled on a monthly basis. During the ethnographic phase of data collection, the researchers learned of several gangs that were monitoring their financial activities. The researchers were not given access to these data until after the gangs had dissolved and word was received that the records could be made available. The general knowledge among those in the city's law enforcement and social service communities that some street gangs record their financial activities, and that many leaders have documented on paper their personal portfolios, provides additional confidence in the data set (indeed, a recent trial of a police officer accused of assisting gang drug operations used a gang's books as part of its evidence).

The question of validity is more problematic. The study data were compiled by hand and stored in notebooks or on scraps of paper. Those responsible for keeping the data had no formal training in accounting. Several possible biases in the data necessitate viewing the results obtained as a lower boundary on the profitability of the gang. First, although used primarily for tracking day-to-day gang operations, the data were also intended to serve as a means by which the gang leader could credibly report to his superiors about profitability or lack of profitability.

This second use of the data raises the possibility that the scale of the operation as a whole was consciously understated—the less money the gang earned, the smaller the monetary tribute that had to be given each month to the leader's superior officer. Also, the gang leader had great flexibility to make "off-the-books" arrangements, such as allowing individual members to sell goods on their own for a small fee payable to the gang, or allowing other local entrepreneurs to sell illicit goods for a similar fee. Finally, the gang also permitted its own members or others in the community to sell marijuana, heroin, or amphetamines in exchange for payment of a monthly "tax." Neither the leader's independent activities nor the sales of these other drugs are reflected in the data. However, both of these revenue sources are likely to be minor when compared with the sale of crack cocaine.

Despite concerns regarding authenticity and validity, ethnographic methods open doors for subsequent policy-relevant research that could be used by social scientists. The receipt of a gang's financial records is one benefit. However, this study's model of the life-course aging process was also a product of ethnographic observation of several gangs throughout the city. Ethnography was used as an initial screening device to gain information about the range of different organizational structures that gangs adopt. Once this "universe" of gang organizational types was formed, it was possible to form a smaller sample and to interview gang members and track their wages/expenditures over an extended period. The outcome was the empirical data on drug trafficking that are representative of gangs throughout the city—not just one region or one organizational type. Moreover, the breadth of ethnographic participation yielded insights into the developmental trajectory of gang members (that is, how they age and at what points particular forms of intervention might be useful).

Although more research of this type is needed, this study offers a preliminary basis from which to analyze the motivations for individual participation in the corporate gang. In light of tremendously skewed wage distribution, a life-course perspective was employed to account for the economic and symbolic incentives of individual corporate gang involvement. Throughout their tenure, gang members move in and out of the service sector and so rely on the gang for both an immediate (but pecuniary) wage and for support and friendship. However, over the course of their involvement in the gang, as members realize that their opportunity to move higher in the gang hierarchy is diminishing, the possibility of lucrative earnings loses its attractive potential and members grow disillusioned with the gang as a viable sphere of economic mobility. Thus, most young adult members withdraw from full-time involvement in the gang's economic activities and become primarily social members.

RECOMMENDATIONS: JOBS ARE KEY

The fact that gang wages are so low and most gang members work at least sporadically in the legitimate sector suggests that public policies designed to encourage greater labor market participation and discourage gang involvement may be successful. To be optimally effective, such policies must recognize the differing motivations for participation among younger drug sellers and those in their adult years. Policies that attempt simply to replace gang-based drug dealing with jobs in the service sector will not be as successful in limiting gang recruitment and countering the dream of underground economic mobility. Indeed, for young members, in addition to peer affirmation, it is the illusion of riches and rewards that is an overwhelming attraction of the corporate gang. For them, the gang must be countered with another meaningful ideal of social mobility and self-efficacy.

As members age, peer group support and identity continue to be important motives for remaining in the gang, but the gang also becomes an employer of last resort, furnishing income in contexts where other opportunities may be limited. For this group, direct job creation may have a more lasting impact in offering a real exit mechanism by which older members can end their involvement in drug economies.

Notes

[1] Taylor, Carl S., *Dangerous Society*, East Lansing, MI: Michigan State Press, 1990.

[2] Padilla, Felix, *The Gang as an American Enterprise*, New Brunswick, NJ: Rutgers University Press, 1992; Bourgois, Philippe, *In Search of Respect*, Cambridge, MA: Cambridge University Press, 1989; and Jankowski, Martin S., *Islands in the Street*, Berkeley: University of California Press, 1991.

13

A Tale of Two Cities
Gangs as Organized Crime Groups

Scott H. Decker, Tim Bynum, & Deborah Weisel

Are street gangs becoming organized crime groups? Do gangs exhibit the characteristics of continuing criminal enterprises? Considerable speculation exists about these issues (Orvis 1996), but hard evidence is more difficult to find. Although law enforcement (Fox and Amador 1993), media sources, and some government agencies (Conley 1993) provide support for this view, little empirical evidence has been gathered to address these questions.

Gang research has exploded in the past decade. Spurred in part by increased federal funding, researchers have "rediscovered" gangs (Bookin-Weiner and Horowitz 1983; Maxson and Klein 1990). Yet despite the abundance of research, a number of important questions remain unanswered. For example, little is known about the evolution of gangs into organized crime groups. Are gangs disorganized aggregations of predatory individuals that commit a number of crimes, or do they purposively engage in crimes motivated and organized by the gang according to formal-rational criteria? The answer to this question has important implications for both prevention and intervention. In addition, it bears on a central question about the nature of criminal behavior—its level of organization.

Decker, Scott H., Bynum, Tim, and Weisel, Deborah, "A Tale of Two Cities: Gangs as Organized Crime Groups." *Justice Quarterly*, Vol. 15, No. 3, pp. 395–425, 1998. Copyright © 1998 by the Academy of Criminal Justice Sciences. Reprinted with the permission of the Academy of Criminal Justice Sciences.

GROUPS, GANGS, AND CRIME

The structure of gangs and gang activity is an important issue in our understanding of gangs specifically, and of crime in general. Indeed, this is one of the most significant topics in criminology and criminal justice today because of its implications for our understanding of both criminal behavior and criminal justice policy. This issue has been framed largely in the context of drug sales.

In their review of the role of gangs in drug sales, Decker and Van Winkle (1995) describe two competing views. The instrumental-rational view is reflected in the work of Skolnick et al. (1988), Padilla (1992), Sanchez-Jankowski (1991), and Taylor (1990). These authors describe gangs as well-organized entrepreneurs who employ traditional economic strategies of marketing, structure, and amassing profits that are reinvested in the gang. The gangs depicted in these works have a vertical structure, enforce discipline among their members, and are quite successful in defining and achieving group values. A contrasting view is found in the work of several well-known gang researchers including Hagedorn (1988), Klein, Maxson, and Cunningham (1991), and Fagan (1989). They describe gang drug sales in sharply different terms, emphasizing the informal-individual characteristics of many youth gangs, and the consequent difficulties in organizing activities, consensus, and investments. According to this view, gangs are diffuse, self-interested, and self-motivated aggregations of individual members, most of whom sell drugs for themselves. The results of Decker and Van Winkle's (1995) St. Louis field study are compatible with the latter conclusion. Their findings support a view of drug sales as a rather haphazard, individually focused activity.

The debate over the organizational nature of drug sales by street gangs offers an important theoretical framework for the current study. That debate also provides a link to a larger issue, the organization of criminal activities. At the heart of this controversy is a question: To what extent can offenders announce and embrace common goals, motivate others to join them in a common enterprise, and maintain a monetary and emotional commitment to the group enterprise of crime? Fortunately the criminological literature is applicable to these issues, and it generally supports a view that street criminals are ineffective in achieving these goals. Einstadter (1969), Conklin (1972), and Wright and Decker (1997), who studied robbers, concluded that armed robbers generally do not plan their crimes, nor do they organize their activities effectively. Bennett and Wright (1984), Wright and Decker (1994), Cromwell, Olsen, and Avery (1992), and Tunnel (1992) interviewed active residential burglars. In each of these studies the researchers concluded that burglars act in a rather disorganized manner—most often caused by drugs, drink, or the desire to impress their friends.

Beyond burglars and robbers lurks a broader group of street criminals, particularly those who engage in petty theft and drug sales. Best and Luckenbill (1994) discuss how street criminals can be grouped into categories. Although they offer several different typologies, these authors add that a typology does not imply obedience or structure among individuals within that typology. Indeed, they suggest that independence among offenders is the norm, and that social organization is largely absent from these individuals' criminal involvement. This view is supported by Irwin (1972), a researcher and ex-inmate who argues that "disorganized criminals" are

> . . . the largest category of active criminals, [which] includes the less skilled, less sophisticated thieves who spend most of their time while not in prison hanging around, waiting for something to come along, and engaging in unplanned, unprofitable petty crimes, often on impulse. (p. 122)

Although Irwin uses the word *group* to refer to these individuals, it hardly reflects the instrumental-rational views of group crime. Similarly, Adler (1985) suggests that although individual drug sellers are enmeshed in an organization, that organization is more a consequence of social life as a series of relationships than the well-orchestrated efforts of a coordinated group.

In this study we examine four gangs: one African-American and one Hispanic in each of two cities, San Diego and Chicago. We seek to determine how extensively these four gangs have taken on the characteristics of organized crime groups. This issue is framed in three specific contexts: (1) the nature of gang organization, (2) the nature of gang activities, and (3) the nature of gang relationships. On the basis of interviews with key informants, some on probation and some imprisoned, we provide both qualitative and quantitative evidence on these issues.

METHODS

We interviewed gang members in two cities. Using the dichotomy developed by Spergel and others, we sought to include one city that represented established gang cities, and another that represented "emerging" gang cities, where gangs were not intergenerational. We chose Chicago because it is widely regarded as the city where gangs have operated continuously for the longest time, are most highly organized, and have begun to penetrate institutional activities such as politics and neighborhood organization. The group of "emerging" gang cities was much larger. As noted by Spergel and Curry (1990), Curry, Ball, and Fox (1994), Curry, Ball, and Decker (1996), and Klein (1995), the number of cities in which law enforcement representatives report the presence of gangs has grown dramatically in the last 15 years. We chose San Diego because it is in California, is easily accessible to Los Angeles (and Los Angeles gangs) by automobile, has a base of knowledge about local gangs (Pennell 1994; Sanders 1994), and is similar to many other emerging gang cities.

We chose these cities and these gangs for strategic reasons. Little comparative research on gangs or gang cities can be found in the literature. Both the Latin Kings and the Gangster Disciples in Chicago have been targeted by the attorney general for federal prosecution. No San Diego gangs have received similar attention, however. This fact strengthens the argument that Chicago and San Diego represent diverse cities and allow for varied tests of the hypothesis of gangs as organized crime groups. The opportunity to compare gangs within and across cities is a strong rationale for the current study because the literature lacks and needs such a comparison.

We asked key law enforcement officials and social service providers in each city to identify their city's most organized gangs. To aid in the identification process, we asked officials to consider variables such as leadership structure, involvement in crime, relationships with other gangs, and relationships with other social institutions. In late 1994 and early 1995, we conducted more than 20 such interviews in each city on two separate occasions. The respondents provided a very short list of gangs in each city. Ethnic composition was an additional criterion for selection. Both Chicago and San Diego contain many African-American and Hispanic gangs; we selected one gang composed primarily of members of each group.

We chose two well-known Chicago gangs, the Latin Kings and the Gangster Disciples. Each has existed in some form for at least two generations; this suggests that they have had substantial impact on neighborhoods. In addition, law enforcement officials and social service providers stated almost unanimously that they were the most highly organized gangs in Chicago. In San Diego we chose the Lincoln Park Piru (also known as the Syndo Mob) and the Logan Heights Calle Treinte (also known as the Red Steps).

Our next task was to design a sampling strategy. We used official agencies as our catchment locations, and within each agency we collected a convenience sample of available and willing subjects. Such samples may not be representative, but in-depth interviews with key informants create a picture of their lives and concerns. Each city has a specialized gang probation unit, and numerous members of each gang were on probation. We believe that gang members on probation are more heavily involved in crime, tend to be older, and consequently would be more knowledgeable respondents about organized gang activities than individuals recruited solely from a street sample. We also believe that many of the most seriously involved gang members, especially in well-organized gangs, are in prison. After all, organized criminal activities are attracting increased attention from law enforcement officials, resulting in more arrests, convictions, and sentences. On the basis of interviews conducted with law enforcement officials, we knew that this was the case in Chicago, and we had reason to believe that the situation was similar in San Diego. Therefore we also interviewed members of each gang who were in prison.

The sampling strategy called for interviews with 10 to 15 members of each gang in probation offices and in prison. This would result in 20 to 30 interviews with members of each gang, approximately half drawn from probation and half from prison. In each case we attempted to recruit "key informants" (McCall 1978)—individuals with long tenure in the gang, and in a position to know about its activities, relationships, and structure. We offered respondents 20 dollars for participation; they could participate only after signing a human subjects consent form. Interviews were conducted by graduate students. In California, the prison interviews were conducted at the R. J. Donovon Correctional Facility; in Illinois they were conducted at the Joliet Prison. At each prison, interviews were held in a private room by an independent researcher. Our sample of subjects is described in table 1.

In all, 85 active gang members were interviewed: 41 from San Diego and 44 from Chicago. In San Diego, a disproportionate share of the total (68 percent) came from probation. The explanation for this deviation from our sampling strategy provides important insights for the primary goal of the study. Our primary goal is to determine whether gangs are becoming like organized crime groups and assuming the features of continuing criminal enterprises: engaging in organized criminal activities, establishing relationships with traditional organized crime groups, and using legitimate activities and relationships to expand influence and control for criminal, gang-related purposes. The differences between an emerging gang city such as San Diego and a traditional gang city such as Chicago are quite evident in these explorations. In San Diego, despite cooperation from a variety of local, state, and federal criminal justice agencies, we could not easily locate members of either gang. The explanation we received from each source we interviewed (including most gang members) was that both

Table 1 Gang Members Interviewed, by City

	Chicago		San Diego	
	GD	Kings	Logan Heights Calle Treinte	Lincoln Park Piru Syndo Mob
Source				
Prison	15	4	10	4
Probation	11	14	10	17
Total	26	18	20	21
Characteristics				
Mean Age	27	24	24	22
Mean Age Joined Gang	13	15	13	13
Percentage Arrested in Gang-related Crime	50	76	80	57
Mean Years of Membership	14	9	11	8

the Logan Heights Calle Treinte and the Lincoln Park Syndo Mob had been dismantled through aging out; splintering; and vigorous law enforcement, prosecution, and incarceration. This point is remarkable because less than a year before initiating interviews with gang members, each of these gangs was identified as the most highly organized and most likely to become like an organized crime group. This situation suggests that even the most highly organized gang, at least in an emerging gang city such as San Diego, can fade rather rapidly from the street gang scene.

In Chicago, our results followed the sampling plan more closely. Twenty-six interviews were conducted with Gangster Disciples, an African-American gang: 15 in prison and 11 on probation. Eighteen interviews were conducted with the Latin Kings, the Hispanic gang selected in Chicago. We were more successful in interviewing Latin Kings on probation than in prison, unlike the Gangster Disciples. This was not unexpected because, early in the study, we met with individuals involved in a project conducted by Irving Spergel in the Pilsen and Little Village areas. The lead interviewers for that project told us that we might find it difficult to gain cooperation from Latin Kings who were incarcerated because gang members, once in prison, became resistant to outsiders' efforts, and gang permission was required to conduct such interviews; consequently we interviewed only four imprisoned Kings and 14 on probation.

A key feature in all gang research is the need to distinguish between the activities of the larger enterprise known as the gang and the activities of individual members or small groups of members who operate outside the gang's influence. Such a distinction has even greater implications for the present study because gang members can engage in behaviors outside their gang that resemble organized crime. We dealt with this crucial issue by prompting respondents to distinguish between their activities as part of the gang and their activities as individuals. Such efforts were aided by specific questions about activities such as racketeering, influence peddling, money laundering, counterfeiting, and prostitution rings, which typically are associated with organized crime. Each gang member was instructed to indicate the activities he engaged in, and whether he did so as an individual or as part of the gang.

FINDINGS

We have organized the results of our interview findings around three major categories: gang structure and organization, gang activities, and relationships with other groups. In examining the extent to which gangs are becoming like organized crime groups, a key indicator is how well organized they are to carry out gang activities. Accordingly, we sought to determine whether gangs had levels of membership and leaders, held regular meetings, had written rules, and owned legitimate businesses. Taken together, such features may indicate a structure similar to those found in organized crime.

The second set of indicators concentrated on the criminal activities pursued by gangs and gang members. Many of these activities centered on drugs, such as selling drugs, organizing drug sales, supplying large quantities of drugs, or using drug money for gang purposes. In addition, we asked questions about firearms, specifically sale and possession of guns by gang members. Finally, we asked whether there were consequences for gang members who left the gang.

A third important element of gangs' increasing organization and sophistication is their relationships with other gangs and with legitimate groups such as neighborhood stores. We probed this area by asking whether gangs met together, sold drugs together, committed crime together, or partied together. We also sought to determine how extensively street gangs maintained relationships with prison gangs and with legitimate political and neighborhood groups. Overall we found a striking consensus between the prison groups and the probation groups within gangs.

To summarize, differences between Chicago and San Diego gangs on most dimensions were much greater than differences between gangs in the same city or between catchment areas for the same gang within a city. In other words, Chicago gangs are considerably more highly organized than their counterparts in San Diego. This finding is not especially surprising, given our selection criteria for cities and gangs. Because of their similarities, we have grouped together the prison and the probation gang members for analysis.

Gang Organization

The gangs from Chicago—the Gangster Disciples and The Latin Kings—are more highly organized than their San Diego counterparts on every measure (see table 2). Between the Chicago gangs, the Gangster Disciples are higher on six of eight indicators; in only one measure (consequences for leaving the gang) is the percentage of King members higher. The cultural significance of the gang to the Latin Kings may account for this difference. San Diego gangs report no written rules, few dues, and virtually no political activities. In Chicago, however, more than three-quarters of members report these activities for their gang. Clearly, the Chicago gangs are more highly organized than their San Diego counterparts. The meaning of these percentages can be seen more fully below, in the gang members' responses.

Levels of Membership

Differentiation within the organization is an important indicator of the level of gang organization. In general, the less differentiation between roles or levels of membership within the gang, the less highly developed the organization, and the less effective it can be in generating goals and

Table 2   Gang Organization

	Chicago		San Diego	
	GD	Kings	Calle	Syndo Mob
Levels of Membership	90% (22)	94% (16)	8% (12)	90% (21)
Leaders	100% (26)	94% (18)	30% (20)	52% (21)
Regular Meetings	85% (26)	82% (17)	30% (20)	29% (21)
Written Rules	81% (26)	81% (16)	0% (17)	0% (18)
Pay Dues	83% (25)	73% (15)	6% (17)	6% (17)
Political Activities	84% (25)	27% (15)	26% (19)	12% (21)
Legitimate Businesses	77% (22)	69% (13)	61% (13)	47% (15)
Consequences for Leaving the Gang	23% (22)	60% (15)	11% (18)	6% (18)

producing compliance among members in the pursuit of those goals. We found well-defined roles among Chicago gangs, but considerably fewer among the gangs in San Diego. This difference reflects the "emerging" nature of the gang situation in San Diego, as well as the longer history of Chicago gangs. Even some Chicago gang members, however, expressed uncertainty about levels of membership.

One imprisoned Gangster Disciple (#003) identified the levels of membership as "King, . . . Board of Directors, the Generals, and First Captains. The rest is just the membership, the enforcers." This view was seconded by several Gangster Disciples from the probation sample. One respondent stated,

> You got the king, you got the chiefs, you got the—wait a minute, let me go down the line. You got the prince . . . next in line. Then you got the don, they call it the don. Something like a war counselor or something. They you got chief of forces, then you got the generals, then the lieutenants. (#010)

Further insight into the Gangster Disciples' level of organization was offered by another incarcerated subject:

> Larry Hoover was king, and that's the highest you can get right there. Coming from him, they go down to BMs, board members. From there, they walk it on down to little generals and lieutenants and all that, and then you have the foot soldiers. (#004)

Despite these Gangster Disciples' claims about different levels of membership, other members were considerably less specific. One (#072, incarcerated) told us that there were "up people, down people"; another (#005) reported that there were "killers, cowards, and ones that party." These insights hardly reflect the role differentiation of a highly organized group.

Gangster Disciples from the probation sample offered a similar perspective on this issue. One member (#051) identified eight different levels of membership, including foot soldiers, first coordinator, second coordinator, literature coordinator, exercise coordinator, regents, governor, and board member.[1] These roles were identified as well by Subject #063, who also added the role of treasurer. Commenting on the overall structure, he noted, "It's pretty cool." Two members of the probation sample denied that there were different levels of membership, and indicated that everyone was equal.

Latin Kings described fewer and less precise distinctions between levels of membership. A probationer (#030) said there were "gangbangers on the street, and the older guys." Another King on probation mentioned "foot soldiers and chiefs." The most common distinction offered was between a lower level of membership (gangbangers on the street, foot soldiers, pee-wees) and leaders (crowns, older guys [OGs]).

San Diego gang members reported considerably lower levels of role differentiation, and described the different roles less precisely. In general, we found no substantial differences in role differentiation between the Lincoln Park Piru and the Logan Heights Calle Treinte. Many members of the San Diego gang seemed confused by the question, as in this exchange:

> INT: Are there different levels of membership in your gang?
>
> #022: Oh yeah.
>
> INT: What levels are there?
>
> #022: I don't know them by name but there are different levels.
>
> INT: Like what kind of levels?
>
> #022: Levels of power.
>
> INT: How many levels of power are there?
>
> #022: I don't know the process, about three or four I would say.
>
> INT: What is the lowest level of power?
>
> #022: Most of those people are youngsters, teenagers barely coming in or trying to hang with them or trying to be cool, I would say.

Other San Diego gang members could name only two or three categories of membership. Usually these were based on age, such as "youngsters" or "old gangsters," "children, teenagers, and adults," "young G, old G, all kinds of stuff" or "young homies and old homies."

Others denied that there were levels of membership. A Lincoln Park member on probation said,

> No. There is nobody called the shot caller.
>
> That's prison shit. That's only in prison. There ain't no shot caller. (#027)

His remarks were echoed by a Logan Heights member, also on probation, who said, "There ain't no shot callers. It's got nothing to do with a gang either. Most Mexicans have respect for our elders. You start growing older, you teach the young ones respect for their elders."

The comments about respect in this Hispanic gang were also evident in the response of an imprisoned member:

> INT: Are there different levels of leadership in your gang?
>
> #029: Not really. It depends on how everybody treats you. If you respect somebody you get that respect back. We don't got no leaders or nothing. Nobody tells anybody what to do.

In sum, our results support the contention that the Chicago and the San Diego gangs show important differences in the degree of organizational differentiation. In the emerging gang city, few members could cite distinctions between levels of membership or duties associated with those levels. In Chicago, however, role differentiation was greatest for the Gangster Disciples, though some of it appeared to take on a "mythic" character.

Leaders

A second characteristic of well-organized groups is the presence of leadership roles. We asked gang members to elaborate specifically on the presence of leaders within their gangs, and whether those leaders had any special roles, responsibilities, or skills. Again, the city was the most important dimension on which our results varied. Gangs in Chicago, especially the Gangster Disciples, told us that their gang had leaders, and those leaders performed functions different than those of regular members. The Latin Kings also described a leadership category, though less clearly defined. In contrast, virtually none of the San Diego gang members could tell us anything about leaders.

Gangster Disciples identified leadership roles in quite distinct terms. Gangster Disciples in prison stated that leaders "make sure all laws and policies are being adhered to" (#009), "give orders" (#003), "are supposed to be the thinkers" (#004), and "sit back and just put out a plan or whatever to [their] generals" (#010). A member on probation (#017) offered an expanded view of the role of leaders, which included making sure members attend school, get a job, and practice good hygiene. The nature of leadership among the Gangster Disciples is not dissimilar to that in many other supergangs, where leadership often reflects a mythic quality.

Latin Kings provided less specific details in identifying the roles and responsibilities of leadership within their gang. Respondent #049, an imprisoned King, told us that leaders "make the overall decisions"; #019, currently on probation, said that the leader "is the one that got the say so." A number of Kings identified a specific leadership role, the Inca, who gives orders to the Cacina. These roles and titles reflect the Latin Kings' strong cultural orientation, a feature common to Hispanic gangs (Moore 1978; Vigil

1988). In general, leaders among the Latin Kings occupied less instrumental, though not less important roles than leaders of the Gangster Disciples.

In San Diego, a less clearly defined picture of leadership emerged. Few Lincoln Park Pirus could specify whether leaders existed. Two Pirus on probation (#022 and #039) reported that leaders could no longer be distinguished from regular members. Logan Heights members provided equally vague definitions of leadership. Leadership roles were defined clearly only in regard to drug sales, where leaders supplied drugs.

We found little evidence of defined leadership roles within these gangs. The lone exception was the Gangster Disciples, where our respondents consistently identified specific leadership responsibilities. In general, highly evolved, effective organizations are characterized by clear leadership roles and responsibilities. This was not true of the other three gangs.

Regular Meetings

Meetings are an important characteristic of organized groups. They accomplish a variety of functions, including enhancing group cohesion, communicating responsibilities, and disseminating information. Almost all of our respondents told us that their gang held meetings, though the character of these meetings varied considerably.

Gangster Disciple members provided the clearest, most consistent answers to our questions about gang meetings; yet even these hardly depict a "businesslike" gathering. A Gangster Disciple on probation (#012) described meetings as "an hour of nonsense talking." Similarly, #017 said, "We talk, we talk. It ain't no meeting, we all just talk." Gangster Disciples in prison described more structured, more purposive meetings. That purpose was variously described as "discussing the programs, problems that may develop" (#003) and "discuss[ing] what's going on and the problems and stuff like that, or finances" (#001).

Latin Kings offered a slightly different view of their meetings. Dues generally were collected, and a concern about the welfare of the neighborhood (reflecting the salience of Hispanic culture) was a usual topic for such gatherings. But these assemblages, too, were informal. "We discuss what has happened, what's been going on, and if a situation occurs we talk about that situation and what we are going to do about it" (#014).

Meetings among San Diego gangs were even more informal; typically they focused on social activities. Lincoln Park gang members talked about holding meetings at a nearby park, which centered around barbecues, drinking beer, and talking to women. Another member (#061) described the meetings as "like a family reunion." The majority of Pirus, however, denied that their gang held meetings.

> INT: Do you have regular meetings or anything?

> #037: Ain't no motherfucking meetings, they ain't organized, none of them.

Logan Heights members had a similar view of their "meetings." They named barbecues and other social gatherings as the occasions when gang members held meetings. Many Calle Treinte members couldn't distinguish between parties or informal gatherings and meetings. One member on probation described meetings (such as they were) in the following terms:

> We just talk about whatever is going on, stuff like that, how we are going to meet girls, what happened to this person or that person, these people are doing this so what are we going to do about it? (#058)

Among the gangs we interviewed, meetings were not formal, nor were they dedicated to achieving specific purposes. More often they reflected their members' informal, social concerns and were held by "happenstance" whenever a number of members ran into each other.

Written Rules

Another characteristic of organized groups is their commitment to formal rules to enforce discipline and maintain order among members. Rules express important organizational values, provide a means of forging consensus, and allow organizations to announce their boundaries by punishing unacceptable conduct. The great majority of the gang members we interviewed stated that their gangs did have rules. When rules existed, their character and their enforcement varied considerably within and between gangs.

Almost all Gangster Disciples reported that their gang had rules; most said that the rules were written. Those rules reflected values central to the gang, and included prohibitions against activities such as "stealing, secrecy, and silence. Secrecy and silence is the first one. That's the one they drill mostly in the head" (#009) Secrecy plays a large role in the Gangster Disciples, as we learned in a number of interviews:

> INT: What were the most important rules?
>
> #010: No stealing, no members . . . hurt each other, no dope, no homosexual activity. The other ones I can't . . . reveal to you. We have an oath we have to swear about certain things we can't say. If we was on the stand [in court] we couldn't say it, we would just have to go to prison.

Many Disciples made references to the "sixteen laws" that each member must study and learn by heart. Although Gangster Disciple rules are written, one member on probation made an observation that nicely captures what many individuals told us about the rules: "Basically it's common sense" (#012).

Latin Kings also identified a number of rules, though these were less formal, and generally were directed toward individual standards of conduct. Respondent #019, currently on probation, told us that the most important rules were related to prohibitions against gang members' use of cocaine and PCP. No King could identify written rules or a constitution, as had their

Gangster Disciple counterparts. A King in prison (#014) said the rules were "Once a King always a King, and don't have no rapists or heroin users."

Not surprisingly, San Diego gangs had very few rules; the rules that existed were more "street norms" than written prohibitions against specific forms of conduct. A Lincoln Park member on probation (#022) said that all the rules were verbal. Another member on probation (#027) denied the existence of written rules.

> INT: Are the rules written down?

> #027: No. It's no bullshit like the whole gang is gonna sit down and listen to some rules. I guess you make up the rules as you go along. It's called a learning process. Everybody knows the rules. Everybody knows you don't go running your goddamn mouth snitching, everybody know you not supposed to be getting your ass whipped and not doing nothing about it.

We made a similar finding for the Logan Heights gang members we interviewed. The rules were informal, not written down, and had the stature of lore. Prohibitions against "snitching" were high on the list. Respondents denied the existence of rules and described them more as "loyalty."

Not surprisingly, the view of rules in these gangs is consistent with the indicators of gang organization discussed above. Only the Gangster Disciples stand apart from the other gangs in that they have a written constitution, acknowledged by all members.

Gang Activities

The general pattern observed for measures of gang organization held for gang activities, though to a lesser degree (see table 3). Though a higher percentage of Chicago gang members reported involvement in criminal activities, the differences between Chicago and San Diego gangs were smaller than in the findings on organization. Although the Chicago

Table 3   Gang Activities

	Chicago		San Diego	
	GD	Kings	Calle	Syndo Mob
Members Sell Drugs	100% (23)	100% (17)	100% (20)	100% (21)
Gang Organizes Drug Sales	74% (23)	80% (15)	63% (19)	72% (18)
Gang Leaders Supply Drugs	62% (21)	67% (15)	29% (14)	37% (19)
Drug Profits Used for Gang Activities	79% (19)	100% (10)	65% (17)	56% (18)
Gangs Sell Guns	67% (24)	77% (13)	74% (19)	71% (17)
Members Own Guns	72% (25)	53% (17)	50% (20)	50% (20)

gangs are more highly organized, their San Diego counterparts hardly lag behind them in criminal activities. One conclusion to be drawn from this set of findings is that levels of organization are not necessarily linked to increased involvement in crime.

We found the greatest difference between gangs in the two cities for the variable measuring whether gang leaders supply drugs for sale: Approximately one-third of each San Diego gang, but nearly two-thirds of Chicago gang members, reported that this was the case. This finding underscores the central and established role of leaders in Chicago gangs. Considerable similarities also exist between gangs in the same city; this fact emphasizes the role of city context for understanding gangs' organization and activities.

Activities are an important measure of gang organization. Here we examine five specific spheres of activity: specialization within the gang, organization of drug sales, use of money made in gang endeavors, ownership of legitimate businesses, and gang involvement in political activities. We do not merely seek to learn whether gang members are involved in these activities; we wish to determine how extensively activities are organized by the gang, involve a large proportion of gang members, and serve gang goals.

Specialization

Specialization in a particular set of activities is a characteristic of organized groups. Specialization requires expertise and technical skills in a defined area, recruitment and development of members with such skills, and establishment of a reputation for that activity. We found little evidence that any of the four gangs we examined had developed such specialization.

The Gangster Disciples we interviewed expressed no consensus about specialized activities of their gang. One (#003) responded that the gang was known as "go-getters" in their housing project (Cabrini Green); others (#010) said they were known for drugs and pistols (#010), "banging" (#004), and "talk" (#013). Responses from Gangster Disciple members on probation were equally diverse and unfocussed: Politics (#012), drug sales (#048), and a form of "neighborhood protection" (#051) were the primary responses. One respondent elaborated:

> Well basically, you know, they ain't really known for nothing special . . . because there is a lot of stores and stuff around there. They probably recognize us for being positive towards the women because we don't mess around like that. Even [when] we see people . . . out there prostituting, we talk to them . . . like, "How come you doing this? How old are you?" One girl actually told me she was 15 years old. I told her, "You know what? If you was my sister, I would beat the shit out of you, just like that." (#051).

The Latin Kings' responses were more focused; a number of members mentioned "drugs" as their specialization. Others mentioned "helping families" (#021), engaging in violence (#031), or sponsoring parties (#050). The Kings, however, expressed little consensus about their areas of specialization.

Responses from the San Diego gangs were equally nonspecific. A number of Lincoln Park Pirus mentioned that their gang specialized in selling drugs, gambling (#075), being "fierce" (#042), and shooting (#035). Two members (#045, #046) told us that the gang didn't specialize in anything. Members of the Logan Heights Red Steps found it equally difficult to identify areas of specialization. Most could not easily comprehend the question, and reported that their gang engaged in diverse activities.

Organization of Drug Sales

Drug sales are a major activity among street gang members, and the four gangs we interviewed were no exception. A majority of the members of each gang told us that the gang played an active role in organizing drug sales, either by providing large amounts of drugs, managing money, or specifying roles in the sales. If gangs are evolving into organized crime groups, they are most likely to do so in areas involving considerable amounts of money, such as street drug sales. By choosing the two most highly organized gangs in Chicago, the city widely acknowledged to contain the most highly organized gangs, we test this hypothesis directly.

The Gangster Disciples are recognized as the most highly organized gang in Chicago (Knox and Fuller 1995). Thus, if any gang should show a high degree of coordination, role differentiation, control, and resource management, it should be this gang. Drug sales by Gangster Disciples sometimes resemble the activity of a well-coordinated corporate giant, though they also display less organized features. A number of subjects told us that members were required to meet certain weekly or monthly quotas of drug sales; and others specified different jobs or roles associated with drug sales. The following comments by imprisoned Gangster Disciples illustrate the level of role differentiation associated with these jobs:

> The guy who picks up the money, the guy who distributes the drugs to the customers, the guy who supplies the guy who distributes. (#003)

> Some of them be making it up, you know, mixing the drugs, some be selling it on the streets, some be distributing it to different members. (#010)

Another imprisoned Gangster Disciple described a virtual franchise operation:

> OK. Say . . . for instance I sold narcotics for eight years for the organization, and I've put away something like $800,000. I would move, take my $800,000, and invest it. . . . Say . . . I move to Alabama and I have $800,000 worth of narcotics. Now I am a member of this organization and I take my concept with me. When I get there, and once I get familiar with the area, if you got a narcotic, you are going to draw attention from those who use it. If you know a lot about the organization you could form GDs in that particular area. (#015)

Although this account hardly resembles a corporate plan for franchising new territories, it shows considerably more organization than comments by those members who indicated that the gang played little or no role in organizing drug sales. An imprisoned Gangster Disciple told us,

> Basically I don't consider [the gang] as being about drug sales. A person sells drugs on they own. The organization don't make them sell drugs. The people sell drugs on they own. (#013)

These views were echoed by several Gangster Disciples on probation.

A large number of Latin Kings participated in drug sales that were both organized by the gang and sales conducted independently. A number of Kings identified different jobs involved in selling drugs; as with the Gangster Disciples, however, these job descriptions were rather general and interchangeable among individuals. Two Kings, both on probation, said that the gang's primary role in organizing drug sales was managing money, as in this description:

> [The gang) collects the money, keeps track of the money. Wants to know exactly where all the money is going, how much profit is coming in, how much profit we will make if we sell different drugs. (#021)

Others, however, were equally eloquent in describing their independence from the gang in selling drugs: "You don't have to tell nobody what you sold. Whatever you sell, you don't have to tell them how much money you made" (#032).

The role of gangs in organizing drug sales in San Diego differed in several ways from that of Chicago gangs. Gangster Disciples and Kings could identify separate roles in drug sales, and some of the Chicago gang members pointed to a role for the gang in overseeing drug profits; San Diego gang members reported no such roles. There were few differences between the two San Diego gangs, and no important differences between the responses we received from probationers and from inmates.

Street gang drug sales in San Diego conform to the balkanized model found in a number of emerging gang cities. The informality of these sales is evidenced in the comments of respondent #024, a Logan Heights member: "They say, do you need money? If you say yeah, they give you the drugs. If you don't need money, you just say no, I don't need no cash."

Most members reported that when it came to selling drugs, they were independent of the gang. Respondent #028 reported, "What I make is mine. I'm the one out there on the street." This comment resonated with many of our subjects: Respondent #061 told us, "Not organized. It's just, you buy some and you sell it and you get your money."

Lincoln Park gang members reported that there was little pressure to get involved in drug sales: Those who wanted to do so, did so, but others chose not to be involved.

Respondent #026 told us that drug sales were organized. He clarified this point by telling us that the basic principle of his gang was "You don't purchase nothing from nobody you don't know." Another gang member offered a similar view of the gang in organizing drug sales:

> INT: Does the gang organize drug sales?

> #034: The gang don't organize nothing. It's like everybody is on they own. You are not trying to do nothing with nobody unless it's with your friend. You don't put your money with gangs.

This sentiment was echoed by respondent #042, an imprisoned member of the Lincoln Park Piru:

> INT: Does the gang organize those [drug] sales?

> #042: Yeah. Let me say this. You said "Do members of the gang sell drugs?" and I said yes. You said "Does the gang organize drug sales?" . . . There is people who sell drugs who are in a gang but they are selling as individuals. A gang never do it as one. Mainly it's just always individuals.

These findings are not particularly surprising, but we must explain the disparity between the fraction of gang members who say that their gang organizes drug sales (between 63 percent and 80 percent) and the responses to specific questions. Clearly gang members are heavily involved in drug sales, and gangs play a role in these sales, largely through contacts that exist within the gang and in cliques or subgroups of friends in the gang. The level of organization, however, is primitive at best, and at worst nonexistent.

Drug Profits for Gang Activities

In understanding any organization involved in financial ventures, one must follow the flow of cash. Thus, understanding how money is managed, its flow through the organization, and how it is spent should clarify the level of gang organization. In general our respondents told us that the money they made from selling drugs remained with them for their own purposes. Most of these purposes involved items for immediate individual consumption, such as clothes, parties, cars, and jewelry.

Only one Gangster Disciple (#003) told us that individuals invested profits from drug sales in gang activities. He said that "holding reunions, buying stores, buying properties, things like that" were the primary uses to which drug profits were put. His response, however, was unique among those of our 85 respondents. Most gang members reported that profits from drug sales went to the individual responsible for selling the drugs. To most respondents this made perfect sense, because they had put themselves at risk to make the money. In a typical comment, respondent #013 said, "I never seen the money that I made go into the organization." Respondent #006 told us that it was "a lie" if anyone said that the gang invested profits from drug sales in anything; the profits were controlled solely by the individual responsible for generating them: "Please not me. If I'm gonna stand up here and sit up here and then use mine [profit] for their benefit, I don't think so. I ain't no sucker." Recall that these responses were received from Gangster Disciples, the most highly organized gang in the most highly organized gang city.

Latin Kings responded uniformly that drug profits went into their pockets. With a single exception (#053), the Kings reported that profits from drug sales went to the individual gang member, not to the gang. They identified parties, trips, bail, or funerals as the most likely uses for such profits.

Reflecting their more disorganized character, members of the San Diego gangs stated that drug profits were used for individual purposes, especially those related to individual consumption. Respondent #029, an imprisoned member of Logan Heights, told us, "A percentage of the drug money [to the gang]? Hell, no. You keep it to yourself." In keeping with the interests of other people their age, our respondents identified items such as fast food and parties as the primary uses for their drug profits. One respondent (#024) said succinctly, "Just round up everyone and let's go eat at Burger King or MacDonald's or something." Others mentioned parties, as in "Buy a keg or something for a homeboy's birthday. Somebody else will have some money and buy another one too" (#028).

Our respondents indicated that the primary (if not the sole) use of drug profits was for individual consumption. Few could identify a common use for the money they made; most denied vehemently that they would share their profits.

Ownership of Legitimate Businesses

One measure of increasing organization would be efforts to find legitimate activities, such as businesses, that the gang could invest in and use to expand its criminal interests. Organized crime groups historically have followed this pattern as a means of finding legitimate roles for members. In addition, legitimate businesses may give gangs the opportunity to exploit their own business-related enterprises for criminal purposes. Indeed, for crime groups, one of the great advantages of owning a legitimate business has been the ability to use that business to pressure other legitimate businesses in ways that lead to illegal profits.

For this measure, more than any other, we observed a distinct difference between the Chicago gangs. Every Gangster Disciple whom we interviewed in prison (and most of those on probation) stated that the gang itself owned legitimate businesses, and that these businesses were not merely providing low-level neighborhood services such as car washes or yard cleanup. Instead they were often quite substantial, involving considerable amounts of capital; the model categories included clothing stores, grocery stores, record shops, cleaning companies, lounges, and apartment buildings. One respondent (#010) reported that the gang had developed a construction business employing several gang members. Another (#063) said that the primary reason for owning legitimate businesses was to "launder your money." Significantly, gang members in prison were generally more aware of these activities than were members on probation. This indicates that access to information about such matters is available to older members and that prison gangs exert some control over events on the street.

The Latin King members' responses regarding the ownership of businesses contrast sharply with those of the Gangster Disciples. Roughly as many Kings told us that the gang owned businesses as told us that they did not. Many of these businesses were associated with automobiles, such as auto detailing shops, body shops, and car washes. Others stated that beeper companies were operated for the benefit of the gang.

The situation in San Diego was quite different: Only five of 41 gang members identified a gang-owned and -operated business. Many of the respondents in San Diego were unsure about the nature of the question, and said that gang members indeed held jobs or had worked in the past. Among Lincoln Park Pirus, gang members mentioned making rap tapes (#022) and working in nightclubs (#037) and at car washes (#078). The few Logan Heights members who identified gang businesses pointed to auto-related operations such as car washes and auto detailing.

This is the first category in which one of the gangs exhibited behavior consistent with higher levels of organization: The majority of Gangster Disciples identified legitimate business owned and operated by their gang. In most cases, these businesses did more than provide small-scale neighborhood services. They generated considerable sums of cash, allowing members of the Gangster Disciples to launder drug money at these locations.

Political Activities

Political involvement is evidence of increased organization on the part of gangs, and facilitates their ability to influence the political process. Because of the number of patronage jobs available to elected officials, especially in cities such as Chicago, efforts to penetrate the political process bring considerable benefits.

Nearly every Gangster Disciple named political activities organized by the gang; these included passing out leaflets backing certain candidates, voter registration drives, soliciting contributions, and raising political awareness. A number of Gangster Disciples mentioned the groups "21st Century Vote" and "Growth and Development" as vehicles for the gang's political activity. These groups have been active in Chicago for the last several years, organizing neighborhood support for candidates sympathetic to their concerns. One such concern, according to respondent #016, was supporting politicians who could help Larry Hoover, the acknowledged leader of the Gangster Disciples (Knox 1995), obtain his release from prison.

By contrast, only one of the Latin Kings told us that he was involved in political activities. The modal response to our question about political involvement was that most members were unable to vote because of felony convictions. The one King who described involvement in political activities said that he had hung posters for a neighborhood candidate.

The San Diego gang members' political involvement is similar to that of the Latin Kings: Not a single Lincoln Park Piru told us that the gang was involved in political activity. One said that voting was the political activity of some members, and only two Logan Heights gang members said that the gang was active in politics. In each case, they became involved as a consequence of Proposition 187, the ballot initiative in California designed to limit immigration.

Relationships with Other Gangs

Relationships between gangs are important in attempting to determine whether gangs have come to resemble organized crime groups. Mutually reinforcing relationships built on instrumental concerns may indicate the evolution of street gangs from relatively disorganized groups to quasi-organized crime groups. Table 4 presents data pertaining to this issue. The San Diego gangs share more relationships with other gangs than do the Chicago gangs on almost every measure, perhaps as a reflection of their social nature. Notably, the percentage of street gang members who report that they have relationships with prison gangs, and the corresponding percentage of prison gang members who report relationships with street gangs, are as high in San Diego as in Chicago, or higher. This finding deserves further exploration; we explore these and other points below, using qualitative data.

One measure of gang organization is a network of relationships between the gang and other groups. Such groups include businesses in the neighborhood, gangs in other cities, prison gangs, and other criminal enterprises that provide roles and opportunities for gangs and gang members. We explored these four areas in an attempt to determine how far gang relationships were expanding beyond the narrow circle of gang members and neighborhoods.

Table 4   Relationships with Other Gangs

	Chicago		San Diego	
	GD	Kings	Calle	Syndo Mob
Meet Together	79% (24)	69% (16)	11% (9)	61% (18)
Sell Drugs Together	43% (23)	53% (15)	44% (9)	53% (17)
Commit Crime Together	61% (23)	50% (14)	44% (9)	53% (17)
Party Together	88% (24)	81% (16)	100% (11)	75% (12)
Street Gangs Maintain Relationships with Prison Gangs	87% (23)	100% (14)	100% (11)	75% (12)
Prison Gang Members Maintain Relationship with Street Gangs	80% (15)	75% (4)	100% (5)	100% (1)

Relationships with Neighborhood Businesses

In addition to a general question about relationships between the gang and neighborhood stores, we asked whether gang members obtained credit from stores, protected stores, received payment to protect stores, extorted money from stores, or sold stolen goods to store owners. A consistent picture emerged: only the Gangster Disciples had made significant inroads into the ownership or control of neighborhood stores. The great majority of members of other gangs (Kings, Lincoln Park Pirus, and Logan Heights Red Steps) seemed to barely understand these questions, as if they had never contemplated such matters.

Gangster Disciples, however, showed considerable evidence that the gang was a presence in the operation of neighborhood stores. This may result from the large number and concentration of Gangster Disciples in many Chicago neighborhoods, as well as from the gang's more extensive ownership of legitimate businesses. Some subjects clearly misunderstood our questions about extortion, and replied that because store owners feared gang members, they and their families enjoyed a certain latitude regarding payments for merchandise. Store owners frequently sought protection against rival gangs from competing neighborhoods. Few Gangster Disciples told us that the store owners bought stolen goods from them. Customers and employees, however, were willing to do so, which may have obviated the need for store owners to engage in such practices (#008). In sum, except for the Gangster Disciple who told us that there weren't any stores left in the neighborhood (#048), this gang appeared actively involved in protection of neighborhood stores.

We found a far different picture for the Latin Kings and the two San Diego gangs. A single King told us that gang members engaged in extortion (#049), but this extortion more closely resembled individual property crime than an effort organized by the gang. Most members of the two San Diego gangs told us that they (and their gang) maintained good relationships with stores in their neighborhood. As a hallmark of these relationships, the respondents regarded themselves as regular customers valued by the store. One member told us that a local grocery extended credit to his family, a privilege that was not offered to him because of his fiscal irresponsibility. One Logan Heights member told us that there was no need to extort money or goods from store owners because "If we were going to do that we would just rob them" (#069). This comment reflects the more primitive level of organization among San Diego gangs.

Relationships with Gangs in Other Cities

Police departments have spoken often about the "spreading tentacles" of gang membership. They imply that gangs are being franchised, primarily out of Los Angeles or Chicago, to virgin gang territory. In this model, gangs from one city find new territory, send veteran members to that territory to start new gangs, and reproduce themselves in the new city. A corollary to this argument is that networks among gangs exist across the country, exchanging cash and goods (primarily drugs and guns) throughout a complex web of cities with interrelated gangs. On the basis of interviews with knowledgeable law enforcement representatives in 1,100 cities, however, Maxson and Klein (1996) found little support for the franchise hypothesis. Instead they concluded that most gang migration occurs as a consequence of normal migratory pressures—family relocation, job opportunities, and the like—rather than because of gangs' concerted efforts to spread criminal activities.

Our results agree with Maxson and Klein's conclusions about gang migration. Nearly every respondent could name other cities that were important to their gang, where relationships with other gangs were maintained. The origins of these relationships, however, lacked the instrumental character associated with the view that gangs actively franchised themselves across the country. Much of the relationship with gangs in different cities had an expressive basis (stemming from family or peer relationships); the ability to buy or sell drugs and guns clearly added an instrumental quality.

Gangster Disciples maintained relationships with gangs in other places; these relationships were based on instrumental benefits. Gangster Disciples named a large and diverse group of such cities, states, and areas: Los Angeles, New York, Orange County (CA), Oklahoma, Hartford, Atlanta, Detroit, Rockford, St. Louis, Arizona, Houston, Miami, Little Rock, Jacksonville, Evanston (IL), Milwaukee, Virginia, The District of Columbia, Minnesota, Indiana, Iowa, Michigan, Mississippi, and the Illinois cities of Springfield, Decatur, East St. Louis, Joliet, Urbana-Champaign, and Elgin. These relationships were built primarily on the exchange of drugs and guns: "It's all about money" (#005); "drug trade, prosperous, cocaine, heroin, marijuana, anything that will sell" (#001); "drugs, money."

One member reported that the gang had been franchised from Chicago to Rockford (IL):

> Set up shop over there with someone from Chicago actually running things over there. They would get the dues, they would get the crime profits, the drug profits, things of this nature. The majority of that would come back to Chicago. (#005)

One Gangster Disciple described why he thought Chicago gangs had an advantage in expanding to other cities:

> People look at guys coming out of Chicago as crazy anyway. They got this Al Capone mentality, that's the way they look at it. (#002)

Latin Kings who commented on this issue told us that there were "Kings all over," but articulated the link between their gang in Chicago and those in other cities in far more tenuous terms. More often than not, family or friends were the basis of such relationships. A smaller number told us that they had relationships with gangs in other cities based on "drugs and money" (#071).

Despite their proximity to Los Angeles, members of both San Diego gangs used general terms to describe their relationships with gangs in other cities. They cited weak connections that provided few instrumental benefits to either party. A number of Lincoln Park Pirus described their relationship with Los Angeles gangs as based on dealing drugs together. This was an exception, however; it was more likely that "hanging out" (#039) or ties to family (#037) formed the basis of such relationships. Logan Heights gang members were divided equally over the basis of such relationships. Respondent #059 told us that "drugs" were at the heart of his gang's relationship with the Mexican Mafia; relatives and family were as important to other members. One respondent expanded on his interest in gangs in Long Beach:

> I have cousins up in Long Beach. I'll go up there with a few friends of mine, kick it there, get fucked up. Take some girls from here up there and meet them. It's a love connection. (#029)

Relationships with Prison Gangs

Because of their involvement in violence and drug sales, many gang members have been sent to prison in the last decade. Because prisons create the need for individual security and protection, they are perfect places for gangs to proliferate. Although the need for protection offers a rationale for the benefits of maintaining gang affiliations, there are other reasons as well. Because large numbers of gang members are imprisoned, inmates can build on existing relationships. Gang members who go to prison have a stake in maintaining ties to fellow gang members on the street because they can depend on them for monetary, influential, or criminal favors. Thus it is no surprise to find that gang members maintain relationships with gangs on the street. The nature of those relationships tells us whether gangs are becoming more highly organized and becoming more like organized crime groups.

To learn more about this subject, we asked gang members about the relationship between the street gang and gang members in prison. We began by determining whether a relationship existed between street and prison gangs, whether prison gangs called the shots on the street, and what kinds of decisions the prison gang made about street gangs' activities.

Prison gangs have operated in Illinois prisons for at least three decades, and Chicago gangs have been at the forefront of such activities. Prison gangs have considerable influence on street gangs in Chicago: Prison gangs often call the shots for the street gang, even specifying targets of violence, locations for drug sales, and other significant aspects of gang activity, criminal and noncriminal. In some ways this finding makes sense because gang leaders are likely to be older, and older gang members face greater odds of being incarcerated because of their extended involvement in criminal activities. In fact, every King and all but two Gangster

Disciples told us that incarcerated gang members played a role in directing the gang's actions on the street.

The primary means of communication were mail, telephone conversations, and visits. Several subjects reported the use of cellular ("cell") phones to which members of gangs had access. One Gangster Disciple told us that his eyes had been "opened" by the prison experience:

> When you come in prison you find out the truth. I found out the people you thought was really your friends, your gang, ain't really nothing to you. It's an economical thing now. They don't believe in brotherhood. They don't believe in it. It's all about the dollar now, the dollars. Let's say you have a guy who was a big drug dealer on the street. If he was already out there on the streets and he come here, he still call the plays. A lot of people do what he tell them to do. (#003)

Those who occupied leadership positions on the street, especially if they were high in the hierarchy, such as regents or governors, exerted considerable influence on street activities from inside the prison. Most Gangster Disciples said that decisions made in prison primarily affected economic matters, especially drug sales, and had a secondary effect on violence, as in identifying targets of gang violence:

> INT: What is the nature of the relationship that you have with the gang on the street?
>
> #005: Monetary, drugs, women, hits, I think that about covers it. This is the Mecca right here. . . . Everybody wants to come to Stateville for that reason.

The view that gang leadership and decisions originate in prison was not confined to the subjects we interviewed in prison. Gangster Disciples on probation also acknowledged imprisoned individuals' active role in decisions about drug sales. Respondent #084 told us, "They are the ones that hand out spots (street locations for drug sales) and I think everything is run from prison, everything." Others stated that going to prison enhanced the members' status, making it more likely that they would assume leadership roles upon release.

Latin Kings expressed similar opinions. Indeed, every King we interviewed, whether in prison or on probation, told us that the prison played a central role in decisions about the street gang's activities. Several told us that the rules governing the gang came from the prison (#019), as did decisions about enforcing the rules and meting out penalties. "They can tell who they want to send them money for clothes and food in there" (#056). Finally, an imprisoned King told us that gangs in prison were so influential as to influence prison management; they played a role in cell assignment for individual gang members.

A different picture emerged from our interviews with the San Diego gangs. Although the great majority told us that they stayed in touch with gang members in prison (just as prison gang members stayed in touch with those on the street), such contacts were more informal and often were based on familial relations. Further, imprisoned San Diego gang members call few "shots" for street activities. Finally, ethnicity appeared to be the primary factor in prison gang association: Imprisoned gang members tended to disregard divisive gang affiliations from the street and to associate primarily on the basis of race.

A number of San Diego gang members told us that family was the primary basis of relationships between prison and street gang members. Respondent #036 said, "We have relationships with people in prison. Most of the people that be in prison be our family, our brothers, our sisters. So yes, we do know people in prison, yeah." Another respondent (#025) told us that they visited prison to see a fellow gang member only if it was a relative—an "uncle, or cousin, or something."

A similar picture emerged when we asked members whether imprisoned gang members "call shots," or order the street gang to perform certain, usually criminal tasks. Here, too, the role of family was important: Respondent #061 informed us that he had ordered such violence from prison in retaliation for someone who had "messed with" his sister. Most respondents from San Diego, however, denied that shots were called from the prison to the street:

> INT: Do the guys in prison still call the shots about drug sales?
>
> #037: They don't call no shots. Too many leaders in every gang, all the gangs like that now, too many leaders.

Respondent #038 told us that giving orders from prison was "movie stuff." Respondent #062, an imprisoned member of Logan Heights, said,

> No. That's the thing that always cracks me up about shot callers. There is no such thing, it's just about respect.

Finally,

> INT: Can a guy in prison, if he is a drug dealer, still call shots and stuff?
>
> #080: That's bullshit. That's the movies, a myth. Not unless you are Al Capone or Scarface or something like that.

Only one San Diego gang member told us that imprisoned members still gave orders to members of the street gang (#077), but he qualified that by saying that the orders were based on respect.

Unlike their Chicago counterparts, Logan Heights and Lincoln Park members pointed to the salience of race for prison gang affiliation. Most stated that race, not prior gang affiliation, was the major unifying factor in prison:

> #041: As far as being locked up, it's a black thing and then it's a white thing and Mexican thing. The main thing is that you are black and you stick with black.

This theme was repeated by a number of respondents, including Hispanic members of the Logan Heights gang.

In sum, street gangs in both cities maintained relationships with imprisoned gang members. For Chicago gangs, these relationships were more instrumental; they provided formal links designed to enable direct input from the prison for the day-to-day operation of the street gang. In San Diego, such communication was more informal, and generally focused on issues of family or friends. Unlike the case in Chicago, few shots were called from prison.

Crime Groups to Join After the Gang

We asked gang members whether their gang had relationships with organized crime groups, and, more important, whether there were criminal gangs with which members eventually could affiliate. This is a key issue in the possible evolution of gangs into more highly organized, more efficient forms of criminal involvement. The results of this line of questioning can be summarized quite succinctly: Not a single respondent could identify a crime group to which he could graduate, nor could any respondent identify an organized crime group with which his gang eventually could affiliate.

CONCLUSION

We have examined a central question in our understanding of contemporary American street gangs: the extent to which such groups are becoming more formal and evolving into organized crime groups. We examined two gangs from an emerging gang city (San Diego), and two gangs from an established gang city (Chicago), choosing one Hispanic and one African-American gang in each city. We used three spheres of gang activity to provide evidence about the nature of gang organization: gang structure, gang activities, and gang relationships.

The results provide a number of important answers to the question that motivated this study. In San Diego, the two gangs identified by law enforcement and social service providers had ceased to be central players on the street within a year of that identification. Little evidence exists to suggest that these gangs ever were on the way to becoming organized crime groups. Their disorganized character is consistent with what Sanders (1994) found in his study of San Diego gangs, and with the results of numerous studies of gangs in emerging gang cities such as St. Louis (Decker and Van Winkle 1996), Milwaukee (Hagedorn 1988), Denver, Cleveland, and Columbus (OH) (Huff 1996), Seattle (Fleisher 1995), and San Francisco (Waldorf 1996).

The story for Chicago is quite different, however. The Gangster Disciples exhibited many characteristics of emerging organized crime groups. In structure, activities, and relationships, this gang has moved well beyond the rather disorganized, informal quality marking groups that have appeared in most American cities in the past decade. Gangster Disciples also apparently have forged effective and solid relationships with gangs in prison and, to a lesser extent, with gangs in other cities. Even so, there seems to be virtually no penetration into traditional organized crime groups. Latin Kings represent a model of the cultural gang: Elements of Hispanic culture have assumed a central role in the gang. Also, although the Kings are more highly organized than their San Diego counterparts, they apparently have not embarked on the course followed by their African-American counterparts.

In addition to the substantive findings presented here, we have demonstrated the importance of comparative studies of gangs. Just as single-city studies have documented the salience of neighborhood characteristics for gang structure, activities, and relationships, important city-level differences and histories affect these features of gang life as well.

Note

[1] It is difficult to imagine the role played by an exercise coordinator. The image of several hundred gang members doing pushups or jumping jacks together doesn't square with what is generally known about gang members.

References

Adler, Patricia. 1985. *Wheeling and Dealing.* New York: Columbia University Press.

Bennett, T. and R. Wright. 1984. *Burglars on Burglary: Prevention and the Offender.* Aldershot, UK: Gower.

Best, Joel and David Luckenbill. 1994. *Organizing Deviance.* Englewood Cliffs, NJ: Prentice Hall.

Bookin-Weiner, Hedy and Ruth Horowitz. 1983. "The End of the Gang: Fad or Fact?" *Criminology* 21:585–602.

Conklin, John. 1972. *Robbery.* Philadelphia: Lippincott.

Conley, Catherine. 1993. *Street Gangs. Current Knowledge and Strategies.* Washington, DC: National Institute of Justice, Issues and Practices.

Cromwell, Paul, Phil Olsen, and D'Aunn Avery. 1991. *Breaking and Entering: An Ethnographic Analysis of Burglary.* Newbury Park, CA: Sage.

Curry, G. David, Richard A. Ball, and Scott H. Decker. 1996. *Estimating the National Scope of Gang Crime from Law Enforcement Data.* Washington, DC: National Institute of Justice.

Curry, G. David, Richard A. Ball, and Robert J. Fox. 1994. *Gang Crime and Law Enforcement Recordkeeping.* Washington, DC: National Institute of Justice.

Decker, Scott and Barrik Van Winkle. 1995. "Slinging Dope: Drug Sales and Gangs." *Justice Quarterly* 11:1001–22.

Decker, Scott and Barrik Van Winkle. 1996. *Life in the Gang: Family, Friends, and Violence.* New York: Cambridge University Press.

Einstadter, Werner. 1969. "The Social Organization of Robbery." *Social Problems* 17:64–83.

Fagan, Jeffrey. 1989. "The Social Organization of Drug Use and Drug Dealing among Urban Gangs." *Criminology* 27:633–69.

Fleisher, Mark. 1995. *Beggars & Thieves.* Madison, WI: U. W. Press.

Fox, Robert W. and Mark E. Amador. 1993. *Gangs on the Move.* Placerville, CA: Copperhouse.

Hagedorn, John. 1988. *People and Folks.* Chicago: Lakeview Press.

Huff, C. Ronald. 1996. *The Criminal Behavior of Gang Members.* Washington, DC: National Institute of Justice.

Irwin, John. 1972. "The Inmate's Perspective." Pp. 117–137 in *Research on Deviance,* edited by Jack D. Douglas. New York: Random House.

Klein, Malcolm. 1971. *Streetgangs and Streetworkers.* Englewood Cliffs, NJ: Prentice Hall.

Klein, Malcolm. 1995. *The American Street Gang.* New York: Oxford University Press.

Klein, Malcolm, Cheryl Maxson, and Lea Cunningham. 1991. "Crack, Street Gangs, and Violence." *Criminology* 29:623–50.

Knox, George and Leslie Fuller. 1995. "The Gangster Disciples." *Journal of Gang Research* 3:58–76.

Maxson, Cheryl and Malcolm Klein. 1986. *Street Gangs Selling Cocaine "Rock."* Los Angeles: University of Southern California, Social Science Research Center.

Maxson, Cheryl and Malcolm Klein. 1990. "Street Gang Violence: Twice as Great or Half as Great?" Pp. 71–100 in *Gangs in America,* edited by C. Ronald Huff. Newbury Park, CA: Sage.

Maxson, Cheryl and Malcolm Klein. 1996. "Street Gang Migration: How Big a Threat?" *National Institute of Justice Journal* 228 (February):26–31.

McCall, George. 1978. *Observing the Law.* New York: Free Press.

Moore, Joan. 1978. *Homeboys: Gangs, Drugs and Prison in the Barrios of Los Angeles.* Philadelphia: Temple University Press.

Orvis, Gregory P. 1996. "Treating Youth Gangs like Organized Crime Groups: An Innovative Strategy for Prosecuting Youth Gangs." Pp. 93–103 in *Gangs: A Criminal Justice Approach,* edited by J. Mitchell Miller and Jeffrey Rush. Cincinnati: Anderson.

Padilla, Feliz. 1992. *The Gang as an American Enterprise.* New Brunswick, NJ: Rutgers University Press.

Pennell, Susan. 1994. *Gangs in San Diego.* San Diego: San Diego Association of Governments.

Sanchez-Jankowski, Martin. 1991. *Islands in the Street.* Berkeley: University of California Press.

Sanders, William. 1994. *Drive-Bys and Gang Bangs.* New York: Aldine.

Skolnick, Jerome, T. Correl, E. Navarro, and R. Rabb. 1988. *The Social Structure of Street Drug Dealing.* Sacramento: Office of the Attorney General of the State of California.

Spergel, Irving and G. David Curry. 1990. *Survey of Youth Gang Problems and Programs in 45 Cities and 6 Sites.* Chicago: University of Chicago, School of Social Service Administration.

Taylor, Carl. 1990. *Dangerous Society.* Lansing: Michigan State University Press.

Tunnel, Ken. 1992. *Choosing Crime: The Criminal Calculus of Property Offenders.* Chicago: Nelson-Hall.

Vigil, Diego. 1988. *Barrio Gangs: Streetlife and Identity in Southern California.* Austin: University of Texas Press.

Waldorf, Dan, Craig Reinerman and Shegha Murphy. 1996. *Cocaine Charges.* Philadelphia: Temple.

Wright, Richard and Scott H. Decker. 1994. *Burglars on the Job.* Boston: Northeastern University Press.

Wright, Richard and Scott H. Decker. 1997. *Armed Robbers in Action.* Boston: Northeastern University Press.

14

Gang Homicide
A Review and Extension
of the Literature

Cheryl L. Maxson

A large number of studies have documented the higher offending pro-
files of gang members compared with similar-aged youths (Esbensen &
Huizinga, 1993; Fagan, 1989; Klein, Maxson, & Cunningham, 1991;
Thornberry, Krohn, Lizotte, & Chard-Wierschem, 1993; Tracy, 1979).
Recent analysis of longitudinal data from interviews with a representative
sample of youths in Rochester, New York, found that gang members, who
constituted 30% of the sample, committed 69% of violent offenses
reported by all youths studied during a 4-year period (Thornberry & Burch,
1997). Similar findings are reported in Denver (14% gang members, 79%
of serious violent offenses [Huizinga, 1997]) and Seattle (15% gang members, 85% of robberies [Battin, Hill, Abbott, Catalano, & Hawkins, 1998]).

Analyses from these types of studies generally support a *facilitation*
model; gang members have higher offending patterns during their periods
of active gang membership than either before they join or after they leave
(Esbensen & Huizinga, 1993; Hill et al., 1996; Thornberry et al., 1993).
Not known, as yet, however, is how gang membership facilitates violent
offending. For example, it is not clear whether membership places youths
in riskier situations, alters individual assessments of appropriate or alternative behaviors, or exposes the youths to group processes (e.g., initiation
rituals, internal status struggles, or territorial threats from rival gangs)

M. D. Smith and M. Zahn (eds.), *Homicide: A Sourcebook of Social Research*, pp. 239–253,
copyright © 1999 by Sage Publications, Inc. Reprinted by permission of Sage Publications, Inc.

that encourage violent behavior (Dodge, 1997). The increased access to and ownership of firearms by gang members are other considerations in determining this relationship (Lizotte, Tesoriero, Thornberry, & Krohn, 1994; Sheley & Wright, 1995).

Youth participation in homicide has increased during the past several years (Fox, 1996). Whether increased levels of youth involvement are the result of higher levels of participation in street gangs is a matter of some debate. The proliferation of gangs across the country, however, means that joining gangs is an option faced by more of our nation's youths than ever before (Klein, 1995; Maxson, 1996; Miller, 1996; National Youth Gang Center [NYGC], 1997).

Although it is recognized that violent activity represents a small portion of crime committed by gang members (Decker & Van Winkle, 1996; Esbensen, Huizinga, & Weiher, 1993; Klein, 1995; Short, 1996) and that gang violence is often overrepresented by sensationalist portrayals in the media (Hagedorn, in press), few dispute the contention that violence committed in the gang context is an appropriate concern. As will be discussed below, data from the gang-entrenched cities of Chicago and Los Angeles document that increasing proportions of homicides reflect aspects of gang membership and, consequently, dramatically increased risks of homicide victimization among those demographic groups disproportionately involved in gang activities.

Several comprehensive reviews on the gang homicide literature are available elsewhere (see Howell, 1995, for the most recent). Therefore, the objective of this chapter is to offer a variety of information about gang homicide by discussing the research literature and, where possible, extending it by presenting previously unpublished data.[1] Major aspects to be discussed here are (a) the national prevalence of gang homicide, (b) changes in the prevalence and in the proportion of all homicides that are gang related in the cities for which these data are available, and (c) comparisons of characteristics of gang homicides with other homicides, using data from several areas within Los Angeles County and deciphering whether these patterns have changed during the last 15 years. Before turning to the data on gang homicide, I first will discuss some methodological issues that affect efforts to better understand the scope and nature of gang homicide.

Methodological Issues in the Study of Gang Homicide

Interviews with representative samples of youth are not useful in investigating the characteristics of homicide because, fortunately, homicide is a rare outcome among all potentially lethal encounters (Block & Block, 1993). Therefore, interviews with incarcerated or chronic offenders, as well as ethnographic studies of individual street gangs, have generated little generalizable knowledge about gang homicides (but see Moore, 1991).

Much homicide research is conducted with national databases such as the Supplementary Homicide Reports (SHR) provided by the Uniform Crime Reporting Program and the mortality data in *Vital Statistics* reported by the National Center for Health Statistics. These are rich sources for answers to other questions, but gang information either is unavailable (as in the death certificate file) or is of questionable use (as in SHR data).[2] Instead, gang homicide scholars must turn to databases maintained by local law enforcement agencies or extract information themselves from homicide case investigation files. Usually, this means that data are available for just one city or police jurisdiction. Studies of homicide that consider multiple cities are the exception, rather than the rule.

Although law enforcement typically devotes more resources to the investigation of homicide than any other crime, the information available in records is limited to that which is known and documented by law enforcement investigators. Information on some coded items may be missing, conflicting, or otherwise so confusing as to challenge the skills of even the most skilled data collectors.[3] Cases involving gang members are among the most difficult to research because the dynamics in these incidents are frequently chaotic and, because of intimidation factors, information from witnesses is often only minimally available. These features, coupled with low levels of gang participation in homicide in most U.S. cities, have discouraged most researchers from investigating the gang aspects of homicide. Chicago and Los Angeles are the most notable exceptions. This lack of attention to gang homicide seems to be changing, however, with studies currently under way in Pittsburgh, Boston, and the three cities included in the work of Zahn and Jamieson (1997).

The most critical methodological issue facing researchers concerns the specific definition of what one calls a *gang-related homicide*. As Huff (1996) notes, "In the history of research and public policy discussions regarding gangs, no single issue has been as controversial as that of defining 'gangs' and what constitutes 'gang-related' crime" (pp. xxi–xxii). It is standard practice for gang researchers to caution their audiences about definitional issues; typically, these are directed to what is meant by *gang, gang membership,* and *gang crime*. Recent extended discussions of gang definitions appear in Klein (1995), Spergel (1995), and Ball and Curry (1995).

Ultimately, the controversy on gang-related crime definitions can be summarized thus: Is gang member *participation* sufficient to designate a crime as gang-related, or is it necessary that the *motive* of the crime be linked to gang function? Law enforcement agencies in Los Angeles and the rest of California have tended to embrace the former approach; the Chicago Police Department is the most cited advocate of the latter. This is not just an academic concern; law enforcement agencies across the country have debated the relative merits of one approach or the other (Spergel, 1988). Generally, gang member-based designation practices place more reliance on adequate listings of active gang members. Motive-based policies require more thorough investigation of the dynamics of the particular incident, a practice that can be problematic for crimes other than homicide. Studies of the implications of the two approaches (Maxson & Klein, 1990, 1996) have found that the choice of approach has substantial effects on prevalence estimates but few differences in the general depictions of incident and participant characteristics. Following the practice adopted in earlier work on this topic in which I was involved, however, the terms *gang member* and *gang motive* will be used for the remainder of this chapter to alert the reader to the two definitional styles.

The reliability of designations made by law enforcement agencies is a matter of concern in the study of gang homicides. When describing the scope and nature of gang homicide, the critical issue is the *type of definition* used in any particular study. Fortunately, considerable consistency has been found in Los Angeles data (Klein, Gordon, & Maxson, 1986). Suggestions of gang motives are quite rare in nongang cases in Los Angeles (Maxson & Klein, 1996) and in Chicago (C. R. Block, personal communication, January 13, 1997). Offenders or victims with gang affiliations explicitly noted in the case file appeared in about 6% and 3%, respectively, of nongang homicides in Los Angeles. Whether the designator of gang incidents is a law enforcement official or researchers, the validity of the designation depends on the case material available.

National Prevalence of Gang Homicide

As yet, there is no national register of gang homicides, although President Clinton's reactivation of the federal effort to establish a national gang tracking network may provide the foundation for such a database (Jackson, Lopez, & Connell, 1997). Walter Miller (1982/1992) provided the first set of tabulations of gang homicides in selected cities across the country. Noting the limitations of definitional variations, dubious recording practices, and considerable missing data, he presented counts of gang homicides for nine gang cities (plus others in aggregate form) for 1967 through 1979.[4] Despite these limitations, Miller's work should be credited as the first effort to document variations in gang homicides between major U.S. cities, to compare rates per population, and to note the vulnerability of law enforcement definitional and reporting procedures to social and political pressures.

National surveys of U.S. cities and towns with street gangs customarily request information about homicide incidence (Curry, Ball, & Decker, 1996; Maxson, 1996; NYGC, 1997). Although such surveys have made great strides in documenting the scope of gang problems in this country, the data gathered on gang homicides remain largely unanalyzed and/or unreported in the literature. In part, this may be due to researchers' reluctance to report such data because of the definitional ambiguities discussed earlier. For instance, the Curry et al. (1996) surveys requested annual counts of gang homicides based on whatever definitional approach was adopted by the reporting agency; in contrast, the NYGC survey asked for the number of homicides involving gang members as perpetrators and, separately, as victims.

The study to be discussed at length here is a survey by Malcolm Klein and me that asked for the number of homicides occurring in 1991 that *involved gang members* (see Maxson, Woods, & Klein, 1995). Findings from this survey are presented in the spirit of offering preliminary baseline information and illustrating various approaches to reporting national prevalence data. No claim is made regarding the validity of this particular approach to measurement or to its superiority of the coverage of U.S. cities and towns with street gangs. On the contrary, the NYGC (1997) survey is more recent and identified 1,492 cities and 515 counties with street gangs. Also, in discussing these results, I readily acknowledge the limitations of law enforcement tabulations of gang members that were used in the survey, limitations that are discussed in detail by Curry and his colleagues in several publications (Curry, Ball, & Decker, 1995; Curry et al., 1996; Curry, Ball, & Fox, 1994).

The Maxson-Klein survey, conducted in 1992, identified 792 cities that reported local street gangs.[5] Four hundred and fifty-three gang cities (60% of 752 responding to this item) stated that they had no gang homicides during 1991.[6] Of the 299 cities with gang homicides, 247—more than 80% of cities with gang homicides—had less than 10 incidents in the targeted year. Another 40 cities had between 10 and 25 homicides, while just 12 reported between 30 and 371 incidents. The homicides reported by these 12 cities represent 40% of the total (2,166 incidents) tallied for the entire sample. Selected characteristics of these cities with relatively high levels of gang homicide are listed in table 1.

The emergence of Los Angeles and Chicago[7] as standouts in the gang homicide arena will be surprising to no one. The city of Commerce, California, might be, because it is highly industrial with a small residential population. Large numbers of gang members living in surrounding communities, however, claim territory in Commerce and thus are identified as Commerce gang members. Most of the cities on this list have the large populations reflective of our nation's urban centers. Three quarters of these cities have chronic, rather than emerging, gang problems (Spergel & Curry, 1990); just four reported the onset of gangs in their communities during or after the 1980s.

A summary description of the U.S. cities with the highest volume of gang homicides is that they tend to be large urban centers with long-standing gang problems. This is hardly a novel statement, yet in the midst of current widespread concern about the proliferation of street gangs to small, less populated areas (Klein, 1995; Maxson, 1996; Quinn, Tobolowsky, & Downs, 1994), it is important to remember that the majority of

Table 1   Cities with Highest Levels of Gang Homicide: Selected Characteristics

City	Gang Homicides (1991)	City Population (1990)	Gang Members	Gang Emergence
Los Angeles, CA	371	3,485,398	55,927	1922
Chicago, IL	129	2,783,726	28,500	1920
Long Beach, CA	53	429,433	11,200	1970
Inglewood, CA	44	109,602	6,500	1961
Commerce, CA	40	12,135	9,000	1925
Cleveland, OH	37	505,616	1,900	1987
San Bernardino, CA	37	164,164	1,550	1988
Kansas City, MO	35	435,146	420	1988
Compton, CA	30	90,454	3,000	1970
Fresno, CA	30	354,202	1,750	1988
Milwaukee, WI	30	628,088	5,000	1976
Oakland, CA	30	372,242	2,500	1966

Source: Adapted from Maxson et al. (1995).

the most violent gang episodes occur in large cities with a long history of gang problems, most notably, Los Angeles and Chicago.

A closer inspection of table 1 reveals apparent anomalies in addition to the Commerce situation already mentioned. The Southern California cities of Compton, Inglewood, and San Bernardino have far lower residential populations than the other cities. Also, Kansas City (Missouri) appears to have relatively few gang members to generate 35 gang homicides. Thus, to compensate for the erroneous impressions that can be conveyed by the use of raw numbers, we computed *rates* of gang homicides per 100,000 population and per 1,000 gang members.[8] These two measures provide a different perspective from the sheer numbers of gang homicides.

The cities with the 10 highest gang homicide rates, as calculated by general population figures, are listed in table 2. The high-incidence cities of Commerce, Compton, and Inglewood represent the only overlap with the cities listed in table 1. With the exception of Compton and Inglewood, all the high-rate cities have relatively low city populations, ranging from around 50,000 to just under 10,000. Seven of these cities are in the county of Los Angeles. All are chronic, rather than emergent, gang cities. The historical nature of gang problems in these cities, like those with high levels of incidents, suggests that their law enforcement agencies may be more attuned to *tabulating gang indicators* through such tactics as assigning officers to special gang units, building gang intelligence, listing gang mem-

Table 2   Cities With Highest Rates of Gang Homicide per 100,000 Population: Selected Characteristics

City	Gang Homicides per 100,000 Population	Gang Homicides (1991)	City Population (1990)	Gang Members	Gang Emergence
Commerce, CA	329.62	40	12,135	9,000	1925
Hawaiian Gardens, CA	109.98	15	13,639	800	1950
East Palo Alto, CA	81.02	19	23,451	375	1984
Artesia, CA	64.67	10	15,464	300	1955
Harvey, IL	63.82	19	29,771	70	1985
East St. Louis, IL	56.17	23	40,944	50	1968
Inglewood, CA	40.14	44	109,602	6,500	1961
Paramount, CA	39.86	19	47,669	1,200	1950
Compton, CA	33.17	30	90,454	3,000	1970
Huntington Park, CA	32.11	18	56,065	1,500	1958

Source: Adapted from Maxson et al. (1995).

bers, and systematically reviewing all homicides for signs of gang involvement. Given this approach, there is a strong likelihood that gang-related homicides will be detected and identified as such. The infrastructure for systematic reporting, particularly among smaller cities with fewer resources, more likely is provided by locations with longstanding concerns about gang violence. For instance, law enforcement agencies within the Los Angeles region have a well-developed infrastructure, and this may explain why so many of these cities appear in table 2. In contrast, newer gang cities might still have been in the assessment phase or in the process of building intelligence capacities at the time of the survey.

With this caveat in mind, the final set of data on homicide rates per 1,000 gang members should be viewed with considerable skepticism. The list of 10 cities with the highest homicide rates per gang population is provided in table 3. All these cities have low counts of gang members (ranging from 50 to 420 individuals), which are particularly questionable among the six cities with populations greater than 100,000. It is interesting to note that no Southern California city appears on this list. Although two cities (Baton Rouge and Kansas City) report the more recent emergence of gangs, and as a group these cities have more recent onset dates than the prior two groups, a number of cities listed in table 3 had gang activity at least 5 years prior to the survey completion. Although some of these cities may have narrow definitions of street gangs and members, this would be inconsistent with the relatively high numbers of gang homicides

Table 3   Cities with Highest Rates of Gang Homicide per 1,000 Gang Members: Selected Characteristics

City	Gang Homicides per 1,000 Gang Members	Gang Homicides (1991)	City Population (1990)	Gang Members	Gang Emergence
East St. Louis, IL	460.00	23	40,944	50	1968
Harvey, IL	271.43	19	29,771	70	1985
Baton Rouge, LA	133.33	20	219,531	150	1989
Saginaw, MI	125.00	20	69,512	160	1986
Durham, NC	110.00	11	136,611	100	1982
Kansas City, MO	83.33	35	435,146	420	1988
New Orleans, LA	76.67	23	496,938	300	1986
Rochester, NY	75.00	15	231,636	200	1985
East Palo Alto, CA	50.67	19	23,451	375	1984
Flint, MI	50.00	15	140,761	300	1978

Source: Adapted from Maxson et al. (1995).

they reported. It was not possible to pursue such anomalies with all survey respondents,[9] and until more information becomes available, the generalizability of these data is highly suspect.

Despite the limitations noted, these data provide a glimpse of the prevalence of gang homicide across the country in 1992. Most gang cities do not report any homicides involving gang members; two fifths of all gang homicides occur in just a dozen cities, mostly urban centers, with gang problems spanning several decades. Cities with the highest homicide rates per city population also have chronic gang problems, but these tend to be smaller cities and towns and are disproportionately located in the Los Angeles region.

Gang violence is a substantial challenge to law enforcement in cities where well-entrenched gang traditions couple with high volumes of lethal gang activity in communities with limited resources. The attempt to identify gang cities with particularly lethal gang populations generated such mixed findings that it is best viewed as a cautionary note for users of law enforcement estimates of gang membership. On the other hand, these data will provide an opportunity for comparison with the NYGC survey when that source's 1996 gang homicide data become available.[10]

Changes in the Prevalence and Proportions of Gang Homicides in Selected U.S. Cities

Coincidental with the proliferation of street gangs and attendant concerns about gang violence, homicide researchers have begun to pay closer attention to gang issues when gathering data from homicide cases. Earlier interest in this topic, however, can be found in the work of C. Rebecca Block and colleagues regarding Chicago and my studies with Malcolm Klein in Los Angeles that extend well through the last decade. The volume of lethal gang activity, its intransigence during an extended period, and the level of law enforcement resources and expertise devoted to gang issues in these two cities have provided the foundation of information that makes such recent research possible. The following section draws from these and other studies to describe the nature of gang homicides, how they contrast with nongang events, and what is known about the proportion of homicides attributable to gang matters. The definitional approach to determining which crimes are designated as "gang" is critical, so I discuss only those studies that provide this information.

Chicago

The Chicago homicide data set maintained by the Illinois Criminal Justice Information Authority (ICJIA) contains information coded from all homicides committed in Chicago between 1965 and 1995. Researchers at the ICJIA code the designation generated by investigators from the Chicago Police Department, applying that department's definition of street gang-related homicide based on the *motive of the offender*. Thus, in Chicago, there must be strong indication that the incident grew from a street gang function (see Block, Christakos, Jacob, & Przybylski, 1996, for a detailed description of possible street gang motives). Thus, *by definition*, Chicago and other jurisdictions employing motive-based categories will report lower volumes of gang-related homicides (and consequently, lower proportions of all homicides as gang related) than departments such as Los Angeles that adopt the broader member-involvement criterion. About 50% to 60% (depending on period and law enforcement agency) of Los Angeles gang homicides meet the more restrictive gang-motivated definition used in Chicago (Maxson & Klein, 1990, 1996).

The trend data on Chicago gang homicides shown in figure 1 reveal several peaks and troughs that Block and her colleagues have noted as characteristic of the spurts or bursts of rival gang activity (Block & Block, 1993; Block & Christakos, 1995).[11] During this period, the total number of homicides in Chicago—gang and nongang combined—showed generally higher numbers in the 1970s than in the 1980s, with marked increases to unprecedented levels in the 1990s, except for the peak year of 962 killings in 1974 (Block & Christakos, 1995). The proportion of all homicides found to be gang motivated averaged 5% during the 1970s, averaged just under 9% during the 1980s, and then nearly doubled to 17% during the first half of the 1990s. Even with year-to-year fluctuations, the trend shown in figure 1 suggests that street gangs have claimed an increasing share of all Chicago homicides since the mid-1970s; in 1994 and 1995, more than one fourth of Chicago homicides were attributed to gang motives.

Figure 1   Gang-Motivated Homicides in Chicago, 1965 to 1995

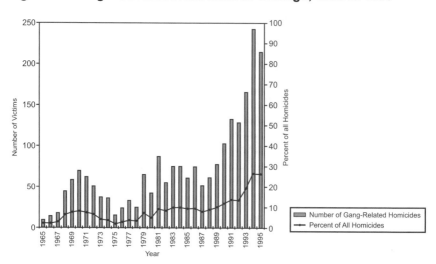

Source: Figures provided by C. Rebecca Block, Illinois Criminal Justice Information Authority.

Los Angeles

Trend data are also available on gang homicides for the Los Angeles area, although several differences from the Chicago data are noted. The Los Angeles data are provided by the Los Angles Sheriff's Department (LASD), which provides *countywide* gang statistics based on the broader, member-involved definitional approach.[12] The *city* of Los Angeles contributed roughly one half of the countywide gang homicide figures.

The Los Angeles County data for 1978 to 1995 are presented in figure 2. The larger area covered and broader definitions of gang homicides yield substantially more gang events than in Chicago. In Los Angeles County, gang homicides decreased during the early 1980s but began to increase steadily from 1985 to 1992, when they leveled off to around 800 incidents per year (with a dip in 1993 and 1994). Preliminary data for 1996 (not shown in figure 2) indicate a dramatic drop in gang homicides; both the Los Angeles Police Department (LAPD) and LASD report a decrease of 20% in the number of gang incidents for that year. In Chicago, gang homicides were rising in the early 1980s, and that city's data do not show the plateau pattern in the first half of the 1990s that is evident in Los Angeles County.

In Los Angeles County, all homicides decreased from 1980 to 1984, whereas the proportion of gang homicides declined also from 19% (1980) to less than 15% (1984). The period from 1985 to 1992 saw a steady increase in total homicides, but the proportion of these homicides with gang aspects increased from 2% to 5% *each* year through 1991. The 1991 proportion of 37% dipped slightly in 1992 and 1993 before jumping to

Figure 2   Gang-Related Homicides in Los Angeles County, 1980 to 1995

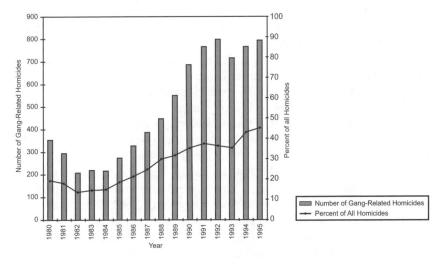

Source: Figures provided by Los Angeles County Sheriff's Department.

43% and 45% in 1994 and 1995, respectively. That nearly half of the homicides in Los Angeles County evidence some type of gang involvement is a statistic not lost on the area's law enforcement, politicians, and social service agencies. This figure is somewhat deceptive, however, because it results largely from declines in the overall number of killings from 1993 to 1995, declines that are *not* mirrored in reduced levels of lethal gang activity. In short, the proportion of gang homicides has increased because the incidence of gang homicides has remained relatively stable at a time that the incidence of nongang homicides has been declining.

The foregoing analysis cannot answer the question of which urban area faces the more severe problem; quite simply, definitional variations preclude such a comparison. Other comparisons can be made, however. For instance, it appears that Chicago figures fluctuate more from year to year. I have discussed elsewhere reported differences in the *structure* of street gangs in the two locations as well as the dangers of comparing the two (Maxson & Klein, 1997). The more organized depictions of Chicago gangs argue for more stability in that city's homicide numbers, but that seems not to be the case. As evidence, African American and Latino gang homicides have been shown to display different patterns, but the overall pattern of fluctuation is evident in gang victimization data for both groups (Block & Christakos, 1995).

Other Cities

As mentioned earlier, researchers in cities other than Chicago and Los Angeles are beginning to investigate levels of gang involvement in homicide. As part of the Boston Gun Project, a team of police, probation officers, and street workers examined lists of homicide victims and offenders, as well as incident locations for 1990 to 1994 to designate incidents as "gang-related" according to a shared consensus of what this meant. According to the researchers' description of this process, the assigned meaning of gang homicides more closely approximated the Chicago than the Los Angeles definition (Kennedy, Braga, & Piehl, 1997).[13] With this definition, nearly 60% of the 155 homicides with victims aged 21 years and younger were attributed to Boston gangs.

Tita, Cohen, and Blumstein (1996) have reported preliminary findings on gang aspects in homicides in Pittsburgh. Data were collected from the Pittsburgh Police Department homicide files for 362 incidents that occurred between 1987 and 1994. Incidents were coded as "gang-motivated" and "gang-involved" (i.e., at least one participant was known to be a gang member, but homicide was not gang motivated). The researchers identified 27 (7%) incidents as gang-involved and 65 (18%) as gang motivated. Eighteen of the 74 homicides coded as drug-motivated included gang members; these are included in the gang-involved (11 cases) and gang-motivated (7 cases) counts above. The researchers found that gang homicides were more likely to involve multiple offenders and large-caliber automatic weapons than were drug homicides. Altogether, 92 (25%) of Pittsburgh homicides would be designated as "gang" according to the "gang member" definition. These figures are surprising for a city whose police department reported no local gang activity on my 1992 survey with Malcolm Klein.

THE NATURE OF GANG HOMICIDE IN LOS ANGELES

In Los Angeles, data have been gathered from police investigation files for samples of gang and nongang homicides for three periods: 1978 to 1982, 1984 to 1985, and 1988 to 1989. Elsewhere, characteristics of these two types of incidents for the first two periods have been discussed, especially the remarkable consistency in the features that distinguish gang from nongang homicides (Klein et al., 1991; Maxson, Gordon, & Klein, 1985). In this section, I offer updated information from the 1988–1989 incidents to address whether the incident and participant descriptors of gang and nongang cases have changed since the earlier period. The 1988–1989 data come from the five station areas in South Central Los Angeles that were studied in 1984 to 1985.[14] Three of the five stations were within the jurisdiction of the LAPD, and two were county areas handled by the LASD; about three fourths of these cases, however, were from LAPD.

Gang and nongang homicides occurring in the five station areas during 1988 and 1989 were sampled using a random stratified approach to yield equal numbers of each type of homicide. Lists of "gang-involved" cases were supplied by each jurisdiction's specialized gang unit. The sampling procedures resulted in 201 gang and 201 nongang homicides, reflecting about two thirds of the population of gang-related homicides and slightly less of the nongang population.[15]

A team of data collectors extracted information from extensive homicide investigation files. Coded items included descriptors of the incident (e.g., setting, automobile involvement, weapons, related case charges, additional injuries, and gang motives); participants (e.g., numbers on each side, relationship, demographics of designated victims and suspects, and stated gang affiliations); and an extensive list of drug indicators (use/sales paraphernalia, drugs found in investigation, autopsy results, drug use or sales by participants, aspects of the location, and drug motives).[16]

Differences in Gang and Nongang Homicides

In previous studies (Klein et al., 1991; Maxson et al., 1985), it was found that gang cases were more likely to take place on the street, to involve firearms, and to have more participants (see also Spergel, 1983). Gang homicide suspects were of younger ages and more likely to be male, although ethnicity did not produce significant gang-nongang differences. The same demographic distinctions hold for homicide victims.

A descriptive comparison of gang and nongang homicides for 1988–1989 is shown in table 4. As expected, each of the variables tested shows significant gang-nongang differences, with the exception of the ethnicity variables.[17] The patterns of differences are similar to those found in the 1984–1985 homicides; the same variables distinguish gang and nongang cases, and there are no directional changes. Data that are not shown in table 4, however, reveal a pattern of *slightly diminishing differences between gang and nongang cases through time*. The percentage of gang cases occurring on the street decreased slightly (67% in 1984–1985; 57% in 1988–1989). Firearms presence remained about the same in gang cases, although it increased slightly in nongang cases (64% in 1984–1985; 75% in 1988–1989). The average number of suspected participants decreased by about one person in gang cases (3.71 in 1984–1985; 2.75 in 1988–1989) and increased slightly in nongang cases (1.50 in 1984–1985; 1.71 in 1988–1989). Victim gender and average age figures remained constant in both types of cases, as did the victim ethnicity in gang cases. In contrast, there was a slight decrease in the percentage of nongang Black victims (85% in 1984–1985; 75% in 1988–1989). Nongang suspects were about 2 years older (29 in 1984–1985; 31.3 in 1988–1989), whereas gang ages remain constant at 20 years. Suspect gender is the same in the two types of cases for the two periods. The only notable ethnic difference is an increase in Hispanic nongang suspects (11% in 1984–1985; 17% in 1988–1989).

Overall, the changes noted are minor and insubstantial relative to the generally consistent patterns of gang-nongang differences through the two periods. Further, this similarity extends to findings derived from the much earlier data collection of homicides occurring from 1978 to 1982 that were drawn from more than 20 station areas within LASD and LAPD (Maxson et al., 1985).

Table 4   Incident and Participant Characteristics in Gang and Nongang Homicides, 1988 to 1989

	Gang (N = 201)	Nongang (N = 201)	Association and Significance[a]
Incident Characteristics:			
Setting			
Street	57% (114)	34% (68)	
Residence	30% (60)	50% (101)	.237***
Other	13% (27)	16% (32)	
Firearms present	95% (191)	75% (150)	.284***
Participants on			
suspect side	2.75	1.71	.302***
(Missing)	(6)	(28)	
Homicide Victims:[b]			
All victims male	90% (180)	77% (155)	.167**
Mean age of victims	24.2	34.4	−.391***
(Missing)	(4)	(4)	
Proportion Black victims	.80	.75	ns
Proportion Hispanic			
victims	.18	.23	ns
Homicide Suspects:			
All suspects male	93% (139)	83% (124)	.163**
(Missing)	(52)	(51)	
Mean age of suspects	20.5	31.3	−.523***
(Missing)	(52)	(52)	
Proportion Black			
suspects	.86	.81	ns
(Missing)	(52)	(51)	
Proportion Hispanic			
suspects	.14	.17	ns
(Missing)	(52)	(51)	

Source: Adapted from Maxson, Klein, and Cunningham (1992).
[a] Levels of association reported are Phi or Pearson's *r*. Significance levels determined by chi-squares or *t* tests. *p < .05; **p < .01; ***p < .001.
[b] Participant characteristics are computed across all homicide victims, or suspects, within a case. Additional victims, or suspects charged with associated case offenses rather than for homicide, are deleted from these calculations. Note that 26% of the homicide cases have no identified homicide suspect.

Drug Involvement in Gang and Nongang Homicides

The level and type of drug involvement in gang as compared with nongang homicides have been matters of concern for the last decade (for a review of this literature, see Howell, 1995; Klein & Maxson, 1994). To provide special attention to this facet of homicide incidents, gang-nongang comparisons for 1988 to 1989 are shown in table 5. In the following discussion, these results will be compared with findings from the 1984–1985 homicide data.

The first question raised is the proportion of cases with drug involvement. The notion of drug involvement was approached quite broadly, and cases mentioning any aspect of drugs were labeled as drug involved. Later analyses will examine the specific nature of the drug involvement.

Of the 402 homicide cases, 64% have some aspect of drugs mentioned, but there are no gang-nongang differences ($p = .350$). The gang figure (124; 62% of cases) is similar to that found in gang cases in 1984 to 1985. On the other hand, the nongang figure (133; 60% of cases) has increased somewhat from the earlier figure of 56%. It appears that the pattern of increasing proportions of drug-involved nongang cases observed earlier in 1984 and 1985 has stabilized to the levels recorded in gang cases (Klein et al., 1991).

Table 5   Drug Characteristics in Gang and Nongang Homicides, 1988 to 1989

All Homicides	Gang (N = 201)	Nongang (N = 201)	Association and Significance[a]
Drug mention	62% (124)	66% (133)	*ns*
Crack mention	19% (39)	30% (60)	−.121
Cocaine mention	34% (68)	48% (97)	−.147**
Sales mention	40% (81)	33% (66)	*ns*
Drug motive mention	17% (34)	27% (55)	−.126*

Drug Homicides	Gang (N = 124)	Nongang (N = 133)	Association and Significance[a]
Crack mention	31% (39)	45% (60)	−.140*
Cocaine mention	55% (68)	73% (97)	−.189**
Sales mention	65% (81)	50% (66)	.159**
Drug motive mention	27% (34)	41% (55)	−.146*

Source: Adapted from Maxson, Klein, and Cunningham (1992).
[a] Levels of association reported are Phi. Significance levels determined by chi-squares.
  *$p < .05$; **$p < .01$; ***$p < .001$.

Given the similar levels of any drug mention in gang and nongang cases, it is appropriate to look more closely at the nature of drug involvement in these cases. Drug information was collected on specific items, most of which did not produce sufficiently high frequencies to support analyses of gang-nongang differences. Alternatively, variables were computed that represent more general aspects of drug involvement and reflect the gang-drug issues in South Central Los Angeles. Most drug mentions were coded to indicate the type of drug involved. From these, a variable was computed for any mention of crack/rock in the case and, because the form of cocaine is often not specified, also any mention of cocaine. The presence of any type of sales or distributional aspect of the case could derive from the nature of the incident location, sales involvement by participants on either side, or motives related to drug distribution. Finally, mention of any drug-related motive for the homicide includes conflicts about drug use, although these are far less frequent than motives stemming from drug distribution.

These aspects of drug involvement are reported in table 5, first for all cases in the sample, then separately for only those homicides with drug involvement. The lower half of the table presents the different percentages and significance tests derived from computations on the smaller set of drug-involved homicides. The patterns in the two halves of table 5 are, of course, similar; the only difference appears in the statistical significance attained by the higher level of drug sales mentions in gang cases when the numbers are reduced to drug-involved cases only.

Specific mentions of crack, or cocaine of any type, are more common in *nongang* than in gang homicides. Both types of drug mentions have increased proportionally over the 1984–1985 figures for nongang cases with drug involvement and have remained stable in gang cases.

On the other hand, presence of drug sales as an aspect of homicide has decreased slightly from the 1984–1985 levels, and in the 1988–1989 homicides, sales are mentioned more commonly in gang drug cases than in the nongang incidents. Finally, drug motives were recorded in about one third of these cases, similar to the findings for 1984 and 1985. *Mentions of drug motives remain proportionally more common in nongang than in gang homicides.*

Overall, 22% of the homicide cases studied had drug motives mentioned in the investigation file. Meehan and O'Carroll (1992) reported the same figure in the Centers for Disease Control and Prevention (CDC) study of 2,162 homicides occurring in the city of Los Angeles between January 1, 1986, and August 31, 1988. Although the CDC study covered a larger area and a slightly earlier (although overlapping) period, neither study provides confirmation of media reports of high levels of drug-motivated homicide in Los Angeles.

In other studies of gang, drugs, and homicide, Block et al. (1996) found that just 2.2% of Chicago street gang-related homicides between

1965 and 1994 involved a drug motive. Equally low proportions are reported by Kennedy et al. (1997) for Boston. Tita et al. (1996) found that 20% of all Pittsburgh gang homicides had a drug component and that 25% of all drug homicides had a gang component. In contrast to these studies, Sanders (1994) attributed an increase in gang-related homicides in San Diego between 1985 and 1988 to competition for turf in cocaine trafficking, but data are not presented to support this contention.

CONCLUSIONS

Investigations into the nature of gang homicide in several large but otherwise diverse U.S. cities find that these homicides most often reflect the dynamics of gang membership such as continuing intergroup rivalries, neighborhood turf battles, identity challenges, and occasional intragroup status threats. The victims in gang homicides are usually other gang members. The commonly stated myths of gang homicides—that they are steeped in drug distribution systemic processes or random acts of expressive outrage against innocent citizens—simply do not hold up. Instead, there is much continuity in findings about the character of gang homicide, despite the growth in numbers. This increase, in the face of the current declining trend in other types of homicide, suggests that the unique aspects of gang violence are especially deserving of more attention.

Far less common, although much more publicized, are the deaths of innocent bystanders. These victims represent collateral tragedies of gang rivalries and membership dynamics, yet mobilize community groups and government officials in ways that the numbing annual statistics of gang homicides apparently do not. The 1995 death of 3-year-old blond-haired and blue-eyed Stephanie Kuhen in Los Angeles was the catalyst for establishing a citywide collaborative task force. The group's findings led local government officials to reassess long-standing practices of allocating funds to unevaluated gang prevention programs in an uncoordinated manner. Recently, the city council launched a new comprehensive prevention effort, the L.A. Bridges project. This program has generated a much-enhanced funding pool ($11 million per year), a longer time commitment to funded programs, and an integrated evaluation component to determine the effectiveness of funded programs.

More often, such catalyzing events provoke large increments in law enforcement responses intended to suppress gang activity. Social scientists, however, can help local policymakers avoid simplistic, ill-designed crisis management reactions (Hagedorn, in press). A small but growing body of alternative efforts uses research knowledge and local empirical data to formulate coordinated and well-targeted responses. The Boston Gun Project, the geographic mapping of crime hot spots in Chicago, and Irving Spergel's Little Village project, also in Chicago, are just a few examples of promising efforts currently under way. Unquestionably, annual tabulations of gang homicides in cities across the country are an important component in recognizing the scope of gang violence. Let us hope, however, that analysts can move rapidly to a better assessment of the character of these lethal (and also nonlethal) events and that these assessments will contribute to the development of solutions targeted to the specific nature of gang-related problems in their communities.

Notes

[1] Previously unpublished data were gathered with support from the Harry Frank Guggenheim Foundation, the Southern California Injury Prevention Center (under the auspices of the Public Health Service Centers for Disease Control and Injury Prevention Grant No. R49/CCR903622) and the National Institute of Justice (No. 91-IJ-CX-K004). Malcolm W. Klein was a coprincipal investigator on all three grants. Views expressed herein are solely mine and do not represent the official position of any of the agencies providing support. I appreciate comments by Mac Klein on an earlier draft and the computer assistance of Karen Sternheimer and Brianna Garcia.

[2] Periodically, researchers have attempted to use the gang information (i.e., victim-offender relationship and gang circumstances) recorded in the Supplementary Homicide Reports but have obtained less than desirable results. In general, the SHR data are thought to underestimate levels of gang involvement, particularly in the past (Bailey & Unnithan, 1994; P. Lattimore, personal communication, January 9, 1997; Riedel & Lewitt, 1996).

[3] I have previously detailed many of the challenges in coding data from gang homicide investigation files, particularly with reference to victim-offender relationships, motives or circumstances, and number of participants (Maxson, 1992).

[4] Wild variations exist between figures provided for Chicago by Miller (1982/1992) and by Block et al. (1996), although both obtained their figures from the Chicago Police Department. For example, Block and her colleagues report 18 gang homicides for 1967, whereas Miller's number is 150. Miller notes the political dimensions of gang homicide reporting (see Appendix D in his 1982 report), a factor that likely accounts for the discrepancy. Convergence between the sources is evident during 1970 to 1974 and 1977 to 1979.

[5] The survey population was 1,019 cities of all sizes, including all U.S. cities with populations greater than 100,000 and other locations with reported gang problems, drawn from a variety of sources. For a detailed description of the study methods and definitions of street gangs, see Maxson et al. (1995), especially Appendix A.

[6] These data were first reported in Klein (1995, p. 116).

[7] Despite the request for counts of homicides involving gang members, the figure of 129 gang homicides in Chicago is consistent with the Chicago Police Department's policy of designating crimes as gang-related only if they are tied directly to a gang function (Maxson & Klein, 1996, but see footnote 2 in that work). Data are not available to assess whether respondents in other cities on this list reported gang homicide figures based on definitional approaches other than those they were requested to use.

[8] In recognition of the fluctuation of gang homicides from one year to the next (Block et al., 1996), rates were calculated only for those cities with at least 10 homicides.

[9] Approximately 5% of all survey respondents were telephoned to clarify ambiguities or conflicting information, but the counts of gang homicides were not a priority item for this process.

[10] The wording of this item on the 1996 NYGC survey (covering homicides in 1995) is not comparable with any other survey. The request of counts of homicides that involved gang members as perpetrators separate from counts of incidents with gang members as victims is problematic. If the NYGC data are limited to city agencies that report at least one homicide in which a gang member was a perpetrator or victim, a simple comparison with the Maxson-Klein 1991 homicide data is possible. NYGC staff identified 366 cities with at least

one homicide so defined (J. Moore, personal communication, January 16, 1997). This number represents about one fourth of all gang cities in the NYGC database. In the Maxson-Klein 1992 survey, just under 300 cities, or about 40% of all gang cities, reported gang homicides during 1991. Thus, the NYGC survey identified nearly twice the number of gang cities in 1995 but just 25% more cities with gang homicides than the earlier survey. A revision of this item on the upcoming NYGC survey of 1996 gang homicides will produce data directly comparable with that gathered in the 1992 survey.

[11] For figure 1, gang homicide tabulations for each year between 1965 and 1994 are taken from Block et al. (1996). The proportions of all homicides were calculated from annual homicide figures printed in Block and Christakos (1995). Data for 1995 were provided by C. Rebecca Block.

[12] Most of the gang homicides in Los Angeles County occur in jurisdictions patrolled by the LAPD and the LASD. The Sheriff Department's Operation Safe Streets gang unit gathers counts of gang homicides that occur in the more than 70 independent police jurisdictions in the county. Uniform definitional practices are used throughout the county.

[13] According to Kennedy et al. (1997),

> Gang-related, as the group understood it, meant in practice that the incident was either the product of gang behavior such as drug dealing, turf protection, a continuing "beef" with a rival gang or gangs, or a product of activity that was narrowly and directly connected with gang membership such as a struggle for power within a particular gang. Not all homicide involvement by gang members counted under this definition. (p. 222)

[14] Case sampling and data collection procedures were similar in the two studies.

[15] The five stations were characterized by high levels of gang activity, with a high proportion of all homicides occurring in their areas being gang related.

[16] Intercoder reliability was assessed by duplicate coding of 10% of the sample; overall, reliabilities were high (greater than .90), but the data collection was closely supervised, with heavy involvement by senior staff in coding decisions.

[17] The high proportion of African American involvement in these cases is a reflection of the ethnic composition of these five station areas and is not representative of homicides in Los Angeles County. Hutson, Anglin, Kyriacou, Hart, and Spears (1995) found that 57% of victims of gang homicides from 1979 through 1994 in the county were Hispanic and 37% were African American. The study of 1978 to 1982 gang and nongang homicides occurring in all unincorporated areas of the county and within three high-activity stations in LAPD, 1979 to 1981, also found that Hispanics were more often victims in gang, than in nongang, homicides (Maxson et al., 1985).

References

Bailey, G. W., & Unnithan, N. P. (1994). Gang homicides in California: A discriminant analysis. *Journal of Criminal Justice, 22,* 267–275.

Ball, R. A., & Curry, G. D. (1995). The logic of definition in criminology: Purposes and methods for defining "gangs." *Criminology, 33,* 225–245.

Battin, S. R., Hill, K. G., Abbott, R. D., Catalano, R. F., & Hawkins, J. D. (1998). The contribution of gang membership to delinquency beyond delinquent friends. *Criminology, 36,* 93–115.

Block, C. R., & Christakos, A. (1995). *Major trends in Chicago homicide: 1965–1994* (Research bulletin). Chicago: Illinois Criminal Justice Information Authority.

Block, C. R., Christakos, A., Jacob, A. P., & Przybylski, R. (1996). *Street gangs and crime: Patterns and trends in Chicago* (Research bulletin). Chicago: Illinois Criminal Justice Information Authority.

Block, R. L., & Block, C. R. (1993). *Street gang crime in Chicago* (Research in Brief: NCJ-144782). Washington, DC: National Institute of Justice.

Curry, G. D., Bail, R. A., & Decker, S. H. (1995). *An update on gang crime and law enforcement record keeping.* St. Louis: University of Missouri, Department of Criminology and Criminal Justice.

Curry, G. D., Ball, R. A., & Decker, S. H. (1996). Estimating the national scope of gang crime from law enforcement data. In C. R. Huff (Ed.), *Gangs in America* (2nd ed., pp. 21–36). Thousand Oaks, CA: Sage.

Curry, G. D., Ball, R. A., & Fox, R. J. (1994). *Gang crime and law enforcement record keeping* (Research in Brief: NCJ-148345). Washington, DC: National Institute of Justice.

Decker, S. H., & Van Winkle, B. (1996). *Life in the gang: Family, friends and violence.* New York: Cambridge University Press.

Dodge, K. A. (1997). *How gang membership increases violent behavior* (National Consortium on Violence Research grant proposal). Nashville, TN: Vanderbilt University, Department of Psychology and Human Development.

Esbensen, F., & Huizinga, D. (1993). Gangs, drugs and delinquency in a survey of urban youth. *Criminology, 31,* 565–589.

Esbensen, F., Huizinga, D., & Weiher, A. (1993) Gang and non-gang youth: Differences in explanatory factors. *Journal of Contemporary Criminal Justice, 9,* 94–116.

Fagan, J. (1989). The social organization of drug use and drug dealing among urban gangs. *Criminology, 27,* 633–669.

Fox, J. A. (1996). *Trends in juvenile violence: A report to the United States attorney general on current and future rates of juvenile offending.* Washington, DC: Bureau of Justice Statistics.

Hagedorn, J. (in press). Gang violence in the post industrial era. In M. Tonry (Ed.), *Youth violence.* Chicago: University of Chicago Press.

Hill, K. G., Hawkins, D., Catalano, R. F., Kosterman, R., Abbott, R., & Edwards, T. (1996, November). *The longitudinal dynamics of gang membership and problem behavior: A replication and extension of the Denver and Rochester gang studies in Seattle.* Paper presented at the annual meeting of the American Society of Criminology, Chicago.

Howell, J. C. (1995). Gangs and youth violence: Present research. In J. C. Howell, B. Krisberg, J. D. Hawkins, & J. J. Wilson (Eds.), *Serious, violent, and chronic juvenile offenders* (pp. 261–274). Thousand Oaks, CA: Sage.

Huff, C. R. (1996). Introduction. In C. R. Huff (Ed.), *Gangs in America* (2nd ed., pp. xxi–xxvii). Thousand Oaks, CA: Sage.

Huizinga, D. (1997, February). *Gangs and volume of crime.* Paper presented at the annual meeting of the Western Society of Criminology, Honolulu, HI.

Hutson, H. R., Anglin, D., Kyriacou, D. M., Hart, J., & Spears, K. (1995). The epidemic of gang-related homicides in Los Angeles County from 1979 through 1994. *Journal of the American Medical Association, 274,* 1031–1036.

Jackson, R. L., Lopez, R. J., & Connell, R. (1997, January 12). Clinton puts priority on curtailing gang crime. *Los Angeles Times,* p. A1.

Kennedy, D. M., Braga, A. A., & Piehl, A. M. (1997). The (un)known universe: Mapping gangs and gang violence in Boston. In D. Weisburd & T. McEwen (Eds.), *Crime mapping and crime prevention* (pp. 219–262). New York: Criminal Justice Press.

Klein, M. W. (1995). *The American street gang: Its nature, prevalence, and control.* New York: Oxford University Press.

Klein, M. W., Gordon, M. A., & Maxson, C. L. (1986). The impact of police investigations on police-reported rates of gang and nongang homicides. *Criminology,* 24, 489–512.

Klein, M. W., & Maxson, C. L. (1994). Gangs and crack cocaine trafficking. In D. L. MacKenzie & C. D. Uchida (Eds.), *Drugs and crime* (pp. 42–58). Thousand Oaks, CA: Sage.

Klein, M. W., Maxson, C. L., & Cunningham, L. C. (1991). "Crack," street gangs, and violence. *Criminology,* 29, 623–650.

Lizotte, A. J., Tesoriero, J. M., Thornberry, T. P., & Krohn, M. D. (1994). Patterns of adolescent firearms ownership and use. *Justice Quarterly,* 16, 51–73.

Maxson, C. L. (1992). Collecting data from investigation files: Descriptions of three Los Angeles gang homicide projects. In C. R. Block & R. L. Block (Eds.), *Questions and answers in lethal and non-lethal violence* (pp. 87–95). Washington, DC: National Institute of Justice.

Maxson, C. L. (1996). *Street gang members on the move: The role of migration in the proliferation of street gangs in the U.S.* Tallahassee, FL: National Youth Gang Center.

Maxson, C. L., Gordon, M. A., & Klein, M. W. (1985). Differences between gang and nongang homicides. *Criminology,* 23, 209–222.

Maxson, C. L., & Klein, M. W. (1990). Street gang violence: Twice as great, or half as great? In C. R. Huff (Ed.), *Gangs in America* (pp. 71–100). Newbury Park, CA: Sage.

Maxson, C. L., & Klein, M. W. (1996). Defining gang homicide: An updated look at member and motive approaches. In C. R. Huff (Ed.), *Gangs in America* (2nd ed., pp. 3–20). Thousand Oaks, CA: Sage.

Maxson, C. L., & Klein, M. W. (1997). Urban street gangs in Los Angeles. In M. Dear & P. Ethington (Eds.), *Los Angeles versus Chicago: Re-envisioning the urban process.* Unpublished report, University of Southern California, Southern California Studies Center, Los Angeles.

Maxson, C. L., Klein, M. W., & Cunningham, L. (1992). *Definitional variations affecting drug and gang homicide issues.* Los Angeles: University of Southern California, Center for the Study of Crime and Social Control, Social Science Research Institute.

Maxson, C. L., Woods, K. J., & Klein, M. W. (1995). *Street gang migration in the United States.* Los Angeles: University of Southern California, Center for the Study of Crime and Social Control, Social Science Research Institute.

Meehan, P. J., & O'Carroll, P. W. (1992). Gangs, drugs, and homicide in Los Angeles. *American Journal of Disease Control,* 146, 683–687.

Miller, W. B. (1992). *Crime by youth gangs and groups in the United States.* Washington, DC: Office of Juvenile Justice and Delinquency Prevention. (Original report issued 1982)

Miller, W. B. (1996). *The growth of youth gang problems in the U.S.: 1970–1995.* Tallahassee, FL: National Youth Gang Center, Institute for Intergovernmental Research.

Moore, J. (1991). *Going down to the barrio: Homeboys and homegirls in change.* Philadelphia: Temple University Press.

National Youth Gang Center. (1997). *1995 National youth gang survey.* Washington, DC: Office of Juvenile Justice and Delinquency Prevention.

Quinn. J. F., Tobolowsky, P. M., & Downs, W. T. (1994). The gang problem in large and small cities: An analysis of police perceptions in nine states. *The Gang Journal,* 2, 13–22.

Riedel, M., & Lewitt, K. N. (1996, November). *Hispanic homicides in Los Angeles: A study of racial and ethnic patterns.* Paper presented at the annual meeting of the American Society of Criminology, Chicago.

Sanders, W. (1994). *Gangbangs and drive-bys: Grounded culture and juvenile gang violence.* New York: Aldine de Gruyter.

Sheley, J. F., & Wright, J. D. (1995). *In the line of fire: Youth, guns, and violence in urban America.* New York: Aldine de Gruyter.

Short, J. F., Jr. (1996). *Gangs and adolescent violence.* Boulder: University of Colorado, Center for the Study and Prevention of Violence.

Spergel, I. A. (1983). *Violent gangs in Chicago: Segmentation and integration.* Chicago: University of Chicago, School of Social Service Administration.

Spergel, I. A. (1988). *Report of the Law Enforcement Youth Gang Symposium.* Chicago: University of Chicago, School of Social Service Administration.

Spergel, I. A. (1995). *The youth gang problem: A community approach.* New York: Oxford University Press.

Spergel, I. A., & Curry, D. G. (1990). Strategies and perceived agency effectiveness in dealing with the youth gang problem. In C. R. Huff (Ed.), *Gangs in America* (pp. 288–309). Newbury Park, CA: Sage.

Thornberry, T. P., & Burch, J. H., II. (1997). *Gang members and delinquent behavior* (NCJ-165154). Washington, DC: Office of Juvenile Justice and Delinquency Prevention.

Thornberry, T. P., Krohn, M. D., Lizotte, A. J., & Chard-Wierschem, D. (1993). The role of juvenile gangs in facilitating delinquent behavior. *Journal of Research in Crime and Delinquency, 30,* 55–87.

Tita, G. E., Cohen, J., & Blumstein, A. (1996, November). *Exploring the gang-drug-gun nexus: Evidence from homicides in Pittsburgh.* Paper presented at the annual meeting of the American Society of Criminology, Chicago.

Tracy, P. E. (1979). *Subcultural delinquency: A comparison of the incidence and seriousness of gang and nongang member offensivity.* Philadelphia: University of Pennsylvania, Center for Studies in Criminology and Criminal Law.

Zahn, M. A., & Jamieson, K. M. (1997). Changing patterns of homicide and social policy. *Homicide Studies, 1,* 190–196.

SECTION IV

Responding to Youth Gangs

Much of the recent response to youth gangs has focused on intervention and/or suppression tactics. Law-enforcement strategies such as the Los Angeles Police Department's CRASH unit (Community Resources Against Street Hoodlums), prosecutorial approaches (including vertical prosecution), and legislative efforts such as California's Street Terrorism Enforcement and Prevention Act (STEP) illustrate the suppression approach. In this section, the first article considers the possibility that the gang problem has been overstated, the next three are devoted to the discussion of approaches to the gang problem other than suppression, while the fifth article describes a relatively new suppression strategy that appears to be receiving increased attention across the United States.

In discussing societal responses to gangs, rarely does the discussion include the possibility that the magnitude of the problem has been exaggerated. Recall some of the definitional issues raised in the first section of this text. Definitions of gangs are important not only for researchers who study gangs, but are perhaps more important for shaping social and political reactions to the presence of gangs. McCorkle and Miethe provide an insightful examination of the emergence of the gang problem in Las Vegas during the late 1980s. Based on law-enforcement and prosecutorial data supplemented with reviews of newspaper articles, they suggest that the police department created and sustained a moral panic for the purpose of

297

securing resources and repairing a tarnished image. The District Attorney's Office, while concerned about gang crime, also supported the panic because it justified funding for additional staff attorneys. This article, and others like it, raises the specter that gang proliferation may not be as extensive, nor as serious, as police data and the media suggest.

Huff's article places gangs and gang violence within the more general context of youth violence. He provides an overview of recent trends in youth violence and establishes that youth violence is a complex phenomenon requiring multiple strategies for successfully reducing violence and associated risk factors. While suppression tactics have been the most common U.S. response to gangs and violence, they may be the least fruitful. Without addressing the underlying causes of youth violence and gang formation, these social problems will continue to manifest themselves. During the 1990s, there was a movement to identify effective programs based on rigorous scientific evaluation designs. The vast majority of these programs focused on prevention efforts—that is, preventing youths from becoming involved in violence rather than treating or responding to youths once they had become problems for the system. Huff introduces some of the issues associated with a prevention approach and laments the absence of a true "national policy" on youth and youth issues. His chapter should provide the reader with some thought-provoking ideas and stimulate discussion about the relative merits of a public health approach to youth violence relative to the suppression-oriented focus of the criminal justice system.

Law-enforcement efforts represent the most common response to gangs. In his article, Greene provides a brief overview of the history of police efforts to regulate and control youth crime. The reactive/suppression model that guided American policing during much of the twentieth century proved ineffective. The 1980s and 1990s witnessed a shift in orientation among many law-enforcement personnel. Community- or problem-oriented policing perspectives were adopted by an increasing number of agencies. This pro-active, problem-solving approach emphasized building partnerships with a focus on prevention rather than intervention. Greene reviews two initiatives that were launched in 1995, the federally funded Youth Firearms Violence Prevention Initiative (YFVI) and the Boston Gun Project. The two initiatives provide an informative contrast in police strategies and outcomes. Based on his review of these two programs, Greene provides a number of policy recommendations that are framed within a theoretical and historical perspective.

Esbensen and his colleagues report findings from their national evaluation of the Gang Resistance Education and Training (G.R.E.A.T.) program, a school-based gang prevention program offered by uniformed law-enforcement officers. The G.R.E.A.T. program utilizes a primary prevention strategy to discourage students from joining gangs by providing them with life skills and knowledge about the negative aspects of gangs. This program, part of a community-oriented policing approach, raises several interesting questions. Can police officers be effective providers of prevention programs? Can a general prevention program that targets the entire adolescent population, similar to previous inoculation efforts to eliminate smallpox, be effective in reducing gang involvement? The results from this national evaluation are promising on both of these counts.

Civil gang injunctions (CGIs) were introduced by southern California law-enforcement agencies in the early 1980s as a tool to combat gangs. During the last few years of the twentieth century, this approach apparently had proliferated across the United States. The 1999 National Youth Gang Survey reported 116 jurisdictions across the country utilizing CGIs. In her chapter, Maxson details the history, theoretical underpinnings, effectiveness, and proliferation of the CGI as a law-enforcement response to gangs.

CGIs are distinct from civil abatement laws. Whereas the latter target specific properties or property owners, CGIs include larger areas and a group of individuals. The CGI generally prohibits gang members from a wide array of activities (some illegal and others not) ranging from use of cell phones and associating with gang members to carrying weapons and selling drugs. One can certainly question the desirability of laws that challenge assumptions of civil liberty (i.e., regulating one's associations and prohibiting individuals from engaging in otherwise legal activities). To date, however, these laws have been upheld in spite of research supporting the efficacy of the laws. Maxson provides an overview of CGIs and provides readers with insight to their implementation.

The Political and Organizational Response to Gangs
An Examination of a "Moral Panic" in Nevada

Richard C. McCorkle & Terance D. Miethe

The past decade has witnessed increasing concern about street gangs and their role in violent crime and drug trafficking. According to a recent national survey, more than 80 percent of prosecutors in large cities now acknowledge that gangs are a problem in their jurisdiction, that their numbers are growing, and that levels of gang-related violence are increasing (Johnson, Webster, and Connors 1995). A seasoned observer of the gang problem has asserted that contemporary street gangs are now "more numerous, more prevalent, and more violent . . . than anytime in the country's history" (Miller 1990:263).

The recognition of a gang problem has not been uniform. Initially, many cities remained in what Huff (1990) calls a state of *denial*, officially disavowing the problem because of public relations fears. Many of these cities now acknowledge gang activity on their streets, a concession that

McCorkle, Richard C., and Miethe, Terance D., "The Political and Organizational Response to Gangs: An Examination of Moral Panic in Nevada." *Justice Quarterly*, Vol. 15 No. 1, pp. 41–64, 1998. Copyright © 1998 by the Academy of Criminal Justice Sciences. Reprinted with the permission of the Academy of Criminal Justice Sciences.

frequently followed the commission of one or more high-profile gang-related crimes (Klein 1995). After the "discovery" of a gang problem, however, public officials react in a standard fashion: gangs are defined as a law enforcement problem, police and prosecutorial "gang units" are formed, and suppression, strategies are promoted vigorously (Huff 1990).

Gangs recently have emerged as a major social problem, it is argued, because of a significant increase in the objective threat posed by such groups. This explanation for the current crisis—overwhelmingly embraced by those who study, police, or prosecute gangs—is characteristic of objectivism, one of two dominant approaches to social problems in general. According to this model, a condition becomes a social problem when it threatens the quality or length of life of a substantial number of people (Manis 1974). Objectivism ignores or minimizes the subjective nature of social problems and assumes that empirical measures of a condition accurately reflect the objective threat it poses. The state acts only in response to that threat and does not attempt to shape or influence public opinion to further its own agenda (Beckett 1994). According to this perspective, the gang problem is real, growing, and deserving of public attention and state resources. Huff's conclusion that public officials typically "overreact" to a gang problem thus should be viewed more as a criticism of the form than of the level of that response; indeed, Huff advocates a massive, "coordinated, comprehensive effort" to address the fundamental social and economic conditions that give rise to gangs (1990:316).

Some observers, however, question the magnitude of the threat posed by contemporary street gangs (Jackson and Rudman 1993; Zatz 1987). Despite surveys suggesting an increase in gang activity across the country, many wonder how such findings should be interpreted, given the lack of a consensus about how even to define a "gang" or what constitutes "gang-related crime." The definitions currently employed are the outcome of an extremely subjective process and vary greatly across jurisdictions, agencies, and researchers; thus it is extremely difficult to make statements about the nature and trends in gang activity (Decker and Kempf-Leonard 1995; Klein and Maxson 1989). Some observers have gone further, asserting that the gang crisis, in certain jurisdictions, was manufactured by social control agencies to obtain resources and expand their authority (Zatz 1987). Public support for state expansion is generated, these critics argue, by creating and promoting images which suggest that the community is under attack from warring tribes of drug-dealing sociopaths.

Those who look askance at the current state and direction of gang policy represent the constructionist approach, the other dominant approach to social problems. According to this model, the objective status of a condition—for example, gang activity—is largely irrelevant in determining what is defined as a social problem. Instead a social problem is understood more accurately as a product derived from the "activities of individuals or groups making assertions of grievances and claims with respect to some putative condition" (Spector and Kitsuse 1977:75). The important point is not the actual nature of the condition, but what claimsmakers *say* about that condition. Conceivably any number of conditions, even those presenting only minor threats, could exist. Yet because public attention and resources are limited, intense competition exists among claimsmakers in public arenas where social problems are framed and funded (Hiltgartner and Bosk 1988). Many apparently are called, but few are chosen.

Gangs have become a major social problem, according to constructionists, because law enforcement officials have been successful in these public arenas. This success has been enhanced by their access to the media and to government officials, by their monopoly of crime information, and by our cultural preoccupations with crime and race. Like other claimsmakers, these officials also have found it "necessary to lie or exaggerate a little" so as to distinguish themselves from other groups seeking recognition and funding (Goode and Ben-Yehuda 1994:120). Unlike the case with most social problems, however, the distortions and exaggerations by law enforcement officials necessarily entail a focus on a particular group of individuals in the community. One possible result is a "moral panic," a situation in which public fears and state interventions greatly exceed the threat posed by the targeted group. Such moral panics purportedly have occurred in response to various groups in American history, as shown by the anti-Catholic movement of the 19th century and the satanic cult scare of the past decade (Hofstadter 1966; Jenkins and Meier-Katkin 1992).

GANGS AND MORAL PANICS

The concept of moral panic actually grew out of research on British youth gangs conducted during the 1960s. Cohen (1972) believed that the term most accurately characterized the reactions of the media, agencies of social control, and the public to a brief melee between the "Mods" and the "Rockers" at a seaside resort. He defined a moral panic as follows:

> A condition, episode, person or group of persons emerges to become defined as a threat to societal values and interests; its nature is presented in a stylized and stereotypical fashion by the mass media; the moral barricades are manned by editors, bishops, politicians and other right thinking people; socially accredited experts pronounce their diagnoses and solutions; ways of coping are evolved or . . . resorted to; the condition then disappears, submerges or deteriorates and becomes invisible. Sometimes the subject of the panic is quite novel and at other times it is something which has been in existence long enough, but suddenly appears in the limelight. (Cohen 1972:9)

A few scattered fistfights and broken windows, according to Cohen, were transformed by the media into "an orgy of destruction," an event characteristic of a wave of hooliganism spreading across the country. Although local law enforcement officials were aware of the embellishment by the media, they played along, seizing the opportunity to increase funds and expand police powers. Even the British Parliament got involved, enacting stiffer sentences against youth offenders and at least entertaining the notion of a return to corporal punishment.

One of the most frequently cited illustrations of a moral panic is taken from events in Britain during the early 1970s (Hall et al. 1978). Britain, at that time, was mired in a deep economic recession, which fomented social unrest and generated challenges to the capitalistic system. To deflect attention from the economic problems, Hall et al. argue, the British ruling class manufactured a moral panic, manipulating the press and the criminal justice system so as to convince the public that street crime had reached epidemic proportions. By exploiting the public's fear of crime, the ruling class shifted the focus from an ailing British economy to street muggings, thereby protecting their own economic interests and legitimating the more strongly authoritarian social control measures employed to quell social unrest.

At least two gang researchers have characterized the reaction to street gangs in the United States as a moral panic. Zatz (1987) accused law enforcement officials in Phoenix during the late 1970s of manufacturing a Chicano youth gang problem as a means of acquiring LEAA funds for a new gang crime unit. Police spokesmen, she contended, exploited the media penchant for violence, sensationalism, and crime "themes" by providing a regular stream of violent, random crimes committed by alleged gang members. Estimates on the number of gangs were ratcheted up by officials regularly and without justification, she reported, and were accompanied by dire warnings of impending social disorder if law enforcement interventions were not beefed up. Analysis of juvenile court records, however, provided little to support law enforcement claims. Chicano youth gang members referred to juvenile court were no more a threat to the community than nongang referrals; most gang youths had been arrested for fighting, primarily among themselves, and for minor property crimes. From interviews with social service agencies in Phoenix that dealt with Chicano youths, Zatz (1987) also concluded that police wildly exaggerated both the number and the size of gangs in the area.

Zatz's designation of the response to gangs in Phoenix as a moral panic may have been premature, however, given that she examined only the criminal activities of youthful gang members. Although there are disturbing accounts of 8- and 10-year old gang members, the upper age range actually has "expanded dramatically" (Klein 1995:105). Because gang violence is primarily a young adult, not a juvenile, problem (Maxson, Gordon, and Klein 1985; Maxson, Klein, and Cunningham 1992; Spergel 1984), Zatz (1987) may have underestimated the nature and level of the threat posed by gangs during that period.

More recently, Jackson and Rudman (1993) suggested that antigang initiatives in California, such as the Street Terrorism Enforcement and Prevention Act, have been excessive and extreme, shaped by stereotypic portrayals of gangs provided by law enforcement and the media. Yet because the authors had not examined actual levels and trends in gang activity in California, they could only conclude that "on the surface," the gang response was "similar to past inquiries finding support for the idea of a 'moral panic'" (Jackson and Rudman 1773:271).

Whether the gang problem in fact constitutes a moral panic in certain jurisdictions thus remains unknown. Certainly a great deal of mythology surrounds gangs: The research simply does not support tales of highly organized, entrepreneurial, drug-dealing urban gangs on the move in search of new markets (Klein 1995). Nonetheless, large numbers of young males grouped in rival factions would pose significant problems for the community. Yet the determination that the response to those groups represents a moral panic requires a more extensive examination of gangs than has been conducted to this point; such an examination must include a detailed analysis of gang activity over a period of years. Moreover, the concept used in previous studies of gang crises has not yet been operationalized adequately. Researchers such as Zatz (1987) and Jackson and Rudman (1989) used the concept in the loosest fashion: They did not properly specify in advance, or subsequently examine, the empirical indicators necessary for demonstrating that a moral panic in fact had occurred.

The concept of moral panics, however, has not been without its critics. For Waddington (1986), the problem is "establishing the comparison between the scale of the problem and the scale of the response to it" (p. 246). At what point, he asks, can we say that a reaction is disproportional to the objective threat, that a "moral panic" has occurred? Furthermore, critics such as Waddington believe that the objective threat of a condition can never be known; consequently, judgments as to whether a reaction was disproportional must remain arbitrary.

In response to such criticisms, Goode and Ben-Yehuda (1994) note that many (if not most) objective threats can be measured, particularly those which are "familiar, ongoing, and based on behavior" (p.43). They further contend that specific criteria can be used to determine the proportionality of a response to a given problem. Indicators of a disproportional response—a "moral panic"—include the exaggeration or fabrication of figures purporting to measure the severity of the problem and wild fluctuations in the attention given to a condition without corresponding changes in its severity. In this study, we gave careful attention to these criteria to determine whether the response to gangs in Las Vegas could accurately be described as a moral panic.

METHODS

In this paper we present the results of a study applying the concept of moral panic to the gang problem in Las Vegas, Nevada. Using a variety of sources, we attempted to understand the process by which gangs, present in the city for more than a decade, came to be defined as a major social problem during the late 1980s. To construct the timetable in which the problem unfolded in Las Vegas, we conducted a search for all gang-related stories published from 1983 to 1994 in the city's two largest newspapers, the *Review Journal* and the *Sun*. We also examined state and local government records including minutes of legislative hearings on gangs, archival data, and law enforcement publications. In reviewing these materials, we identified and subsequently interviewed key actors—police officers, school officials, prosecutors, and politicians active in the definition and response to gangs in Las Vegas. These interviews provided further details about the history of the gang response in Las Vegas.

To assess the appropriateness of that response to gangs, we examined all felony charges filed in Clark County district courts from 1989 through 1994. Previous studies did not use prosecutors' filings as a measure of the objective threat posed by gangs; gang crime typically was measured by self-reports (Esbensen and Huizinga 1993; Hagedorn 1988; Thornberry et al. 1994) or by arrest data (Maxson, Klein, and Cunningham 1992; Tracy 1987). We believe that prosecutors' filings are at least as valid an indicator of gang crime as self-reports or arrest data, if not more so.

One of the surest paths to overstating gang members' criminal activity is to take the accounts provided by the gang members themselves (Klein 1995; Spergel 1995). They are prone to exaggerate their own criminal activity, and possess unreliable and biased information on the scope of the group's crimes. Arrest statistics suffer a different set of problems: Because gangs consist primarily of minorities (Klein 1995), and because race is not independent of the decision to arrest (Black 1971; Smith and Visher 1981; Smith, Visher, and Davidson 1984), arrest statistics may be a more accurate indicator of enforcement patterns than of criminal activity. Indeed, the higher rejection and dismissal rates for members of minorities strongly suggest that police often use arrests for nonlaw enforcement purposes: for example, to harass or punish troublesome, disrespectful populations (Hepburn 1978; Petersilia 1985; Pope 1978).

On the other hand, there is little or no evidence that race is a factor on a prosecutor's decision to file charges (Albonetti et al. 1989; Miethe 1987; Miethe and Moore 1986). That decision is a function primarily of the severity of the offense and the quality of the available evidence. Consequently we believe that prosecutors' filings are a valid measure of the objective threat posed by gangs over the period in question.

One problem with using felony charges, of course, is that the juvenile gang members' delinquent acts would not be included in our assessment of gang activity during the period under study; those acts are under the exclusive jurisdiction of the juvenile court. Thus the measure of objective gang threat used in this study underestimates the threat posed by these groups, but not by much. Research has confirmed that serious gang activity is attributable primarily to older adolescent and young adult males (Spergel 1995). Furthermore, juveniles age 15 and older in Nevada, when charged with committing serious violent crimes, are automatically certified as adults and prosecuted in the adult court system.

Some might argue that our measure actually overstates the threat posed by gangs. By labeling any crime committed by a known gang member or associate as a "gang-related" incident, we are employing the broader of the two definitions in use (Klein 1995; Spergel 1995). As a measure of gang activity, these crimes did not necessarily spring from intergang rivalries, turf conflicts, or efforts to increase gang revenues. A crime was committed, an arrest was made, and the suspect's name showed up in the gang file. The alleged crime may have been independent of gang affiliation: For example, an individual robbed a convenience store not to help the gang but to purchase his next fix or put gas in his car. This "member-based" definition, in fact, is used by law enforcement officials in Las Vegas and is the basis of reports on the incidence of gang crime in the city (C. Owens, June 12, 1995, personal communication). Using a "motive-based" definition, and counting a crime as gang-related only if it was gang-motivated, might have reduced the reported incidence of gang crime in the city by as much as half (Klein 1995).

GANGS AND MORAL PANIC IN LAS VEGAS

Before the mid-1980s, Las Vegas essentially had no gang problem (M. Hawkins, March 3, 1995, personal communication). Gangs existed, but they were few, were not particularly troublesome, and were confined to public housing projects and minority communities, particularly on the west side of the city (Nerlander and Ferguson 1990). Nonetheless, in 1985 the Las Vegas Metropolitan Police Department (LVMPD) assigned two officers full-time to an experimental Gang Diversion Unit (GDU). The unit's function was largely intelligence gathering; officers made no arrests, arranged no drug busts, and answered no dispatches. Procedures for identifying and recording gang members and their associates were also developed. These provided the first official "count" of gangs in late 1985: 15 gangs with some 1,000 members ("Special Police Units" 1985). The GDU reports also concluded that Las Vegas gangs were not heavily involved in the illicit drug market.

Early in 1986 the Gang Diversion Unit abruptly announced that there were now 4,000 gang members in 28 distinct gang sects; many were involved heavily in selling illicit drugs ("Group Examines" 1986). More disturbing than the increased number was the apparent movement of gang activity, reported in the media, from the traditionally "troubled" neighborhoods to recreation centers, theaters, and public schools across the city. GDU officers now also reported that area street gangs, in addition to drug trafficking, were involved increasingly in burglary, vandalism, animal abuse, and satanism ("Group Examiner" 1986).

Concern about the gang problem increased quickly, as indicated by trends in media coverage during the late 1980s. Figure 1 presents the trend in gang coverage by the two major Las Vegas newspapers over that period. In 1983, only 4 stories on gangs appeared in local papers; at its peak in 1989, the number of gang-related stories reached 174. Local papers continued to carry well over 100 stories a year through 1991. The growing apprehension was also reflected in a public survey of Las Vegans in 1989 (Center for Survey Research 1989): 77% of residents were "very concerned" about gangs in the community, up from 67 percent from 1987. Moreover, 89% of those polled believed that the gang problem was worsening and perhaps was out of control.

Figure 1   Gang Stories in Clark County (NV) Newspapers, 1983–1994

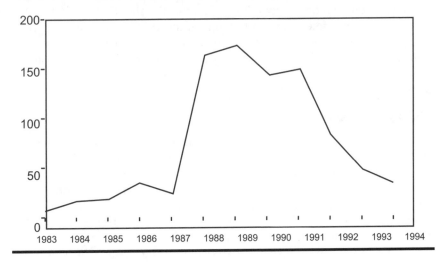

The Law Enforcement Response

The official response to gangs began to take shape in early 1988, when the county provided funding for an additional 16 officers for the Gang Diversion Unit. That mobilization of forces was accompanied by a radical shift in strategy, from an emphasis on intelligence gathering and selective enforcement to a harder position on deterrence and punishment. Gang-infested areas were to be targeted; aggressive sweeps were to be conducted, which would "rid Las Vegas of hoodlum gangs" once and for all ("Metro Mobilizes" 1988). Throughout the year, press reports trumpeting the success of the new GDU appeared in local papers. Television news reporters frequently accompanied police on drug sweeps of areas purportedly controlled by gangs, filming raids of crack houses and the arrests of "high-level" gang leaders. Because of this sustained assault, law enforcement officials (while not declaring victory), claimed that the tide had turned; gangbangers were retreating in the face of "superior forces" ("Gang Diversion Unit" 1988).

Talk of victory would have been premature, particularly because of the outbreak of gang violence on high school campuses in spring 1989 (J. Lazzarotto, September 29, 1995, personal communication). Law enforcement officials offered an explanation for the disruptions, claiming that gangs were moving from the street to the campus to recruit new members and expand drug distribution networks. In response, the Las Vegas Metropolitan Police Department (LVMPD) stepped up patrols, undercover police officers wandered on and near campuses, and school district police, usually unarmed, were allowed to carry weapons ("Bonanza students" 1989).

Calm eventually returned to high school campuses; only a few, very minor interruptions were reported in the spring semester of 1990. The alarm was sounded once again, however, after the shooting death of a student in a school cafeteria on the first day of the 1990–1991 academic year. The gunman, a 15-year-old Hispanic male, was arrested and charged with murder. Police described his act as a "gang-related slaying," an accusation never substantiated despite repeated challenges from the attorney assigned to represent the youth ("Eldorado Teen" 1990).

The Legislative Response

During the 1989 session, state lawmakers had enacted a number of statutes targeting gang crime, particularly that which occurred on school property (Nerlander and Ferguson 1991). The cafeteria slaying of 1990 was viewed as part of a larger pattern of gang activity, suggesting that gang members were not deterred by the passage of this legislation. In an impassioned speech delivered on the day after the cafeteria shooting, the governor of Nevada announced what he believed would be the *coup de grace*: a complete ban on gang membership. The statute, he promised, would be written broadly to ensure that "wearing gang colors, hanging around gangs, or even bragging about being in a gang" would be a criminal offense and subject to swift, severe sanctions ("Governor Miller" 1990). The initial draft of this "Gang Abolishment Act" drew sharp criticism from local ACLU officials, who claimed that the bill had disturbing racial overtones because the majority of gang members were members of minorities (C. Kendrick, July 18, 1995, personal communication).

The initial draft consequently underwent major revisions; the LVMPD and the Clark County Prosecutor's Office were placed in charge of producing a workable gang bill. Redactors relied heavily on California's Street Terrorism and Enforcement and Prevention Act, a comprehensive piece of gang legislation that had withstood the scrutiny of California's appellate court (Committee on Judiciary 1991). In the new version (known as the

Gang Enhancement Statute), gang membership in Nevada would not be criminalized. Any person, however, who committed a crime "knowingly for the benefit of, at the direction of, or in association with a criminal gang" would be subject to a term of incarceration in addition to, and consecutive to, the term prescribed by the statute for the crime (Committee on Judiciary 1991:316). For felonies, prison sentences would be doubled. The bill sailed through the state senate and assembly; it drew only four opponents, the most critical a black senator who characterized the legislation as a "veiled effort to incarcerate more minorities" (J. Neal, August 13, 1995, personal communication). In fall 1991, a specialized gang prosecution unit was developed, which would apply the statute more effectively.

The Abatement of the Panic

By 1992 the Special Enforcement Detail was asserting that it had "control over the gang problem" (Hartung and Roberts 1993:32). Hundreds of gang members reportedly had been imprisoned; the sentences of many were doubled under the Gang Enhancement Statute as a result of their expert testimony. In the months following the passage of the Gang Enhancement Statute and the creation of a gang prosecution unit, media attention to street gangs in Las Vegas declined sharply (see figure 1). The problem of gangs apparently had been addressed. Even if it had not, the media now were dominated by more dramatic issues: deepening state budget deficits, an unscrupulous battle between a university president and the basketball coach, the federal government's plan to store radioactive waste only 90 miles from the city.

ASSESSING THE OBJECTIVE THREAT POSED BY GANGS

Perhaps the declining criterion of a moral panic is the lack of proportionality between the objective threat posed by a condition and the reaction to that threat. To assess the appropriateness of the response to gangs in this jurisdiction, we examined data on all felony charges filed in Clark County District Courts from 1989 through 1994. We obtained a list of all known gang members and associates from the Gang Investigation Section (GIS) of the LVMPD. The list contained the identification numbers (no names) of 4,752 individuals, assigned at their first contact with GIS officers in the field. Individuals also were distinguished by whether they were juveniles or adults. When a gang member or associate had been arrested by LVMPD, a defendant identification number also was recorded. The Clark County District Attorney's Office uses these numbers to monitor the flow of cases through the court system. We excluded the 2,152 juveniles on the list, and then matched the remaining 2,600 adults with the case-monitoring data. By doing so, we could document the level and the trends of officially recorded gang crime during the period of the ostensible moral panic.

Table 1 presents the percentage of UCR index crime and felony drug charges filed against known gang members from 1989 to 1994. For violent offenses in general, the objective threat posed by gangs increased during that period. The proportion of violent index crimes attributable to gangs more than doubled from 1989 to 1993. Despite this disturbing trend, however, the percentage of violent crime linked to gangs was (and remained) quite low. When the gang panic erupted in 1989–1990, known gang members accounted for only about 3 percent of all reported violent crimes committed in the county. Gang members were responsible for even a smaller share of property crimes, although again the data show increased activity. Perhaps most striking are the figures related to drug crimes, which law enforcement officials have linked closely to the gang phenomenon: Official court records give no indication that gangs were particularly active in the illicit drug market during this period.

Table 1   Proportion of Index Crimes and Felony Drug Charges[a] Filed against Known Gang Members, 1989–1994[b]

	1989	1990	1991	1992	1993	1994
Violent Index	.03	.04	.05	.07	.07	.05
Offenses	(4,032)	(4,771)	(5,017)	(5,904)	(6,349)	(6,195)
Murder	.13	.08	.18	.18	.19	.15
	(266)	(355)	(346)	(493)	(488)	(354)
Rape	.01	.00	.03	.09	.02	.05
	(181)	(135)	(66)	(70)	(126)	(79)
Aggravated	.02	.03	.03	.03	.04	.05
Assault	(2,945)	(3,597)	(3,550)	(4,402)	(4,507)	(4,493)
Robbery	.04	.06	.08	.14	.16	.14
	(640)	(684)	(1,055)	(1,299)	(1,228)	(1,269)
Property Index	.02	.04	.06	.06	.05	.03
Offenses	(3,604)	(3,558)	(3,967)	(4,915)	(5,629)	(7,564)
Burglary	.02	.03	.04	.05	.04	.03
	(1,716)	(1,736)	(2,003)	(2,461)	(2,400)	(2,932)
Larceny/theft	.01	.05	.04	.04	.03	.01
	(1,104)	(1,001)	(1,141)	(1,396)	(2,206)	(3,467)
Motor vehicle	.04	.06	.12	.11	.12	.10
Theft	(774)	(800)	(819)	(1,054)	(1,010)	(1,161)
Arson	.00	.05	.00	.25	.08	.00
	(10)	(21)	(13)	(4)	(13)	(4)
Drug Offenses						
Drug sales	.02	.01	.02	.03	.05	.04
	(1,419)	(1,111)	(700)	(992)	(775)	(929)
Drug	.02	.03	.03	.07	.05	.05
Trafficking	(639)	(787)	(1,054)	(1,415)	(1,349)	(1,479)

[a] Includes attempted crime and conspiracy to commit crime.
[b] Numbers in parentheses represent the total number of charges for the specific offense filed during the year.

Having concluded that traditional criminal statutes were inadequate for prosecuting crimes typically committed by gangs the legislature (as discussed above) enacted several pieces of antigang legislation (Nerlander and Ferguson 1990). Table 2 shows that some of these laws were useful, but most were rarely, if ever, applied. The most frequent charges based on the antigang statutes were those directed at the random and reckless use of firearms, typical of gang retaliatory crimes. (These figures represent the total number of charges filed; they are not separate criminal events in which the law was invoked.) It was not uncommon for 15 or more charges under this law to be filed against a gunman who (for example) fired a single shot in the air near a crowd. Most of these charges, of course, would be dismissed during plea negotiations.

The number of defendants actually convicted under each of these antigang statutes is shown in parentheses in table 2. Although these statutes, with the exception of the Gang Enhancement Statute, were enacted to deal with "gang crimes," most of those convicted under the antigang laws had not been identified as members of street gangs.

The Gang Enhancement Statute was used only once in the year after it was signed into law. Prosecutors undoubtedly needed some time to research the attendant legal issues, cultivate expert witnesses, and plot trial strategies. In 1993, 84 charges were filed with the statute as an enhancement; in 1994 the number had risen to 117. Ninety percent of the Gang Enhancement charges, however, were dismissed before final disposition. As of 1994, only 18 defendants had been convicted of felonies under the Gang Enhancement Statute.

UNDERSTANDING THE GANG PANIC IN NEVADA

The reaction to gangs in Las Vegas fits the pattern established in previous studies of moral panics. Questions remain, however. Why did the gang hysteria break out in 1988? In the absence of a gang crime wave, why did gangs become the focus of a moral panic? How can we account for the end of the gang crisis? Two complementary perspectives, drawn from the moral panic literature, provide insight into such questions (Ben-Yehuda 1986).

The first perspective focuses on the *timing* of moral panics and requires us to consider the social, political, and economic motivations behind the creation and cultivation of the gang crisis in Las Vegas. This perspective emphasizes the role of established interest or pressure groups, particularly those with direct access to policy makers and legislators.

The second perspective emphasizes issues of *morality* as a means of understanding moral panics. Panics purportedly emerge when society's deeply held moral values are threatened. The reaction to the deviant group constitutes "boundary maintenance" and represents a collective effort to reinforce socially approved behaviors (Ben-Yehuda 1986; Cohen 1972; Gusfield 1963; Trebach 1982).

Table 2   Number of Charges Filed and Persons Convicted[a] under Anti-gang Legislation, 1989–1994[b]

	1989	1990	1991	1992	1993	1994
Additional penalty for procurement or solicitation of minor to commit certain violations as agent (effective 7/6/89)	0	0	0	0	0	0
Additional penalty for commission of certain violations at or near school, school bus stop, or recreational facilities for minors (effective 7/6/89)	0	0	0	0	0	0
Additional penalty: Felony committed on school bus (effective 7/6/89)	0	0	0	0	0	0
Possession of dangerous weapon on property or in vehicle of school (effective 10/1/89)	0	0	0	7 (2)	27 (1)	15 (0)
Discharging of firearm out of motor vehicle (effective 6/28/89	0	3 (1)	2 (2)	12 (6)	47 (5)	89 (3)
Aiming firearm at human being; discharging weapon where person might be endangered	27 (2)	205 (26)	193 (16)	247 (29)	377 (36)	392 (40)
Gang Enhancement Statute: Felony committed to promote activities of criminal gang	—	—	0	1 (1)	84 (9)	117 (8)

[a] Includes attempted crimes and conspiracy to commit crimes.
[b] Numbers in parenthesis represent number of persons convicted.

The Inspiration for the Gang Panic

The response to gangs in Las Vegas can be understood only in the broader national context of the gang phenomenon during those years. Street gangs were deemed "unnewsworthy" for more than a decade. In the late 1980s, however, the national press began to focus considerable attention on gangs, linking them to the distribution of illicit drugs and to senseless acts of violence. From Hollywood came powerful and frightening dramatizations of urban gangs, such as *Colors, Boyz in the Hood,* and *Warriors*. These films often depicted the "supergang" Crips and Bloods of Los Angeles engaged in urban guerilla warfare, turning communities into war zones over reputations and drug turf, and regularly taking the lives of innocent bystanders. These images were disturbing to the people of Las Vegas, only a four-hour drive away.

The national and local media clearly played a role in the moral panic examined here, similar to that documented in previous studies of moral panics (Cohen 1972; Goode and Ben-Yehuda 1994). Yet the moral panic in Las Vegas could not have been inspired by the media; what reporters and filmmakers knew about gangs came from the police. A number of studies have directly implicated the police in moral panics, revealing how law enforcement used its control of crime information to serve its own bureaucratic interests (Ben-Yehuda 1986; Fishman 1978; Zatz 1987).

The possibility that the local Las Vegas police instigated the moral panic is further suggested by the intense and sustained lobbying efforts of police organizations during that period. At county and state hearings, police representatives testified on the growing threat posed by gangs; they fostered the impression that war-weary officers were outgunned and outstaffed in street confrontations with gangbangers; they helped to draft new gang legislation and lobbied vigorously for its passage ("Senate Airs" 1991; "Senate Judiciary" 1991). In short, police representatives were extremely active in politicizing the gang problem.

There is nothing unusual about LVMPD's activity; law enforcement in the United States has always been extremely active politically (Benson 1990). The unique position of enforcement bureaucracies—easy access to legislative and executive leaders, the potential for creating social disorder, the monopoly of information about crime—grants them a great deal of political power, which they have wielded successfully to protect and advance their own interests (Ben-Yehuda 1986; Fishman 1978; Glaser 1978; Jackson and Rudman 1993; Roby 1969; Zatz 1987). Police activism invariably is accompanied by repeated references to the public safety, and certainly there is much truth to that claim. All bureaucracies, however, are subject to strong pressures to conflate public and organizational interests, particularly during periods of retrenchment or threats to legitimacy (J. Wilson 1989).

Las Vegas police operated under such pressures throughout the 1980s. A deep and prolonged recession early in the decade forced hiring freezes and reductions in operating budgets in law enforcement, as well as in other government agencies across the state (Nevada Employment Security Department 1983). Even after economic recovery in 1983, wary public officials continued to exercise tight fiscal policies for fear of being caught unprepared once again. By 1987, because of this situation and a population boom during the decade, the officer-civilian ratio in Las Vegas was only about half the national average ("New Positions" 1987).

In February 1988, in response to these social and economic conditions, top law enforcement officials introduced the "Four-Year Plan," an ambitious long-range budget calling for (among other things) 200 additional police officers. The requisite funding would come from four consecutive years of property tax increases, a measure to be decided by referendum in the November elections ("Metro Seeks" 1988). Over the next several months, police officials campaigned heavily to increase public awareness of the need for more officers ("LV Police" 1988). During this campaign the public was informed of the growing menace posed by criminal street gangs, largely through a steady stream of "gang-related" crimes released to the media. In November 1988, voters approved the property tax increases needed to fund the Four-Year Plan and bolster police resources in the war on gangs.

During the late 1980s, local police also faced a crisis of legitimacy, dogged by persistent allegations of police harassment, brutality, and warrantless searches (known in the LVMPD as "home visits") ("Police Trample" 1990). The number of citizens' complaints filed against LVMPD officers skyrocketed from less than 300 in 1984 to nearly 900 in 1989. Alleged victims of police brutality—transients and tourists, prostitutes and preachers, cab drivers and corporate attorneys—also received increased media coverage (figure 1). Across the valley, police lawlessness was denounced in organized rallies featuring nationally known speakers such as Jesse Jackson, Angela Davis, and Nation of Islam leader Louis Farrakhan ("Farrakhan" 1990). Organizations such as the NAACP and ACLU filed numerous suits seeking redress in federal courts.

Revelations of the gang menace in the late 1980s directed the public attention back to the streets and away from the police department. Local media coverage of police misconduct moved from the front page, to be replaced by stories of drive-bys, turf wars, and drug deals. Suddenly the police were once again the "good guys," arresting gangbangers, busting crack houses, and generally making the world safe again for decent people. In keeping with moral panics, the threat posed by gangs overshadowed other social problems.

Gangs and Morality

The above discussion suggests that the local police department created and sustained a moral panic to obtain needed resources and to repair a badly tarnished image. The District Attorney's Office also supported the panic, in part because of a genuine concern about gang crime, but also because its association with the gang panic brought funding for additional staff attorneys (Lucherino 1995).

The emotional intensity that defines a moral panic, however, derives not from perceptions of physical danger per se but from more fundamental threats to the "moral-symbolic universe" (Goode and Ben-Yehuda 1994). Street gang crime constitutes such a threat, much more so than crime in general. Gangs are the most visible manifestation of a subculture typically associated with the underclass found in inner cities across the country (Anderson 1990; W. Wilson 1987). The values and lifestyle of the underclass are perceived as antithetical to those of the larger community, and its apparent resistance to state and market-oriented interventions has only intensified public fear and anger (Magnet 1993). Gangs have become the media icons of the underclass, flaunting the values perceived to be endemic to the underclass culture itself: the glorification of violence, the rejection of the work ethic, irresponsible sexuality, and drug abuse. Gangs' rejection of mainstream culture is accentuated by their street language, their manner of dress, and their music.

Thus it is not surprising that gangs provoke such hostility in the public. More disturbing, however, are perceptions that the gang culture is diffusing into the middle class. White middle-class youths now routinely "play the dozens," the highly stylized, sexually explicit repartee traditionally engaged in primarily by lower-class black males (Majors and Billson 1991). White youths who talk and dress black have become so common as to constitute a new hybrid of American teenagers, known on the streets as "wiggers" (Bernstein 1995). Rap or "gangsta" music, inspired by and reflecting the deprivations of the inner city, now finds its largest market among white youths despite their parents' denunciation of its angry, violent, and misogynistic lyrics (Nelson 1995). Gangster clothes—baggy pants, Pendleton-type wool shirts, and starter jackets—are the rage on junior high school and high school campuses across the country; mainstream retailers now offer a full line of "ghetto wear" for those who seek the pretense of oppression. In effect, today's celebration of the gang culture by middle-class youths is blurring moral boundaries and fostering "in-group" deviance even in the best-ordered communities.

CONCLUSIONS AND IMPLICATIONS

On the basis of the sources examined here, we believe it is fair to conclude that events in Las Vegas during the late 1980s and early 1990s indeed constituted a moral panic. Street gangs, composed primarily of Hispanic and African-American males, became the focus of intense concern and hostility throughout the community. The crisis came suddenly, then disappeared almost as quickly as it had emerged. Despite its relatively brief duration, the intensity expressed at the height of the gang panic had a significant and enduring impact on the community: an expansion of social control agencies, new legislation, metal detectors on school campuses, more liberal juvenile certification procedures, and a proliferation of public and private antiviolence programs targeting at-risk youths.

The actual threat posed by gangs, however, was less real than imagined. Two specific findings reported here support this claim. First, despite an increase in the proportion of charges attributed to gang members during the period, court data reveal that this figure never exceeded 15 percent for any type of violent crime. Second, and contrary to law enforcement claims, gangs played only a minor role in the Las Vegas drug market: Not even 4 percent of charges filed for drug sales from 1989 to 1994 involved known gang members.

Even so, the figures presented here suggest that gang-related crime increased during the period; thus, perhaps, the response by authorities was proportionate to the objective threat. The proportion of violent crime attributable to gangs more than doubled, increasing from 6 percent in 1988 to 14 percent in 1993. Whether these numbers constitute a "wave" of gang crime is debatable. We believe, however, that such figures greatly exaggerate the actual level of gang members' criminal activity during those years.

Because law enforcement officials in Las Vegas use a "member-based" definition, the levels of "gang-related" crime during the period are almost certainly overstated. Furthermore, as in most jurisdictions across the country, the method by which offenders are identified as "gang members" in Las Vegas is highly questionable; as a result, marginal gang members or "wannabes" are placed on official lists of known gang members (Huff 1990). According to GIS officers in Las Vegas, distinctions among minority males—who is a gang member and who is not—can be made accurately on the basis of clothing (e.g., "saggy pants"); monikers (a nickname given by the gang; this is usually written on the inside of a baseball cap, standard headware for gang members); and hand signs ("a manipulation of the hands, arms and fingers to form a cryptic message") (Hartung and Roberts 1993:26). Though they may have originated in gangs, such dress, sobriquets, and gestures are no longer confined to those groups. The glamorization of the gang culture through music and movies has popularized certain mannerisms and styles of clothing once peculiar to street gangs. Consequently the markers used to identify gang members are no longer valid. In certain neighborhoods, residents may even feel pressured to adopt certain styles or colors for defensive purposes, to avoid being mistaken for rival gang members.

Other identifiers are equally suspect. According to a federal public defender in Las Vegas, a veteran of several high-profile gang cases, "minorities are often identified and entered into the record as gang members or associates, without being informed, simply because they happen to be in the company of a known gang member, and that member probably got labeled in a similar fashion" (F. Forsman, September 30, 1995, personal communication). In subsequent contact with police, she added, such persons are often genuinely surprised to find that they have been placed in LVMPD's "gang file." The problem of overlabeling gang members is further indicated by the comments of a gang unit officer who asserted, "It is safe to assume that when you run across a young, black drug dealer, he's probably a gang member" ("Police Units" 1986). This mindset makes the problem of "false negatives" (gang crime not labeled as such) seem unlikely. Coupled with organizational pressures to identify and respond to gangs, such stereotypes make it likely that a young minority male would be labeled a gang member.

Our suspicions regarding the official data on gang-related crime were confirmed by sources in the District Attorney's Office. The chief deputy prosecutor admitted that he was not "comfortable" with the way LVMPD labeled gang members, and suggested that we "take whatever numbers they give you and divide them by two" (W. T. Koot, August 30, 1995, personal communication). In view of the problems surrounding the identification and labeling of gang members, a "ripple," not a wave, may be a better characterization of the trend in gang activity during the period examined. The additional resources allocated to police and prosecution agencies during those years, as well as the organizational restructuring within those agencies, thus appear to be vastly disproportionate to the objective threat posed by gangs.

The infrequency with which antigang legislation was used during those years also suggests that the threat from gangs was exaggerated. For example, under the Gang Enhancement Statute, the most forceful of the laws, only 18 defendants were convicted from 1991 to 1994. Given the alleged magnitude and nature of the threat posed by criminal street gangs, why was the law not used more frequently and more effectively? According to criminal justice officials interviewed for this study, supporters of the statute made assumptions about gangs that simply proved to be false. Lawmakers had been influenced strongly by media stereotypes of gangs as highly organized, routinely violent, and dominating illicit markets in drugs and weapons. The language of the Gang Enhancement Statute targeted this type of criminal organization. In the course of prosecuting gangs, however, prosecutors discovered that the reality of gangs was far from the stereotype. Gangs were not "criminal enterprises" but simply loose, shifting associations without stable leadership, role expectations, or collective goals. In most cases processed, "gang crime" amounted to little more than the impulsive acts of marginal persons attempting to gain immediate, easy, *individual* short-term pleasure. Nor have officials "cracked down" on gang members who commit conventional street crimes. In Las Vegas, gang defendants actually stand a greater chance than nongang defendants that the charges against them will be dismissed. If prosecuted and convicted, they are less likely to be sentenced to prison (Miethe and McCorkle 1997).

Law enforcement officials figured prominently in the creation of such a stereotype, and in the moral panic itself. The timing of the panic corresponded to a vigorous public campaign aimed at bolstering police resources, a campaign hindered by perceptions of lawlessness and violence within the police department itself. The "discovery" of a gang problem in the late 1980s diverted public attention from ongoing police scandals, and also provided a justification for increased agency budgets. Officially acknowledging a gang problem might discourage tourists from visiting Las Vegas and injure LVMPD's efforts to obtain additional revenues. That risk, however, was probably minimized; gangs and tourism appeared to coexist in Los Angeles, only a short drive away (Huff 1990).

In addition, law enforcement officials certainly believed that the politicization of gangs served the public interest; many abhorrent and irrational acts of violence, in fact, were committed by offenders with gang affiliations. Yet the threat posed to the community by such persons was subject to interpretation, and it is generally accepted that the function and interests of any organization necessarily influence the manner in which its members perceive, interpret, and respond to the environment (Edelman 1988; J. Wilson 1989). Moreover, in many organizations, and certainly in law enforcement, the development of expertise leads to a sense of dedication that often is erroneously identified with the public interest (Niskanen 1971). Thus, in short, bureaucrats attempting to protect and advance the organization's interests can "easily persuade themselves of the rationality and morality of their appeals" (Edelman 1988:22).

Despite the nature of organizational behavior, generalizations from this study to other jurisdictions can only be speculative. Estimates regarding the prevalence and activity of gangs will be affected by the distinctive political and economic environments in which law enforcement agencies operate. Conditions in one jurisdiction may exert pressure to overestimate the problem; in another, circumstances may dictate a "denial" of any gang problem (Huff 1990).

A necessary, but not sufficient, condition for a moral panic is some level of public fear toward certain minority groups, which Goode and Ben-Yehuda (1994) call the "raw material" for moral panics. Because of the tremendous growth of minority populations in Nevada during the 1980s, the raw material for the crisis was in ample supply; a scratch probably would have been sufficient to ignite the moral panic examined here. During the decade, the number of unemployed black and Hispanic males age 16 to 24 in Las Vegas nearly doubled (U.S. Bureau of the Census 1983, 1992). Nonetheless, according to the moral panic concept, public concern about such "threatening" populations would have remained at the level of general unease without the activities of claimsmakers.

In this regard we believe that the concept of moral panic may be useful in refining the "threat hypothesis" (Liska 1992), an essentially objectivist perspective that posits a link between the growth of minority populations and the expansion of social control agencies. Missing from the threat hypothesis is a comprehensive examination of the "sequence of events by which threatening acts, people, and distributions of people influence social control . . . why specific acts, people, and distributions of people are perceived as threatening" (Liska 1992:176). The moral panic concept provides this level of analysis by examining how control agencies advance their political and organizational interests by labeling certain groups as "threatening" to the community. By ignoring the social construction of threatening populations, the threat hypothesis remains unembedded in more general theories of social structure and social process.

Although generalizations from this study are limited, we can say that law enforcement agencies, like organizations in general, struggle constantly to maintain legitimacy and to protect and increase the flow of resources (Meyer and Rowan 1983). In that struggle, the pursuit of organizational interests can easily obscure the public good. The findings of this study clearly show that in addition to responding to crime, law enforcement agencies are involved in the social construction of crime itself. Law enforcement, in some sense, creates the demand for its services; therefore we cannot discount the possibility that gangs are the object of a moral panic in other jurisdictions.

References

Albonetti, C., J. Hauser, J. Hagan, and I. Nagel. 1989. "Criminal Justice Decision-Making as a Stratification Process: The Role of Race and Stratification Resources in Pretrial Release." *Journal of Quantitative Criminology* 5:57–82.

Anderson, E. 1990. *Street Wise: Race, Class, and Change in an Urban Community.* Chicago: University of Chicago Press.

Beckett, K. 1994. "Setting the Public Agenda: 'Street Crime' and Drug Use in American Politics." *Social Problems* 41:425–47.

Benson, B. L. 1990. *The Enterprise of Law: Justice without the State.* San Francisco: Pacific Research Institute.

Ben-Yehuda 1963, cited p. 22.

Ben-Yehuda, N. 1986. "The Sociology of Moral Panics: Toward a New Synthesis." *Sociological Quarterly* 27:495–513.

Bernstein, N. 1995. "Goin' Gangsta, Choosin' Cholita." *Utne Reader* 68:87–90.

Black, D. 1971. "The Social Organization of Arrest." *Stanford Law Review* 23:63–77.

Center for Survey Research. 1989. Department of Sociology, University of Nevada at Las Vegas.

Cohen, S. 1972. *Folk devils and Moral Panics: The Creation of the Mods and Rockers.* London: MacGibbon and Kee.

Committee on Judiciary, 1991. "Minutes of the Joint Senate and Assembly Committee on Judiciary." February 13, 1991. Mimeographed copy.

Decker, S. and K. Kempf-Leonard. 1995. "Constructing Gangs: The Social Definition of Youth Activities." Pp. 112–37 in *The Modern Gang Reader*, edited by M. Klein, C. Maxson, and J. Miller. Los Angeles: Roxbury.

Edelman, M. 1988. *Constructing the Spectacle.* Chicago: University of Chicago Press.

Esbensen, F. P. and D. Huizinga. 1993. "Gangs, Drugs, and Delinquency in a Study of Urban Youths." *Criminology* 68:262–73.

Fishman, M. 1978. "Crime Waves as Ideology." *Social Problems* 25:531–43.

Glaser, D. 1978. *Crime in Our Changing Society.* New York: Holt, Rinehart and Winston.

Goode, E. and N. Ben-Yehuda. 1994. *Moral Panics: The Social Construction of Deviance.* Cambridge, MA: Blackwell.

Gusfield, J. R. 1963. *Symbolic Crusade: Status Politics and the American Temperance Movement.* Urbana: University of Illinois Press.

Hagedorn, J. 1988. *People and Folks: Gangs, Crime, and the Underclass in a Rust Belt City.* Chicago: Lake View Press.

Hall, S., C. Critcher, T. Jefferson, J. Clark, and B. Roberts. 1978. *Policing the Crisis: Mugging, the State, and Law and Order.* London: Macmillan.

Hartung, V. and L. Roberts. 1993. "Identification of Hispanic Gangs." Las Vegas Metropolitan Police Department, (Nov/Dec).

Hepburn, J. 1978. "Race and the Decision to Arrest: An Analysis of Warrants Issued." *Journal of Research in Crime and Delinquency* 15:54–73.

Hiltgartner, S. and C. Bosk. 1988. "The Rise and Fall of Social Problems: A Public Arenas Model." *American Journal of Sociology* 94:53–78.

Hofstadter, R. 1966. *The Paranoid Style in American Politics and Other Essays.* New York: Knopf.

Huff, R. 1990. "Denial, Overreaction and Misidentification: A Postscript on Public Policy." Pp. 310–17 in *Gangs in America*, edited by R. Huff. Beverly Hills: Sage.

Jackson, P. and C. Rudman, 1993. "Moral Panic and the Response to Gangs in California." Pp. 257–75 in *Gangs: The Origin and Impact of Contemporary Youth Gangs in the United States*, edited by S. Cummings and D. Monti. New York: SUNY Press.

Jenkins, P. and D. Meier-Katkin. 1992. "Satanism: Myth and Reality in a Contemporary Moral Panic." *Crime, Law and Social Change* 17:53–75.

Johnson, C., B. Webster, and E. Connors. 1995. *Prosecuting Gangs: A National Assessment.* Washington, DC: GPO.

Klein, M. 1995. *The American Street Gang: Its Nature, Prevalence, and Control.* New York: Oxford University Press.

Klein, M. and C. Maxson. 1989. "Street Gang Violence." Pp. 198–234 in *Violent Crime, Violent Criminals*, edited by M. Wolfgang and N. Weiner. Beverly Hills: Sage.

"Special Police Units Probe Gangs in Southern Nevada." 1985. *Las Vegas Sun,* May 9, p. B2.

"Group Examines Gang Problem." 1986. *Las Vegas Sun*, Mar. 13, p. B2.

"Metro Mobilizes Against LV Gangs." 1988. *Las Vegas Sun*, March 24, p. B1.

"Gang Diversion Unit Called a Success." 1988. *Las Vegas Sun*, May 3, p. B1.

"Gov. Miller Wants Gangs Outlawed." 1990. *Las Vegas Sun*, August 28, p. B1.

"Farrakhan: Stop Killing." 1990. *Las Vegas Sun*, October 22, p. B6.

"Senate Judiciary committee Considers New Anti-Gang Bill." 1991. *Las Vegas Sun*, March 6, p. B3.

"Police Units Target Increasing Gang Activity." 1986. *Las Vegas Review Journal*, April 4, p. B2.

"New Positions Cut From Metro Budget." 1987. *Las Vegas Review Journal*, February 24, p. B4.

"Metro Seeks 79.4 Million, 50 New Officers." 1988. *Las Vegas Review Journal*, February 25, p. B1.

"LV Police Urge Voters to Approve Property Tax Hike." 1988. *Las Vegas Review Journal*, August 7, p. B3.

"Bonanza Students Fear More Violence." 1989. *Las Vegas Review Journal*, March 14, p. B1.

"Eldorado Teen Gunned Down: Gunfire Erupts in Gang-Related Cafeteria Fight." 1990. *Las Vegas Review Journal*, August 27, p. B1.

"Police Trample Rules in Searches." 1990. *Las Vegas Review Journal*, September 18, p. B1.

"Senate Airs Metro-Designed Bill to Target Crimes Committed By Gangs." 1991. *Las Vegas Review Journal*, February 2, p. B1.

Liska, A. 1992. "Developing Theoretical Issues." Pp. 165–90 in *Social Threat and Social Control*, edited by A. Liska. New York: SUNY Press.

Lucherini, R. 1991. "Gang Unit Proposal." Clark County District Attorney Office. Mimeographed document.

Magnet, M. 1993. *The Dream and the Nightmare: The Sixties' Legacy to the Underclass*. New York: William Morrow.

Majors, R. and J. M. Billson. 1991. *Cool Pose: The Dilemmas of Black Manhood in America*. New York: Lexington Books.

Manis, J. 1974. "The Concept of Social Problems: Vox Populi and Sociological Analysis." *Social Problems* 21:305–15.

Maxson, C., M. Gordon, and M. Klein. 1985. "Differences between Gang and Nongang Homicides." *Criminology* 23:209–22.

Maxson, C., M. Klein, and L. Cunningham. 1992. "Defining Gang Crime: Revisited." Presented at the meetings of the Western Society of Criminology, San Diego.

Meyer, J. and B. Rowan. 1983. "Institutionalized Organizations: Formal Structure as Myth and Ceremony." Pp. 199–215 in *Organizational Environments: Ritual and Rationality*, edited by J. Meyer and W. Scott. Beverly Hills: Sage.

Miethe, T. 1987. "Charging and Plea Bargaining Practices under Determinate Sentencing: An Investigation of the Hydraulic Displacement of Discretion." *Journal of Criminal Law and Criminology* 78:155–76.

Miethe, T. and R. McCorkle. 1997. "Gang Membership and Criminal Processing: A Test of the 'Master Status' Concept." *Justice Quarterly* 14:407–427.

Miller, W. 1990. "Why the United States Has Failed to Solve Its Youth Gang Problem." Pp. 263–87 in *Gangs in America*, edited by R. Huff. Beverly Hills: Sage.

Nelson, H. 1995. "Hip-Hop Jumps Cultural Lines." *Billboard* (November), p. 34.

Nerlander, D. and J. Ferguson. 1990. "Street Gangs." Unpublished manuscript. Research Division of the Legislative Counsel Bureau, Carson City, NV.

Nevada Employment Security Department. 1983. *Economic Update*. Quarterly Report. Carson City: Nevada Employment Sec. Department.

Niskanen, W. A., Jr. 1971. *Bureaucracy and Representative Government*. Chicago: Aldine.

Petersilia, J. 1985. "Racial Disparities in the Criminal Justice System: A Summary." *Crime and Delinquency* 31:15–34.

Pope, C. E. 1978. "Post-Arrest Release Decisions: An Empirical Examination of Social and Legal Criteria." *Journal of Research in Crime and Delinquency* 15:35–53.

Roby, P. 1969. "Politics and Criminal Law: Revision of the New York State Penal Law on Prostitution." *Social Problems* 17:83–109.

Smith, D. and C. Visher. 1981. "Street-Level Justice: Situational Determinants of Police Arrest Decisions." *Social Problems* 29:167–77.

Smith, D., C. Visher, and L. Davidson. 1984. "Equity and Discretionary Justice: The Influence of Race on Police Arrest Decisions." *Journal of Criminal Law and Criminology* 75:234–49.

Spector, M. and J. Kitsuse. 1973. "Social Problems: A Reformulation." *Social Problems* 21:145–59.

Spergel, I. A. 1984. "Violent Gangs in Chicago: In Search of Social Policy." *Social Service Review* 58:199–226.

———. 1995. *The Youth Gang Problem: A Community Approach.* New York: Oxford University Press.

Thornberry, T., A. Lizotte, M. Krohn, M. Farnsworth, and S. Joon Jang. 1994. "Delinquent Peers, Beliefs, and Delinquent Behavior: A Longitudinal Test of Interactional Theory." *Criminology* 32:47–83.

Tracy, P. 1987. "Race and Class Differences in Official and Self-Reported Delinquency." Pp. 87–121 in *From Boy to Man, from Delinquency to Crime,* edited by M. Wolfgang, T. Thornberry, and R. Figlio. Chicago: University of Chicago Press.

Trebach, A. S. 1982. *The Heroin Solution.* New Haven: Yale University Press.

U.S. Bureau of the Census. 1983. *Census of the Population, 1980.* Washington, D.C.: U.S. Government Printing Office.

———. 1992. *Census of the Population, 1990.* Washington, D.C.: U.S. Government Printing Office.

Waddington, P. A. J. 1986. "Mugging as moral Panic: A Question of Proportion." *British Journal of Sociology* 37:245–59.

Wilson, J. Q. 1989. *Bureaucracy: What Government Agencies Do and Why They Do It.* New York: Basic Books.

Wilson, W. J. 1987. *The Truly Disadvantaged.* Chicago: University of Chicago Press.

Zatz, M. 1987. "Chicago Youth Gangs and Crime: The Creation of a Moral Panic." *Contemporary Crisis* 11:129–58.

Youth Violence
Prevention, Intervention, and Social Policy

C. Ronald Huff

Although most violent crime in the United States is committed by adults, juveniles also are far too often involved in violent behavior, with more than 15 percent of those arrested for violent crimes being under 18 years of age (U.S. Department of Justice, 2002), as well as 9 percent of all *known* homicide offenders (Centers for Disease Control and Prevention, 2002). We also know that those in gangs are disproportionately responsible for the violence attributable to youths in our society (Esbensen and Huizinga, 1993; Thornberry et al., 1993; Huff, 1996). Moreover, in the 1990s, homicide became the second leading cause of death for adolescents ages 15–19 in the United States—and the leading cause of death for African-American male adolescents (Centers for Disease Control and Prevention, 2002). The apparent "epidemic of youth violence" that occurred between 1983 and 1993 prompted calls for the adoption of a public health perspective on the part of scholars (see, for example, Prothrow-Stith, 1995) and policymakers alike.

In addressing the problem of youth violence, several important points must be noted. First, violent behavior by youths is a complex phenomenon that results from multiple factors. Therefore, it is important that we approach the problem of youth violence from multiple perspectives and disciplines, because violence stems from multiple sources of risk including

Prepared especially for *American Youth Gangs at the Millennium* by C. Ronald Huff.

neurobiological, individual, family, neighborhood, ecological, and socio-economic factors (see, for example, Flannery and Huff, 1999).

Second, we must view violence as occurring along a developmental continuum. Different points along this continuum represent different opportunities for prevention or intervention efforts (Loeber, et al., 1991). Longitudinal research suggests that there are at least two different kinds of life-course trajectories leading to violence—early onset (violence beginning prior to puberty) and late onset (violence beginning after puberty, or around age 13). These two life-course trajectories have very different implications for prevention and intervention strategies, as noted in the U.S. Surgeon General's (2001) report on youth violence. Youths who become violent before about age 13 generally commit more crimes, and more serious crimes, for a longer period of time. Their violence tends to escalate throughout childhood and sometimes continues into their adult years.

Third, an integrated, systematic, longer-term approach that includes multiple disciplines and intercedes at multiple levels is necessary if we are to have sustainable and generalizable change. We will not effectively prevent or substantially ameliorate youth violence if we depend on rigid approaches from any single perspective.

The recent report by the Surgeon General (2001) summarized some of the major findings from the extant research on youth violence and set forth important policy and programmatic recommendations for addressing the problem. In addition to the finding noted above concerning two different life-cycle trajectories, some other major findings and conclusions of the report were:

- Most youth violence begins in adolescence and ends with the transition into adulthood;
- Most highly aggressive children or children with behavioral disorders do not become serious violent offenders;
- Surveys consistently find that about 30 to 40 percent of male youths and 15 to 30 percent of female youths report having committed a serious violent offense by age 17;
- Serious violence is part of a lifestyle that includes drugs, guns, precocious sex, and other risky behaviors. Youths involved in serious violence often commit many other types of crimes and exhibit other problem behaviors, presenting a serious challenge to intervention efforts. Successful interventions must confront not only the violent behavior of these young people but also their lifestyles, which are teeming with risk;
- The differences in patterns of serious violence by age of onset and the relatively constant rates of individual offending have important implications for prevention and intervention programs. Early childhood programs that target at-risk children and families are critical

for preventing the onset of a chronic violent career, but programs must also be developed to combat late-onset violence; and

- The importance of late-onset violence prevention is not widely recognized or well understood. Substantial numbers of serious violent offenders emerge in adolescence without warning signs in childhood. A comprehensive community prevention strategy must address both onset patterns and ferret out their causes and risk factors (Surgeon General, 2001).

IMPLICATIONS FOR PREVENTION

A great deal of violent behavior is learned behavior. In reviewing the extant literature on violence, it is clear that a substantial body of empirical research has demonstrated that violence for most individuals is learned behavior (Eron et al., 1971; Bandura, 1973; Lefkowitz et al., 1977). Biological factors, of course, also play an important role (Raine, 2002). In fact, recent research has shown that chronic exposure to violence and victimization from violence can directly alter neural pathways and impact the ways in which a child reacts to threatening stimuli (Osofsky, 1997).

If we accept the fact that violent behavior is, for the most part, learned behavior, then this has significant implications for prevention and intervention. Parents can be taught to be more effective monitors of their children's whereabouts, thus decreasing a child's opportunity to commit violent acts (and to risk being victimized). Adults can be taught that relying on aggressive discipline only tends to teach children over time that aggression is acceptable by "modeling" that behavior for them. Parents can be better informed about the impact of abuse and neglect on children. Children can be taught social competence and problem-solving skills that will improve their ability to resolve conflicts (Embry et al., 1996). Aggressive children can be taught to reinterpret neutral or ambiguous environmental cues in a less hostile way. Even at-risk and delinquent youth can be taught strategies that can improve their anger control and enhance their pro-social skills (Goldstein, 1999).

Aggression is generally stable and chronic. Aggression is a relatively stable, self-perpetuating behavior that often begins early in life for children who get into fights, do not get along well with their peers (and may be actively rejected by their peers), and demonstrate poor impulse control and poor frustration tolerance. They are often bullies at school and in play groups. They should not be ignored, and their behavior should not be dismissed as "typical" or "expected" ("boys will be boys"). Although certainly not all children who are in this group grow up to be violent adolescents, the majority of violent adolescents, in retrospect, are discovered to have been part of this group of youths who felt rejected and responded aggressively.

Prevention must be multilevel and multifaceted. As noted above, violent behavior is complex and results from multiple factors. Therefore, effective prevention and intervention efforts must address risk at multiple levels. They need to include families and peers, and they should address a child's psychological needs as well as school adjustment difficulties. Where possible, they also should address the neighborhood disorganization and ecological contexts that affect the child.

Prevention and intervention efforts need to be systematic and long-term. Programs need to last at least two years before they demonstrate significant, sustainable change in youth behavior (Yoshikawa, 1994). Primary prevention efforts, such as those that target an entire classroom without labeling any individual child, are very important and often represent the best single investment we can make (see, for example, Gottfredson, 1986; Gottfredson et al., 2002). However, they cannot adequately address the complex needs of high-risk children, so we need to include interventions for those youths as well. An example of how to do this is to offer a primary prevention program in the schools, for example, while at the same time offering training for parents of at-risk youths and group or individual interventions for youths already identified as aggressive or delinquent.

IMPLICATIONS FOR INTERVENTION

For those interventions at the individual level, it is very important to have a good developmental history of the youth, as well as a good understanding of the risk factors that the child faces and his or her relationships and functioning in different kinds of settings. This is essential, since risk for violence is often identifiable at an early age and is affected by parenting and the parent-child relationship. Peer-group affiliation, including gangs of course, is a very important factor to be considered because of its tremendous influence on the decisions and behaviors of young people.

In addition, reducing risk or managing aggressive behavior will not be as effective, in the longer-term, as interventions that focus on building social competence, improving pro-social and problem-solving skills, and teaching a youth how to resolve conflicts. Developing a youth's skills in these areas can result in lifelong "tools," as opposed to short-term behavioral change. It is also highly desirable to work with families whenever possible, since they can either positively or negatively reinforce the desired behavioral changes. As desirable as macrolevel changes would be, it is not necessary to make radical changes in a youth's neighborhood, social status, or economic conditions in order to improve that child's home environment and social networks. It is also important to work with the school to help reinforce the skills that we want to instill in the child.

IMPLICATIONS FOR SOCIAL POLICY

Isn't it ironic that our nation's future depends on the healthy, pro-social development of our youths but we have no national youth policy per se? Moreover, we need to ask ourselves whether our communities or our states have anything that we could reasonably call "youth policy"—policy that attempts to address the developmental needs of our youths in a coordinated, integrated manner that *cuts across* bureaucracies, agencies, and jurisdictions. Instead, we have developed policies and programs (often with categorical funding requirements that ignore the holistic needs of our youths) that are fragmented and are largely designed to establish systems of social control to which youths (and often their families) can be assigned only *after* they have come to society's attention as "failures." By then, of course, it is often too late.

The effectiveness of these systems of social control (such as social welfare, prosecution, courts, corrections) is generally limited. Moreover, although we have begun to learn that the most cost-effective approaches to health care focus heavily on *prevention*, we have not yet learned to appreciate that fact in the juvenile and criminal justice systems, where we persist in spending vastly disproportionate amounts of public funds to finance expensive new correctional institutions. We have focused far too heavily on that end of the continuum. In a recent speech to the American Bar Association discussing incarceration in the United States, Supreme Court Justice Anthony Kennedy commented, in part:

> . . . Consider its remarkable scale. The nationwide inmate population is 2.1 million people. In countries such as England, Italy, France, and Germany, the incarceration rate is about one in 1,000 persons. In the United States it is about one in 143. (Kennedy, 2003)

In addition, the funding of expensive correctional facilities and their staffing and operations is coming increasingly at the expense of state education budgets, leading to a circularity by which the quality of education continues to erode, leading to poorly prepared students and potentially more costs related to social welfare and crime which, in turn, leads to a call for even more correctional facilities and other expensive systems of social control. What, then, can we do?

Strengthen neighborhoods and communities by implementing the "Communities That Care" approach advocated by Hawkins and Catalano (1992). Many of the problems associated with youth violence have important linkages to communities and neighborhoods that are often described as "disorganized." The social and economic isolation of some neighborhoods can have criminogenic effects, and these are made worse by a society in which the individual, rather than the community, is emphasized; an economy that focuses on individual companies and individual workers rather than their families and their communities; and a political system that pays little attention to those living in marginal socioeconomic circumstances with little political influence.

Consider some of the data concerning important socioeconomic "facts of life" in the contemporary United States. According to the U.S. Census Bureau's 2001 Supplementary Survey (U.S. Bureau of the Census, 2002), an estimated 12 percent of the population were living in poverty and 16 percent of related children under 18 were living in poverty. Nine percent of all families were below the poverty level and, even worse, 27 percent of all female-headed single-parent families present lived in poverty. Another important factor contributing to poverty is lack of education. Among those 25 and older, only 82 percent have completed a high school education. The fact that nearly one in five Americans who are 25 or older have not completed high school clearly represents a major failure in preparing citizens to find employment in an increasingly complex world.

The "Communities That Care" model developed by Hawkins and Catalano (1992) advocates a communitywide prevention focus, including prevention councils for each community. These councils are responsible for conducting prevention assessments at least every two years and establishing community task forces to help design and implement strategies to improve prevention by increasing the protective factors afforded youths living in troubled neighborhoods and in other neighborhoods as well. This model also builds on community empowerment and partnerships rather than relying on the traditional top-down method of policy development and implementation, which has generally failed.

Strengthen support for families. Our policies for health care, education, juvenile justice, social welfare, and compensation and benefits are viewed as lagging behind those of many other nations with more family-friendly approaches. The quality of U.S. health care and education is too closely tied to wealth, status, race, and ethnicity. Justice policy in the United States criminalizes many youths who are not felons and whose difficulties are often rooted in family problems that are more amenable to social service intervention.

Social welfare policies have historically provided "perverse incentives"—providing incentives for males to leave their families so that their families could receive public assistance; providing more financial assistance to foster parents than to biological parents in need of assistance; and providing incentives for young girls to become pregnant rather than to complete school and likely face bleak employment prospects. Employers in the United States generally lag behind a number of other nations' employers in developing reasonable childcare and family leave benefits. The development of a fully integrated youth policy would reconsider how all federal, state, and local policies impact families and children and would be designed to strengthen, nurture, and support them rather than fragment them and subject them to social control interventions that reflect our failures.

Strengthen our efforts to control youth access to firearms. A number of studies have shown that youths generally have fairly easy access to fire-arms (see, for example, Sheley and Wright, 1995). Compared with Canada, for example, the age-specific homicide rates for the United States are vastly higher at each age level. This means that we have far too many young murderers and young victims. Although many gun owners in Canada have not complied with that nation's licensing requirements (Jacobs, 2002: 149), Canada does indeed have more strict nationwide gun-control policies than does the United States. Because we also know that young people can obtain guns from multiple sources, it is important that in each community we determine in what ways young people are obtaining weapons and then, through collaborative efforts, develop and implement policies that will interdict these weapons and punish those responsible for providing guns to young people. Such efforts should be accompanied by well-coordinated media publicity in order to maximize the effects.

Strengthen our efforts to prevent youths from joining gangs and to assist youths who wish to desist from gang involvement. Research has consistently demonstrated that youths involved in gangs are far more extensively engaged in serious delinquent and criminal behavior than are their non-gang peers and that they are more involved in crime and delinquency while they are in the gang than either before they join or after they leave the gang (Esbensen and Huizinga, 1993; Thornberry et al., 1993). We also know that it is probably easier for gang-involved youths to leave the gang than was previously thought (Decker and Lauritsen, 2002). We should emphasize the development and implementation of public policy that dis-courages gang involvement and offers activities and incentives for pro-social activities that meet the needs of young people—the same needs that are attracting them to gangs (belonging to a peer group, having a sense of "family," fun, and "protection"—although the latter is illusory, of course, since joining the gang actually increases their risks rather than providing protection). Working with the community prevention councils, local sur-veys could be conducted to develop data to be used in planning activities and incentives for young people. At-risk youths should certainly be repre-sented in such planning groups, since programs and activities designed by adults often are not met with enthusiasm by their intended target group of young people.

Strengthen our investment in the rigorous evaluation of policy and pro-grammatic initiatives and use evaluation research to refine those initiatives. All too often, we are operating programs and following policies that have never been adequately evaluated. Why do we continue to invest public and private funds in initiatives that may not be working effectively or effi-ciently? We won't know unless we subject them to careful evaluation. Without such evaluation (and often, even with it!), decisions will be based on politics, political pressure, and anecdotes. A good general rule of thumb is that about 10% of all grants and awards for policy and programmatic initiatives ought to be set aside for evaluation. It is only in this manner that we can ever hope to pursue our goal of formulating and implementing effective youth policy at the federal, state, and local levels to address the problem of youth violence.

Again, it is critical that we bear in mind that violence results from multiple factors. That being said, it is highly unrealistic to concentrate so much of our public-policy response on suppression alone and yet, in the past decade, some of the main policy responses we have seen in our country include such things as "three strikes" sentencing for adults; "boot camps"; and waivers, or bindovers, to adult criminal court for juveniles. There are no convincing empirical data that demonstrate the effectiveness of these approaches but, like so many other popular trends, they became policy fads that swept the nation. At this time, what we need is a "coalition of the willing" in communities across the nation to develop more progressive and balanced policy approaches that lead to healthy communities where young people's developmental needs are given a high priority and where young people have hope. Such communities have a much greater chance of reducing youth violence. However, the development of these nationwide community-based initiatives takes time, and the efforts to do so must overcome a number of constraints, including legislative term limits and other pressures that focus solely on short-term actions.

A broad, community-based approach that is focused on developing "healthy communities" is consistent with the growing public health perspective on violence and its prevention. This approach depends, in part, on identifying the problem and its causes, then developing, implementing, and evaluating programs for prevention and intervention. When the data warrant, model programs can then be identified and attempts can be made to implement them, with appropriate local modifications where necessary, in other communities.

Existing research conducted by the Center for the Study and Prevention of Violence (2003) at the University of Colorado has identified a number of programs that are considered "model programs" and others that may be considered "promising programs" in need of further study. The project, called Blueprints for Violence Prevention, has thus far identified 11 prevention and intervention programs that meet a strict scientific standard of program effectiveness from among more than 600 that have been reviewed. The determination of program effectiveness is based on an initial review by the Center and a final review and recommendation from a distinguished advisory board, comprised of seven experts in the field of violence prevention. The 11 model programs are known as "blueprints," and they have been effective in reducing adolescent violent crime, aggression, delinquency, and substance abuse. Model programs currently include:

- Prenatal and infancy home visitation by nurses
- "The Incredible Years" series

- Promoting alternative thinking strategies
- Bullying prevention program
- Big Brothers/Big Sisters of America
- Life Skills Training
- Midwestern Prevention Project
- Functional family therapy
- Multisystemic therapy
- Multidimensional-treatment foster care
- Project "Towards No Drug Abuse"

Detailed descriptions of these programs can be found on the Center's Web page that is dedicated to the Blueprints program (http://www.colorado.edu/cspv/blueprints). Another 21 programs have also been identified as promising programs.

Through careful program development, based on sound developmental theory and followed by equally careful program implementation and rigorous program evaluation, we can make progress in addressing the problems posed by youth violence and youth gangs. Such progress is more likely to be made in those enlightened communities that commit themselves to a broader approach to "youth policy" that regards our youths as our most important natural resource to be developed for the good of our communities and our society. In a free democratic society such as the United States, it is vital that we socialize our youths to be responsible, law-abiding citizens, since we grant our citizens extensive freedom—freedom that can be used in either pro-social or antisocial ways.

References

Bandura, A. 1973. *Aggression: A Social Learning Analysis*. Englewood Cliffs, NJ: Prentice-Hall.

Centers for Disease Control and Prevention. 2002. *Best Practices of Youth Violence Prevention*. Atlanta, GA: Centers for Disease Control and Prevention.

Center for the Study and Prevention of Violence. 2003. *Blueprints for Violence Prevention*. Boulder, CO: Center for the Study and Prevention of Violence (http://www.colorado.edu/cspv/blueprints/).

Decker, S. H., and J. L. Lauritsen. 2002. Leaving the gang. Pp. 51–67 in C. R. Huff (ed.), *Gangs in America III*. Thousand Oaks, CA: Sage.

Embry, D., D. Flannery, and A. Vazsonyi. 1996. PeaceBuilders: A theoretically driven, school-based model for early violence prevention. *American Journal of Preventive Medicine* 12:91–100.

Eron, L. D., L. O. Walder, and M. M. Lefkowitz. 1971. *The Learning of Aggression in Children*. Boston: Little, Brown.

Esbensen, F., and D. Huizinga. 1993. Gangs, drugs, and delinquency in a survey of urban youth. *Criminology* 27:565–589.

Flannery, D. J., and C. R. Huff (eds.). 1999. *Youth Violence: Prevention, Intervention, and Social Policy*. Washington, DC: American Psychiatric Press.

Goldstein, A. P. 1999. Teaching prosocial behavior to antisocial youth. Pp. 253–273 in D. J. Flannery and C. R. Huff (eds.), *Youth Violence: Prevention, Intervention, and Social Policy.* Washington, DC: American Psychiatric Press.

Gottfredson, D. C. 1986. An empirical test of school-based environmental and individual interventions to reduce the risk of delinquent behavior. *Criminology* 24:705–731.

Gottfredson, D. C., D. B. Wilson, and S. S. Najaka. 2002. The schools. Pp. 149–189 in J. Q. Wilson and J. Petersilia (eds.), *Crime: Public Policies for Crime Control.* Oakland, CA: ICS Press.

Hawkins, J. D., and R. F. Catalano. 1992. *Communities That Care.* San Francisco: Jossey-Bass.

Huff, C. R. 1996. The criminal behavior of gang members and nongang at-risk youth. Pp. 75–102 in C. R. Huff (ed.), *Gangs in America* (2nd ed.). Thousand Oaks, CA: Sage.

Jacobs, J. B. 2002. *Can Gun Control Work?* New York: Oxford University Press.

Kennedy, A. M. 2002. Remarks to American Bar Association. San Francisco, August 2. As cited in *Criminal Justice Newsletter,* August 15, 2003, p. 2.

Lefkowitz, M. M., L. D. Eron, and L. O. Walder. 1977. *Growing Up to Be Violent.* New York: Pergamon.

Loeber, R., M. Stouthamer-Loeber, and W. B. Van Kammen. 1991. Initiation, escalation, and desistance in juvenile offending and their correlates. *Journal of Criminal Law and Criminology* 82:36–82.

Maruna, S. 1999. *Making Good: How Ex-Convicts Reform and Rebuild Their Lives.* Washington, DC: American Psychological Association.

Osofsky, J. 1996. *Children in a Violent Society.* New York: Guilford.

Prothrow-Stith, D. 1995. *Deadly Consequences.* New York: Harper Collins.

Raine, A. 2002. The biological basis of crime. Pp. 43–74 in J. Q. Wilson and J. Petersilia (eds.), *Crime: Public Policies for Crime Control.* Oakland, CA: ICS Press.

Sampson, R., and J. Laub. 1992. *Crime in the Making.* Cambridge, MA: Harvard.

Sheley, J. F., and J. D. Wright. 1995. *In the Line of Fire: Youth, Guns, and Violence in Urban America.* Hawthorne, NY: De Gruyter.

Surgeon General of the United States. 1999. *Youth Violence: A Report of the Surgeon General.* Washington, DC: U. S. Department of Health and Human Services.

Thornberry, T. P., M. D. Krohn, A. J. Lizotte, and D. Chard-Wierschem. 1993. The role of juvenile gangs in facilitating delinquent behavior. *Journal of Research in Crime and Delinquency* 30:55–87.

U. S. Bureau of the Census. 1999–2001. *Supplementary Survey.* Washington, DC: U.S. Bureau of the Census.

U. S. Department of Justice. 2002. *Crime in the United States: 2001.* Washington, DC: Federal Bureau of Investigation.

Yoshikawa, H. 1992. Prevention as a cumulative protection: Effects of early family support and education on chronic delinquency and its risks. *Psychological Bulletin* 115:28–54.

Police Youth Violence Interventions
Lessons to Improve Effectiveness

Jack R. Greene

POLICE PROBLEM SOLVING: NEW METHODS FOR OLD PROBLEMS

Crime and delinquency research has clearly established that those below the age of majority account for a sizable proportion of criminal justice problems (see Greenwood, 2002, 76–79). As youths continue to account for a significant proportion of offending and victimization, the police invariably must deal with issues involving young people.

While issues of youths and crime have clear historic roots, since the late 1960s youth crime has also taken on significant symbolic value. Beginning in the early 1960s, "youth culture" has come to be intimately connected to social problems, most especially those of crime. The "hippie," "counterculture," "drug," "gang violence," "hip hop," and "gangsta" descriptions of youth culture have contributed considerably to public fear of crime as well. For the past 40 years or so youths have been linked both overtly and symbolically to crime.

In the mid-1980s and into the mid-1990s the more generalized problems of youths and social disorder yielded to problems of youth violence,

Prepared especially for *American Youth Gangs at the Millennium* by Jack R. Greene.

most particularly gun violence (Blumstein and Rosenfield, 1998). The intersection of youthfulness, drugs, and gun violence led some to predict phenomenal increases in youth violence, in particular gang violence.

By the 1980s youth culture had become synonymous with violence, forging a strong association between real and imagined fears of youth crime. In the mid-to-late 1980s, the rise of a visibly violent youth culture called into question criminal justice and police efforts to prevent youth crime. During that period it became clear that there were significant gaps in the capacity of the police to deal with youth problems. Since the 1980s those in the criminal justice system, including the police, have become increasingly focused on youth crime and violence.

Recognizing a link between youths and crime would seem to lend great credibility for proactive police interventions with youths. Accordingly, police programs to intervene, either to prevent crime or to suppress it, were expected to gain national prominence. In spite of national awareness, however, police youth-focused programs were often poorly conceived and implemented. The history of American policing has witnessed only fragmentary attempts to effectively deal with crime and disorder among youths.

Most of the early youth interventions were associated with youth clubs emphasizing recreational and sports activities. These efforts, often seen as prevention focused, combined some sense of role modeling for youths with the more direct concern of keeping youths occupied when they were not in school. Such programs continue to the present, despite inconsistent data on their effectiveness. While the central focus of these efforts is to *prevent* youth crime, most efforts rest on incomplete or unspecified notions of youth development theories. And, it is not clear that the police are the appropriate social agency to sponsor such intervention strategies.

Since the late 1980s most police efforts have focused almost entirely on crime *suppression*, an after-the-fact youth crime-control policy. These programs often include "rousting" youths hanging out on street corners, targeting gangs for police and other legal interventions, and police "zero-tolerance" programs emphasizing a get-tough crime control policy (see Fritsch, et al., 1999; Decker and Curry, 2000; and Decker, 2003). Such practices have been largely short lived and had limited impact on youth-crime problems.

In a few places, however, more thoughtful and more likely effective approaches to youth crime and violence have emerged. How the police have approached problems of youth crime, our understanding of the effects of these interventions, and their import for police-focused crime prevention strategies are the subject of this chapter.

A shift from a reactive, suppression-oriented model of policing to one advocating partnerships and analytic problem solving has enabled the police to be more effective in dealing with many crime and disorder problems, including those associated with youths. This shift has set the stage for renewed and coordinated efforts to address chronic gang, drug, and violence problems, particularly in major American cities. This article examines two "models" on how the police deal with youthful offenders. These models contrast traditional police responses to youth violence with those that have embraced a community- and problem-oriented approach. The contrast arising from these two models and their implications is reviewed with particular concern for assessing the effectiveness and long-term viability of these approaches. To provide context for this assessment, historical and current shifts in policing are considered. Such context is important as it speaks to how policing is shifting toward more thoughtful and analytic interventions with youths.

REACTIVE POLICING AND A SHIFT TOWARD PROBLEM SOLVING

A reactive and ineffective model of law enforcement dominated policing in much of the twentieth century. Police responses to crime and victimization, whether youth related or not, were largely after-the-fact—that is, in reaction to events which had already occurred. This reactive approach was closely tied to the historical development of the police in the United States (see Kelling and Moore, 1988; Greene, 2000).

Early twentieth-century policing was influenced by the "child-saving" efforts of progressives. Youths were processed differently from adults as they were seen as in need of a form of "parental" supervision, even if that supervision was provided by juvenile courts. The police often "rounded up" wayward youths and funneled them to the court. While youths were indeed well represented among those who committed crime, police contact with youths focused mainly on infractions of the law. Otherwise, youths who contributed to social disturbances or lower-level crime were often given a "swift kick in the seat of the pants" and returned home. Youth-serving programs were just emerging and not well focused, and as a consequence police efforts to "prevent" youth crime were unorganized and never matured.

By the 1950s the police had emerged institutionally by separating themselves from local politics (as best as possible), and by adopting a "professional" ideology suggesting a social and clinical distance from their "clients." Prevention was largely the by-product of individual and general deterrence assumptions wherein the police, in their deployment and rapid response to crime situations, were thought to also prevent crime, particularly among youths. (Either you were deterred from committing a crime for fear of the police catching you, or you were caught.) This reactive model dominated policing between the 1940s and the 1980s and continues to influence policing to this day. Institutionally the police have "sold" the public on the model of crime suppression and deterrence and are often hard pressed to abandon it, even in the face of poor results.

Despite the tendency of the police to cling to the past model of reactive response, nearly 50 years of research suggests that reactive and generalized policing simply doesn't work (see Cordner and Hale, 1992). Responding to calls for service without understanding their genesis and providing a generalized roving patrol capacity alone do not reduce crime and disorder, nor are they clearly associated with fear reduction. While this style of policing had the appearance of efficiency and effectiveness (see Manning, 1977), the day-to-day reality of policing was much less impressive—the police were neither effective nor efficient.

To one degree or another, by the 1980s American policing had become a singular response to complex and multiple problem sets. In many ways policing had a "one-size-fits-all" philosophy; roving patrol, rapid response, and follow-up criminal investigations were the mainstay of this approach. Consequently, policing efforts more often missed than hit their intended marks.

THE RISE OF COMMUNITY-ORIENTED AND PROBLEM-ORIENTED POLICING

Community- and problem-oriented policing (commonly referred to as COP and POP, respectively) have shifted the dominant paradigm of American policing from reactive to proactive, distant to involved, process to results oriented, and from addressing generalized problems (crime) to specific problems (e.g., robbery) or locations where specific problems are located (neighborhoods or business locations) (see Greene, 2000). Such a shift in focus and response provides police with an opportunity to develop strategies and tactics that differ by the nature of the problems addressed.

Problem- and community-oriented policing focus on developing in-depth understanding of a wide range of crime, disorder, and fear problems and then crafting responses to those problems, focusing specifically on the particular characteristics of these differing problems. In each case—problem definition and response—the complexity of the problem and the solution to the problem are central concerns. Understanding the problem's complexity should lead to an individualized solution that addresses each problem as unique. In turn, knowing the range of problems and their complexity should lead to a range of more complex police interventions.

Understanding this complexity, and therefore being more successful in addressing problems, is thought to be a major incentive for police agencies to adopt community- and problem-oriented policing as a central way of "doing business." However, after nearly 20 years of development, community- and problem-oriented policing still struggle for footing within many police agencies (for a review of the process and adoption problems see Goldstein, 2003).

Community-oriented policing has sought to mobilize the community and other invested institutions to address the problems of crime, disorder, and fear (for a review see Greene, 2000). COP has focused efforts on building coalitions of effort that bridge the multiple agencies serving the public and that touch on issues of crime and victimization, especially those involving youths.

From the perspective of the police, COP is an outreach strategy—focused on building external alliances that both report and amplify crime and disorder problems, while at the same time providing support for their resolution. From the perspective of external others, COP is a strategy of investment (social, institutional, and community) where the community at large takes some responsibility for addressing crime and disorder.

Community-oriented policing programs have the effect of broadening the institutional reach of the police as formal agents of social control. At the same time, COP has the benefit of including others as partners to more effectively address youth-crime problems. These others include a wide array of formal and informal social control agents.

Central to the philosophies and practice of COP is the idea that such coalition building strengthens a community's capacity to prevent, deter, or suppress crime. While it may take a village to raise a child, that same village is central to supervising and controlling that child as well.

In contrast to COP, problem-oriented policing has as its root the recognition that for policing to be effective it must be intelligent and analytic (see Goldstein, 1990). Historically, police were organized as a response-based system, largely activated by the public. While much of policing remains response-driven to this day, problem solving has interjected an analytic framework focused on four discrete analytic and evaluative elements. Collectively, these four problem-solving elements frame the analytic requirements of "good policing" (Goldstein, 2003). The problem-solving process has been linked to the *"SARA"* (scanning, analysis, response, assessment) model emphasizing the application of a scientific approach to policing (Eck and Spelman, 1987).

Scanning, a process of environmental assessment, is an externally focused attempt to glean information about the causes and conditions that lead to crime and disorder problems. Scanning is meant to be broadly focused, not only on the crime problems in any location but also on other social or economic conditions that support or give rise to the crime or disorder problems witnessed. It suggests that the police should assess social problems from a multivariate perspective, as a means to better understand crime and other social linkages to it. Scanning also has implications for identifying those in the environment who might be useful in providing solutions to problems the police encounter.

Following scanning activities, police agencies operating within a problem-solving framework should *analyze* closely the crime or disorder problem they are encountering. This is seen as a data-driven exercise, where discrete crime or disorder problems are analytically illuminated and analyzed. Sophisticated computer analysis and crime-mapping regimes, now commonplace in U.S. police agencies, focus on understanding the local dynamics of the identified problem.

Once analyses are completed they should lead to a *response* mode, where police and other resources are brought to bear on the identified problem. The response mode in problem solving seeks a targeted response to a targeted problem set. Rather than the generalized patrol strategies the police have used in the past, problem-solving responses are thought to lead to better and more direct police interventions—generally involving other agencies or communities.

Finally, *assessment* is an important component of problem solving, focusing on the effect(s) of the intervention selected—the response. The thought is that if the police are to become more effective in dealing with crime and disorder problems, they must subject their tactics and interventions to close scrutiny to better understand the effects over a wide array of problems. One can think of the police as building a problem-solving repertory of interventions, linking problems with interventions that have a higher probability of success (see Knuttson, 2003). Figure 1 presents the problem-solving model and the focus of each of its stages.

Figure 1   The SARA Model for Problem Solving (adapted from Eck and Spelman, 1987)

Stage	Focus	Data
Scanning ⟶	External environment	Social/economic/demographic/ crime and delinquency
Analysis ⟶	Specifically identified problem	Crime pattern/time location/ offender/victim
Response ⟶	Range of appropriate responses	Benchmarks from other programs
Assessment ⟶	Implemented program	Program/process and outcome

It can be said that problem solving has brought an analytic rigor to policing that has been historically absent. Such analytic thinking has led to a consideration of the causal chains within which the police seek to operate (see Greene, 2003).

Figure 2 presents a simple cause-and-effect model used to identify points where interventions can occur. Such a model is often used to determine appropriate places for medical interventions. Extrapolating this model to police interventions with youths suggests that a primary intervention—called *prevention*—typically occurs between the preconditions that give rise to the problem and its proximate (or closest) associated cause (see Greene, 2003).

Youth interventions may focus on identifying youths from high-risk families or youths with social or behavioral problems that may indicate "risk factors" potentially leading to delinquency and crime. There is con-

---

Figure 2 Levels of Police Intervention (adapted from Suchman, 1968; Greene, 1998; Greene, 2003)

Preconditions ⟶ Proximate Cause ⟶ Effects ⟶ Consequences

Primary intervention
(prevention)

Secondary intervention
(treatment)

Tertiary intervention
(rehabilitation)

---

siderable criminological literature identifying such risk factors (for a review see Farrington, 2002) that seeks to increase youth "protective" factors as a way of preventing youth crime and delinquency.

At the secondary level, called *treatment*, an intervention is sought between the proximate causes of the behavior or problem and its effects. Focus is on treating problems once they have occurred as opposed to preventing them. The police have been most focused within the treatment intervention arena. At this stage, youth-focused efforts are almost entirely suppression or deterrence oriented, emphasizing saturated patrol, follow-up criminal investigations, and/or youth/gang intervention teams.

The last point of intervention depicted in figure 2 is a *tertiary intervention* focused on rehabilitation. Here the focus is on the downstream consequences of the problem behavior with the view of redressing problems or repairing harm. Such activities as gang mediation, victim assistance, dispute resolution, and re-integrative strategies form the core of interventions within this category.

Using the model depicted in figure 2, it can be asserted that most police interventions are neither preventive nor rehabilitative. Rather, policing has come to largely embrace "treatment" defined rather narrowly in terms of traditional law-enforcement activities. Since these interventions address neither prevention nor rehabilitation, in all likelihood they are doomed to a cycle of repetition in that they do not address core issues about cause, nor do they address effects and consequences of delinquency and crime among youths. They are indeed "mid-range" interventions that stabilize the patient but generally ignore how he or she came to need services in the first place as well as how those services benefited (or failed to benefit) the patient. This has been the historical approach of policing youth problems. Recognizing where in the cause → effect chain the police are attempting to intervene greatly enhances their capacity for analytic problem solving. Although such thinking is beginning to shape police intervention strategies, the historical legacy of "treatment-focused" policing have yet to be overcome.

Despite difficulties in assessing appropriate points of intervention for the police, successful problem solving can be associated with several identifiable activities and focuses that collectively concentrate the analytic efforts of the police on indefinable problems or problem sets.

First, successful problem solving is clear in the specification of the target of the intervention. That target can be a neighborhood, a business district, a discrete household, a problem bar or drinking establishment, or a particular group of youths, typically those associated with gang activities.

Second, successful problem-solving efforts are clear in the interventions selected and used to address the identified problem. Here the focus is on how the police choose to intervene, either alone or in concert with others, and what they do when they intervene.

Third, problem-solving efforts that are successful appear to mobilize others for responses to complex social and criminal problems. The focus is on gathering community and other social support, as well as the resources that can be brought to bear on the identified problem. At times the police will be the lead agency for such interventions, but on many occasions they will need to play a support role to other agencies and institutions better suited to addressing the problem.

Finally, problem-solving efforts are successful to the extent that they can measure their success. Recognition that the problem is indeed solved, mitigated, or still unsolved rests largely on the ability to measure outcomes and effects. The measurement of *effort* (e.g., patrol officers assigned or calls received and dispatched) is not the same as *outcome* measurement. For problem-solving to become a mainstay of policing, outcome assessment is a priority matter (see Knuttson, 2003).

Taken together, the elements of the problem-solving process provide an analytic and data-driven framework that continues to shape policing to this day. Its application in addressing youth problems is now considered.

TWO APPROACHES TO YOUTH VIOLENCE

Recently there have been several expansions of the police role in dealing with youth problems. Contrasting two of these approaches highlights the importance of problem solving to this process. Youth interventions by police can be reactive or proactive, and they can involve primary, secondary, and tertiary interventions.

The two interventions discussed here, the Youth Firearms Violence Initiative and Boston's Gun Project, are in many ways both secondary—that is, they were both initiated by police in response to problems of youth handgun violence. Beyond this basic similarity, these two programs significantly differ in how the police approached the problem, how they defined intervention methods, and how these efforts were implemented. They also differ in long-term institutional improvements realized.

Youth Firearms Violence Initiative

In 1995 the National Institute of Justice, through the Office of Community Oriented Policing Services (COPS), launched a national program focused on youth and gun violence. The Youth Firearms Violence Initiative (YFVI) sought to demonstrate effective approaches to reducing youth gun violence in 10 American cities: Baltimore, MD; Birmingham, AL; Bridgeport, CT; Cleveland, OH; Inglewood, CA; Milwaukee, WI; Richmond, VA; Salinas, CA; San Antonio, TX; and Seattle, WA (see Dunworth, 2000; Greene et al., 1998).

The YFVI was initiated in the face of dramatic increases in youth firearms violence between 1984 and 1995, a period characterized by a decline in firearms violence among adults. The YFVI program provided up to $1 million for 10 jurisdictions to combat youth firearms violence. The sites were chosen, in part, to demonstrate various "community-policing" approaches as a means of stemming youth firearms violence, and, in part, for the level of violence they were experiencing.

While the YFVI program varied considerably across these cities, its focus was on:

- separating kids from guns,
- reducing gun violence among youth,
- stimulating innovative police interventions, and
- broadening range of police interventions.

The summative assessment of the YFVI program suggested that it had a "mixed" impact in terms of arrests, incidents, and gun crime, despite its considerable expense. Comparisons made between the local "sites" of these efforts (in all but one site these were typically sections of a single city) and the citywide experiences suggested that the YFVI had significant impact in some areas and less of an impact in others (see Dunworth, 2000). In many of the sites increased police efforts produced more arrests and gun seizures, but this was seen as more likely an impact of increased police resources to a small section of the community rather than as an impact of the program. Perhaps more important, once the federal funds were expended, most of these sites returned to their "traditional" ways of responding to crime and violence, suggesting that the YFVI had little long-term impact on how these agencies policed their communities (see Dunworth, 2000; Greene, et al. 1998).

The limited impact of this program was often associated with two important issues: (1) the YFVI sites were quite limited in the level of analysis they used in defining and addressing youth firearms-violence problems; and (2) most of these programs failed to build attachments to the youth-serving agencies in their communities, thereby missing opportunities to strengthen their implementation and effectiveness. Problems in analysis and implementation were to be the significant limitations for the YFVI program.

At the analytic level, the YFVI program anticipated that the participating agencies would integrate computer analyses of crime (spatially and temporally) as part of the scanning and analysis activities associated with problem solving. In practice, however, many of the sites failed to acquire and implement such techniques and relied more on traditional patrol deployment information. Moreover, many of the sites were not well equipped to provide analysis in this intervention. Because analysis was not a well-grounded institutional premise in many of the recipient agencies, YFVI suffered from an underdeveloped use of analytic capability in these agencies.

In addition to the lack of technical and analytic support for the YFVI program, from its onset the program seemed to struggle in many sites between enforcement and prevention ideologies and tactics. The original program emphasized a need for the police to broaden their response from traditional patrol and investigation-based approaches to youth violence to a more preventive emphasis in police strategy and tactics. Nonetheless, most of the programs were enforcement oriented, emphasizing directed patrol within designated areas and follow-up criminal investigations, or offender-specific investigations typically focused on identified youths.

Furthermore, although it has been increasingly recognized that many agencies and institutions have a stake in youth development outcomes—including crime prevention—the YFVI program typically involved the police acting alone or within very restricted frameworks. While some of the units had a connection with local schools, most were not rooted in the youth-serving networks that existed within their targeted communities. Rather, the singular police focus of these programs often became a major barrier to forming external partnerships. The largest proportion of these efforts had little appreciation for, or attachment to, the communities within which they operated. Community partners, as well as other government youth-serving programs, had limited roles—if any—in these efforts. As a result, existing local capacities to address youth violence problems (schools, family services, probation, juvenile court, community-based youth agencies, and the like) were generally non- or limited participants to the YFVI program. The upshot of this process was to limit success in most of the YFVI sites.

The YFVI program sites also struggled with several external and internal issues that ultimately limited its success. Most of these issues show that in many of the YFVI sites the police approached youth-related problems without a clear analytic focus or set of partners. While crime analysis played a limited role in most of the projects, much of the tactical focus was on patrol solutions to youth and gun problems. This typically took the form of saturation or directed patrol in areas of these cities that had histories of gun violence among youths. In most instances these were "place-based" responses, with little specific analysis of the types of offenders that were represented in these areas. Toward the conclusion of the assessment of the YFVI program some of the sites began to build information systems that would create greater opportunity to identify and track offenders, but the most general of police tactics remained at the core of police interventions—patrol response followed by follow-up investigations.

In addition to a lack of strategic focus, these programs also suffered from a lack of connection and cooperation within their own police agencies. For the most part YFVI units were located in patrol and were generally unconnected to the larger efforts within their host departments. They often lacked internal support and were quite distant from upper-level police decision makers whose policies affected the YFVI effort. In many ways the YFVI programs actually competed with other internal police units for attention, and the "elite" status so often attached to specialized operations often hampered YFVI personnel in their attempts to work within the larger police organization.

The upshot of the analytic and connectivity limitations of many of the YFVI efforts was a lack of consistent impact. To be sure, many of the participating agencies claimed and could substantiate increased effort by the police (arrests and confiscation of guns). However, most could not demonstrate safer and less violent communities.

Finally, a large proportion of these efforts struggled to maintain support within their hosting departments and communities, and most were disbanded when federal funding was exhausted. Moreover, neither the police nor other youth-focused agencies within most of the YFVI communities gained a capacity for prospectively addressing youth problems as a result of this program.

Boston's Gun Project

Boston's Gun Project came about as a response to a significant youth-violence problem in that city in the late 1980s. This effort grew into a more elaborate series of interventions named "Operation Ceasefire" and "Operation Nightlight" (Kennedy, Piehl and Braga, 1996).

Prior to the late 1980s, there has been a long history of gang problems and interventions (see Miller, 1957, 1959). For a decade (1976–1986) violence attributed to gangs had been relatively stable, with between 30 and 35 youth homicides (age 24 and under) each year (see McDevitt et al., 2003, 57). Such stability created the impression that this problem was small and perhaps manageable using traditional police approaches.

Beginning in about 1988 and continuing through 1990, the number of youthful homicide victims skyrocketed, nearly doubling from the previous year (see Kennedy, Braga and Piehl, 1997). Analyses conducted by the Boston Police Department and Harvard University's Kennedy School of Government revealed that youthful victims were predominantly minority males and that the sudden rise in homicide among youths was clearly firearms related (Kennedy, Braga and Piehl, 1997). Such violence, depicted frequently in the *Boston Globe*, caused great public concern.

In early 1995 the Boston Gun Project was funded by the U.S. National Institute of Justice. From its onset the project sought collaboration in building effective responses to youth firearms violence in Boston. This collaboration took two forms—a research and evaluation partnership, established between the John F. Kennedy School of Government at Harvard University and the Boston Police Department, and a series of intervention partnerships involving several youth-service and criminal justice agencies that had been working on matters of youth crime for some time.

The Boston Gun Project had five central elements, each of which supported an analytic and collaborative approach to addressing youth-crime problems, especially violence. As a consequence, the Boston project clearly embraced the central tenets of community- and problem-oriented policing (see Braga, Kennedy, Waring and Piehl, 2001).

First, the project sought to create an interagency "working group" composed of line-level criminal justice professionals from the police department as well as probation and parole services, youth services, U.S. and District Attorney representatives, federal agency representatives, and the Boston Schools and Youth Centers. The focus of the project was on building a broader "team" to address youth problems.

Second, this project sought to better understand the particular dynamics of youth violence in Boston through the use of quantitative and qualitative research. Researchers from Harvard focused attention on the nature and location of youth-violence problems and began a sophisticated analysis by isolating the specific gangs and gang territories that were most likely to witness violence. As the analysis unfolded, it became clear that a small number of gangs and gang members accounted for a disproportionate amount of the observed violence in Boston.

Third, this effort also focused on specifying the precise "treatment" that could be employed in the identified places and with the identified gang members. Tying interventions to short-term impacts was a central feature in the selection of interventions.

Fourth, the Boston Gun Project focused on the proper implementation and later the adaptation of the intervention, assuring that the effort would not fail and that once implemented the program could adapt to changing environmental circumstances. This element proved to be very important as the Boston Gun Project gained momentum and formed larger numbers of external partnerships.

Finally, the Boston Gun Project also included an evaluation component, headed by the research team from Harvard. Documenting the progress as well as the outcomes and impacts of this effort was a design component from the very beginning of the project. All too often such research design discussions are brought to action projects only after they have been designed and are actually operational.

The Boston Gun Project was first an analytic effort, trying to better understand the dynamics of youth violence in the city. The analyses shed light on the depth of the city's gun problems, the linkage between youths and firearms, the gang connections to these problems, and the nature and source of the firearms used (Kennedy, Braga and Piehl, 1997).

The analysis led to the design of several interventions that were grouped under the heading "Operation Ceasefire," which had two primary intervention strategies. First, this effort focused directly on the firearms marketplace, targeting those trafficking in firearms to youths. Second, it focused on building a community consensus and a strong message to youths that such violence would not be tolerated. The objective was to create a climate of deterrence, while at the same time channeling youths to social service programs for assistance.

The first of these initiatives (firearms tracking) involved the joint efforts of many local and federal law enforcement agencies. Information on gun access was obtained from many sources, including gang members who had been arrested. Combined law-enforcement efforts proved useful in identifying and then disrupting gun markets, hence limiting illegal gun access in Boston.

The second element of Operation Ceasefire involved building a coalition of government, private, and community leaders to present a united front for a message of "no tolerance" in matters of youth gun violence (see Kennedy, 1997). Such a message, coupled with aggressive criminal justice action, was thought to produce a climate for deterring and preventing handgun violence among those most prone to handgun use.

This part of Operation Ceasefire involved several activities, including the identification and visiting of gang members on probation—"Operation Nightlight"— as a means of keeping high-risk youths off the streets particularly in rival gang territories and at times when violence was most likely. Efforts centered on reducing the risk factors for any particular youth.

In addition to police or criminal justice interventions, social-service street workers in Boston were charged with identifying at-risk youths and connecting them to services like job training, substance-abuse counseling, and education. Increasing the protective factors for youths was viewed as a means of preventing future delinquency and violence.

Third, and perhaps most important, in 1992 leaders from many community, civic, and religious groups joined this effort to provide an even broader "community base" for these interventions (see McDevitt, et al., 2003, 60–62).

The history of police and minority relations in Boston is not a pleasant one. Minority communities had substantial distrust of the police, yet these same communities were victim to the gang violence that this effort sought to end. The Ten-Point Coalition, created by a group of black clergy, forged a community alliance to address youth violence and specific at-risk youths in their communities. The Coalition's link to the police and other agency interventions was exceedingly important because it created a supporting climate within these communities that had not previously supported police actions.

In joining this effort the Ten-Point Coalition helped to communicate and interpret police actions in minority communities. This interpretation was bi-directional: To the community, the Coalition stressed that police actions were necessary if violence was to be controlled and if neighborhood youths were to be safe—the message was that police action was needed, and that such actions were not in and of themselves racist. In communicating the community concerns to the police, the Coalition stressed the aggressive and often disrespectful police actions. Fear of the police and a community concern with racial motivation underlying police actions were the central issues. The Coalition thus was able to help shape police interventions as well as community acceptance of these interventions.

The Boston Gun Project achieved remarkable results on two fronts. One is the short-term impact of the project on youth handgun violence.

First, youth homicide dropped dramatically in Boston after the implementation of the program. By 1997 youth homicides in Boston numbered 17, a dramatic decrease from the peak in 1990 of 73. The impact of this change, while dramatic, cannot be directly attributed to this program. However, it is clear that the coordinated efforts of many armed with analysis that pointed them to the appropriate areas, gangs and people, contributed to the success achieved. These reductions continue to this day with the youth-violence level rising slightly but not near the record levels seen in 1990.

A second and more long-term impact of this project for Boston was a shift in police thinking about how to address complicated crime problems. Like many cities prior to the 1990s Boston had a small analytic capability, mostly focused on patrol deployment. With the advent of problem solving and its link to the Boston Gun Project, the Boston Police Department has significantly invested in the "thinking systems" of the department. Part of the legacy of the project was to demonstrate the power of thoughtful analysis as a precursor to police action, including whom they invite into partnerships to solve those problems.

A related legacy of this effort is an increased coherence in the coalition within Boston that deals with matters of crime. While Boston has had a long history of youth programs and efforts (see Prothrow-Stith, 1992), this project served as a vehicle for strengthening what was a loosely connected set of agencies and service providers. The strength of this coalition continues to the present, with considerable interaction among these agencies and their service providers. Perhaps more important is the recognition that for Boston to successfully address youth-violence problems, participating agencies must "engage the problem-solving process to develop an interagency, comprehensive intervention that fits both the nature of the city's youth-violence problem and the available array of the city's operational capacities" (McDevitt et al., 2003).

THE FUTURE OF POLICE/YOUTH INTERVENTIONS

In all likelihood policing and youth problems will remain intertwined. Crime, after all, is a young persons' game, and policing will invariably confront shifts in youth culture—now and in the future. Nonetheless, in the twenty-first century policing has shed part of its reactive response to social problems, becoming more of a force for proactive and preventive interventions, including those with youths. This shift is not complete, however, and much remains to be accomplished (Goldstein et al., 2003).

To make such a shift in strategy and tactics the police can learn from the failure of the Youth Firearms Violence Initiative and the success of Boston's Gun Project. Several of the lessons learned from these efforts that are now shaping police responses to youth and violence can be grouped under five broad headings.

The first lesson in the comparison of YFVI and Boston's approach is the need to understand the nature of the community in which the intervention may occur. Several studies of community social structure and the level of informal social organization suggests that community-focused interventions first need to understand the contexts in which they are introduced. Understanding community social context is indeed part of the environmental analysis that should precede police interventions.

A second analytic issue confronting police interventions, including those focused on youths, is in understanding the nature of the intervention. Police interventions can be targeted at individuals, small groups, organizations (generally illegal ones), and communities. Each form of intervention addresses a different level of social organization, and each makes certain assumptions about cause and effect within these levels. For the police to be effective in their pursuit of safer communities, they must first understand the level of social organization in which they intervene.

This leads to a third analytic issue, that of matching interventions to individuals, small groups, illegal organizations, and communities. This assures at the onset that some consideration has been given to what level of social organization is in need of intervention and that the intervention selected has some chance of affecting the problem and level of social organization identified. This, of course, would also include a concern for matching interventions to problems. In sum, the analytic requirement for the police to be effective in dealing with youth problems, including those associated with violence, is to assess the social network most likely causing the problem and then to match a response to that network.

In addition to improving the analytic capacity of the police, it must be recognized that community- and problem-oriented policing does not occur in a vacuum. Rather, many activities and efforts characterize policing in the broadest sense of the term. Coordinating police activities and efforts with other agency interventions is necessary in any response to the targeted problem and/or level of social organization. For the police to be effective, as seen in the Boston example, the coordinated efforts of many agencies are a necessary condition for program success. Such effort requires a focus on the dominant problem (through an analytic process) and the willingness to partner with others who have some overlapping responsibility for the target audience, location, or problem. In Boston such coordination was the hallmark of the program; in contrast, for many of the YFVI programs, such interaction among youth-serving agencies was lacking.

Finally, some recommendations can be made about modeling police-youth interventions. First, to be effective, the police need to identify and understand the problem they seek to address. Problems have many causes, outcomes and implications, and only through thoughtful and thorough analysis can problems be made visible and thereby understood. Good policing will not advance without such analysis.

Second, once problems are analytically understood, the police need to be able to specify the treatments they propose in clear terms. This means knowing where in the cause-and-effect chain their efforts should be directed, and with what intended effects and long-term outcomes. In addition, the police must be prepared to assess the outcomes of their interventions, whether they are primary, secondary, or tertiary, to provide the foundation for "validating" chosen interventions.

Third, in addressing complex social problems like juvenile crime and violence, the police need to link multiple services and providers if they are to be effective. The Boston program reveals that the sustained capacity of the program was due in large part to the many agencies that participated in the process (before and after this program).

The long-term relationships built through individual interventions will also ultimately strengthen the network of those who have an investment in solving the problem. In the case of youth violence, this includes many government, private, and community agencies and organizations. Building community confidence in the ability of these networks to competently address youth and other problems is an important long-term institutional matter for the police, and a more likely outcome in community policing and problem-solving approaches.

Finally, for policing to become effective it must identify the impact of its interventions in clear terms. This is accomplished through both formative and summative program assessment. All too often programs offered by the police fail to impact the problems they were meant to address. Whether this failure is conceptual, theory-related, or associated with program implementation will be revealed through formative and summative program assessment.

This is not just an academic distinction. All police interventions are rooted in assumptions about cause and effect and are therefore theory driven. Understanding the nature of the theory pursued is important. When programs fail, we want to know if they were just bad ideas or whether they were simply poorly implemented. Until the police can distinguish conceptual or theory failure from program failure (implementation), their interventions will not be well understood, nor will they be capable of replication. In the youth crime and violence arena such considerations are central to effective service and safer communities.

References

Blumstein, A., and R. Rosenfield. 1998. "Explaining Recent Trends in U.S. Homicide Rates," *Journal of Criminal Law and Criminology* 88(4): 1175–1216.

Braga, Anthony A., David M. Kennedy, Elin J. Waring, and Anne M. Piehl. 2001. "Problem-Oriented Policing, Deterrence, and Youth Violence: An Evaluation of Boston's Operation Ceasefire." *Journal of Research in Crime and Delinquency* 38(3).

Cordner, G. W., and D. C. Hale (eds.) 1992. *What Works in Policing?* Cincinnati, OH: Anderson.

Decker, S. H. (ed.) 2003. *Policing Gangs and Youth Violence.* Belmont, CA: Wadsworth/Thomson.

Decker, S. H., and G. D. Curry. 2000. "Responding to Gangs: Does the Dose Match the Problem?", in J. Sheley (ed.) *Criminology.* Belmont, CA: West/Wadsworth.

Dunworth, T. 2000. "National Evaluation of the Youth Firearms Violence Initiative," *Research in Brief.* Washington, DC: National Institute of Justice.

Eck, J. E., and W. Spelman. 1987. *Problem Solving: Problem-Oriented Policing in Newport News.* Washington, DC: Police Executive Research Forum.

Farrington, D. 2002. "Families and Crime," in Wilson, J. Q., and J. Petersilia (eds.) *Crime: Public Policies for Crime Control.* Oakland, CA: ICS Press.

Fritsch, E. J., T. J. Caeti, and R. W. Taylor. 1999. "Gang Suppression Through Saturation Patrol, Aggressive Curfew and Truancy Enforcement: A Quasi-Experimental Test of the Dallas Anti-gang Initiative," *Crime & Delinquency* 45:122–139.

Greene, J. R. 1998. "Evaluating Planned Change Strategies in Modern Law Enforcement," in J. P. Brodeur (ed.) *Good Policing: Problems and Issues.* Thousand Oaks, CA: Sage.

Greene, J. R. 2000. "Community Policing in America: Changing the Nature, Structure and Function of the Police," in Horney, J., et al. (eds.) *Criminal Justice 2000. Volume 3. Policies, Processes, and Decisions of the Criminal Justice System.* Washington, DC: National Institute of Justice.

Greene, J. R. 2003. "Gangs, Community Policing and Problem Solving," in S. H. Decker (ed.) *Policing Gangs and Youth Violence.* Belmont, CA: Wadsworth/Thomson.

Greene, J. R., T. Dunworth, T. Rich, S. Cutchins, J. Frank, A. Garrett, K. Jacoby, and R. Kling. 1998. *National Evaluation of the Youth Firearms Violence Initiative: Final Cross-Site Report.* Cambridge, MA: Abt Associates.

Greenwood, P. W. 2002. "Juvenile Crime and Juvenile Justice," in Wilson, J. Q., and J. Petersilia (eds.) *Crime: Public Policies for Crime Control.* Oakland, CA: ICS Press.

Goldstein, H. 1990. *Problem-Oriented Policing.* New York: McGraw-Hill.

Goldstein, H. 2003. "On Further Developing Problem-Oriented Policing: The Most Critical Needs, The Major Impediments, and a Proposal," in J. Knuttson (ed.) *Problem-Oriented Policing: From Innovation to Mainstream. Crime Prevention Studies,* Vol. 15. Monsey, NJ: Criminal Justice Press.

Kelling, G. L., and M. H. Moore. 1988. "The Evolving Strategy of Policing," *Perspectives on Policing* No. 4. Washington, DC: National Institute of Justice.

Kennedy, D. M. 1997. "Pulling Levers: Chronic Offenders, High-Crime Settings, and a Theory of Prevention," *Valparaiso University Law Review* 31:449–484.

Kennedy, D. M, A. A. Braga, and A. M. Piehl. 1997. "The (Un)Known Universe: Mapping Gangs and Gang Violence in Boston," in Weisburd, D., and T. McEwen (eds.) *Crime Mapping and Crime Prevention.* New York: Criminal Justice Press.

Kennedy, D. M., A. M. Piehl, and A. A. Braga. 1996. "Youth Violence in Boston: Gun Markets, Serious Youth Offenders, and a Use-Reduction Strategy," *Law and Contemporary Problems* 59:147–196.

Knuttson, J. (ed.) 2003. *Problem-Oriented Policing: From Innovation to Mainstream.* Monsey, NJ: Criminal Justice Press.

Manning, P. K. 1977. *Policework: The Social Organization of Policing.* Cambridge: MIT Press.

McDevitt, J., A. A. Braga, D. Nurge, and M. Buerger. 2003. "Boston's Youth Violence Prevention Program: A Comprehensive Community-Wide Approach," in Decker, S. H. (ed.) *Policing Gangs and Youth Violence.* Belmont, CA: Wadsworth/Thomson.

Miller, W. B. 1957. "The Impact of a Community Group Work Program on Delinquent Corner Groups," *Social Service Review* 41(4): 390–406.

Miller, W. B. 1959. "Preventive Work with Street Corner Groups: Boston Delinquency Project," *Annals of the American Academy of Political and Social Science* 322:97–106.

Prothrow-Stith, D. 1992. *Deadly Consequences: How Violence is Destroying Our Teenage Population and a Plan to Begin Solving the Problem.* New York: HarperCollins.

Suchman, E. A. 1968. *Evaluative Research Principles and Practice in Public Service and Social Action Programs.* New York: Russell Sage Foundation.

Gang Prevention

A Case Study of a Primary Prevention Program

Finn-Aage Esbensen, Dana Peterson, Terrance J. Taylor,
Adrienne Freng, & D. Wayne Osgood

OVERVIEW

Youth delinquent gangs received considerable attention during the 1990s. Much of this attention focused on the violence and drug dealing in which gang members are involved. Despite widespread concern about gangs, there has been a paucity of research and evaluation of prevention and intervention programs. In this chapter, we report on a multiyear, multifaceted evaluation of one school-based gang prevention program in which uniformed law enforcement officers teach a nine-week curriculum to middle-school students.

The Gang Resistance Education and Training (G.R.E.A.T.) program was developed in 1991 by law-enforcement agencies in the greater Phoenix area. According to the G.R.E.A.T. Officers' Instructor's Manual, the primary purpose of the G.R.E.A.T. program is "to reduce gang activity" and "to educate a population of young people as to the consequences of gang involvement."

From October 1994 through December 2001, the National Institute of Justice (NIJ) funded a National Evaluation of the G.R.E.A.T. program. Two

Prepared especially for *American Youth Gangs at the Millennium* by Finn-Aage Esbensen, Dana Peterson, Terrance J. Taylor, Adrienne Freng, and D. Wayne Osgood.

separate objectives guided the evaluation design. The first objective was to conduct a process evaluation, that is, to describe the program and its components, and to assess the program's fidelity. The second objective was to assess the effectiveness of G.R.E.A.T. in terms of attitudinal and behavioral consequences through an outcome evaluation.

The process evaluation consisted of two different components: (1) assessment of the G.R.E.A.T. officer training; and (2) observation of officers actually delivering the program in school classrooms. For the outcome analysis, three different strategies were developed. First, a cross-sectional study was conducted in which 5,935 eighth-grade students in eleven different cities were surveyed to assess the effectiveness of the G.R.E.A.T. program. Second, a five-year longitudinal, quasi-experimental study was conducted in six different cities. Third, parents, teachers, and law enforcement officers were surveyed to determine their level of satisfaction with the program and its perceived effectiveness.

PROBLEM STATEMENT

In spite of years of research and years of suppression and intervention efforts, the American gang scene is poorly understood and far from being eliminated. There is a lack of consensus about the magnitude of the gang problem; the extent and level of organization of gangs; and, importantly, what should be done to address the gang issue. Some of the epidemiological and etiological confusion can be traced to different methodologies and different theoretical perspectives. Disagreement about policy can be attributed largely to political agendas and to a shortage of evaluations of strategies enacted to address the gang phenomenon. To address the latter issue, a number of gang-specific programs with evaluative components were implemented at both the local and national level during the 1990s. Of particular interest in this article, however, is discussion of the extent to which a gang prevention program can be implemented in middle schools and with what degree of success.

THE G.R.E.A.T. PROGRAM

The G.R.E.A.T. program is a school-based gang prevention program taught by uniformed police officers. G.R.E.A.T. was developed in 1991 by Phoenix Police Department officers in cooperation with officers representing other Phoenix area police departments (see Winfree, Lynskey, and Maupin, 1999 for a history of the program). The Bureau of Alcohol, Tobacco, and Firearms, the Federal Law Enforcement Training Center, and representatives from five local law enforcement agencies (Phoenix, AZ; Portland, OR; Philadelphia, PA; La Crosse, WI; and Orange County, FL) share responsibility for and oversight of the current program. Since its inception, G.R.E.A.T. has experienced rapid acceptance by both law enforcement and school personnel. Evidence for this is its adoption by numerous law-enforcement agencies across the country; by the conclusion of data collection for this National Evaluation (December 1999), more than 3,500 officers from all fifty states and the District of Columbia had completed G.R.E.A.T. training.

The stated objectives of the G.R.E.A.T. program are: (1) "to reduce gang activity" and (2) "to educate a population of young people as to the consequences of gang involvement" (G.R.E.A.T. Officer Instructor's Manual). The curriculum consists of eight lesson plans offered over a nine-week period to middle-school students, primarily seventh graders. Officers are provided with detailed lesson plans containing clearly stated purposes and objectives. In order to achieve the program's objectives, the eight lessons cover such topics as conflict resolution, goal setting, and resisting peer pressure. Discussion about gangs and how they affect the quality of people's lives are also included. The eight lessons are listed below.

1. Introduction—Students get acquainted with the G.R.E.A.T. program and officer.

2. Crime/Victims and Your Rights—Students learn about crimes, victims, and the impact on their school and neighborhood.

3. Cultural Sensitivity/Prejudice—Students learn how cultural differences impact their school and neighborhood.

4. Conflict Resolution (2 lessons)—Students learn how to create an atmosphere of understanding that would enable all parties to better address problems and work on solutions together.

5. Meeting Basic Needs—Students learn how to meet their basic needs without joining a gang.

6. Drugs/Neighborhoods—Students learn how drugs affect their school and neighborhood.

7. Responsibility—Students learn about the diverse responsibilities of people in their school and neighborhood.

8. Goal Setting—Students learn the need for goal setting and how to establish short- and long-term goals.

More information about the G.R.E.A.T. program can be found at the following Web site: http://www.atf.treas.gov/great/index.htm.

PROCESS EVALUATION

Of primary importance in the process evaluation was determining whether the program described in written documents was, in fact, the program delivered. During the first year of the evaluation, members of the research staff observed five officer training sessions. In addition to enhancing the researchers' understanding of the program, these observations allowed for assessment of the training program and the appropriateness of instructional techniques. The overall consensus of the evaluators was that these training sessions were well organized and staffed by a dedicated group of officers (Esbensen and Osgood, 1997).

Our next concern was to assess the extent to which the officers brought the materials learned at training to the classroom. A total of 87 lessons was observed by one or two trained observers in six different cities and 14 different schools. Each observer noted the extent to which the officers adhered to the lesson outline and the extent to which they conformed to the lesson content. As with the training sessions, the overall consensus was that the officers did a commendable job of presenting the materials as they were taught in the G.R.E.A.T. officer training. Based on these two observational components, we concluded that the program was delivered with a high degree of conformity to the written description (Sellers, Taylor, and Esbensen, 1998).

Outcome Evaluation

Although the development of the G.R.E.A.T. curriculum was not theory driven, the design of the National Evaluation was. The theories judged to be most relevant to the program were social learning theory (Akers, 1985) and self-control theory (Gottfredson and Hirschi, 1990). The identification of relevant theoretical constructs is critical to the short-term evaluation of prevention programs because prevention necessarily takes place well before the outcome of major concern (gang membership) is likely to occur. Thus, the evaluation placed considerable emphasis on theoretical constructs that were logically related to the program's curriculum and that were both theoretically and empirically linked to gang membership and delinquency (Grasmick, Tittle, Bursik, and Arneklev, 1993; Hawkins and Catalano, 1993; Huizinga, Loeber, and Thornberry, 1994; Winfree, Vigil-Backstrom, and Mays, 1994). It was maintained that if the program had positive effects on those variables in the short term, then it held promise for long-term benefits of reducing serious gang delinquency. Decisions about the potential value of G.R.E.A.T. could not wait for research that would track program participants through their entire adolescence to determine whether they ever joined gangs or participated in serious delinquency, nor would the expense of such research be justified without evidence of short-term effects.

Winfree, Esbensen, and Osgood (1996) elaborated on the relationship between the G.R.E.A.T. curriculum and the theoretical constructs included in this evaluation. For example, lesson 4 (conflict resolution) deals with concepts closely linked to self-control theory's anger and coping strategies.

Lesson 5 (meeting basic needs) has conceptual ties to the risk-taking element of self-control theory. Lessons 6, 7, and 8 include elements addressing delayed gratification and impulsive behavior by attempting to teach responsibility and goal setting, including personal and career goals.

Elements of social learning theory appear in lessons 1, 3, and 4. These lessons introduce definitions of laws, values, norms, and rules supportive of law-abiding behavior. Tolerance and acceptance (lesson 3), for instance, are presented as values that reduce conflict and subsequently violence. Further, lesson 4 addresses conflict resolution and steps students can take to ward off negative peer influences.

Measures

The questionnaires administered to students participating in both the cross-sectional and longitudinal studies were identical. Measures included in the student questionnaires can be divided into three main categories: attitudinal, cognitive, and behavioral. While the attitudinal measures included in these instruments can be classified as measures of five different theoretical perspectives (social learning, social control, social strain, labeling, and self-concept) and have been used for testing theoretical propositions in other publications (Deschenes and Esbensen, 1999; Esbensen and Deschenes, 1998; Lynskey, Winfree, Esbensen, and Clason, 2000; Miller, Esbensen, and Freng, 1999; Peterson, Miller, and Esbensen, 2001; Winfree and Bernat, 1998), they will be referred to as attitudinal variables in the subsequent discussion. The following questionnaire items are representative of the diversity of questions answered by the student respondents:

"There are gang fights at my school."
"My parents know who I am with if I am not at home."
"Sometimes I will take a risk just for the fun of it."
"Police officers are honest."
"If your group of friends was getting you into trouble at home, how likely is it that you would still hang out with them?"
"I'll never have enough money to go to college."
"It's okay to tell a small lie if it doesn't hurt anyone."
"I try hard in school."
"Being in my gang makes me feel important."

In addition to attitudinal items, the students were requested to complete a self-report delinquency inventory. This technique has been used widely during the past forty years and provides a good measure of actual behavior rather than a reactive measure of police response to behavior (e.g., Hindelang, Hirschi, and Weis, 1981; Huizinga, 1991; Huizinga and Elliott, 1986). The types of behaviors comprising this 17-item inventory included status offenses (e.g., skipping classes without an excuse), crimes against property (e.g., purposely damaging or destroying property; stealing or trying to steal something worth more than $50), and crimes against persons (e.g., hitting someone with the idea of hurting them; attacking someone with a weapon). Additionally, students were asked about drug use, including tobacco, alcohol, and marijuana. Given that the focus of the G.R.E.A.T. program was on gang prevention, a series of questions asked the students about their involvement in gangs and the types of gang activities in which they and their gangs were involved.

Analysis Issues

Prior to a discussion of program effectiveness, several methodological issues need to be addressed. G.R.E.A.T. is a school-based program, delivered simultaneously to entire classrooms rather than separately to individual students. For analysis of program effectiveness, this poses a problem concerning the appropriate unit of analysis: individuals, classrooms, or schools. If students from the same classroom tend to be more similar to one another than to students from other classrooms, then treating individuals as the primary unit of analysis is likely to violate the standard statistical assumption of independence among observations (Judd and McClelland, 1989:403–416). When this assumption does not hold, we risk the possibility of concluding that there is a reliable treatment effect when it is, in fact, idiosyncratic to only a few classes, or we may fail to establish the statistical significance of a small but very consistent effect.

For the independence assumption to hold, *all* similarity within classes must be explained by the treatment effect and control variables. In most cases there are many other sources of similarity as well, such as which trainer delivered the program, the teacher's classroom management style, and all extraneous factors that determine which students end up in which classrooms. Although it is possible that an analysis would succeed in accounting for all such differences between classes, it is more prudent to assume that this may not be the case. While it would be ideal to use an analysis strategy that allows for the possible nonindependence within classrooms by including classrooms as a unit of analysis, we could not do this with the cross-sectional data. It was not possible to reconstruct the seventh-grade class configuration with the available data. It was possible, however, to use school as a level of analysis and thus be able to control for school differences and, indirectly and more limitedly, officer and teacher characteristics. In the longitudinal survey, we randomly assigned classrooms to G.R.E.A.T. or non-G.R.E.A.T. and were thus able to conduct those analyses using the classroom as a unit of analysis.

CROSS-SECTIONAL DESIGN—1995

The first outcome analysis was based on the cross-sectional survey completed in the spring of 1995. In this cross-sectional design, two ex post facto comparison groups were created to allow for assessment of the effectiveness of the G.R.E.A.T. program. Since the program was taught in seventh grade, eighth-grade students were surveyed to allow for a one-year follow-up while at the same time guaranteeing that none of the sample was currently enrolled in the program. Eleven cities met all the required conditions for participation in the National Evaluation (functioning G.R.E.A.T. program, contribution to the geographical diversity of the study, and cooperation from the school district and law enforcement agencies): Las Cruces, NM; Omaha, NE; Phoenix, AZ; Philadelphia, PA; Kansas City, MO; Milwaukee, WI; Orlando, FL; Will County, IL; Providence, RI; Pocatello, ID; and Torrance, CA. These sites provide a diverse sample. One or more of the selected sites can be described by the following characteristics: large urban area, small city, racially and ethnically homogeneous, racially and ethnically heterogeneous, East Coast, West Coast, Midwest, inner-city, working class, or middle class.

Within the selected sites, schools that offered G.R.E.A.T. during the past two years were selected and questionnaires were administered to all eighth graders in attendance on the specified day. This resulted in a final sample of 5,935 eighth grade students from 315 classrooms in 42 different schools. Passive parental consent procedures (students were included unless specifically prohibited by parents) were approved in all but the Torrance site. The number of parental refusals at each of the passive parental consent schools ranged from zero to two percent. Thus, participation rates (the percent of students in attendance on the day of administration actually completing questionnaires) varied between 98 and 100 percent at the passive consent sites. (For further description of the consent process in the cross-sectional study, consult Esbensen, Deschenes, Vogel, West, Arboit, and Harris, 1996.)

Sample Characteristics

Approximately half of the sample was female (52%) and most lived in two-parent homes (62%)—respondents indicated that both a mother and father were present in the home, including stepparents. The sample was ethnically diverse, with Whites accounting for 40 percent of respondents, African Americans 27 percent, Hispanics 19 percent, Asians 6 percent, and other 8 percent. As expected with an eighth-grade sample, most of the respondents were between 13 and 15 years of age, with 60 percent being 14 years old. The vast majority reported having parents with a minimum educational level of a high school diploma, with a sizable number having mothers and/or fathers with some college-level education. Approximately 25 percent of the respondents did not know their father's highest level of education, while 20 percent did not know their mother's.

With respect to gang affiliation, some interesting insight to self-reported gang membership is revealed. As with most social phenomena, definitional issues arise. In the current research, two filter questions introduce the gang-specific section of the questionnaire: "Have you ever been a gang member?" and "Are you now in a gang?" Given the current sample, with most of the respondents under the age of 15, even affirmative responses to the first question followed by a negative response to the second may still have indicated a recent gang affiliation. Relying upon responses to the first question as an accurate reflection of the magnitude of the gang problem, fully 17 percent (994 youths) of the sample indicated that they had belonged to a gang at some point in their lives. This contrasts with nine percent (522) indicating that they were currently gang members (review article 2 in this volume for a discussion of definitional issues).

Comparison Group

A primary concern for assessing program impact was determining whether the students who participated in the G.R.E.A.T. program were comparable to those who did not. The treatment group (G.R.E.A.T. participants) and comparison group (nonparticipants) were defined through answers to the question, "Did you complete the G.R.E.A.T. program?" Of the 5,836 respondents who answered the question (99 students did not respond), 2,629 (45%) reported they had completed the program. The 3,207 (55%) who did not became the comparison group.

The schools varied substantially in the number of students who reported they had completed and who had not completed the G.R.E.A.T. program. Since the precision with which program impact can be established at each school depends on the number of students in *both* participant and nonparticipant groups, schools with few students in one of the groups could contribute relatively little to the evaluation. Therefore, analysis of the treatment and comparison groups was replicated using a restricted sample of 28 schools in which there were at least 15 students in each group, participants and nonparticipants.

Because data were gathered on only a single occasion, a year after completion of the program it was necessary to compare the participants and nonparticipants, using statistical controls to rule out the possibility that differences between them were attributable to various background characteristics. Questions were asked in the survey to determine five background characteristics that could be associated with the outcome measures. The analysis controlled for: gender; race (White, African American, Hispanic, Asian-American, and other); age (because only eighth-grade students participated in the evaluation, there was little variation in age); family status (as reflected in the adults with whom the youths resided); and parental education (defined as the highest level attained by either parent).

Background Characteristics

Not surprisingly, there were differences among the 42 schools in terms of racial composition and socioeconomic status (as reflected by family status and parental education). The analysis, which controlled for differences between schools, found a few small but statistically significant differences in background characteristics between the treatment and comparison groups.

Ideally, the treatment and comparison groups should have been matched, but this could not be expected in a post hoc evaluation such as this study. The pattern of group differences in background characteristics was ambiguous, but it did not appear especially problematic to determining the impact of the G.R.E.A.T. program. Comparisons of the treatment and comparison groups revealed no systematic bias. Demographic characteristics indicating high or low risk for delinquency and/or gang membership were found in both groups. In the comparison group, 15-year-old students were overrepresented while in the treatment group African-American youths were overrepresented. Similarly, there were fewer females in the comparison group but more youths from single-parent homes. Given this inconsistent pattern and the small size of group differences, it was concluded that the outcome measures were not a product of pre-existing differences between the G.R.E.A.T. and comparison students.

Outcome Results

Findings from the cross-sectional study indicated that G.R.E.A.T. appeared to be meeting its objectives of reducing gang affiliation and delinquent activity. The students who reported completing the G.R.E.A.T. program reported *lower* levels of gang affiliation (9.8 percent of G.R.E.A.T. students reported gang membership compared to 11.4 percent of the comparison group) and self-reported delinquency. These differences were small but statistically significant. Not only was the aggregate measure of delinquency lower for the G.R.E.A.T. group, but so were most of the subscales, i.e., drug use, minor offending, property crimes, and crimes against persons. No differences between the groups were found for rates of victimization or selling drugs.

A number of differences also were found for attitudinal measures. As discussed above, G.R.E.A.T. lessons are aimed at reducing impulsive behavior, improving communication with parents and other adults, enhancing self-esteem, and encouraging students to make "better" choices. The cross-sectional survey results revealed that one year after completing G.R.E.A.T., the G.R.E.A.T. students reported better outcomes—that is, more positive attitudes and behaviors than students who did not complete the program (see figure 1).

LONGITUDINAL RESEARCH DESIGN

The cross-sectional evaluation of the G.R.E.A.T. program reported above contains several methodological limitations. That design lacked a pretest measure and required the ex post facto creation of a comparison group. While statistical procedures were used to strengthen the validity of that design, it is generally considered a weak design (e.g., Sherman, Gottfredson,

---

Figure 1   Cross-Sectional Design Outcomes

Students completing the G.R.E.A.T. program reported more positive attitudes and behaviors than did the comparison group of students. They reported:

- Lower rates of self-reported delinquency
- Lower rates of gang affiliation
- More positive attitudes toward the police
- More negative attitudes about gangs
- Having more friends involved in prosocial activities
- Greater commitment to peers promoting prosocial behavior
- Higher levels of perceived guilt at committing deviant acts
- More commitment to school
- Higher levels of attachment to both mothers and fathers
- More communication with parents about their activities
- Fewer friends involved in delinquent activity
- Lower likelihood of acting impulsively
- Lower likelihood of engaging in risky behavior
- Lower levels of perceived blocks to academic success (see Esbensen and Osgood, 1999 for further discussion of these results)

MacKenzie, Eck, Reuter, and Bushway, 1997). The longitudinal research strategy implemented in the second phase of the National Evaluation, with a quasi-experimental research design and random assignment of classrooms to treatment, serves two very important functions. First, this assignment process should create groups of G.R.E.A.T. and non-G.R.E.A.T. students at equal risk for future delinquency and gang involvement. Second, the longitudinal research design greatly increased statistical power for detecting program effects by controlling for previous individual differences and examining change over time.

Site Selection

Six cities were selected for inclusion in the longitudinal phase of the National Evaluation. The first criterion was the existence of a viable G.R.E.A.T. program. A second criterion was geographical location. It was desired to include an East Coast city (Philadelphia, Pennsylvania), a West Coast location (Portland, Oregon), the site of the program's inception (Phoenix, Arizona), a Midwest city (Omaha, Nebraska), a nongang city (Lincoln, Nebraska), and a small "border town" with a chronic gang problem (Las Cruces, New Mexico). Clearly, some consideration was given to proximity to the location of the research office (Lincoln). A third criterion was the cooperation of the school districts and the police departments in each site.

Quasi-experimental Research Design

The longitudinal study includes relatively equal-sized groups of treatment (G.R.E.A.T.) and control (non-G.R.E.A.T.) students in the seventh grade at five of the sites and sixth-grade students in the sixth (Portland). Because G.R.E.A.T. is a classroom-based program, assignment was implemented for classrooms rather than for individual students. When data were pooled across sites, there was a large enough sample of classrooms for confidence in our results, even when classrooms were used as the unit of analysis. The longitudinal sample consists of 22 schools, 153 classrooms, and more than 3,000 students (all students whose names appeared on class lists at the beginning of the school year).

The quasi-experimental design was a critical feature of this research design. During late summer and early fall of 1995, procedures for assignment of classrooms to experimental and control conditions were developed at each of the 22 middle schools participating in the longitudinal study. Since the G.R.E.A.T. program was implemented differently at each site, unique solutions were required to assign classrooms at each site and, in some situations, at each school. The exact nature of the process was dependent on what was possible at each site, but in all cases the goal was to minimize the potential for differences between the sets of treatment and control classes. Working in conjunction with principals, teachers, and G.R.E.A.T. officers, treatment and comparison samples were derived at each site. These various procedures resulted in 76 G.R.E.A.T. classrooms representing 1,871 students and 77 control classrooms with 1,697 students.

Active Consent Procedures

The University of Nebraska Institutional Review Board approved a research design that allowed passive parental consent (students were included unless specifically prohibited by parents) during the pre- and post-test data collection. These surveys were conducted two weeks prior to and two weeks following completion of the G.R.E.A.T. program. Active parental consent (students were excluded unless written approval for participation was obtained from parents) was planned for the subsequent annual surveys. These procedures were also approved by each of the participating school districts.

A modified Dillman (1978) total design method was utilized to obtain the active consent forms, although the specific procedures varied slightly in terms of timing and sequencing across the six sites. Below is an "ideal type" of the procedures that were followed. Three direct mailings were made to parents of survey participants. Included in the mailings were a cover letter (both English and Spanish versions were included in Phoenix and Las Cruces), two copies of the parent consent form for student participation, and a business reply envelope. All parents not responding after the second mailing were contacted by telephone. School personnel also cooperated by distributing consent forms and cover letters at school.

The results of the active consent process led to an overall retention of 57 percent of the initial sample (for a more detailed discussion of the active consent process and examination of the effects of active consent procedures on the representativeness of the sample, consult Esbensen, Miller, Taylor, He, and Freng, 1999). Altogether, these efforts cost in excess of $60,000 in terms of supplies, personnel time, telephone, and mailing costs.

Questionnaire Completion Rates

The completion rates for the student survey were excellent. Of the 2,045 active consents obtained at the six sites, 1,758 (86%) surveys were completed during the one-year follow-up, 1,550 (76%) in the two-year follow-up, 1,419 (69%) in year three, and 1,377 (67%) in year four. Given the multisite, multischool sample, combined with the fact that respondents at five of the six sites made the transition from middle school to high school between the year-one and year-two surveys, this completion rate is commendable. Hansen, Tobler, and Graham (1990) examined attrition in a meta-analysis of 85 longitudinal studies and reported an average completion rate of 72 percent for the 19 studies with a 24-month follow-up period. Few of these 19 studies included multisite samples. Tebes, Snow, and Arthur (1992) report on the attrition rates from middle school to high school. In their study examining differential attrition for different age groups, they report losing 41.3 percent of their sample between eighth and ninth grade.

Outcome Results

The longitudinal sample differs from the cross-sectional sample on some of the demographic characteristics. Those students participating in the longitudinal study were recruited in the sixth and seventh grade and as such are younger than the cross-sectional sample comprised of eighth-grade students. The longitudinal sample also consists of a higher percentage of White students (46%), fewer African Americans (17%), but approximately the same representation of Hispanics (19%) and others (16%). With respect to gender and family structure, the longitudinal sample is virtually identical to the cross-sectional, with 51 percent females and 61 percent living in two-parent households.

The assignment of classrooms to G.R.E.A.T. and non-G.R.E.A.T. was relatively successful in establishing comparable groups. Some differences were noted but the only statistically significant difference was for race; more White youths were in the comparison group while the treatment group consisted of proportionately more African-American and Hispanic youths. A review of attitudinal and behavioral measures collected in the pretest indicated that the comparison group was slightly more pro-social than the G.R.E.A.T. group (e.g., more positive attitudes to police, more negative attitudes about gangs, more peers involved in pro-social activities, and lower rates of self-reported delinquency). The analysis strategy, however, controls for school, classroom, and preexisting differences between groups (for discussion of analysis issues, consult Esbensen, Osgood, Taylor, Peterson, and Freng, 2001).

The research design involved four nested levels of analysis: waves of data collection are nested within *individual students* who are followed *over time*, those students are nested within *classrooms* where the program was (or was not) delivered, and the classrooms are nested within *schools*. The multilevel statistical program developed by Goldstein (1995) allows for examination of four levels or analysis and was utilized in the assessment of program effect. Analyses conducted with the second year of follow-up data failed to replicate the previous positive findings of the cross-sectional study. No differences were found between the G.R.E.A.T. and non-G.R.E.A.T. groups. In the spirit of sharing information with the G.R.E.A.T. administrators, these null findings were reported in October 1998. Rather than shoot the messenger, the National Policy Board called for a critical review of the G.R.E.A.T. curriculum (see figure 2).

Subsequent analyses including all five years of data revealed small but systematic beneficial program effects that emerged gradually over time. It was not until four years after program exposure, however, that statistically significant differences between the groups were discernable. On average, we found more pro-social changes in the attitudes of G.R.E.A.T. students than the non-G.R.E.A.T. students. The program effect is statistically significant for five of the outcome measures. G.R.E.A.T. students reported:

- lower levels of victimization,
- more negative views about gangs,
- more favorable attitudes toward the police,
- more peers involved in pro-social activities, and
- lower levels of involvement in risk seeking behaviors.

Although these five outcomes are a fraction of the total set of 32 outcomes measures, they are a greater number than would be expected by chance. More importantly, in all cases the direction of the difference favors participants in G.R.E.A.T. (e.g., less victimization and more pro-social peers). Indeed, all but four of the 32 estimates of program impact are in the direction favorable to G.R.E.A.T., and this preponderance is far greater than would be expected by chance. Thus, we conclude that the beneficial direction of the program impact is statistically reliable. At this same time, it is important to realize that the magnitude of this positive impact is small. The average standardized program effect for the five significant outcomes is only .11, and the average across all measures is only .04.

Figure 3 illustrates the pattern of positive program effects that held for all the variables with significant program effects on change from the pre- to post-program periods. In the first of these examples, the overall rate of victimization declined throughout the study. With respect to pro-social peers, a different trend is observed; our respondents first suffered an over-all loss of pro-social peers, followed by an increase in the final two years. For both outcomes, participants in G.R.E.A.T. had somewhat less favorable adjustment prior to the start of the program, meaning a higher rate of vic-timization and fewer pro-social peers. With each assessment after the com-pletion of the program, the participants' adjustment improved relative to the control group, until the initial difference was reversed in the final two years. Although the change is small, note that it is in a pattern generally

---

Figure 2   The G.R.E.A.T. Review

Because of the contradictory findings from the cross-sectional and the two-year longitudinal study results, the National Policy Board (NPB) of the G.R.E.A.T. pro-gram expressed a desire to have the G.R.E.A.T. curriculum reviewed and assessed by a board of experts. In response, the National Institute of Justice (NIJ) funded a review of the G.R.E.A.T. program, and in 1999 the G.R.E.A.T. Review Workgroup was convened to conduct a critical assessment of G.R.E.A.T. This review process was extraordinary in that the G.R.E.A.T. program administrators' willingness to subject the program to a critical review is quite uncommon and demonstrates the G.R.E.A.T. administrators' serious commitment to the preven-tion of gangs and violence.

The G.R.E.A.T. Review Workgroup was comprised of G.R.E.A.T. officers and administrators, staff members from the National Evaluation, and experts in gangs and/or school-based prevention programs. The Workgroup carefully examined the overall objectives of the program as well as the content of each of the lessons in the G.R.E.A.T. curriculum. In contrast to suppression and intervention programs, which are directed at youths who already are gang members, G.R.E.A.T. is a uni-versal prevention program intended to provide life skills to empower adolescents with the ability to resist peer pressure to join gangs. This strategy is meant to be a cognitive approach that seeks to produce attitudinal and behavioral change through instruction, discussion, and role playing. However, the Workgroup found many of the elements necessary for effective delinquency prevention to be lacking in the current G.R.E.A.T. curriculum (e.g., teachers not integrated into the program delivery, insufficient focus on teaching social competency skills, and inadequate use of cooperative and active learning strategies).

Following a comprehensive review of the curriculum, a series of recommenda-tions for programmatic changes was submitted to the NPB. These recommenda-tions were accepted by the NPB, and by August 2000 an "enhanced" curriculum was written by a group of G.R.E.A.T. officers, curriculum writers, gang research-ers, and experts in school-based prevention programs. During the fall of 2000, a small cadre of officers were trained to teach the revised curriculum and partici-pated in a pilot test of the "enhanced" curriculum during the spring of 2001. By the fall of 2002, the new G.R.E.A.T. curriculum had replaced the original version. To date, no evaluation of this "enhanced" program has been conducted.

For a detailed discussion of this program review process, consult Esbensen, Freng, Taylor, Peterson, and Osgood (2002).

Figure 3 Program Impact for Two Outcome Measures: Victimization and Pro-social Peers

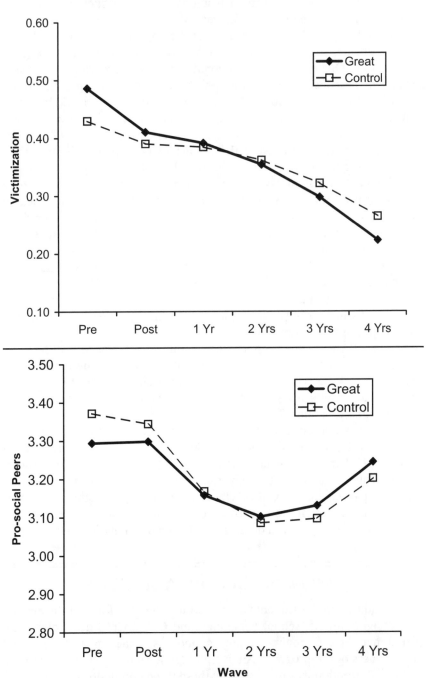

considered to be interpretable as a program effect, even if the initial difference was genuine. As Cook and Campbell note (1979:111), the reversal of an initial group difference cannot result from artifacts such as regression to the mean, ceiling effects, or maturation.

We also explored the possibility that the impact of the G.R.E.A.T. program might depend on students' levels of risk for delinquency and gang membership. Our earlier cross-sectional analyses of program impact had examined the consistency of program effects across demographic groupings (Esbensen and Osgood, 1997, 1999). There we found evidence that G.R.E.A.T. was more effective with groups that are at higher risk for delinquency, specifically males and minority-group members. In the present longitudinal analysis assessing the impact of G.R.E.A.T., no more than chance differences were found between high- and low-risk youth.

Three additional analyses were conducted to test whether the finding of program benefits might be attributable to weaknesses in the research design rather than to genuine effects of G.R.E.A.T. The purpose of these additional analyses was to further insure that the apparent program effects were genuine. These three methods consisted of: controlling for preprogram risk for negative outcomes; bolstering the comparability of the treatment and control groups based on propensity scores (Rosenbaum and Rubin, 1983; Winship and Morgan, 1999); and restricting the analyses to five sites at which pre-test and attrition differences between treatment and control groups were minimal.

Each of these three approaches reduced the pre-test differences between G.R.E.A.T. participants and the control groups, though none eliminated them. Using risk scores as a control variable was most effective in this regard. Despite the greater pretest comparability, the magnitudes of the estimated program effects were essentially unchanged. Indeed, the very small changes that occurred favored the treatment group at least as often as the control group. Furthermore, though two of these strategies sacrificed sample size, there were virtually no meaningful changes in statistical significance. Thus, it appears unlikely that our findings showing a positive impact of participating in G.R.E.A.T. could be due to preexisting differences between the treatment and control groups. This increases our confidence that the G.R.E.A.T. program does have some modest beneficial effects.

ALTERNATIVE OUTCOME ASSESSMENTS

In addition to the student surveys, which were the focus of the evaluation design, parents, school personnel, and G.R.E.A.T. officers also completed mail questionnaires inquiring about satisfaction and perceived effectiveness of the program. An overall high level of satisfaction with the G.R.E.A.T. program was expressed by these three populations.

Parent Survey

During the summer of 1998, questionnaires were mailed to parents of each of the students participating in the longitudinal phase of the outcome evaluation (see Freng, 2001). A total of 647 (32%) parents completed the surveys and returned them to the research office. The sample consisted mainly of White (70%) or Hispanic (14%) mothers who reported living in their neighborhoods for more than nine years. One-third reported that they had completed some college and about half (52%) stated that the primary wage earner in the household held a managerial or professional position.

Questions were asked to explore parents' perceptions of not only prevention programs in general, but the G.R.E.A.T. program in particular. They were also asked their opinions regarding crime and gangs in their neighborhoods, the role of law enforcement officers in schools, and the environment of their child's school. The results indicate that regardless of where the individual lived, crime and gangs were not seen as serious problems in their neighborhoods. Additionally, parents generally reported that they were safer in their neighborhoods (76%) and their child was safer at school (68%) when police officers were present. Furthermore, the majority of respondents reported that uniformed officers belong in schools (80%) and that they make good instructors in schools (71%).

When asked about the school environment, most parents believed that their child was safe at school (52%) and only one-third of parents reported that there was a gang problem in their child's school. Parents also stated that they believed prevention programs were effective (79%), that schools should be involved in prevention programming (69%), and that there should be more prevention programming in schools (73%). However, a majority of parents (60%) also stated that basics such as reading, writing, and arithmetic should be the focus of schools. Of the parents who reported that they were familiar with the G.R.E.A.T. program, the majority thought that G.R.E.A.T. taught valuable lessons (88%) and helped students stay out of gangs (60%). Overall, parents reported positive attitudes towards G.R.E.A.T., believed the program was effective, and reported high satisfaction with the program.

School Personnel Survey

During the summer of 1999, 1,006 anonymous, self-report questionnaires were distributed through contact persons at 21 middle schools originally involved in the longitudinal evaluation (see Peterson, 2001). (One of the original 22 middle schools had since been restructured to serve only elementary school students.) Questionnaires were distributed to all administrators, teachers, and counselors employed at the schools with an overall response rate of 67 percent. The resultant sample was largely White (81%) and female (72%); as expected, teachers (86%) comprised the majority of the sample.

Results indicate that middle school personnel feel that schools are a suitable place for delinquency prevention efforts and that law enforcement officers are an appropriate medium through which to transmit prevention program lessons. Overall, the G.R.E.A.T. program was received and evaluated positively by educators. The majority agreed that the curriculum appeals to students (64%), is appropriate to the students' age and comprehension levels (77%), and produces positive results in terms of teaching skills to avoid gang and delinquency involvement (72%), improving students' attitudes about law enforcement officers (76%), and addressing problems students face (78%). Despite these favorable perceptions, there was less agreement from educators that the G.R.E.A.T. program had reduced actual gang participation in their schools (43%) and communities (44%).

Teachers and administrators had somewhat dissimilar views of their schools' environment, both inside and outside, with administrators perceiving the environment more favorably. Further, teachers were more likely than administrators to agree that prevention programs are disruptive to teaching, and they were less likely than administrators to agree that they should incorporate prevention program lessons into their own curricula.

Law Enforcement Officer Survey

To examine officer satisfaction with the G.R.E.A.T. program, all officers who had completed the G.R.E.A.T. officer training (GOT) prior to July 1999 ($n = 3,925$) were identified by the Bureau of Alcohol, Tobacco, and Firearms (BATF) staff. Anonymous questionnaires were sent to these officers with 1,224 (31%) responding (see Taylor, 2001). This sample represents a diverse group of individuals (80% male; 71% White, 13% African American, and 9% Hispanic) and agencies (70% local/municipal, 22% county; 31% fewer than 50 sworn officers, 35% 51–250 sworn officers, and 34% more than 250 sworn officers).

Officers were overwhelmingly supportive of the approach of the program, with approximately 75 percent indicating that G.R.E.A.T. dealt with problems relevant to students in their communities, adequately addressed risk factors associated with youth gangs, and taught students the skills necessary to avoid gangs. Officers also felt that the program improved relationships with youths (89%), schools (89%), and the community as a whole (77%) but were less confident that the program reduced their communities' gang (47%) and crime (39%) problems. Levels of satisfaction and perceived program effectiveness were found to vary by gender and race (with males more supportive than females and officers from racial and ethnic minority groups more supportive than Whites) but, overall, officers of both genders and all racial/ethnic backgrounds were generally supportive of the G.R.E.A.T. program.

DISCUSSION

The Gang Resistance Education and Training program is a school-based prevention program that seeks to reduce adolescent involvement in gangs. Uniformed law-enforcement officers teach this primarily cognitive-based program to middle-school students. Of primary interest in this evaluation was the question: can a cognitive-based prevention program produce a measurable treatment effect? A related issue of considerable policy interest concerns the role of law enforcement in such programs; that is, are officers suitable deliverers of prevention programs in schools? Previous evaluations of similar law-enforcement prevention efforts have provided mixed results. For example, the DARE program has been the object of numerous evaluations with what can be described, at best, as mixed results (e.g., Lynam et al., 1999; Rosenbaum and Hanson, 1998). Another program, law-related education (LRE), has not been as widely evaluated as DARE, but the extant evaluations have generally been positive (see Gottfredson, 2001, for a discussion). Contrary to the mixed reviews of DARE, the previously published outcome evaluations of the G.R.E.A.T. program have been modestly positive (Esbensen and Osgood, 1997, 1999; Palumbo and Ferguson, 1995). The four-year results reported here are consistent with those of the previous G.R.E.A.T. studies.

The consistency of these findings about G.R.E.A.T. is important given that different research designs and slightly different methods were utilized in the three studies. Here the focus is on the two studies that were conducted as part of the National Evaluation. The cross-sectional evaluation of the G.R.E.A.T. program was completed in 1995 in eleven cities using *anonymous* questionnaires completed by students under *passive parental consent* procedures. The longitudinal evaluation was conducted in six cities (four that were included in the cross-sectional study) from 1995 through 1999 using *confidential* questionnaires restricted to those students for whom *active parental consent* had been obtained. In spite of these methodological differences, results from the two evaluations were remarkably similar. Those students participating in the G.R.E.A.T. program expressed more pro-social attitudes after program completion than did those students who had not been exposed to the G.R.E.A.T. curriculum.

In spite of these consistent yet modest positive effects of the G.R.E.A.T. program, two issues need our attention. First, the program's primary stated objective is to reduce gang activity. While the cross-sectional evaluation did find slightly lower rates of gang membership and self-reported delinquency, this was not the case in the longitudinal study. Second, while the cross-sectional findings reflected a difference between groups *one year* after program completion, the longitudinal design did not produce any significant group differences until *three to four years* after program exposure. Had the evaluation been concluded after a one- or two-year follow-up period, our conclusions would have been different. The two graphs presented in figure 3 reveal that it was not until the third year that the groups began to diverge. Each of these issues will be discussed more fully below.

The dual goals of the G.R.E.A.T. program (as stated in the G.R.E.A.T. Officer Instructor's Manual) are "to reduce gang activity, and to educate a population of young people as to the consequences of gang involvement." Additional inquiries of the G.R.E.A.T. management staff determined that another objective of the program was to develop positive relations with law enforcement. These three objectives are addressed through the eight-lesson curriculum that targets both attitudinal and behavioral change. At the outset of the National Evaluation, the research team developed a questionnaire that would allow examination of the effectiveness of program content as well as the stated objectives. Two of these program objectives appear to have been met through the curriculum; the G.R.E.A.T. students reported more favorable attitudes toward the police and more negative attitudes about gangs than did the non-G.R.E.A.T. students. Of the five evaluation outcomes that achieved statistical significance, it is worth noting that neither gang membership nor rates of self-reported delinquency were lower for the G.R.E.A.T. students than for the control group. All but one of the seven behavioral measures, however, were in the direction suggesting a program effect.

The finding that the benefit of G.R.E.A.T. became evident only gradually and over many years can be considered curious and unexpected. For a short-term program such as this, many would expect any impact to be strongest immediately and to be subject to decay over time. However, other evaluations have reported similar lagged or long-term effects (e.g., Berrueta-Clement, Schweinhart, Barnett, Epstein, and Weikart, 1984; Hawkins, Guo, Hill, Battin-Pearson, and Abbott, 2000; Olds et al., 2001; Tremblay et al., 2001). *Why* this delayed effect occurs is less clear than the fact that it *does* occur. Several possible explanations come to mind. First, young adolescence is a stressful and anxiety-filled stage of life during which most adolescents experience considerable ambiguity with regard to appropriate attitudes and behaviors. Second, the organizational structure of American schools may contribute to this stress; at ages 11 or 12, children move from the comfort of relatively small and stable elementary schools to larger, more diversified middle or junior high schools, and then at ages 14 or 15 the young adolescent is forced to make another transition to an even larger, more diverse high school setting. As the child reaches the age of 16 and 17, some of the angst of adolescence is resolved and the child has adapted to the high school setting (tenth or eleven grade). Thus, prior prevention or intervention experiences may, at this time, begin to manifest themselves.

The lagged effects found in this research, when considered in the context of other similar program effects, suggest that program development and associated evaluations may well benefit from adopting a developmental or life-course perspective. Outcomes related to attitudinal and behavioral change may not be discernable in the short run and may well be mediated by specific developmental issues such as peer group affiliation, growing independence from family of origin, and school transitions. As noted by Tremblay and colleagues:

> If a preschool intervention aims at preventing delinquency, the impact of the intervention must obviously be measured when the delinquent behavior usually appears, that is, no earlier than preadolescence. Clearly, we must expect interventions that aim to change the course of human development will have long-term effects. In fact, there may be more long-term effects than short-term effects. (2001:335)

From this perspective, these lagged effects do not appear either curious or unexpected.

To conclude, we would like to pose three summary statements and recommendations. First, to test for program effectiveness, a developmental perspective may be beneficial. This would entail longitudinal research designs that allow for examination of both short- and long-term program effects, capturing lagged effects that would be important in assessing program success.

Second, evaluations need to consider not only stated program goals, but implied goals as well. The G.R.E.A.T. program, for instance, is generally described as a gang prevention program with stated objectives of reducing gang membership and teaching students about the negative aspects of gangs. As mentioned above, a third goal of the program was the development of positive relationships with law enforcement. Had we assessed program effectiveness from the rather restricted perspective of reducing gang membership, we would have concluded the program to be ineffective. Including measures of attitudes toward the police and attitudes about gangs allowed for a more comprehensive assessment of program effectiveness.

Third, with respect to the issue of whether law enforcement officers can be effective deliverers of prevention curricular in schools, results of this evaluation suggest that they can be effective teachers and they are positively received by stakeholders. With the current pro-active, community-oriented policing emphasis of law enforcement, prevention and/or school resource officers may play a beneficial role in crime prevention. Our findings of a positive program effect indicate that evaluations of officer-taught, school-based, cognitive prevention programs need not be restricted to "feel-good" or satisfaction measures; such programs can have a measurable impact on students' attitudes and limitedly on behaviors.

This article is a compilation of evaluation results published or presented in various venues. Our sincere thanks and indebtedness are due to our colleagues, without whom this research would not have been possible: Lesley Brandt, Chris Sellers, Tom Winfree, Libby Deschenes, and Fran Bernat. Additionally, we would like to thank the numerous respondents (students, parents, teachers, and law enforcement officers) who provided their time and assistance in the completion of this evaluation. This research was supported under award #94-IJ-CX-0058 from the National Institute of Justice, Office of Justice Programs, U.S. Department of Justice. Points of view in this document are those of the authors and do not necessarily represent the official position of the U.S. Department of Justice.

References

Akers, Ronald L. 1985. *Deviant Behavior: A Social Learning Approach,* 3rd Edition. Belmont, CA: Wadsworth.

Berrueta-Clement, John R., Lawrence J. Schweinhart, W. Steven Barnett, Ann S. Epstein, and David P. Weikart. 1984. *Changed Lives: The Effects of the Perry Preschool Program on Youths through Age 19.* Ypsilanti, MI: High/Scope Press.

Cook, Thomas D., and Donald T. Campbell. 1979. *Quasi-Experimentation: Design & Analysis Issues for Field Settings.* Boston, MA: Houghton Mifflin Company.

Deschenes, Elizabeth Piper, and Finn-Aage Esbensen. 1999. "Violence and Gangs: Gender Differences in Perceptions and Behavior." *Journal of Quantitative Criminology* 15:53–96.

Dillman, Don A. 1978. *Mail and Telephone Surveys: The Total Design Method.* New York: Wiley.

Esbensen, Finn-Aage, and Elizabeth Piper Deschenes. 1998. "A Multisite Examination of Youth Gang Membership: Does Gender Matter?" *Criminology* 36:799–828.

Esbensen, Finn-Aage, Elizabeth Piper Deschenes, Ronald E. Vogel, Jennifer West, Karen Arboit, and Lesley Harris. 1996. "Active Parental Consent in School-Based Research: An Examination of Ethical and Methodological Issues." *Evaluation Review* 20:737–753.

Esbensen, Finn-Aage, Adrienne Freng, Terrance J. Taylor, Dana Peterson, and D. Wayne Osgood. 2002. "Putting Research Into Practice: The National Evaluation of the Gang Resistance Education and Training (G.R.E.A.T.) Program." In Winifred L. Reed and Scott H. Decker (eds.) *Responding to Gangs: Evaluation and Research.* Washington, DC: U.S. Department of Justice.

Esbensen, Finn-Aage, Michelle H. Miller, Terrance J. Taylor, Ni He, and Adrienne Freng. 1999. "Differential Attrition Rates and Active Parental Consent." *Evaluation Review* 23:316–335.

Esbensen, Finn-Aage, and D. Wayne Osgood. 1997. *Research in Brief: National Evaluation of G.R.E.A.T.* Washington, DC: U.S. Department of Justice.

Esbensen, Finn-Aage, and D. Wayne Osgood. 1999. "Gang Resistance Education and Training (G.R.E.A.T.): Results from the National Evaluation." *Journal of Research in Crime and Delinquency* 36:194–225.

Esbensen, Finn-Aage, D. Wayne Osgood, Terrance J. Taylor, Dana Peterson, and Adrienne Freng. 2001. "How Great is G.R.E.A.T.? Results from a Longitudinal Quasi-experimental Design." *Criminology and Public Policy* 1:87–118.

Esbensen, Finn-Aage, and L. Thomas Winfree, Jr. 1998. "Race and Gender Differences Between Gang and Non-Gang Youth: Results from a Multi-Site Survey." *Justice Quarterly* 15: 505–526.

Esbensen, Finn-Aage, L. Thomas Winfree, Jr., Ni He, and Terrance J. Taylor. 2001. "Youth Gangs and Definitional Issues: When Is a Gang a Gang and Why Does it Matter?" *Crime and Delinquency* 47:105–130.

Freng, Adrienne. 2001. "Parents Speak Out: Parent Questionnaires from the Gang Resistance Education and Training (G.R.E.A.T.) Evaluation." Paper presented at the Annual Meeting of the Academy of Criminal Justice Sciences, Washington, DC, April.

Goldstein, Harvey. 1995. *Multilevel Statistical Models*. London: Arnold.

Gottfredson, Denise C. 2001. *Schools and Delinquency*. New York: Cambridge University Press.

Gottfredson, Michael R., and Travis Hirschi. 1990. *A General Theory of Crime*. Palo Alto, CA: Stanford University Press.

Grasmick, Harold G., Charles R. Tittle, Robert J. Bursik, Jr., and Bruce J. Arneklev. 1993. "Testing the Core Empirical Implications of Gottfredson and Hirschi's General Theory of Crime." *Journal of Research in Crime and Delinquency* 30:5–29.

Hansen, William B., Nancy S. Tobler, and John W. Graham. 1990. "Attrition in Substance Abuse Prevention Research." *Evaluation Review* 14:677–685.

Hawkins, J. David, and Richard F. Catalano. 1993. *Communities that Care: Risk-Focused Prevention Using the Social Developmental Model*. Seattle, WA: Developmental Research and Programs, Inc.

Hawkins, J. David, Jie Guo, Karl Hill, Sara Battin-Pearson, and Robert Abbott. 2000. "Long Term Effects of the Seattle Social Development Intervention on School Bonding Trajectories." Seattle, WA: University of Washington, Social Development Research Group.

Hindelang, Michael J., Travis Hirschi, and Joseph G. Weis. 1981. *Measuring Delinquency*. Beverly Hills, CA: Sage Publications.

Huizinga, David. 1991. "Assessing Violent Behavior with Self-Reports." In Joel Milner (ed.) *Neuropsychology of Aggression*. Boston, MA: Kluwer.

Huizinga, David, and Delbert S. Elliott. 1986. "Reassessing the Reliability and Validity of Self-Report Delinquency Measures." *Journal of Quantitative Criminology* 2:293–327.

Huizinga, David, Rolf Loeber, and Terence P. Thornberry. 1994. *Urban Delinquency and Substance Abuse*. Washington, DC: U.S. Department of Justice.

Judd, Charles M., and Gary H. McClelland. 1989. *Data Analysis: A Model-Comparison Approach*. New York: Harcourt Brace Jovanovich.

Lynam, Donald R., Richard Milich, Rick Zimmerman, Scott P. Novak, T. K. Logan, Catherine Martin, Carl Leukefeld, and Richard Clayton. 1999. "Project DARE: No Effects at 10–Year Follow-Up." *Journal of Consulting and Clinical Psychology* 67:1–4.

Lynskey, Dana Peterson, L. Thomas Winfree, Jr., Finn-Aage Esbensen, and Dennis L. Clason. 2000. "Linking Gender, Minority Group Status, and Family Matters to Self-Control Theory: An Analysis of Key Self-Control Concepts in a Youth Gang Context." *The Juvenile and Family Court Journal* 51(3):1–20.

Miller, Michelle Hughes, Finn-Aage Esbensen, and Adrienne Freng. 1999. "Parental Attachment, Parental Supervision and Adolescent Deviance in Intact and Non-Intact Families." *Journal of Crime and Justice* 23:1–29.

Olds, David, Charles R. Henderson, Jr., Robert Cole, John Eckenrode, Harriet Kitzman, Dennis Luckey, Lisa Pettitt, Kimberly Sidora, Pamela Morris, and Jane Powers. 2001. "Long-term Effects of Nurse Home Visitation on Children's Criminal and Antisocial Behavior." In Alex Piquero and Paul Mazerolle (eds.) *Life-Course Criminology*. Belmont, CA: Wadsworth.

Palumbo, Dennis J., and Jennifer L. Ferguson. 1995. "Evaluating Gang Resistance Education and Training (GREAT): Is the Impact the Same as That of Drug Abuse Resistance Education (DARE)?" *Evaluation Review* 19:591–619.

Peterson, Dana. 2001. "G.R.E.A.T. Prevention: School Personnel Perspectives." Paper presented at the Annual Meeting of the Academy of Criminal Justice Sciences, Washington, DC, April.

Peterson, Dana, Jody Miller, and Finn-Aage Esbensen. 2001. "The Impact of Sex Composition of Gangs and Gang Member Delinquency." *Criminology* 39:411–440.

Rosenbaum, Dennis P., and Gordon S. Hanson. 1998. "Assessing the Effects of School-Based Drug Education: A Six-Year Multilevel Analysis of Project D.A.R.E." *Journal of Research in Crime and Delinquency* 35:381–412.

Rosenbaum, Paul R., and Donald B. Rubin. 1983. "The Central Role of the Propensity Score in Observational Studies for Causal Effects." *Biometrika* 70:41–55.

Sellers, Christine S., Terrance J. Taylor, and Finn-Aage Esbensen. 1998. "Reality Check: Evaluating a School-Based Gang Prevention Model." *Evaluation Review* 22:590–608.

Sherman, Lawrence W., Denise Gottfredson, Doris MacKenzie, John Eck, Peter Reuter, and Shawn Bushway. 1997. *Preventing Crime: What Works, What Doesn't, What's Promising.* Washington, DC: National Institute of Justice.

Taylor, Terrance J. 2001. "What Makes G.R.E.A.T. Officers Think G.R.E.A.T.'s Great?" Paper presented at the Annual Meeting of the Academy of Criminal Justice Sciences, Washington, DC, April.

Tebes, Jacob K., Davis L. Snow, and Michael W. Arthur. 1992. "Panel Attrition and External Validity in the Short-Term Follow-Up Study of Adolescent Substance Use." *Evaluation Review* 16:151–170.

Tremblay, Richard E., Frank Vitaro, Lucie Bertrand, Marc LeBlanc, Helene Beauchesne, Helene Boileau, and Lucille David. 2001. "Parent and Child Training to Prevent Early Onset of Delinquency: The Montreal Experimental Study." In Alex Piquero and Paul Mazerolle (eds.) *Life-Course Criminology.* Belmont, CA: Wadsworth.

Winfree, L. Thomas, Jr., Teresa Vigil-Backstrom, and G. Larry Mays. 1994. "Social Learning Theory, Self-Reported Delinquency, and Youth Gangs: A New Twist on a General Theory of Crime and Delinquency." *Youth and Society* 26:147–177.

Winfree, L. Thomas, Jr., and Frances Bernat. 1998. "Social Learning, Self-Control, and the Illicit Drug Use Patterns of Eighth Grade Students: A Tale of Two Cities." *Journal of Drug Issues* 28:539–558.

Winfree, L. Thomas, Jr., Finn-Aage Esbensen, and D. Wayne Osgood. 1996. "Evaluating a School-Based Gang Prevention Program: A Theoretical Perspective." *Evaluation Review* 20:181–203.

Winfree, L. Thomas, Jr., Dana Peterson Lynskey, and James R. Maupin. 1999. "Developing a Local Police and Federal Law Enforcement Partnership: The Sometime Tortuous Journey from a Great Idea to Implementation of G.R.E.A.T." *Criminal Justice Review* 24:145–168.

Winship, Christopher, and Stephen L. Morgan. 1999. "The Estimation of Causal Effects from Observational Data." *Annual Review of Sociology* 25: 659–707.

Civil Gang Injunctions

The Ambiguous Case of the National Migration of a Gang Enforcement Strategy

Cheryl L. Maxson

In July 2003, Los Angeles city officials filed a nuisance complaint in civil court against the Rolling Sixties street gang—the seventeenth implementation in Los Angeles of a gang enforcement tool known as Civil Gang Injunctions (CGI). CGIs—suing targeted street gangs in civil court for a judicial order to prohibit gang members from myriad illegal and otherwise legal behaviors—has been touted by law enforcement officials as a means to produce safer neighborhoods and to promote residents' quality of life. Police and prosecutors in numerous southern California jurisdictions, along with public officials and some community residents, have embraced this concept of targeted gang enforcement, despite a flurry of challenges by the American Civil Liberties Union, legal scholars, and community activists. In the last eight years of the twentieth century, at least 30 gang injunctions were issued in the region (Maxson, Hennigan, and Sloane, 2003).

Systematic evaluation of the effectiveness of CGIs lags far behind the anecdotal pronouncements in the media of the strategy's success. We don't yet have sufficient evidence about whether injunctions "work" and, if they do, the types of gangs or the types of communities where their use might

Prepared especially for *American Youth Gangs at the Millennium* by Cheryl L. Maxson.

be optimal. Moreover, we have only clues as to why they might accomplish their intended consequences of the reduction of crime and neighborhood improvement. These compelling unknowns stand in juxtaposition with the clear evidence that the use of injunctions is proliferating. Several articles in the law-enforcement practitioner literature have surfaced (for example, Cameron and Skipper, 1997; Genelin, 1998; Mazza, 1999) and the California District Attorney's Association sponsors workshops on how to get and implement injunctions for law enforcement throughout the state.

My colleagues and I have tracked the increasing popularity of CGIs in California, but little is known about their use in other regions of the country. In an earlier report, we noted the numerous inquiries received by Los Angeles injunction practitioners from law enforcement across the country (Maxson et al., 2003). National press coverage and the extensive national network of gang-enforcement training activities suggest that other locales would experiment with the strategy. The 1999 National Youth Gang Survey provides the first data on the national proliferation of the use of CGIs. The objective of this chapter is to report on this initial attempt to document the national use of injunctions and on the results of a follow-up study designed to clarify the scope and nature of activities subsumed under the rubric of "civil gang injunctions." This investigation revealed that the concept is not well understood by the national law-enforcement community and that the national survey clearly overestimated the prevalence of injunction use. Prior to discussing the results of the study, I'll describe how gang injunctions are obtained and used, and what we know thus far about their impact. In the conclusion, I focus on the role that community members might play in injunctions, and how this level of civic engagement might influence the ultimate effectiveness of injunctions.

WHAT ARE CIVIL GANG INJUNCTIONS?

Beginning in 1980, law enforcement in Orange and Los Angeles counties obtained a series of civil court injunctions to prohibit gang activity at specific locations in Santa Ana (1980), Pomona (1981), West Covina (1982), and East Los Angeles (1986).[1] The first injunction against a gang and its members is credited to the Los Angeles city attorney (1982). Injunction activity increased at a moderate pace but dramatically accelerated beginning in 1996. Maxson and her colleagues report, "From 1996 to 1999, a Southern California gang was enjoined, on average, every two months" (2003:250). More than two-thirds of the 31 injunctions granted in Southern California in the 1990s were in Los Angeles County.

Typically, local prosecutors work with police to develop evidence to support a suit brought before a civil court judge. The suit alleges that a certain gang presents a public nuisance to its community; in California, this violates Civil Code sections 3479 and 3480. The evidence is a series of declarations supported by criminal histories of gang members that document that the gang is an unincorporated association responsible for creating and maintaining the public nuisance. The suit asks that named members (and usually the rest of the gang) be prohibited, within a specified geographic area, from a range of activities. Some prohibited activities are illegal, such as selling drugs, carrying weapons, committing vandalism, and trespassing on private property, while others are not (wearing gang clothing, throwing hand signals and, most troublesome from a civil rights perspective, associating with other gang members).

If the judge agrees, a temporary restraining order is issued and these individuals can be arrested for violating a court order, prosecuted either in civil or criminal court, and given fines up to $1000 and/or incarcerated for up to six months. Later on, prosecutors may ask for modifications to the order, such as adding more participants, expanding the area, or changing prohibited activities. In some states, prosecutors may request a permanent injunction. All named defendants are notified of the initial hearing date and served with notice when the injunction is issued. While defendants can be represented in injunction development proceedings, publicly funded counsel is generally not provided in civil court. There is no systematic recording of the number of arrests in gang injunctions; interviews conducted for this and an earlier study (Maxson et al., 2003) suggest that relatively few arrests and prosecutions typically result from injunctions.

HOW EFFECTIVE ARE CGIs?

If injunctions produce few arrests, how can they be effective in reducing crime and making neighborhoods safer? Amidst the many anecdotal claims of success, only three studies have attempted to use empirical data to assess the impact of injunctions, all three using reported crime data trends before and after injunctions were implemented. The first two studies (Maxson and Allen, 1997; ACLU, 1997) each targeted an individual injunction and found no clear impact, and perhaps a negative effect on crime. Both studies had serious flaws in methodology and analysis.

In the most thorough and rigorous test to date, Grogger (2000) investigated changes in reported Part I violent and property crimes for 14 injunctions imposed in Los Angeles County between 1993 and 1998. He compared crime trends in the five quarters preceding the injunctions with trends in the following year (including the quarter the injunction was imposed). He also looked at neighboring areas to detect spillover, or displacement effects, and at matched comparison areas to identify whether crime changes were attributable to injunctions. It's unfortunate that data limitations required that all 14 injunction areas be pooled together. Grogger was not able to determine the impacts of specific injunctions, or the characteristics of implementation, that might be more or less effective.

From his analysis, Grogger concluded that reported violent crimes fell somewhere between 1.4 and 3.0 crimes per quarter in the average injunction target area. This translates to a decline of roughly 5 to 10 percent when compared with the preinjunction period. Further analysis revealed that the effect was concentrated in reductions in assault rather than in robbery, and no positive effects were detected for property crime. Finally, this study uncovered no evidence of the displacement of criminal activity into adjoining areas.

The Grogger study provides clear evidence of an effect of injunctions on reported violent crimes, but no indication of what it is about injunctions that produces this effect. Maxson et al. (2003) draw from the criminological and social psychological literatures to suggest three mechanisms by which injunctions might have salutary effects. The first, and most obvious, is through deterrence. While the penalties for injunction violations are not severe, the notifications of hearings and injunction papers might increase the perception of targeted gang members that they are being closely watched and likely to be apprehended and prosecuted for violations (Klein, 1993). Low arrest rates would presumably erode this perception, but practitioners contend that issuance of the injunction has a profound effect on gang members. Longtime community gang intervention activist Father Greg Boyle was cited in a recent press report, "I mean, eight minutes after one was filed here on the Eastside, I had kids in my office saying, 'Get me a job'" (Fremon, 2003).

This perceived effect of the injunction might result not from fear of punishment as suggested by deterrence theory, but through a process of individuation that decreases identification with the gang (Zimbardo, 1969). Social psychological theory suggests that individuals may feel less responsible for their behavior when they strongly identify with a group (Erikson, 1968). Being served with injunction papers might send the message, "We are watching you closely, it is your name on these papers, and you will be held responsible for your behavior." In this process, individual member identification with the gang might decrease, as could the overall gang cohesiveness that is associated with violent gang activity (Klein, 1995).

A third mechanism by which injunctions might work derives from social disorganization theory (Bursik and Grasmick, 1993). The process of developing and implementing a gang injunction may engage community members in an overall effort to build informal social control, social capital, and supportive organizational structures in deteriorating neighborhoods. Direct effects may derive from community resident empowerment processes, while reducing the level of the immediate threat of the gang to community residents may lay a foundation for shoring up community control that reduces criminal activity. These anticipated effects are often noted in the injunction practitioner literature. For example, an injunction manual explicitly advances the community policing/prosecution perspective as the ideological foundation for CGIs:

Instead of relying chiefly on arrests and convictions, community-based law enforcement is premised upon the fact that the quality of life of a neighborhood cannot improve unless residents actively participate with police and elected officials in the restoration of the neighborhood. (L.A. County District Attorney, 1996:2)

The goals of injunctions typically are couched in community policing terms, such as solving specific community crime, disorder, and fear problems (Greene, 2003). Higher levels of community involvement and greater impact on community environments might be expected from injunctions developed and implemented with this philosophical orientation as compared with other forms of gang enforcement (Decker, 2003). A community survey currently underway will assess changes in physical and social disorder, fear of crime, and gang visibility in an injunction area. Thus far, though, no researchers have investigated the impact that injunction might have on communities. A related issue, discussed later in this chapter, is the role that community members play in injunction activity.

A NATIONAL STUDY OF THE PREVALENCE OF CGIS

The National Youth Gang Center has conducted annual surveys of law enforcement about gang matters since 1995. The survey includes a nationally representative sample of 3,018 law enforcement agencies, including all cities and counties with populations of more than 25,000 and a representative random sample of smaller jurisdictions with populations between 2,500 and 25,000 (see article 4 by Egley, Howell, and Major). The results from these annual surveys, and secondary analyses by gang scholars, are widely distributed to law-enforcement and social service practitioners, policymakers, and researchers. The National Youth Gang Surveys (NYGS) are generally regarded as the best source of gang information on a national scope, although not without problems (see Curry, Ball, and Decker, 1996, and Maxson, Curry, and Howell, 2002, for discussion of definition and recording issues). Participation by the law-enforcement community is quite strong, and 86 percent of the targeted jurisdictions completed the 1999 survey (Egley, 2000).

As a result of the burgeoning interest in civil law as a gang-enforcement tool, the 1999 NYGS included the following item in the 1999 survey:[2]

14. Use of abatement ordinances and civil injunctions are two currently popular legal ways of combating youth gang problems.

   a. Has your city council (or county government) enacted a gang-related abatement ordinance?   Yes   No   Don't Know

   b. Has your city/county attorney developed a civil injunction against gang behavior?   Yes   No   Don't Know

Item 14b is a direct measure of the prevalence of CGIs; respondents in 116 jurisdictions indicated "yes" to this question. Strikingly, 82 of these jurisdictions were outside California—the first empirical evidence of the migration to other states of CGIs as a gang-enforcement tool. These 82 non-California jurisdictions should provide a broad laboratory for investigating the range of gang situations and implementation practices for this relatively untested strategy. Together with students[3] from the University of California, Irvine, I began calling these NYGS respondents to gather more detailed information about these injunctions. The questions in the interview guide ranged along the following topics:

1. Context for initiation: Was there a precipitating event? What were the community/police/prosecutor/public official/media roles in the decision to develop the CGI?

2. Injunction target: Description of the gang, number, and type (sex and age) of members targeted. What was the area covered? What behaviors were enjoined?

3. Implementation: How many violations or arrests? What type of officer training occurred? Were special units tasked with enforcement? How did the community react to enforcement?

4. Impact: What was the impact on the targeted community? The gang (i.e., gang activity, composition, and structure)?

5. Opinion about CGIs: Would you do it again? What are the appropriate conditions and targets of CGIs?

We attempted this contact one to two years after the survey was submitted, so not surprisingly, a number of the original respondents were no longer in positions of gang enforcement. We tried to track respondents to their current positions, and if not available, then we interviewed a person in the agency who was thought to be most familiar with the local gang situation. After repeated attempts, we were able to conduct interviews with officers in all 116 agencies. In all cases, the interviews began with the statement that the department had responded to the NYGS indicating that a civil injunction against gang behavior had been developed in the jurisdiction.

Many of the officers we spoke with simply didn't know what a civil gang injunction is, and some of them had never heard of the term. To make sure the respondent understood the technique about which we were asking, we offered the following definition:

> A civil gang injunction is an antigang strategy where a prosecutor asks a civil court judge to issue an injunction or restraining order against gang members to prohibit a list of activities.

Many officers confused this strategy with other forms of civil abatement. Others used our phone call (and presumably, the NYGS survey) as an opportunity to "be counted" for any antigang program they had in place.

Many of the activities described to us were not gang focused or relied on criminal, rather than civil, statutes. Other descriptions were ambiguous and, given the flexible nature of this tool, could be considered injunctions. All the responses could be placed in one of four categories.

CGI Jurisdictions

Thirty of the 116 agencies described activities that could reasonably be placed under the injunction rubric. It is striking that only one-fourth of agencies that responded, "yes, our local prosecutor has developed a civil injunction against gang behavior" in the national survey could recount injunction activity one year or so after the survey was completed!

The geographic distribution of these jurisdictions confirms that California is the site of most injunction activity. Exactly half of the 30 injunction jurisdictions were located in southern California, another four in northern California. Many California jurisdictions have acquired more than one injunction, but the city of Los Angeles tops the list with 17.

The state with the second highest number was Texas; five agencies correctly identified injunctions in their jurisdictions: the cities of San Antonio, Corpus Christi, Abilene, and League City, as well as Bexar County.[4] The remaining six CGI jurisdictions were Phoenix (AZ), Cicero (IL), Madison (WI), Beaver County (PA), Fall River (MA), and Albany (GA).

The CGIs that respondents described covered a wide variety of activities. The number of targeted gang members ranged from five to almost 300 individuals. The targets were overwhelmingly male and primarily over the age of 18 years. Some of the injunctions, for example, in Abilene, specified all gang members (about 100) in the city.

The covered geographic area might be a park, a few blocks, an apartment complex, a housing project, and in one case a county fair. The Fall River injunction targeted a street and park contiguous to a particular church whose members were harassed by a gang. Other injunctions spanned an entire city or county.

The prohibitions articulated in the injunctions varied as well. Many prohibited association with other gang members and other legal behaviors, such as using public pay phones, cells, or pagers. Most included a list of prohibited illegal acts like vandalism, selling drugs, and trespassing on private property. Some of the injunction prohibitions are fairly restrained as compared with those with which we were already familiar in California. For example, League City targeted only smoking, drinking, and marking graffiti.

Confirming previous work in California (Maxson et al., 2003), many of these interviews revealed only minimal community involvement in the injunction development or implementation. Other respondents described phone calls from the parents of gang members to report prohibited gang activity or community reports of incidents as the catalyst to enforcement. The Corpus Christi injunction targeted specific residences. That city's interview respondent noted that residents gave trespass warnings to prohibited gang members: "If they revisited the area, they went to jail for six months." A few agencies reported that community members not only instigated, but also obtained, injunctions in a process quite similar to domestic violence victims getting a restraining order. In Madison, the owner of a troubled apartment complex went to court and secured an injunction. In Stockton, the police assisted residents of a housing project to get an order that enjoined nine gang members from coming within 1,000 feet of the property.

Civil Abatements

Officers in twelve jurisdictions (10 percent) described civil abatement strategies to target gang members and/or drug sellers. Gang membership and drug sales are inextricably intertwined for many law-enforcement practitioners, so it is not surprising that the distinction between the two is lost in the reports of the application of civil code violations. Typical of these efforts are going after residential property owners that permit drug sales, often via violations of housing codes, eviction procedures, and attempts to shut down businesses that attract gang members and/or visible drug sales. The activities described by officers in this category expand the typical reach of gang enforcement into the arena of civil law, and CGIs might well be considered as one strategy within a larger toolbox umbrella of civil gang abatement. However, these other civil abatement projects are more narrowly conceived and limited in scope. Immediate targets are property owners rather than gang members and individual properties rather than larger gang territories.

Miscellaneous Criminal Penalties for Gang Activity

Officers in 18 agencies (about 15 percent of the 116) related antigang responses that used criminal statutes to enhance incarceration for gang-related crimes or special conditions of probation or parole to target gang association. In 1989, the California legislature enacted the Street Terrorism, Enforcement, and Prevention (STEP) Act that codified a legalistic definition of criminal street gangs (see Klein, 1995, for an extended critique of this definition) and specified a laundry list of crimes for which convicted gang defendants could have periods of incarceration extended by several years. Over the years, the legislature has added more crimes to the list and more years to the penalty enhancement. Prosecution of the STEP Act is now widespread in California; "STEPing" gangs, the initial phase of notification to gang members that their group has been declared a "criminal street gang," is the common parlance among gang officers. As with other California gang enforcement innovations, STEP Act procedures have been adopted in a variety of other states, including Florida, Georgia, Illinois, Ohio, and Louisiana. The use of statutory enhancements or property forfeiture for gang-related crimes is fairly common, but what is noteworthy for our purposes here is that officers in seven jurisdictions framed this response as civil gang injunction activity—a clear misperception of the legal foundation of both STEP and CGIs.

The other 11 respondents in this category reported "No Gang Contact" conditions of probation and/or parole as the exemplar of injunction activity. The prohibition of associating with gang members is a standard condition of probation in California for all gang-involved youths, and violation can precipitate revocation of community placement and return to correctional facilities. This procedure falls entirely within the criminal or juvenile court jurisdiction and has no semblance to the civil suit process embodied by CGIs.

No Specialized Antigang Enforcement

Officers in 56 agencies, or just under half of the sample of 116 jurisdictions that marked "yes" to the NYGS item on injunctions, could not describe any specialized antigang activity in their agencies. Their jurisdictions had neither civil gang abatements, nor other special gang-enforcement programs like STEP nor gang probation conditions. Interviewers pressed these respondents for antigang program descriptions and asked for other officer informants that might have different perspectives. Occasionally we gathered information about other types of gang enforcement activity and placed the agency in another category. One officer suggested that a student survey about gang matters was likely the basis for marking the survey item. A few officers reported that their agencies had been considering a civil gang injunction and one was helping to enforce another city's CGI. Most often, the officers in this group stated clearly that they had nothing approximating injunction projects in their jurisdictions and could offer no explanation for the survey response.

CONCLUSIONS AND RESEARCH TOPICS FOR THE NEW MILLENNIUM

This study found that a total of 86 agencies answered this particular item on the 1999 NYGS incorrectly. This is a nearly 75 percent false positive rate. One obvious explanation was the timing of the follow-up study: the study team attempted to verify the reports of gang injunctions by telephone one to two years after the agency completed the NYGS. Although one would expect that awareness about the implementation of an innovative, labor-intensive, and visible gang-intervention strategy would permeate the law-enforcement agency, officer turnover and the acceptance of replacement respondents is a plausible explanation for the high false positive rate. However, more than half of the 86 officers in this group were listed as completing the 1999 NYGS, so respondent turnover isn't a complete explanation.

A more likely explanation for the high false positive rate stems from the lack of understanding within the national law-enforcement community regarding what a civil gang injunction is, and what types of enforcement activities might reasonably fall within this rubric. Agencies that implement innovative gang interventions, particularly those that draw on civil code enforcement, may lack the program terminology to categorize these out-of-the-ordinary efforts and thus grasp the best fit with the CGI rubric. Our research team struggled with a few descriptions, uncertain whether to categorize the site as having an injunction or civil abatement. Also, we can't dismiss the possibility of a positive response bias in the NYGS. Perhaps agencies want to be counted among law enforcement jurisdictions that are "doing something" to discourage gang activity.

Interviewers asked only about the responses to this single survey item. Staff at the National Youth Gang Center has contacted survey respondents to clarify answers on numerous occasions, but there has been no systematic study of the reliability of the annual surveys. As policymakers, practitioners, and researchers increasingly rely on NYGS data for both national and regional depictions of gang prevalence, trends, and characteristics, the assessment of the reliability of these data is critical. It is quite likely that since CGIs are a relatively new gang-enforcement strategy, that this survey item presented special difficulty to respondents. The survey's sponsor should consider providing a definition similar to that used in the follow-up study. Moreover, a retest of a sample of all items with a sample of respondents should be a standard practice for a routine survey of this magnitude.

The foregoing discussion concerns the likely overestimate of CGI activity in the United States as derived from the 1999 NYGS, but it's also true that all jurisdictions with CGIs are not included in our study. Such jurisdictions may have inaccurately indicated "no" to the survey item (either due to the ambiguity of the term, or simply by error), or may not have returned the 1999 survey, or may not have been asked to participate in the survey. The 30 CGI jurisdictions identified by our study are only a starting point to assessing the national scope of injunction activity and pertain only to activity up to and including 1999.

The National Youth Gang Center included a question about CGIs again in the 2001 NYGS. In the more recent survey, respondents were asked to indicate whether a "civil injunction against gang behavior" was currently being used in the jurisdiction. Of the 30 jurisdictions reporting CGIs in 1999 and confirmed in the follow-up study, 16 stated that they were still in use in 2001 and six agencies reported that they were not. Two of the 30 agencies indicated that they no longer had gang activity. The remaining six jurisdictions reported "don't know" to the item or did not respond to the 2001 survey. Twenty-eight new agencies, 23 of which are outside California, identified an injunction in 2001. Without further investigation, we can't be sure whether this is new injunction activity, or whether these jurisdictions might be more accurately placed in one of the other categories identified in the follow-up study.

Our interviews with the 1999 survey respondents determined that most—about two-thirds—of injunction jurisdictions are located in California. California has more jurisdictions reporting gangs, and reports more gangs and gang members, than any other state (Miller, 2001), so the finding that California agencies more often use this intervention devised by California law enforcement is not surprising. We found only modest evidence of the migration of this intervention technology to other states (most frequently Texas) and to other widely geographically dispersed locales. It does not appear that this strategy is widely practiced elsewhere—at least, so far.

Opinions on the impact of injunctions among those who have used them are uniformly positive and several jurisdictions have obtained multiple injunctions. For example, Abilene has acquired a series of these orders since 1992 and that city's interview respondent noted, "Overall, the injunctions have been very successful. We still use them today and we are most likely going to use them tomorrow." The enthusiastic respondent from San Antonio, having secured four injunctions since 1999, provided a pithy summary: "It *is* a cure-all for gang ills." While trends of gang activity ebb and flow, it is quite likely that more jurisdictions outside California will experiment with this intervention, particularly where traditional gang-enforcement activities fail to curb serious, violent gang activity.

For those jurisdictions considering injunctions, we can offer the following observations:

1. The meager empirical evidence suggests that injunctions may be effective in reducing violent crime. Just one study (Grogger, 2000) has generated positive results, and reductions were relatively modest. Due to the pooling of effects, we cannot learn from this study which of the 14 injunctions he studied were more or less effective. Furthermore, all studies conducted have relied on crime as the indicator of success. The practitioner rhetoric on the purpose of obtaining injunctions is to make neighborhoods safer and reduce fear, but we don't yet know whether injunctions impact community quality of life.

2. These interviews and our prior interviews with southern California gang unit personnel suggest that injunctions are labor intensive and therefore very costly. Many informants suggest they be considered as a last resort. Janet Moore, the current head of the Los Angeles District Attorney's Hardcore Gang Division, was recently quoted in a newspaper article on diverse opinions regarding injunctions. Moore warned that without heavy investments of time and resources, "virtually all gang injunctions are doomed to failure" (Briscoe, 2003).

3. We don't know the type of gang situations that are most amenable to injunctions. Again, our interviews suggest that territorial gangs are best suited to injunction activity. Injunctions limit activity only within a well defined geographic area, so gangs that move freely across a wide area to commit crimes may not be affected.

4. The pesky "why" question could be critical to this issue. If deterrence is at work, then given the minor penalties involved, one assumes that swiftness and certainty of punishment is key. This reinforces the argument that the allocation of resources to continuing implementation would be important to achieving positive results. If it's individuation, then identifying the targeted gang members most likely to be affected and providing resources for alternative avenues of addressing individual and social needs becomes paramount. Finally, if it is social disorganization, then community involvement could be the critical element.

Most of the interviews in this and the prior study suggest that community participation is minimal. Typically the decision to get an injunction, selection of the gang and area to be targeted, activities to be prohibited, and enforcement of the injunction are solely in the hands of law-enforcement agencies. Sometimes community members may provide declarations of the nuisance caused by gang members, but there is some debate as to whether even this level of involvement is really necessary.

Consider the following two models of comprehensive gang intervention:

Model 1: Community residents are actively engaged in collaboration with school personnel, law enforcement, and youth service providers. Here, the CGI is one of an array of gang prevention and intervention activities. Residents might identify the gang and area to be targeted and select the prohibitions appropriate to that particular nuisance situation. They might also participate in enforcement, especially in informal ways like apprising law-enforcement partners about neighborhood gang activity. Community-based organizations might participate in the service of notice of injunction and counsel targeted gang members about alternative activities and program services.

Model 2: Several law-enforcement agencies join forces to target a particularly troublesome area. Probation and parole agents ride along with police, conduct home searches, and look for violations. Police work closely with prosecutors who work in vertical prosecution teams. Police gang experts identify a gang and gather evidence on the most active gang members for inclusion in an injunction petition. Here, an injunction is just one of several suppression activities among a team focused on one area.

As the reader may have guessed, Model 1 is rare in practice. A variation of this model appears to have been implemented in the southern California community of Redondo Beach (Cameron and Skipper, 1997). Far more common is the implementation of Model 2, which is the operating model for LA's Community Law Enforcement and Recovery (CLEAR) program. This model has been practiced in six different regions of the city, and a recently announced infusion of 2.5 million federal dollars will permit expansion to two more areas (Winton, 2003). While the community component of CLEAR varies from one area to the next, program observations and descriptions indicate that community roles and program resource allocations to community functions are quite minor.

Gang and community research over the last several decades would indicate that injunctions would be more optimally practiced within the context described in Model 1. Thus far, so little research has been conducted that suggestions of how injunctions might best be practiced are wholly speculative. There is no indication that the charm of civil gang injunctions is on the wane among southern California law enforcement. Many city officials, prosecutors, police, and some community members are enamored. We can anticipate that as other jurisdictions become increasingly familiar with this intervention, they too will begin to experiment. Father Boyle offered the following cautiously optimistic assessment of CGIs: "At its best, an injunction creates a kind of vigilant heat that moves kids toward the light" (Fremon, 2003). The "best" form of CGIs remains an open question. One only hopes that these ventures will be accompanied by an independent research component that might contribute to our overall understanding of the gang situations and injunction forms that are most effective in reducing gang activity and making neighborhoods more safe.

Finally, the social costs of an intervention that erodes the foundation of civil rights of individuals under our legal system must be weighed against the effectiveness of such strategies in addressing the social harm caused by gang members. Noted scholar Gilbert Geis cautions against the "superficial sense of safety" derived from the use of civil law against gang members:

> There is no question that juvenile gangs can be unruly and can make life wretched and sometimes dangerous for people who live in their midst. But there is a good deal of question concerning the validity of the idea that laws that target gang members and that at best are only arguably acceptable in a free society are the most effective way to deal with problems that gangs may present. (Geis, 2002:270)

Notes

[1] This information was gathered for a prior study from documents prepared by prosecutors (see particularly Castorena, 1998; and Whitmer and Ancker, 1996), newspaper articles, and interviews with police gang experts and injunction practitioners (see Maxson et al., 2003).

[2] The National Youth Gang Center, directed by John Moore, provided these data. Center analyst Arlen Egley offered assistance in development of analysis files. Jurisdictions with no gang activity for a given year complete only the initial screening portion of the survey.

[3] The author gratefully acknowledges the assistance of undergraduate students Priscilla Pasion, Avita Jaswal, Misha Nubia, and Arash Gheytanchi, who helped to develop the interview guide and conducted interviews.

[4] Bexar County cited an injunction area that included a portion of San Antonio but described features different from the response obtained by the latter agency. Therefore, we don't consider this a duplication of injunction jurisdictions.

References

American Civil Liberties Union. *False Premises, False Promises: The Blythe Street Injunction and Its Aftermath.* Los Angeles: ACLU Foundation of Southern California, 1997.

Briscoe, Daren. "Agencies Differ Over Tactics to Combat Gangs." *Los Angeles Times*, August 13, 2003.

Bursik, Robert J., and Harold G. Grasmick. *Neighborhoods and Crime: Dimensions of Effective Community Control.* Lexington, MA: Lexington Books, 1993.

Cameron, Jeffrey R., and John Skipper. "The Civil Injunction: A Preemptive Strike Against Gangs." *The FBI Law Enforcement Bulletin*, November 1997, pp. 11–15.

Castorena, Deanne. "The History of the Gang Injunction in California." Los Angeles: Los Angeles Police Department Hardcore Gang Division, 1998.

Curry, G. David, Richard A. Ball, and Scott H. Decker. "Estimating the National Scope of Gang Crime from Law Enforcement Data." In C. Ronald Huff (ed.), *Gangs in America,* Second Edition, pp. 21–36. Thousand Oaks, CA: Sage Publications, Inc., 1996.

Decker, Scott H. *Policing Gangs and Youth Violence.* Belmont, CA: Wadsworth, 2003.

Egley, Arlen. Highlights of the 1999 National Youth Gang Survey. *OJJDP Fact Sheet.* Washington, DC: Office of Juvenile Justice and Delinquency Prevention, 2000.

Egley, Arlen, James C. Howell, and Aline K. Major. "Recent Patterns of Gang Problems in the United States from the 1996–2002 National Youth Gang Survey." In Finn-Aage Esbensen, Larry Gaines, and Stephen G. Tibbets (eds.), *American Youth Gangs at the Millennium*, pp. 90–108. Long Grove, IL: Waveland Press, 2004.

Erikson, E. H. *Identity: Youth and Crisis.* New York: Norton, 1968.

Fremon, Celeste. "Flying the Flag: The Debate Over the Latest Gang Crackdown." *L. A. Weekly,* July 18–24, 2003.

Geis, Gilbert. "Ganging Up Against Gangs: Anti-Loitering and Public Nuisance Laws." In C. Ronald Huff (ed.), *Gangs in America,* Third Edition, pp. 257–270. Thousand Oaks, CA: Sage Publications, Inc., 2002.

Genelin, Michael. "Community Prosecution: A Difference." *Prosecutor's Brief* (3):13–17, 1998.

Greene, Jack C. "Gangs, Community Policing and Problem Solving." In S. H. Decker (ed.), *Policing Gangs and Youth Violence*, pp. 3–16. Belmont, CA: Wadsworth, 2003.

Grogger, Jeffrey. "The Effects of the Los Angeles County Gang Injunctions on Reported Crime." Los Angeles: University of California, Department of Policy Studies, 2000.

Klein, Malcolm W. *The American Street Gang.* New York: Oxford University Press, 1995.

Klein, Malcolm W. "Attempting Gang Control by Suppression: The Misuse of Deterrence Principles." *Studies in Crime and Crime Prevention: Annual Review,* 88–111, 1993.

Klein, Malcolm W. *Street Gangs and Street Workers.* Englewood Cliffs, NJ: Prentice Hall, 1971.

Los Angeles County District Attorney. *SAGE: A Handbook for Community Prosecution,* June 1996.

Maxson, Cheryl L., and Theresa L. Allen. "An Evaluation of the City of Inglewood's Youth Firearms Violence Initiative." Los Angeles: Social Science Research Institute, University of Southern California, 1997.

Maxson, Cheryl L., G. David Curry, and James C. Howell. "Youth Gang Homicides in the United States in the 1990s." In W. L. Reed and S. H. Decker (eds.), *Responding to Gangs: Evaluation and Research*, pp. 103–107. Washington, DC: National Institute of Justice, 2002.

Maxson, Cheryl L., Karen Hennigan, and David C. Sloane. "For the Sake of the Neighborhood? Civil Gang Injunctions as a Gang Intervention Tool." In S. H.

Decker (ed.), *Policing Gangs and Youth Violence*, pp. 239–266. Belmont, CA: Wadsworth, 2003.

Maxson, Cheryl L., and Malcolm W. Klein. "Investigating Gang Structures." *Journal of Gang Research* 3(1):33–40, 1995.

Mazza, Susan. "Gang Abatement. The San Diego Experience." *Law Enforcement Quarterly* 288(11), Spring 1999.

Miller, Walter. "The Growth of Youth Gang Problems in the United States: 1970–1998." Washington, DC: Office of Juvenile Justice and Delinquency Prevention, 2001.

Whitmer, John, and Deanne Ancker. "The History of the Injunction in California." In Los Angeles County District Attorney's *SAGE: A Handbook for Community Prosecution*, Appendix M, June 1996.

Winton, R. "L.A. Expands Gang Program with U.S. Funds." *Los Angeles Times*, August 7, 2003.

Zimbardo, P. G. "The Human Choice: Individuation, Reason, and Order Versus Deindividuation, Impulse and Chaos." In W. J. Arnold and D. Levine (eds.), *Nebraska Symposium on Motivation* (Vol. 17). Lincoln: University of Nebraska Press, 1969.